LETs and NESTs:
Voices, Views and Vignettes
Edited by Fiona Copland, Sue Garton and Steve Mann

ISBN 978-086355-804-7

Contents

Foreword
John Knagg OBE.. 3

Introduction: positions, experiences and reflections on the native speaker issue
Fiona Copland, Steve Mann and Sue Garton.. 5

1   **Responsibility without power: native-speaker experiences of team teaching in Japanese secondary schools**
Luke Lawrence 21

2   **Fostering better collaborative relationships between Native English Speaker Teachers and Local English Teachers for a more effective Native English Teacher (NET) Scheme in Hong Kong**
Elaine Hau Hing Tang 39

3   **Native or non-native English-speaking professionals in ELT: 'That is the question!' or 'Is that the question?'**
Ali Fuad Selvi 53

4   **Employment advertisements and native-speakerism in Japanese higher education**
Damian J. Rivers 71

5   **Bilingualism and globalisation in Latin America: fertile ground for native-speakerism**
Adriana González and Enric Llurda 93

6   **Native teachers' perspectives on co-teaching with Korean English teachers in an EFL context**
Sung-Yeon Kim 113

7   **NEST schemes and their role in English language teaching: a management perspective**
Greg Keaney 129

8   **Native English-Speaking Teachers (NESTs) in Taiwan: policies and practices**
Tzu-Bin Lin and Li-Yi Wang 151

9   **Power, balance and identity: an insight into intercultural team teaching**
Jaeyeon Heo 169

10   **Managing relations in cross-national team teaching pairs: insights from rapport-sensitive incidents**
Trần Thị Minh Khánh and Helen Spencer-Oatey 185

11   **From an assistant to a team member: a perspective from a Japanese ALT in primary schools in Japan**
Chiyuki Yanase 201

12   **Problematising the paradigm of 'nativeness' in the collaboration of local (NNEST) and foreign (NEST) teachers: voices from Hong Kong**
Mary Shepard Wong, Icy Lee and Andy Gao 217

13   **'Almost' native speakers: the experiences of Visible Ethnic-Minority Native English-Speaking Teachers**
Eljee Javier 233

14   **Opinions and positions on native-speakerism**
Sue Garton, Fiona Copland and Steve Mann 247

Contributors 267

British Council statement

This publication is a collection of essays. While all reasonable efforts have been made by the writers to ensure that the information contained herein is accurate, the British Council accepts no liability for such information, or for the views or opinions presented.

Foreword

The British Council's mission is to build a friendly knowledge and understanding of the United Kingdom and to build trust through a variety of activities and programmes around the world. This book connects with a number of our activities in English language teaching (ELT), including our direct teaching of English to students in many countries, our collaboration with education authorities internationally to improve their English teaching and our support to schemes in which students and teachers travel to work or study in other countries for mutual benefit.

We believe that teachers should be judged on how well they can do their job, not on where they come from or on what they look like. Our understanding of what makes a good teacher has developed, and our British Council model now revolves around a set of professional practices such as understanding learners, designing and managing courses and lessons, using multilingual approaches and providing an appropriate linguistic model. As an organisation that pays increasing attention to the benefits of a diverse profession and workforce, we are opposed to discrimination of all kinds, and that includes native-speakerism. Our Accreditation UK quality assurance scheme for ELT does not recognise the distinction between native and non-native speakers. We are aware of the importance of a deep understanding of a learner's social, educational and linguistic background, the experience of having learned additional languages well and the value of offering an attainable model for learners. These qualities are often associated with the model Local English Teacher (LET), which accounts for the vast majority of the millions of English teachers in the world. The future of ELT lies in the hands of these teachers.

We also believe in the value of teachers, inexperienced and experienced, engaging in professional exchange between the UK and other countries. The model of the Native English-Speaking Teacher (NEST) that we prefer is not monolingual and unqualified but increasingly multilingual, multicultural and expert. We believe that NEST schemes and the teachers on them should work to that objective. The fact that NEST schemes have existed for so long, with new ones continuing to be created, shows that they are perceived to be of value by national authorities. However, we are very clear about the mutuality of the schemes; the individual NEST participants also have much to gain from the experience – linguistically, socially and in their overall development as global citizens. We would like to look forward to a global ELT profession where the NEST/LET divide and native-speakerism is a thing of the past, but one in which ELT professionals still benefit from international exchange. The success of that international exchange depends to a large extent on the quality of relationships between NESTs and LETs, as this book shows us.

This book grew out of a research project on NEST schemes around the world (*Investigating NEST schemes around the world: Supporting NEST/LET collaborative practices*) by the same team from the Universities of Aston, Stirling and Warwick. That research project also led to a set of freely available training materials to promote understanding and collaboration between LETs and NESTs. This book discusses the issues involved in greater depth. Our thanks go to Fiona Copland, Sue Garton and Steve Mann for developing the initial concept and bringing it to fruition, and to all the contributors to the book. I feel sure that this work can make a substantial contribution to the future of English language teaching internationally.

John Knagg OBE
Senior Adviser, English
British Council

Introduction: positions, experiences and reflections on the native speaker issue

Fiona Copland, University of Stirling, UK
Steve Mann, Centre for Applied Linguistics, University of Warwick, UK
Sue Garton, Aston University, Birmingham, UK

Let us put our cards on the table. We, the editors of this book, are all Native English-Speaking Teachers (NESTs). We have all taught English overseas and in the UK, and we have all found our teaching experiences at various times engaging, exciting, painful, stressful, challenging and, in the end, life-enhancing. We have all, too, worked with Local English Teachers (LETs), sometimes in team teaching relationships. These LETs have been colleagues, bosses, friends, research participants and students, depending on working contexts.

Through our experiences, both in and out of the classroom, we have become increasingly interested in the native-speaker teacher issue, as it applies to us as (now) British academics and as it applies to NESTs, LETs and students in various classrooms and contexts around the world. By the 'native-speaker teacher issue', we mean the discourses of enquiry, criticism and evaluation that surround any discussion of the native speaker, and the Native English-Speaking Teacher in particular. This interest led to our obtaining research funding from the British Council to investigate collaborative practices between LETs and NESTs. The outputs from this study – a research report, an audit of a range of government-backed NEST schemes and a set of materials for developing more successful co-working between LETs and NESTs – are now free to download from www.teachingenglish.org.uk. However, as we carried out our research and prepared the outputs, our interest in the topic grew, not least because our classroom observations and the data from interviews with LETs and NESTs did not always chime with the positions in the academic literature, particularly those which argue from a theoretical position that the native speaker no longer exists, that 'native-speakerism' always works in favour of NESTs, or that the clash of educational cultures makes co-teaching a particularly challenging educational practice. Academic debate has undoubtedly made significant and valuable contributions to our theoretical understanding of native-speakerism, linguistic imperialism, team teaching and related issues. Nonetheless, many of the experiences of NESTs and LETs who took part in our study seemed not dissimilar to our own experiences as NESTs, the earliest being 30 years ago, suggesting to us that, despite the important debate in the academic literature, in classrooms perhaps little has changed in recent years.

It was this awareness that inspired us to edit a book on NESTs and LETs from a 21st century perspective. We wanted to share current voices from teachers and academics working and researching in contexts where NESTs are employed and work on a daily basis with LETs. We also wanted to better understand the daily practices of LETs and NESTs, and consider how LETs and NESTs can work together more successfully. Finally, we wanted to have a better understanding of the issues pertaining to the employment of NESTs from the perspectives of both NESTs and LETs. The chapters, therefore, offer a range of perspectives, which we shall shortly describe. Before doing so, however, we would like to share some of the discussions that arose when we were conducting our research and then editing this volume, all of which are pertinent to any discussion of NESTs and LETs.

Labels

How should we describe the teachers we are talking about? In the literature, 'NEST' seems to be a fairly well-established term, although others have been used (e.g. 'expatriate teachers', 'overseas teachers', or, as one editor has recently requested, 'native English teachers'). It traditionally denotes a teacher from an 'Inner Circle' country (Kachru, 1985), such as Australia, the UK and the USA, who has learned English from childhood and was educated in English. This is the kind of NEST many employers have in mind when they advertise teaching positions. Increasingly, however, positions are not all being filled by traditional NESTs. Instead, teachers who themselves have learned English subsequent to their 'first' language are taking on the role. Sometimes teachers who are fluent speakers of the language of their students, perhaps sharing it as a first language (L1), are also employed as NESTs (see, for example, the chapters in this volume by Yanase, a bilingual teacher with Japanese as her first language, and Javier, who describes a NEST who can speak the students' L1 fluently). Interestingly, these teachers are sometimes asked to disguise their bilingual skills, sometimes to detrimental effect (see Wong, Lee and Gao, this volume). A third group comprises teachers from Kachru's (op cit) 'Outer Circle' countries, such as Nigeria, India and the West Indies. In these countries, English is an official language and children are often schooled in English, becoming bilingual (or, more often, multilingual) in the process. In his chapter, Keaney argues that, as the demand for NESTs continues to rise, teachers from Outer Circle countries will be needed to make up any recruitment shortfall. According to Davies (2003), these teachers may already describe themselves as native English speakers and so it is likely that they will apply for NEST roles if recruitment criteria are relaxed. (At present, many NEST schemes require teachers to have been at least educated in an Inner Circle country; see Copland et al., 2015.) Whether employers respond positively to these teachers remains to be seen, but the response of Japanese schools to Filipino teachers suggests that the road ahead may be bumpy (Jo, 2010).

These examples provide evidence that the term 'native speaker' may no longer be valid. Indeed, in 1997, Leung et al. challenged the notion from a sociolinguistic perspective, arguing that there is no one-to-one correspondence between ethnicity and language. Leung et al.'s prediction that as the world becomes increasingly superdiverse notions such as 'native speaker' will become increasingly less accurate seems to us entirely sensible. Other sociolinguists have endorsed this position. For example, Piller (2001) calls the idealisation of the native speaker 'useless' (in terms of the descriptor) but also 'debilitating' and 'unfair'. Nevertheless, while sociolinguists may avoid the term because of its inaccuracy, Doerr (2009: 1) points out that 'the notion of the "native speaker" is used widely, not only in "second", "foreign" or "heritage" language education, but also in daily life', where the term 'native speaker' is neither problematised nor contested and perhaps provides an accurate label. For these reasons, we use it in this volume (rather than one of the other terms that sociolinguists have suggested), although we hope the final chapter in the volume in particular (see section below) demonstrates an engagement not only with the term but also with its limitations and its pedagogical and linguistic consequences.

If the term NEST is problematic, a label for describing the situated English teachers is even more difficult. NNEST, that is, 'Non-native English-Speaking Teacher', has been the most common label: indeed the TESOL Interest Section calls itself Nonnative English Speakers in TESOL (NNEST-IS) (see Selvi, this volume). However, the 'non-' prefix signals deficit and may also suggest deviance from what is often perceived as the norm, which, in this case, is the NEST. It is also quite a difficult acronym to say. As with NEST, other terms have been suggested and used by other writers (e.g. bilingual teachers) but these are less widely used.

In this introduction and in the final chapter (and in our research outputs), we have decided to use the acronym LET, standing for 'Local English Teacher'. This was the term that was most commonly used by the teachers we spoke to and interviewed for the research project. Unlike NNEST, it is not a word that is negatively framed in relation to another term (NEST). However, this does not mean that LET is value-free: the word 'local' might have connotations that could be considered negative in the context of describing English-teaching professionals, for example, 'craft', 'small-scale' and 'limited' (thanks to Julian Edge for useful discussions about this label). On the other hand, 'local' undoubtedly has some positive connotations, such as having 'local knowledge'. All things considered, its emic quality made it the best choice from a limited (and limiting) selection.

Another label often applied in discussions of NESTs and LETs is ALT, which stands for 'Assistant Language Teacher'. ALT is the label commonly used in Japan to describe a NEST on the JET (Japan Exchange and Teaching) programme. These NESTs are, for the most part, inexperienced and lack qualifications, so Assistant Language Teacher would seem to be appropriate. The label is interesting in two ways. First, an ALT is not necessarily a NEST. Although the two terms are often used synonymously, the ALT role can be filled by anyone suited to the job. In her chapter, Yanase describes how she was recruited to the ALT role because her bilingual and bicultural skills were recognised as highly suited to working in primary schools, where few teachers could speak English and where overseas ALTs (from Expanding Circle countries) had not fitted in.

Second, the ALT label does not always match the role NESTs (and others) are required to play out. NESTs are sometimes qualified and experienced (in the local setting as well as in other overseas contexts) and may also be bilingual. In his chapter, Lawrence explores what happens when NESTs of this calibre – whom Keaney (this volume) calls the 'prima donnas' of the NEST/LET world – are recruited by the British Council to work on a co-teaching scheme in Tokyo. For many of the teachers he interviews, status is an issue. They believe their hard-won experience and qualifications earn them the right to be considered more than mere ALTs and they resent being considered by some LETs as equivalent to their non-trained, inexperienced counterparts. Lawrence also considers what the ALT label means to LETs: do they stress the 'assistant' part of the label or has 'ALT' become a single lexical item, a convenient term to describe the (usually) foreign teachers who support the English language teaching endeavour of the school? This conundrum highlights the situated nature of labels and suggests that what they index may differ across contexts.

Who is a NEST? Who is a LET?

Debates about 'who is a native speaker' and associated discussions, such as 'what is a first language', have been circulating in the literature for years and have interested linguistic scholars such as Chomsky, who tend to take 'language' as their unit of analysis, as well as scholars of linguistics and applied linguistics who are interested in how social context affects language acquisition (for example, Halliday, 1978; Davies, op cit). Academics tend to pin their flags to one of two masts: the mast that recognises the existence of the native speaker (for example, Davies, 2003) and the mast that does not (for example, Paikeday, 1985; Piller, op cit; Luk and Lin, 2010), although, as Davies (op cit) points out, some scholars avoid the terms and prefer to focus on the 'mother tongue' instead (for example, Halliday, op cit). For us, the issue in this book is not so much an intellectual one or an academic one; rather it is about how the term comes to be used in the communities we have investigated and by the writers of the chapters. In these contexts, the concept of the native speaker is alive and kicking, although, as our chapters show, what being a 'native speaker' entails is contextual and contested.

The discussion of who a native speaker is inevitably links to issues of identity. As we have suggested, NEST describes a concept rather than being a fully accurate description (see also Leung et al., op cit). For example, one of the NESTs mentioned in Wong, Lee and Gao's chapter is Eastern European and has learned English as a second/additional language. He recognises the irony in how he is positioned by the school as a NEST but also questions a labelling which means he cannot present himself to the children and staff as a successful English language learner. A similar situation affects Yanase, who, as she recounts in her chapter, is recruited for her bilingual and bicultural skills but must pretend in school either not to understand or speak Japanese or to speak a 'broken' version.

Javier's chapter draws our attention to an area that will continue to impact on discussions of NESTs and LETs in our increasingly superdiverse world (Blommaert and Rampton, 2011): Visible Ethnic-Minority Native English-Speaking Teachers (VEM-NESTs). Javier challenges us to think about how this group of teachers faces questions of race and identity in contexts where what you look like defines your identity to a great extent. In his chapter, Rivers, too, highlights race as an issue in recruitment of NESTs in Japan when he points to the requirement in many advertisements for applicants to send a photograph with their letters of application and CVs. While race is not explicitly mentioned by Keaney in his chapter, his suggestion discussed above – that growing demand for NESTs will result in teachers needing to be recruited from Outer Circle countries – could, in the future, present a challenge for countries where multiethnic diversity is limited and where linguistic and racial stereotyping tend to be unquestioned.

In some ways, the LET is easier to describe. Usually, LETs are brought up in the country in which they teach and have learned English through the school system in these countries, occasionally studying in an 'English-speaking' country for a period of time. However, here similarities between them end. As Keaney (this volume) points out, there is no universally accepted level of English language that teachers need to obtain before they can start teaching English, and demand in some countries has led to the employment of many LETs whose English level is low. On the other hand, some LETs, like their NEST counterparts, are bi- or multilingual and hence have a range of linguistic resources on which to draw in the classroom.

Furthermore, national qualifications in English language teaching tend to be patchy. While some governments require their teachers-in-training to study methodology, in other countries, little teacher training is required and much of what is offered is theoretical. Dormer (2010: 287) notes that in Indonesia, schools, 'usually seek teachers who are considered proficient in English – regardless of their educational background'. Furthermore, the increasingly young age at which children are now being required to study English in schools has meant that many teachers are being forced to teach English despite either not knowing English or not knowing how to teach it, or, in worst-case scenarios, both (Copland et al., 2014). The discrepancy between the well-trained, experienced and linguistically skilled LET and the untrained, inexperienced and linguistically challenged LET can be huge, and so discussing them as a homogeneous group (like their NEST counterparts) should be avoided. Indeed, Heo (this volume) explains how some LETs are so experienced and skilful that they act as trainers and mentors for the NESTs. In contrast, other team teaching pairs in Heo's study feature a much more experienced NEST who takes on a mentor role for a much less experienced LET. In his chapter, Lawrence also describes how NESTs on the project he features acted as trainers for the LETs.

Roles

The editors of the current volume have all had experience as NESTs in state education systems. They have worked both as the sole teacher in charge of a class and as team teachers collaborating with LETs. It came as something of a surprise to them to discover during their research that on most of the current government-sponsored schemes, NESTs and LETs co-teach (a clear exception is the CfBT scheme in Brunei). The rationale for co-teaching (or team teaching) was different on each scheme, as was how co-teaching was organised. As we observed, it could even vary from classroom to classroom in the same school. At one end of the team teaching scale (see Luo, 2010, citing Maroney, 1995), the LET and NEST fully collaborated in class, taking responsibility for different sections of the lesson and for different aspects of classroom management (Tajino and Tajino, 2000, call this the 'strong' version of team teaching). They dialogued in front of the students and asked each other questions, sometimes even negotiating in English about who would do what next. At the other end of the scale (the 'weak' version of team teaching), the LET conducted most of the lesson, with the NEST acting as what has become known as the 'human tape recorder' (Tajino and Tajino, op cit), that is, reading out the English sections of the coursebook. Alternatively, the NEST conducted the whole lesson while the LET sat at the back of the class, sometimes marking books, sometimes disciplining students if required.

A number of researchers have commented on and discussed the issue of role from different perspectives. For example, Chung, Min and Park (1999) and Park (2010) describe how teachers on the EPIK (English Program in Korea) are not clear about their roles while Tajino and Tajino (op cit) and Kumabe (1996) discuss similar issues on the JET programme. Luo (2010) explains that, in many of the classes she observed in Taiwan, the weak version of team teaching prevailed, particularly when the LET was inexperienced. In this volume, Kim shows how, in her context, NESTs and LETs worked in parallel rather than in teams, and that collaboration was rare, often because time for planning was limited, a point also made by Lin and Wang in their chapter. Indeed, lack of planning for team teaching is an issue raised by many researchers and emerged in most of the schemes we investigated in our project (see Copland et al., op cit).

Relationships between NESTs and LETs

An area that has figured prominently in the literature is the relationship between NESTs and LETs (for example, Moote, 2003; Carless, 2006; Carless and Walker, 2006; Lee, 2009). It is almost inevitable that when two sets of teachers from very different cultural, linguistic and pedagogic backgrounds are put together in one institution – often in one classroom and sometimes without consulting the LET – the relationship between them will be of paramount importance to effective collaboration. During research for our project, we observed what seemed to be excellent relationships between NESTs and LETs but also some instances where there was minimal evidence of a relationship. In addition, during interviews, we were told on numerous occasions of relationships that had deteriorated. It is no surprise, then, that a number of chapters in this volume deal in detail with relationship issues. Heo and Khánh and Spencer-Oatey, for example, both use critical incident analysis to examine relationship breakdown, particularly in terms of cross-cultural clashes. Heo also features examples of conflicts and tensions that were the cause of stress and challenge in co-teaching working relationships. Tang's interview study of LETs (this volume) elicits examples of similar cultural misunderstandings. On the other hand, good relationships can exist in these educationally engineered contexts. Lin and Wang's chapter features NESTs with very positive attitudes to the educational culture in Taiwan and the teachers they work with, although other aspects, such as educational administration, fare less well (see also Khánh and Spencer-Oatey, this volume).

Native-speakerism

Native-speakerism was the original title for this book, but when we shared the title with colleagues, we realised that the title suggested a volume with a critical scope throughout, which was not our aim. The book certainly engages with native-speakerism as a concept and as a troubling and sometimes pernicious set of values and prejudices. However, the chapters included provide a range of voices and perspectives, which do not fit well under the umbrella term 'native-speakerism'. Nevertheless, it is impossible to conduct a research project or edit a book about NESTs and LETs without addressing 'native-speakerism', however briefly, and it is to this that we now turn.

As Keaney, drawing on Johnston (2003), shows in his chapter, concerns about native-speaker teachers in terms of their impact and their possible influence on local values were recorded in Roman times. However, more recent discussions of native-speaker teachers' influence have tended to be critical of the advantages NESTs enjoy as a result of their linguistic skills alone (Seidlhofer, 1999) leading to what Phillipson (1992: 217) and others refer to as the 'native speaker fallacy', that is, 'the belief that the ideal teacher of English is a native speaker' (see Selvi, this volume, for a full discussion). Untrained, inexperienced NESTs from Inner Circle countries (what Keaney, in his chapter, calls 'backpacker' NESTs) have long been able to pick up teaching jobs in Expanding Circle countries (Kachru, op cit) on arrival. Slightly savvier (and better-off) NESTs enrol on a one-month English language teaching certificate course, such as a CELTA or Trinity Certificate, before setting off, which will usually allow them to attract better terms and conditions. According to Brandt (2006), around 7,000 people take a CELTA annually and the vast majority go overseas to teach. Keaney (this volume) notes with some alarm that teachers who hold one of these certificates are often considered 'qualified' in the field. They might even be perceived as more qualified than LETs who have trained for years and have years of experience.

Courses such as CELTA promote a particular pedagogy based on communicative language teaching (CLT). This approach was developed for teaching small classes of adult learners (Holliday, 1994) who were often learning English in an Inner Circle country or in private language schools overseas. The approach aimed to develop students' conversational skills. However, many NESTs draw on CLT regardless of the kind of classroom they find themselves in, ignoring its (lack of) suitability for large classes, for schoolchildren studying for exams or its fit with local educational norms. In 2005, Holliday coined the term 'native-speakerism' to refer to the widespread belief that '[n]ative speakers represent a "Western culture" from which spring the ideals both of the language and of language teaching methodology' (ibid.: 49). Since then, the criticism of NESTs, or at least of the privileges they enjoy, has, at times, been vitriolic (although see Waters, 2007, for a different perspective).

Jenkins (2007) takes a slightly different line in her discussion of English as a Lingua Franca (ELF). Her argument is that the variety (or varieties) of English spoken by native English speakers is not the variety most easily understood by those using ELF among themselves (that is, non-native English speakers). This may well be true and provides support to the position that LETs are ideal language teachers (see the discussion below) as they will be better able to understand and work with their students' utterances. (Jenkins provides an example of such a situation in practice in her 500-word piece in the final chapter of this book.) However, we are less convinced by Jenkins's claim that:

> the future may turn out to be more problematic for many English native speakers – unable to speak other languages or to adapt their English for international communication – than for many non native speakers. (ibid.: 237)

In our experience, most NESTs are, at least, excellent communicators with both students (who speak very little English) and colleagues (who sometimes only speak slightly more), and often have to communicate with more than one colleague using ELF. Furthermore, many NESTs learn the language of their hosts. It is unlikely that NEST schemes would survive if communication turned out to be too difficult. (See Lawrence's chapter in this volume for a discussion of NESTs who have learned Japanese and, in some cases, are fluent speakers.)

The realisation that NESTs have tended to enjoy benefits because of the circumstances of their birth rather than because of their teaching skills or qualifications was mirrored by the growth of the 'NNEST movement'. Pivotal to its establishment was a paper by Peter Medgyes called 'Native or non-natives: who's worth more?' (Medgyes, 1992). In this paper, Medgyes argued that Non-native English-Speaking Teachers are able to be as successful as their 'native' counterparts and, in fact, have a number of advantages over them (for example, being able to anticipate language-learning problems and acting as a model of a successful learner of English). These realities, felt by LETs for many years but not expressed in such explicit terms (in a Western journal, at least), are now well established, and a number of publications have successfully taken up the LET cause (e.g. Mahboob, 2010; Clark and Paran, 2007) and influential bodies such as TESOL USA now have an active and dynamic NNEST interest section (see Selvi, this volume). While much discrimination still exists (see, for example, González and Llurda, this volume), some inroads have been made, and most of the large, international applied linguistics and TESOL organisations, for example, no longer allow employers to advertise for NESTs on their websites and in other publications. Indeed, in 2014, the BAAL mailing list debated at length terminology that should be avoided in language teaching advertisements.

There is no doubt that discriminatory practices are mostly targeted at LETs. However, NESTs can also be subject to prejudice, a topic which Houghton and Rivers (2013) examine in detail and which Rivers revisits in his chapter. For example, employers in Japan continue to advertise for NESTs, but once they have joined an institution, NESTs (and other non-Japanese nationals) may be subject to less favourable conditions than their 'Japanese' counterparts. NESTs in other parts of the world report similar inequitable practices (indeed, Garton, one of the editors of this volume, and her NEST colleagues had to go through the courts in Italy and the European Union to gain employment rights afforded to her 'Italian' colleagues).

Geography

Our original research project examined government-sponsored NEST schemes such as the JET programme and VSO (Voluntary Service Overseas), as we were interested in both policy and practice. The majority of the schemes are to be found in Asia, with those in Hong Kong, Japan, South Korea, Brunei and Taiwan all being well established. Inevitably, much of the empirical and investigative work has been carried out on these schemes and this is reflected in the geographical reach of the chapters in this volume. However, as González and Llurda establish in their chapter, many countries in South America are now taking their lead from Asian countries and introducing their own schemes, such as Heart for Change, an organisation which recruits volunteers to teach in Colombia. It is also true that in the United

Arab Emirates and other parts of the Middle East, NESTs form part of a multilingual, multicultural workforce, often managing educational establishments as well as being responsible for learning and teaching. However, less is written about these contexts from the NEST/LET perspective, perhaps because staffrooms are made up of expatriate teachers using English as a lingua franca, often with LETs being in the minority. Nevertheless, whatever the geographical location, similar issues pertain, particularly when NESTs and LETs work collaboratively, and it is hoped that the chapters presented here will resonate with readers whatever their pedagogic context.

Writing for this collection

There is an enormous body of work on NESTs and LETs, from theoretical work that challenges the native speaker concept (for example, Leung et al., 1997) and the value of native-speaker English teachers (Phillipson, op cit) to empirical work that garners opinions and beliefs (for example, Llurda, 2005) or provides discourse analyses on related documentation or classroom discourse (for example, Sato, 2009; Train, 2009; Luk and Lin, op cit) or investigations of pedagogies for team teaching (for example, Tajino and Tajino, op cit; Carless and Walker, op cit). Our aim in this volume has been to focus for the most part on empirical work and investigations of classroom teaching. This is because we want to provide readers with a contemporary insight into the NEST/LET world in order to uncover current issues in the field. Many of our papers, therefore, have been written by emerging researchers or by teachers developing an academic career. Many of these are, or have recently been, negotiating the various challenges of working collaboratively. However, we also have contributions from well-established writers who continue to challenge injustices or misconceptions in the area through their empirical work.

Our final chapter is innovative. We invited a number of scholars who have previously produced seminal work in the area to contribute 500 words on their current thinking. We are delighted with the responses, which are diverse, insightful and forward-looking. We have collated the contributions by theme and examine them in light of the chapters in the collection. We also consider what these contributions suggest in terms of future research and directions that those interested in the field might take.

We turn now to introducing the chapters in the volume in terms of theme.

Teaching on government schemes

The majority of the chapters in this volume focus in one way or another on government schemes. On these schemes, teachers – generally from Inner Circle countries (Kachru, op cit) – are recruited to teach in schools where English is taught as a foreign language. Two of the writers, Tang and Kim, point to the lack of research carried out in such institutional contexts, examining in detail the classrooms and experiences of the two groups. All of the writers address to some degree the tensions that can exist between LETs and NESTs, although chapters examine and respond to these tensions in different ways.

Cultural clashes

Khánh and Spencer-Oatey's chapter, like Heo's, uses critical incident analysis to examine cultural tensions between the two groups. Khánh and Spencer-Oatey describe these critical incidents as 'rapport-sensitive incidents' and focus on the kind of cultural misunderstandings that affect NESTs and LETs in tertiary institutions in Vietnam. Through a series of vignettes, drawing on diary, interview and observational data, they show how the actions of the LETs can alienate the NESTs and upset their sense of fairness and appropriate behaviour. The LETs, for their part, are often totally oblivious to the upset they have caused, or at least are unaffected by it. Khánh and Spencer-Oatey argue that concepts from intercultural theory can explain why certain incidents cause particular problems and suggest that these concepts and rapport-sensitive incidents are integrated into training programmes for both LETs and NESTs.

Heo also uses critical incident analysis in her chapter, this time to examine the experiences of LET and NEST primary school teachers in South Korea. However, she focuses on how power and identity are negotiated in these critical incidents and is particularly interested in how the NESTs and LETs resolve their intercultural clashes.

Collaboration

In their chapters, Yanase and Kim both focus their lenses on the collaborative practices of team teachers. Yanase presents an auto-ethnography of her experiences over a month as a quasi-NEST in a Japanese primary school. In fact, Yanase was hired as an ALT because she was both bilingual and bicultural, which the hiring local government believed would reduce the issues arising from hiring someone who could not function in Japanese in the young learner workplace. Yanase explores a number of fascinating themes in her chapter, not least issues of identity, which her role and background often foreground. However, the main theme is how she negotiates her role with a number of different teachers who all behave differently and expect slightly different things of her.

Kim concludes in her chapter that NESTs in South Korean middle and secondary schools are professionally isolated in the institutions in which they work. Drawing on observational data and in-depth interviews with NESTs and LETs, she realises that lack of cooperation in planning (and, in some cases, in executing) lessons means that co-teaching is not a team activity at all, but rather features two teachers working at best in parallel and at worst in isolation. Kim also calls for better training of both LETs and NESTs to ensure that the aims of the EPIK scheme in Korea can be more successfully fulfilled.

Wong, Lee and Gao focus on the Hong Kong context in their chapter and report on two cases studies from an in-depth research project into collaborative practice between NESTs and LETs. Like Tang (this volume), they are careful to outline Hong Kong's complex linguistic heritage and its uneasy relationship with its (sometimes) bilingual educational system. Using a series of metaphors to describe the NESTs, they argue that collaborative practice between NESTs and LETs is hampered by a native-speaker paradigm that limits the participating teachers' roles linguistically, pedagogically and professionally.

The view from one side

Tang (this volume) only interviews LETs in her study of the NET scheme in Hong Kong, but given that LETs' views and opinions are often marginalised or even ignored in studies of NESTs, her decision allows her to explore in detail the opinions of the teachers who have to work with NESTs, whether they wish to or not. The LETs in the study express a number of concerns about the NESTs they work with, particularly in terms of the curricula they teach, which they feel are often prioritised over their own curricula. These teachers also experience cultural insensitivity. However, they all agree that the NESTs offer useful language support to students which they do not always feel they can provide themselves, particularly at the primary level.

Lin and Wang (this volume) probed the decision-making processes of six NESTs who chose Taiwan as their place of work. Their chapter is insightful in two ways: first, it shows that choices are often carefully made, drawing on a range of factors, with remuneration not always being a primary consideration. Second, it suggests that NESTs can be culturally curious and sensitive, showing an appreciation of the educational culture in which they find themselves. That is not to say that the NESTs do not face challenges. As in many of the co-teaching contexts reported on in this volume, finding time to plan lessons is difficult and, as roles have not been decided in advance, means that true collaboration in class cannot be achieved. Another common challenge is a school administration that is perceived to be 'inefficient' by NESTs' standards, as Khánh and Spencer-Oatey also report, among other things, in their chapter (see also Copland, Garton and Mann, 2016).

Lawrence's chapter examines a scheme in Japan which, unlike many NEST schemes (e.g. JET, EPIK or FETRP), employed English language teachers who were experienced (in that the teachers had worked as language teachers for many years) and qualified (in that the teachers had certificates, diplomas and higher degrees in TESOL from Western awarding bodies). In his discussion of an interview study with four NESTs who had worked on the scheme, Lawrence tries to reconcile two views of native-speakerism: one which positions LETs as deficit teachers because they have not learned English as their first language and do not teach according to Western principles of communicative language teaching (e.g. Medgyes, op cit; Pennycook, 1994; Mahboob, 2010), and the other, which exposes the less attractive aspects of being a NEST, for example discriminatory hiring practices (see also Houghton and Rivers, 2013; Rivers, this volume).

Native-speakerism and discrimination

Selvi, in his chapter, brings a new set of perspectives to the NEST/NNEST debate, reconceptualising its politically driven and ideologically based underpinnings through reviewing key myths and misconceptions such as the idea that NNEST-IS are only open to NNESTs and that students prefer NESTs. He argues against a 'them and us' approach to discussing issues of native-speakerism and instead suggests that the groups should work together to establish a more democratic, participatory, professional and egalitarian future for the ELT profession.

González and Llurda are less optimistic in their chapter about native-speakerism in Latin America. They describe how a number of emerging economies are embarking on similar routes to those taken by Asian counterparts a few years ago, employing NESTs to support ambitious programmes aimed at creating bilingual (in Spanish and English) citizens. Through an analysis of newspaper articles in Chile, Colombia, Ecuador and Mexico, the writers uncover the discourses that are constructed around these recruitment policies and focus in particular on how publications deal with the native speaker myth. They conclude that these countries are a fertile ground for the promotion of native-speakerism, a phenomenon that they argue is spreading in the language education agendas in Latin America.

Rivers takes a slightly different approach to discussing the issue of native-speakerism in his chapter. Drawing on his own previous work and a corpus of Japanese job advertisements, he makes the case for reconsidering native-speakerism, moving the definition towards configuration as a contemporary social problem rather than an ideological one. He argues that this configuration brings greater attention to the ways in which a wide range of practices share a common foundation in stereotyping and in-group/out-group classification dynamics. The 292 advertisements he discusses recruit within the context of Japanese higher education; Rivers suggests that the use of the native-speaker criterion in the majority of the advertisements constitutes 'native-speakerism' and shows how and when they disadvantage potential applicants on the basis of their speakerhood status.

Javier (this volume) draws on critical race theory in her discussion of VEM-NESTs. Her chapter discusses how the association between the notion of the 'native speaker of English' and 'White' racial identities can affect the way VEM-NESTs are perceived in specific contexts. The VEM-NESTs in her study have to negotiate how they are positioned by teachers and students from monocultural countries, where language, culture and race are fairly synthesised. Javier's chapter, therefore, provides classroom data to develop discussions of the denotation of native speaker.

Keaney manages the CfBT NEST scheme in Brunei, which employs 267 NEST teachers. His chapter reports on one of the longest-running NEST schemes globally and shows how the aims of the scheme have developed over the years as its partnership with the Brunei Ministry of Education has deepened. A key feature of the scheme nowadays is the promotion of bilingual education (rather than the sole promotion of English language). In his discussion, Keaney examines the skills and attributes that both LETs and NESTs bring to the profession, suggesting that the language proficiency skills of qualified and experienced NESTs are balanced by the sociocultural knowledge base of qualified and experienced LETs, but that both groups provide students with excellent language learning opportunities.

The final chapter

We have already discussed in brief the final chapter. In order to conclude the book, we asked a number of scholars who have contributed over the years to the NEST/LET debate from either a sociolinguistic or pedagogical perspective to provide a statement of 500 words on their current thinking on the issue. We are very grateful to those we asked for responding so generously and positively. We believe that, taken together, this is a unique, insightful and challenging collection of positions and perspectives. We hope it makes a thought-provoking read.

References

Blommaert, J and Rampton, B (2011) Language and superdiversity. *Diversities* 13/2: 1–22.

Brandt, C (2006) Allowing for practice: A critical issue in TESOL teacher preparation. *ELT Journal* 60/4: 355–364.

Carless, D (2006) Good practices in team teaching in Japan, Korea, and Hong Kong. *System* 34/4: 341–351.

Carless, DR and Walker, E (2006) Effective team teaching between local and native-speaking English teachers. *Language and Education* 20/6: 463–477.

Chung, GJ, Min, CK and Park, MR (1999) A study of team teaching for the utility of native English teachers in the elementary and the secondary school. *English Teaching* 54 (2): 201–227.

Clark, E and Paran, A (2007) The employability of non-native-speaker teachers of EFL: A UK survey. *System* 35/4, 407–430.

Copland, F, Garton, S and Burns, A (2014) Challenges in teaching English to young learners: Global perspectives and local realities. *TESOL Quarterly* 48/4: 738–762.

Copland, F, Garton, S and Mann, S (2016) *Investigating NEST schemes around the world: supporting NEST/LET collaborative practices*. London: The British Council.

Copland, F, Mann, S and Garton, S with Davis, M (2015) *Investigating NEST schemes around the world: Supporting NEST/LET collaborative practices*. London: The British Council.

Davies, A (2003) *The native speaker: Myth or reality?* Basingstoke: Multilingual Matters.

Doerr, MN (2009) 'Introduction' in Doerr, MN (ed) *The native speaker concept: Ethnographic investigations of native speaker effects*. Berlin: Mouton De Gruyter, 1–10.

Dormer, JE (2010) 'Strength through difference: Optimising NEST/NNEST relationships on a school staff' in Mahboob, A (ed) *The NNEST lens: Non native English speakers in TESOL*. Newcastle upon Tyne: Cambridge Scholars Publishing, 285–304.

Halliday, MAK (1978) *Language as a social semiotic: The social interpretation of language and meaning.* London: Edward Arnold.

Holliday, A (1994) *Appropriate methodology and social context.* Cambridge: Cambridge University Press.

Holliday, A (2005) *The struggle to teach English as an international language.* Oxford: Oxford University Press.

Houghton, SA and Rivers, DJ (2013) *Native-speakerism in Japan: Intergroup dynamics in foreign language education.* Basingstoke: Multilingual Matters.

Jenkins, J (2007) *English as a lingua franca: Attitude and identity.* Oxford: Oxford University Press.

Jo, M (2010) Why do English teachers have to be native speakers? *The Japan Times.* Available online at: www.japantimes.co.jp/life/2010/04/15/lifestyle/why-do-english-teachers-have-to-be-native-speakers/#.VfwahEJVikp (accessed 28 February 2016).

Johnston, B (2003) *Values in English language teaching.* Mahwah, NJ: Lawrence Erlbaum Associates.

Kachru, B (1985) 'Standards, codification and sociolinguistic realism: The English language in the Outer Circle' in Quirk, R, Widdowson, H and Cantu, Y (eds) *English in the world, teaching and learning the language and literatures.* Cambridge: Cambridge University Press, 11–30.

Kumabe, N (1996) ALT donyu ga motarashita mono (What the introduction of ALTs has brought). *Modern Language Teaching* 336: 13.

Lee, KWY (2009) *Pathways to collaboration: A case study of local and foreign teacher relationships in a South-Eastern Chinese university.* Unpublished Master's thesis, University of Toronto, Canada.

Leung, C, Harris, R and Rampton, B (1997) The idealized native speaker, reified ethnicities, and classroom. *TESOL Quarterly* 31/3: 543–560.

Llurda, E (2005) (ed) *Non-native language teachers: Perceptions, challenges and contributions to the profession.* New York, NY: Springer.

Luk, JCM and Lin, AMY (2010) *Classroom interactions as cross-cultural encounters.* London: Routledge.

Luo, WH (2010) 'Collaborative teaching of EFL by native and non-native English speaking teachers in Taiwan' in Mahboob, A (ed) *The NNEST lens: Non native English speakers in TESOL.* Newcastle upon Tyne: Cambridge Scholars Publishing, 263–284.

Mahboob, A (ed) (2010) *The NNEST lens: Non native English speakers in TESOL.* Newcastle upon Tyne: Cambridge Scholars Publishing.

Mahboob, A (2010) *The NNEST lens: non-native English speakers in TESOL.* Cambridge: Cambridge Scholars Publishing.

Medgyes, P (1992) Native or non-native: Who's worth more? *ELT Journal* 46/4: 340–349.

Moote, S (2003) Insight into team teaching: The English Teacher: An International Journal 6/3: 328–334.

Paikeday, T (1985) *The native speaker is dead!* Toronto: Paikeday Publications Inc.

Park, HY (2010) An analysis of native and non-native English teachers' perception on their role in elementary school settings of co-teaching. *English Language Teaching* 22(4): 133–163.

Pennycook, A (1994) *The cultural politics of English as an international language.* Harlow: Longman.

Phillipson, R (1992) *Linguistic imperialism.* Oxford: Oxford University Press.

Piller, I (2001) Who, if anyone, is a native speaker? *Anglistik. Mitteilungen des Verbandes Deutscher Anglisten* 12: 109–121

Sato, S (2009) 'Communication as an intersubjective and collaborative activity: when the native/non-native speaker's identity appears in computer-mediated communication' in Doerr, MN (ed) *The native speaker concept: Ethnographic investigations of native speaker effects.* Berlin: Mouton De Gruyter, 277–296.

Seidlhofer, B (1999) Double standards: Teacher education in the Expanding Circle. *World Englishes* 18/2: 233–245.

Tajino, A and Tajino, Y (2000) Native and non-native: what can they offer? Lessons from team-teaching in Japan. *ELT Journal* 54 (1): 3–11.

Train, R (2009) 'Toward a "natural" history of the native (standard) speaker' in Doerr, MN (ed) *The native speaker concept: Ethnographic investigations of native speaker effects.* Berlin: Mouton De Gruyter, 47–80.

Waters, A (2007) Native-speakerism in ELT: Plus ça change...? *System* 35/3: 281–292.

1

Responsibility without power: native-speaker experiences of team teaching in Japanese secondary schools

Luke Lawrence, Yokohama City University, Kanagawa, Japan

Introduction

ALTs (Assistant Language Teachers) have been firmly established within the Japanese education system since the introduction of the Japan Exchange and Teaching (JET) programme by the Japanese government in 1987. This project has been widely criticised as establishing an unequal hierarchy between the Native English-Speaking Teacher (NEST) and Local English Teacher (LET) working together in the same classroom, with the NEST in the subordinate role. One year before the introduction of the JET programme, in 1986, the British Council Japan contracted with one government ward in Tokyo to supply NESTs to teach alongside Japanese LETs. British Council NESTs now teach in 23 secondary schools and one elementary school across the ward. In contrast to the government-run JET programme, British Council NEST teachers were described as 'team teachers' and were to be responsible for the preparation and the bulk of the delivery of lessons. This inverse hierarchy, or at least more equal footing, should have resulted in a more cooperative, collaborative working relationship between NESTs and LETs. However, through insight gained from four semi-structured interviews with British Council NESTs past and present, this chapter will show that this has not necessarily been the case.

Concepts of native-speakerism in Japan

It is no surprise that the first serious challenge to Holliday's widely cited conception (2005) and subsequent clarification (2006) of native-speakerism (that posits the NEST as the belligerent colonialist forcing 'their' ways on the Local Teacher in thrall to the infallible NEST) came from within Japan. The redefinition by Houghton and Rivers in 'Native-Speakerism in Japan' (2013) turned Holliday's theory on its head by portraying the NEST as often an impotent victim, unable to have any real say in policies and practices in the culture and environment within which they are working. Japan is an overwhelmingly homogenised culture where clear distinctions between local population and foreigners (*gaijin*, literally 'outside people') are taken for granted and are part of everyday discourse. At the same time, the native speaker is held up as the ideal English teacher. These realities put

Japan in a prime position for the tensions between the two definitions of native-speakerism to come to the surface.

During the three years that I spent working within the Japanese education system as a NEST working alongside a Japanese Local English Teacher (LET), I saw these tensions played out on an everyday basis. I often felt isolated and discriminated against but powerless to do anything because of my status in the schools. However, at the same time, I enjoyed the teaching and was given responsibility, entrusted as the lead teacher in all classes and respected for my teaching knowledge and ability. I found this juxtaposition confusing and started to look for academic studies that recognised and discussed my own experiences. However, I found that academic papers either perpetuated Holliday's stereotype of the young, clueless, incompetent NEST and the all-knowing, highly qualified LET (e.g. Boecher, 2005; Tajino and Tajino, 2000) or described NESTs as the lead teacher usurping the implied natural authority of the anxious LETs. Even when these papers acknowledged the power imbalance between NESTs and LETs, they tended to suggest that this was not due to the actual skills or qualifications of the NESTs but was the product of the native speaker fallacy, whereby the NEST is regarded as superior simply because he/she is a native speaker (Miyazato, 2009; Butler, 2007). Neither of these scenarios fitted my own experience and that of my British Council NEST colleagues, many of whom were highly experienced and qualified, with either PGCEs from UK institutions or postgraduate degrees in teaching and linguistics. There were also many teachers who were long-term residents of Japan and well versed in cultural and linguistic matters and the needs and idiosyncrasies of Japanese learners. I began to wonder whether there was a significant difference between the experiences of my colleagues and myself and those of JET programme teachers that I had read about. I also wondered whether or not these differences were related to new conceptions of native-speakerism.

To help put the following discussion of these issues into context, it is perhaps useful to first give some background details regarding both the government-run JET programme and the British Council team teaching project.

The JET programme

The original intent of the JET programme was for Japanese students to increase their cultural awareness of foreign countries and, concomitantly, to develop their appreciation of their own Japanese language and culture. The programme pairs young-ish (the age limit of 35 years old has recently been raised to 40), untrained and new-to-Japan native speakers with LETs to work together as team teachers within the same secondary school classroom. The handbook for new NESTs produced by the Ministry of Education, Culture, Sports, Science and Technology (MEXT) in collaboration with the British Council defines team teaching simply as 'having two teachers in the classroom, rather than the usual one' (British Council, 2013: 8).

It was also envisaged that students would benefit from being exposed to 'real' English and cultural insights from the native speaker. The LET would support students when misunderstandings occurred and deal with classroom management, including discipline. As NESTs were generally untrained – in contrast to their LET counterparts, who had gone through the Japanese training programme – they were designated as *Assistant* Language Teachers (ALTs). The ALT Handbook itself states that it is 'important to remember that the JTL (LET) is a qualified teacher of language, and knows the schools, students and local culture far better than you do, as a newcomer' (ibid.). This positioning has tended to ensure that ALTs take a subordinate role, even when they have training or experience. At the same time, many LETs have complained that classes with ALTs are a mere sideline to the real business of teaching English, citing the youth and inexperience of ALTs as problematic (McConnell, 2000).

The British Council project

In the British Council/local ward project, NESTs were designated as 'team teachers', rather than ALTs, and were responsible for planning and preparing lessons as well as for the delivery of the majority of class activities. In a model that has remained more or less in place since the project's inception in 1986, one lesson period is set aside each week for the NEST and LET to meet and plan forthcoming lessons and, if necessary, to review and adapt lessons currently being taught. This approach was designed to ensure that the planning and teaching of all lessons would be a collaborative process between the British Council NEST and the LET.

In addition, but perhaps in juxtaposition to this collaborative ethos, the British Council has also offered an annual week-long Teacher Development Workshop for LETs. This features a number of sessions on different pedagogical themes delivered by British Council teachers and attended voluntarily by LETs.

Teacher distribution

Until 2012, it was common for one NEST to teach at one or two schools, depending on the size of the school, and for each student to receive one team-taught lesson per week for the whole of the school year. However, in 2012, due to changes in funding, the number of lessons pupils received was halved, and NESTs began to teach in three to five different schools on a two-week rotation system (i.e. pupils now received two team teacher lessons per month). The knock-on effect of this was that British Council teachers were present in each school less, which not only increased the workload for British Council teachers but may also have had some influence on the ability of NESTs and LETs to forge relationships and for NESTs to feel accepted as the only foreign worker in each school.

Lesson content

All lessons utilise original materials created by British Council teachers, which are subject to approval by LETs. At present, these lessons closely follow the language and themes of the students' regular coursebook, but they take a task-based approach, focusing on speaking and listening and encouraging communication between students. In order to standardise classes across the project, a core set of 20 lessons for each school grade were chosen and created by British Council teachers. Individual teachers are responsible for creating lessons, which are then shared with other teachers on the project via a shared computer drive. These can be adapted and personalised at will or at the request of a LET.

The present study

In order to explore whether the 'hybrid' experience I described at the beginning of the chapter was shared by others, and to investigate more fully the attitudes and experiences related to being a NEST working alongside a LET in the context of a public secondary school in Japan, I carried out semi-structured interviews with four British Council teachers.

Due to the small sample size and the open-ended nature of my enquiry, I felt that semi-structured interviews were the best way to explore the issues at hand. Following Richards (2003), I approached the interviews as a 'professional conversation' (Kvale, 1996: 5, cited in Richards, 2003: 50), with an awareness of the need to collaborate with the interviewees as I would do in any conversation. Richards makes the distinction that, unlike in conversation, interviews should aim to encourage the speaker without offering the interviewer's opinion in order to focus on 'drawing from the speaker the richest and fullest account possible' (ibid.). I wanted the interviewees to feel that they could expand and steer the interview in any direction they liked, while at the same time keeping to an approximate planned interview schedule (see Appendix). Additionally, the fact of my own background on the project meant that I already had a good overview of the field being analysed and was able to formulate relevant questions in advance without limiting the 'depth and breadth of the respondent's story' (Dörnyei, 2007: 136), which the semi-structured interview is well suited to.

It was also important to acknowledge the importance of co-construction that permeates all human interactions and the fact that both interviewer and interviewee are 'unavoidably active' (Holstein and Gubrium, 1995: 4). Mann (2011) states that '*all* interviews are already sites of social interaction where ideas, facts, views, details and stories are collaboratively produced by interviewee and interviewer' (2011: 8, *italics his*). Although I attempted to keep my own responses to a minimum at all stages, every utterance by both interviewer and interviewee is inextricably linked to the next (ibid.), which makes the final product a communicative event, rather than simply isolated opinions from interviewees. The fact that in this study there were no concrete hypotheses that I was seeking to prove or disprove meant that there was little temptation to steer the conversation one way or another. However, the underlying human impulse to share and corroborate our own experiences may have had an effect on the overall tone and direction of the interviews.

An additional element was that in this study the interviewees were colleagues of mine. This gave a different experience to a typical scenario of an outside interviewer coming into a research arena and interviewing volunteer participants. Acquaintance interviews (Garton and Copland, 2010) can have both benefits and drawbacks. The fact that I had a 'prior relationship' with all of the interviewees that had evolved outside of the narrow scope of a research context meant that some of the usual practices associated with interviewing did not apply. For example, asking softer questions to begin in order to make the interviewee relaxed and open was not necessary as we were already comfortable with one another. There was also no need for lengthy explanations of factual information as I was already familiar with the background and context they were working in. At the same time, this intimacy may lead to complexities in the roles of interviewer and interviewee (ibid.), which could mean that what is understood is not stated or that themes introduced by the interviewer may be misjudged and lead to misunderstandings or misrepresentation. I sought to deal with these issues by not responding directly to phrases from interviewees such as 'as you know' and by pressing for clarification of statements that could be construed as ambiguous.

Participants and interview themes

Two of the teachers had worked on the British Council project previously and two were currently active on the project. They were selected in order to gain both an immediate and a longer-term perspective on the team teaching experience and to highlight and offset current issues that may influence the individual experience of teachers. The participants were:

Teacher A
A highly experienced and qualified teacher who spent a total of eight years working on the project but stopped over four years ago. At the time he began he had been in Japan for two years and had lower-intermediate Japanese ability. By the end of his time on the project, he had been in Japan for ten years and therefore his knowledge of Japanese school culture was very thorough and his language ability had also improved.

Teacher B
Another very experienced and qualified teacher (he holds a teaching diploma and a Master's degree in TESOL and linguistics) with a good knowledge of Japanese language and culture. He worked on the project for six years over five years ago.

Teacher C
Currently working on the project, he has taught in Japan for ten years and previously worked as a full-time solo teacher in a private Japanese high school for five years. This background has given him a good knowledge of Japanese school culture and the particular needs of Japanese young learners. His Japanese language ability is upper-elementary/lower-intermediate.

Teacher D
A teacher new to the project who has previously worked in secondary schools in Europe in a similar capacity. He has been in Japan for six years and describes his Japanese speaking ability as intermediate, with lower levels of reading and writing skills. Although reasonably familiar with Japanese culture in general, this is his first experience of teaching in the Japanese school system.

The interviews focused on five main themes: relationships with LETs, the classroom role of the NEST, the NESTs' perception of themselves in relation to their designation as team teacher as opposed to ALT, issues around being a native-speaker teacher in Japan and suggestions for change and improvement in the project.

Relationships with Local English Teachers

All participants reported a diversity of experiences in terms of relationships with LETs. Although experiences were generally positive overall, all interviewees were readily able to cite exceptions. In some cases, these were due to personality clashes which may be expected in any professional context. However, a number of examples of negative relationships seemed to be a direct result of conflicting role expectations, of disagreements in pedagogical procedure, or even of NESTs' perceptions of having been treated negatively by LETs precisely because of their status as a native-speaker teacher.

Teacher D felt very strongly that Local Teachers did not show the same level of professionalism that was expected of him. Examples of this were making last-minute changes to the teaching schedule without informing the NEST, or the LET calling the NEST on his day off and demanding changes to lessons planned for the following morning. As well as finding practices such as these intrusive and unprofessional, the NESTs felt that LETs did not understand that they had other teaching commitments outside the British Council project. Similar scenarios were reported by Teacher C, who gave an example of a LET who stopped him halfway through a class and changed the activity as he did not approve of it. Teacher C explained to the LET that this action was both unprofessional and humiliating as it was done in front of the students.

There was a feeling that some of the LETs' attitudes and practices, as reported by NESTs, were the result of LETs viewing NESTs as service providers. This is perhaps to be expected from a private contract scenario. However, interviewees also suggested that they would not have been treated in a similar manner if they were Japanese teachers under contract in similar arrangements.

Other tensions emerged due to disagreements over pedagogical practice. All interviewees gave examples of times when they were asked to do something that they personally objected to on a pedagogical basis, and that they felt undermined what the British Council and local government ward was attempting to achieve through the project.

The most striking example of this was given by Teacher A, who was asked by the LET to point to Japanese sentences on the board and elicit the corresponding sentences in 'correct' English from the students. He explained that this mechanical approach to teaching and learning English may damage the students' love of English and their whole attitude towards English education. He reported feeling 'fake' as he could not read the sentences perfectly himself and was confident that the same target language could have been taught in a more communicative way. He refused to do what was asked and instead stayed at the back of the classroom whilst the LET performed the activity. Although he was not admonished for his refusal at the time, the following academic year all British Council teachers on the project were told that they were required to do all activities asked of them by the LET, even if they disagreed with them on a pedagogical basis. This suggests that the British Council management had received feedback about the incident from the LET.

Disagreements such as these were often played out in the allocated weekly planning meeting. The idea behind the weekly meeting time between NESTs and LETs was to encourage more equal collaboration and to share ideas about the lessons. This proved to be effective in many cases as it provided a time for respite and communication between NESTs and LETs on both a personal and a professional level. As well as providing an opportunity to share ideas and negotiate lesson plans, weekly meetings were also used for general chat and, in some cases, to allow LETs to practise speaking English. However, some interviewees also viewed these meetings negatively as they highlighted the inequality of the relationship. For example, Teacher C preferred to keep his lesson plans open in order to allow room for flexibility and adaptation during the class. However, he felt that LETs often went through the plans with a 'derogatory attitude' and that they did not trust that the lesson would be successful without a precise plan. Teacher C also reported that he invariably yielded to the LET in all demands but felt that it was unfair that LETs were able to decide *what* was to be done, without giving any input as to *how* it could be put into practice. Teacher D also greatly resented the fact that, as he saw it, LETs exercised 'power without responsibility'.

The belief that LETs wield the ultimate power and have the final say without having to design activities or prepare worksheets can have a negative impact on NESTs' relationships with LETs. Teacher D felt strongly that LETs' attitudes needed to change if there was ever going to be equality, while Teacher C thought that these attitudes were 'unfair, but not unreasonable' given the nature of the client/contractor relationship. Teacher B was similarly resigned, stating that his proposals were refused from time to time, which he just accepted.

In contrast, both Teacher A and Teacher B reported a number of positive working relationship experiences in the planning and teaching process and, in some cases, a reversal of the power structure experienced by Teacher C and Teacher D. At the start of his time working on the project, Teacher B was able to learn some useful techniques and activities from the LETs. Meanwhile, Teacher A made sure to coordinate his lesson plans with what the LETs were doing, without specifically being asked to, in order to make the situation more team-like, instead of him 'calling the shots'. This required a heightened awareness of the power relations between LETs and NESTs and relied on subtlety and diplomacy in order not to offend the LET. He believed that a combination of his being a native speaker, working for a reputable company and having many years' experience teaching in Japanese secondary schools meant that LETs may have been reluctant to question his ideas and lesson plans and perhaps hesitant to suggest their own ideas in case he did not agree with them. As Teacher A speculated, 'I think, you know, if I was fresh off the boat, no teaching experience, working for a company that was not so well known, it might have been different.'

Classroom roles

Three of the four interviewees reported that in all classes they were the lead teachers and that they basically taught the whole lesson. Only Teacher A reported that he was able to get a fairly even split between himself and the LET teaching in the classroom.

In Teacher B's case, there were two LETs at the start of his time on the project that took the lead and controlled the class. They also prepared the lessons in terms of content and materials. He confessed that he did not mind this at the time, but that he may have been 'put out' if it had happened later on in his career on the project. Like the other NESTs, Teacher B felt it natural that he should be leading the lessons.

Indeed, Teacher C and Teacher D both preferred a hands-off approach by LETs in the classroom and wanted to be left alone to teach the class without interference from the LET. Teacher D recalled one LET who 'just looks in the fish tank' for the entire lesson and Teacher C mentioned a time that a LET actually sat outside the classroom and did marking while he taught the class by himself. The NESTs saw these as positive scenarios. When asked to give an example of a good relationship that he has with a LET, Teacher C talked about a LET who was new to the area and to the British Council project. After watching Teacher C's initial classes and recognising his ability as a teacher, he was happy to take a back seat and let Teacher C teach the class. Teacher C felt that in the large classes that he teaches (up to 40 students) the LET's role should be 'a more disciplinarian role, or just, you know, monitoring, meandering and helping out the kids that are a bit slow.'

This was qualified to some extent by Teacher A, who stated that he always tried to involve the LETs as much as possible in the lessons and that he was usually able to do so but that they sometimes needed 'a bit of a push'. These reports imply that some LETs were reluctant to become involved in the delivery of team-taught lessons.

The issue of classroom management came up in three out of the four interviews. It is understood – and indeed forms part of the initial orientation that British Council teachers new to the project receive – that NESTs are not to get involved in disciplining students. This area of direct classroom management is the sole domain of the LET. Teacher C saw this situation as 'unfortunate', as it meant less authority for the NEST in the eyes of the students. Teacher B recognised it as a problem, particularly when the LET lacked the ability to control or discipline a class, but did not think that discipline and punishment should be part of the NEST's role. As he explained, each school has its own unique culture within which different forms of behaviour are acceptable and of which the NEST, as a visitor in the school, may not be aware. On top of this is the fact that NESTs only see the students a couple of times a month and, subsequently, are not aware of any issues that the students may be having in their lives, or of the school's policy towards that particular student.

There was also a general feeling among the NESTs that they were not regarded as proper teachers by the LETs. NEST lessons were always used by LETs to review previously taught grammar or language points. In fact, lesson plans were often rejected on the grounds that the students had not covered the relevant grammar or language. If the NEST suggested that they could introduce the new language in the team-taught lesson, they were refused. As Teacher C succinctly put it, 'I feel like I'm a reinforcer, as opposed to a teacher.' This is a revealing insight. It shows that, on the one hand, the NESTs in this study are respected and given autonomy to plan, create and teach the majority of the lesson by themselves; on the other, they are not trusted to input and explain how new language works, which remains the domain of the LETs.

Although some NESTs resented the lack of trust and respect this positioning suggested, it was justified by Teacher A, who believed that his role as a native speaker was to get students producing language. He thought that it was more important for the NEST to be leading the production stage than the input stage, which he believed was relatively easy for anyone to teach.

'Team teacher' versus 'ALT'

One of the biggest distinctions between this unique British Council project and other similar government-run initiatives is the use of the term 'team teacher' to describe the NEST's role, as opposed to the more common ALT (Assistant Language Teacher).

It was clear from the interviews that this distinction was important to NESTs. Teacher C stated that being referred to as a team teacher was definitely better than being called an ALT, but that both were inferior to being embedded within a school simply as a 'teacher', as in his previous job. Teacher A felt that the distinction was important in order to highlight the fact that British Council teachers do not do what 'normal ALTs' do, which is the whole point of the project. He also felt that it was important for students to recognise the NEST and LET as a team. Teacher B felt that it was not important to him as an individual to distinguish between 'ALT' and 'team teacher' and that teachers who were offended by the term 'ALT' or saw it as pejorative were being somewhat precious. Furthermore, in terms of the overall project, it was important for the British Council to make the distinction clear. It seems that in this respect, however, it has not been successful, as other interviewees confirmed that they were usually referred to as an ALT by the LET and by other members of the school staff. For example, pigeonholes and desk spaces provided for British Council teachers were often labelled 'ALT'.

Issues around working as a native speaker in Japanese schools

The NESTs interviewed gave a mix of positive and negative responses when asked if they had experienced any problems or negative reactions as a result of their status as the only non-Japanese staff member working in the schools in which they taught.

On the positive side, Teacher A reported that he always felt welcome and that other teachers in the schools went out of their way to help him. Similarly, Teacher B said that he did not feel discriminated against and that it helped that he always made a point of introducing himself on the first day. He also socialised with other teachers during the lunch break and took part in general conversations. This level of interaction was only possible because he is able to speak Japanese and he believes that he would not have enjoyed these social situations at all if he had not been able to do so. Tellingly, despite this positivity, both teachers were readily able to cite examples of discrimination they had faced. Teacher A recounted an incident when his students had wanted to ask him a question. It transpired that another teacher in the school had told the students, somewhat derogatorily, that when a 'Westerner' crashes into your car, they will not apologise. The students wanted to know whether this was true. Teacher A reported that he had answered the question as well as he felt he could under the circumstances but that he had felt uncomfortable being the spokesperson for and defender of 'Westerners'.

Teacher C and Teacher D were less positive about their experiences, both as a native speaker working in Japan and, in the case of Teacher D, specifically within their role as a NEST working on this project.

Teacher C had experienced outright hostility and 'borderline racism' when working as a solo teacher in a private upper secondary school, and said that although he had not experienced any kind of hostility working on this project, he felt very isolated in his working environment. The nature of the schedule, he believes, does not allow time or opportunity to build relationships, either with individual teachers or with the school itself. When asked if he was treated differently from the Japanese part-time teachers at the schools, he originally said he was not but later qualified his comment by saying that he was not sure.

Teacher D disagreed and thought that he was definitely treated differently from Japanese part-time teachers and that no attempt was made either by other teachers or by the school management to make him feel part of the school. As with Teacher C, this had led to feelings of isolation and a lack of engagement and enthusiasm for the job. Additionally, Teacher D also believed that he was not treated as an equal by the LETs, who regularly questioned his authority regarding accurate English language use. As a new teacher to the project, he was shocked by this treatment, as he had never experienced it before. He said he believed it was a direct result of his being a native teacher and the preconceptions that some LETs may have around the abilities and status of NESTs.

Suggestions for change and improvement

As the interviews wound down, I asked the NEST interviewees for some suggestions as to how the project could be improved. This was left as an open question and a wide range of answers were given that encompassed ideas to improve the daily working lives of both NESTs and LETs as well as wider issues around being a foreigner working in Japan.

Teacher D would like to see joint training of NESTs and LETs. As well as fostering improved communication, this would also ensure that both sides were on the same page pedagogically speaking, which would reduce the chances of tensions or disagreements. In conjunction with this, Teacher D also recommended that LETs contribute to making teaching materials. As Teacher A pointed out, this would contribute not only to LETs' skills development but also to building confidence in LETs who may be afraid of making mistakes with English. Presenting their own original materials (as opposed to textbook exercises) would help LETs to see themselves on a more equal footing with NESTs in terms of their ability to present and practise language in the production stage. At present, LETs described in this project do not contribute at all to worksheet and materials development, and, as Teacher A reported, they never offer to do so (with the exception of the two teachers cited by Teacher B at the start of his time on the project). Given the terms of the agreement between the British Council and the local government ward, it may be that LETs believe this work to be the responsibility of the NEST and part of what the ward is paying for by hiring expensive British Council teachers rather than cheaper ALTs.

In order to counteract the problem of isolation, Teacher C stated that he would like to see more than one NEST in a school at the same time. This would allow for natural and spontaneous sharing of ideas and opinions regarding lesson plans and activities, which he believes the LET is supposed to provide but does not. It is not clear whether, in this case, this is because NESTs do not solicit opinions from LETs or whether LETs do not offer them. (When I was teaching, I was often able to bounce ideas and opinions off LETs in a natural and spontaneous manner, which helped relieve isolation.) Neither does Teacher C believe the irregular meetings organised for NESTs by the British Council to share ideas and give each other feedback on teaching materials are effective. He felt that the forced, fixed sharing of ideas lacked the real-time urgency of on-the-spot discussion.

In order to have the opportunity to form more meaningful relationships with LETs, both Teacher C and Teacher B believed it was imperative that NESTs were in the same schools on a full-time basis and that students should receive one team-taught lesson a week. This would maximise the effectiveness of the impact of teaching on students as well as providing more opportunities for the NEST and LET to work together to better fine-tune their roles and gain more practice of working in a team.

In parallel with this, Teacher B also thought that NESTs should be more involved in the life of the school. They could attend sports days and school assemblies, assist form tutors and attend social events with other teachers. This approach would allow NESTs to become more integrated in the fabric of the school, which should go some way towards their feeling less marginalised. It should also help to normalise the presence of NESTs for the LET and other teaching and administration staff. This familiarity may help eliminate any prejudices, preconceptions or fears that school staff may have about NESTs in particular or 'foreigners' in general.

Discussion

The experiences and opinions of my colleagues on this project past and present suggest that my own feelings of being trapped between the two sides of the native-speakerism debate were not unique. Although British Council NESTs enjoy more freedom and responsibility than their ALT counterparts, there was a pronounced feeling of 'them' and 'us' that emerged during the course of the interviews.

In terms of the relationship between NESTs and LETs, it appears that although for the most part there are no overt problems, in many cases the relationship is far from ideal. As mentioned previously, the fact that all interviews can be seen as co-constructed communicative events (Holstein and Gubrium, op cit; Mann, op cit; Talmy and Richards, 2011) means that my questions and answers, and the lines of inquiry that I chose to pursue, had a direct impact on the interviewees. It may be the case that in encouraging the interviewees to expand more on their negative experiences, a distorted picture emerged that placed LETs in a less favourable light than an alternative line of questioning may have produced. Also, the fact that I, as the interviewer, was also one of 'us' may have also contributed to, and even helped create, the 'them' and 'us' mindset that was apparent. This 'discursive' (Talmy and Richards, ibid.) view of interviews should be borne in mind as the data is interpreted and analysed.

The observation that LETs enjoyed 'power without responsibility' and examples given by NESTs of being at the beck and call of the LET can make NESTs feel that they are the unequal partner. However, when we consider the fact that the British Council is a service provider in what is essentially a client/contractor relationship, this inequality is understandable, however undesirable it may be for NESTs. Similar examples of this inequality were found within the JET programme (Miyazato, op cit), which is not a private contract, and from other private dispatch companies (McEvoy, 2014). However, in these cases, NESTs are generally not experienced or qualified so it is perhaps understandable that they have less status in the classroom.

Additionally, accusations levelled at LETs of unprofessionalism and lack of contribution to lesson planning is the reverse of what has been found in other studies (Hasegawa, 2008) and could be due to a number of factors. For instance, they may not have the time or even the expertise to produce lesson materials in the British Council style. The widely held stereotype that LETs are the highly trained and experienced half of the team (Boecher, op cit; Tajino and Tajino, op cit) is not borne out by reality in the cases described here with regard to practical English language activities. The teachers on the JET scheme receive very little practical training outside their initial two-week on-the-job period shadowing an older, experienced teacher. In contrast, all British Council teachers hold the practical teaching-based Cambridge CELTA, many hold the higher-level DELTA, some hold PGCE certificates from the UK and increasing numbers are taking postgraduate qualifications in teaching and linguistics-related fields.

It seems to be the case that rather than the LETs being frustrated by the NESTs' lack of teaching ability, as found in other studies (Tajino and Tajino, ibid.), it is the NESTs who are irritated by the LETs' lack of teaching competence and awareness of seemingly obvious, basic pedagogical principles.

Of course, these principles may embrace Western ideals of CLT-focused pedagogy, which may or may not have a place in the Japanese secondary school classroom. Furthermore, championing these principles would suggest that NESTs are engaging in what Holliday calls 'othering' (2006: 385), 'especially when LETs have difficulty with the specific types of active, collaborative, and self-directed "learner-centred" teaching-learning techniques that have frequently been constructed and packaged as superior within the English speaking West' (Holliday, ibid.). On the other hand, it simultaneously supports the more recent re-definition of native-speakerism that recognises the abilities of NESTs and empathises with the frustration of being a skilled and experienced teacher but having all power and authority stripped away (Houghton and Rivers, op cit).

A less complex explanation, put forward by McEvoy (op cit), may simply be that the respective roles are not clearly defined and that neither the NEST nor the LET is sure to what extent each should be contributing or how they should be communicating their needs and intentions to one another.

Indeed, in this study, there seemed to be little empathy towards the LETs from some of the NESTs. Although complaining of unfairness and of being treated unprofessionally, they showed little awareness of the impact their presence may have on the professional and practical day-to-day lives of the LETs. For example, in Japan, teachers take responsibility for school administration and after-school sports clubs as well as their own teaching duties, with up to 40 to 50 per cent of teachers' time being spent on activities other than preparing and teaching classes (Sakui, 2004). Although this was mentioned briefly by interviewees, it was not taken into account when considering reasons why LETs may be unwilling or unable to contribute more equally with the time-consuming process of materials development.

Another factor may be the degree of Japanese language ability and cultural sophistication that the NEST possesses. The teachers in this study with comparatively lower Japanese skills, or less experience or knowledge of Japanese school culture, reported a more negative overall experience. This may have been a contributing factor to the lack of communication and support in the planning stages and to the ineffectiveness of the weekly meeting hour.

It seems clear from the answers given by Teacher B in particular that efforts were made by some LETs to integrate NESTs smoothly into the life and culture of the school and, from my own experience, this was done in a multitude of subtle ways that only became apparent with hindsight. One example of this was the fact that in all schools I was always given the various handouts, announcements, updates and weekly student news-sheets that all staff received regularly. This was despite the fact that they were written entirely in Japanese and it was assumed that I was unable to read them. I was puzzled by this at the time and threw a lot of them away without even attempting to read them. I now believe that this was done deliberately to help me feel included in the life of the school. In some schools, I was also included in staff photo sessions and invited to participate in sports days and culture festivals.

In this study, classroom roles were found to be generally one-sided, with NESTs leading classes and teaching the majority of the lessons. This is consistent with studies of other team teaching programmes (Miyazato, op cit), but differs in the sense that the NESTs in this study felt that this was a natural state of affairs and were even demanding more autonomy and less 'interference' from LETs. This outcome can be seen as going against the collaborative ethos of the original aim of the British Council project. However, it may also be part of what sets it apart from other schemes.

In terms of native-speakerism, elements from the debate are apparent. On the one hand, it could be argued that NESTs are arrogantly disregarding collaboration in order to dictate their own agenda and methodologies to LETs, reinforcing the political inequalities that Holliday (2006) perceives as prevalent throughout the EFL world. Alternatively, it could be argued that, in this case, the skills and experience of the NESTs, dispatched from a company that is recognised worldwide as an expert in education, are simply receiving their due recognition and being enhanced to the full. Seen from this viewpoint, the project can be held up as a pioneer in combating the negative effects of Houghton and Rivers' (op cit) definition of native-speakerism, with NESTs standing up for themselves against institutional and societal suppression. However, it should be noted that this deference/recognition of skill and expertise only goes so far. The fact that the role of NESTs in this project can be seen as that of a reviewer or 'reinforcer', rather than of a teacher of original input, shows that some in-built perceptions of either the role or the capability of NESTs continue to exist.

Whatever the underlying causes of this imbalance, there seems to be a fundamental flaw in the set-up of the entire project. By having a system that allows the NEST to prepare and deliver the majority of the lesson, the concept of team or collaborative teaching is undermined. In addition, the fact that the British Council offers workshops to LETs, led by the project NESTs, may well contribute to LETs' understandings of the different roles LETs and NESTs are expected to adopt in the classroom. This would seem to confirm Holliday's view of the native speaker taking control and assuming dominance over the compliant LET.

The decision to refer to NESTs as 'team teachers' rather than 'ALTs' seems to have had a very positive effect in terms of how NESTs view themselves, particularly vis-à-vis 'normal' ALTs. However, according to the interviewees, the underlying values inherent in the term have not filtered through to schools and LETs, who, NESTs believe, often treat them as ALTs (overriding their decisions and not allowing them to input new language). However, it could be that, from the point of view of the LET, the terminology itself is neutral and relatively meaningless and they do not perceive the same nuances in the labels as the NESTs; 'ALT' may just be a handy generic word used to describe the foreign teachers they work with. LETs are prepared to entrust much of the responsibility for their classes (for which the LET is ultimately accountable) to British Council NESTs. Were they also to entrust inputting new language and overall control of the lesson to the NESTs, they would be in danger of disenfranchising themselves. This is understandable, but could be seen as confirmation of the glass ceiling that Houghton and Rivers (op cit) imply. NESTs are allowed some responsibility, but only so much.

As we have seen, the roles and relationship between NESTs and LETs on this project suggest that definitions of native-speakerism are perhaps more complex than the dichotomy suggested at the beginning of the chapter.

Conclusions

Although this study was very small and limited in scale, only taking into account the views of selected NESTs and no LETs, the insights gained reveal a multitude of issues to be explored further in terms of practical improvements that can be made to this project and potentially to other team teaching programmes within Japan and elsewhere. From my personal point of view, although the experiences of my colleagues did not entirely chime with my own, this study has helped me to put the confusion I felt over being stuck between two definitions of native-speakerism into perspective. It has also shown that the debate over who can be considered as perpetrator or victim is far from over and is more complex than the discussion so far in the literature seems to suggest.

Future studies in this area would benefit from including opinions from LETs as well as NESTs (see Copland et al., 2016). In order to better identify the extent to which tensions around working relationships and classroom roles can be attributed to native-speaker status, it would be useful to run comparative studies of part-time Japanese teachers' experiences of teaching in secondary schools. It would also be useful to conduct case study research on different NESTs, particularly those who are able to use Japanese and are culturally sophisticated in terms of Japanese culture in general and Japanese schooling in particular. Do these skills positively affect the experiences of NESTs or not?

For this long-running and unique British Council project to thrive and prosper into the future, it is essential for both NESTs and LETs to understand the complexities of the native-speakerism debate and how each group perceives the other. Furthermore, it would be helpful for NESTs and LETs to share their perceptions, their fears and their expectations. Through such discussions, perhaps the 'them' and 'us' mentality will dissipate and mutual respect and true collaboration will emerge.

References

Boecher, Y (2005) Native and Non-native English-Speaking Teacher distinctions: From dichotomy to collaboration. *The CATESOL Journal* 17/1: 67–75.

British Council (2013) *ALT Handbook.* www.britishcouncil.jp/sites/britishcouncil.jp/files/alt-handbook-en.pdf (accessed 18 February 2016).

Butler, YG (2007) Factors associated with the notion that native speakers are the ideal language teachers: An examination of elementary school teachers in Japan. *JALT Journal* 29/1: 7–40.

Copland, F, Garton, S and Mann, S (2016) *Investigating NEST schemes around the world: supporting NEST/LET collaborative practices.* London: The British Council.

Dörnyei, Z (2007) *Research methods in applied linguistics.* Oxford: Oxford University Press.

Garton, S and Copland, F (2010) 'I like this interview; I get cakes and cats!': The effect of prior relationships on interview talk. *Qualitative Research* 10/5: 533–551.

Hasegawa, H (2008) Non-native and native speakers' perceptions of a team-teaching approach: Case of the JET programme. T*he International Journal of Language, Society and Culture* 26: 42–54.

Holliday, A (2005) *The struggle to teach English as an international language.* Oxford: Oxford University Press.

Holliday, A (2006) Native-Speakerism. *ELT Journal* 60/4: 385–387.

Holstein, JA and Gubrium, JF (1995) *The Active Interview.* California: SAGE.

Houghton, SA and Rivers, DJ (eds) (2013) *Native-speakerism in Japan: Intergroup dynamics in foreign language education.* Bristol: Multilingual Matters.

Mann, S (2011) A critical review of qualitative interviews in applied linguistics. *Applied Linguistics* 32/1: 6–24.

McConnell, DL (2000) *Importing diversity: Inside Japan's JET program.* London: University of California Press.

McEvoy, J (2014) An analysis of the perspectives of dispatch (haken assistant) language teachers regarding the status quo of the ALT system. *Sophia TESOL Forum 6.*

Miyazato, K (2009) Power-sharing between NS and NNS teachers: Linguistically powerful AETs vs. culturally powerful JTEs. *JALT Journal* 31/1: 35–62.

Richards, K (2003) *Qualitative inquiry in TESOL.* Basingstoke: Palgrave Macmillan.

Sakui, K (2004) Wearing two pairs of shoes: Language teaching in Japan. *ELT Journal* 58/2: 155–163.

Tajino, A and Tajino, Y (2000) Native and non-native: what can they offer? Lessons from team-teaching in Japan. *ELT Journal* 54/1: 3–11.

Talmy, S and Richards, K (2011) Theorizing qualitative research interviews in applied linguistics. *Applied Linguistics* 32/1: 1–5.

Appendix

Interview schedule

1	In general, what is/was your relationship with the Local Teachers like? Can you give one positive example and one negative example?
2	Do/Did you feel that you can't/couldn't express your true opinion or ideas? Was there a time when a proposal or idea was denied or refused?
3	Do/Did you ever feel discriminated against in the schools you were teaching in?
4	How would you describe your role in the classroom?
5	Does the 'team teacher' label make a difference to you?
6	What do you think are/were the student expectations of you as a native speaker? What are/were the Local Teacher expectations?
7	Have you had any general problems as a native-speaker teacher in Japan? Is this project any different?
8	Is there anything (in terms of teaching or something else) that you would like to do/have done, but feel that you can't/couldn't do?
9	What would you like to see change about the project?

2

Fostering better collaborative relationships between Native English Speaker Teachers and Local English Teachers for a more effective Native English Teacher (NET) Scheme in Hong Kong

Elaine Hau Hing Tang, English Language Teaching Unit,
The Chinese University of Hong Kong

Introduction

In the past two decades, Hong Kong society has been experiencing numerous challenges and transformations. These are due to the fast-changing and competitive economic environment in the Asia-Pacific Region as well as the political transition in July 1997 from being a British colony to a Special Administrative Region of China. Policy-makers and the public have increasing expectations of the role and functions of school education (Cheng, 2009). English is often the chief educational concern, it being 'a habitus for the community, a way of life to the millions of westernised, cosmopolitan local residents' (Chan, 2002: 282). Also, the new language policy put in place in 1997, which stipulated that most public sector secondary schools must use Chinese as the medium of instruction (MOI) instead of English, has led to long-term changes to the teaching and learning of languages in Hong Kong. It is within this context that a Native-speaking English Teacher (NET) scheme started to be implemented in secondary and primary schools in the 1998/99 and 2002/03 school years respectively.

Language use and English language teaching in Hong Kong

For the majority of Hong Kong (HK)'s population, the mother tongue and the language medium for everyday communication has always been Chinese, mainly Cantonese (Education Department, 1997). Following British colonisation in 1842, English became the official language in HK (Ho, 2006) and the language of administration, law and education (Cheng, 2004). Although at least 95 per cent of the population are ethnically Chinese (ibid.), Chinese (although undefined but generally believed to be written Chinese and spoken Cantonese) was only added as another official language with the declaration of the Official Language Ordinance in 1974 (Ho and Wong, 2004). Unlike other ex-colonies such as Singapore, HK Chinese do not use English among themselves unless some members of the group do not speak Cantonese (ibid.). In fact, according to the 2011 Population Census findings, Cantonese was the most commonly spoken language at home for almost 90 per cent of the HK population aged five and over (Census and Statistics Department, the Government of the Hong Kong Special Administrative Region, 2012).

In the 1980s, as many as 90 per cent of secondary schools used English as the MOI (Ho, op cit), although in these schools, mixed-code (Chinese and English) teaching was very common (Crooke, 2000); while all textbooks and examinations were in English, classes were mostly conducted in Cantonese (Cheng, op. cit.). Nevertheless, Leung and Lee (2006) suggest that English has failed to take root in HK as people are determined to maintain their cultural identity and choice of lingua franca. Cantonese has therefore always overshadowed the coloniser's language, English. Some also began to wonder if English should continue to be the MOI in most schools, as this was believed to impose barriers when students expressed views and asked questions (Education Department, op cit). According to the department, only 33 per cent of pupils were capable of learning effectively in both English and Cantonese.

Finally, in May 1997, right before the change of sovereignty, the Legislative Council decided that Chinese was to be used as the MOI in all public sector secondary schools, starting from the Secondary 1 intake of the 1998/99 school year. At the same time, there were indicators showing that HK after 1997 was becoming a less plurilingual society and that English was declining in importance (Leung and Lee, op cit). For example, English speeches given in Legislative Council are given little coverage in the media. Also, from 1993 to 2003, English television programmes very seldom entered the list of the top 20, exceptions being the very short ones helping locals learn English (with the use of Cantonese) (ibid.). In order to maintain the city's position as an international financial centre, the government's language education policy has been for young people to be 'biliterate (Chinese and English) and trilingual (Cantonese, Mandarin, and English)' (Education Department, op cit; Education Bureau, 2009). The government has thus provided support measures and additional resources for schools (Ho and Wong, op cit) in order to prevent any possible lowering of students' standard of English due to reduced exposure to the English language (Education Department, op cit).

The Native-speaking English Teacher (NET) Scheme in Hong Kong

In the midst of these educational reforms and English language teaching challenges, a Native-speaking English Teacher (NET) Scheme has been implemented in public sector secondary and primary schools since the 1998/99 and 2002/03 school years respectively to 'enhance the teaching of English Language and increase exposure of students to English' (Education Bureau, 2015: 2). At the same time, it can be seen from the objective statements of the Primary NET Scheme and the Secondary NET Scheme (officially called Enhanced NET Scheme in Secondary Schools) that the government has different expectations for the schemes at the two levels and hence for the NESTs too.

According to the Education Bureau (ibid.), the objectives of the Primary NET Scheme are to:

- provide an authentic environment for children to learn English
- develop children's interest in learning English and establish the foundation for life-long learning
- help Local English Teachers (LETs) develop innovative learning and teaching methods, materials, curricula and activities suited to the needs of local children
- disseminate good practices in language learning and teaching through region-based teacher development programmes such as experience-sharing seminars/workshops and networking activities.

Meanwhile, the objectives of the Secondary NET Scheme are to:

- enrich the English language learning environment in schools
- enhance the learning and teaching of English with linguistically and culturally authentic materials and resources
- strengthen teaching capacity through school-based professional development and collaboration between NETs and English Panel Members.

A key difference observed from the two lists is that Native English Speaker Teachers (NESTs) teaching in primary schools are expected to resource Local English Teachers (LETs) and disseminate good practices not only in school-based events but also in region-wide ones (which seems to suggest that NESTs are linguistically and pedagogically superior) whereas those teaching in secondary schools are to collaborate with the LETs (perhaps suggesting a more equal partnership). In the Primary NET Scheme, schools are also supported by Advisory Teachers (ATs) from the NET Section of the Education Bureau, who facilitate the deployment of the NESTs and provide support for effective teaching strategies and curriculum resources (ibid.).

In terms of the mode of deployment of the NESTs, the Primary NET Scheme is a lot more structured and some would perhaps say more rigid than the secondary one because of the necessity for a primary school to hire a NEST through the Education Bureau's NET Scheme and then to follow a prescribed syllabus developed by the bureau. In 2004, the HK Curriculum Development Council recommended including a Reading Workshop component for as much as 40 per cent of English lesson time in primary schools. Consequently, the Primary Literacy Programme – Reading (Key Stage 1) (PLP-R (KS1)) was developed and piloted in the same year. The PLP-R (KS1) uses teaching strategies such as Storytelling, Reading Aloud, Shared Reading, Guided Reading and Independent Reading, and it is believed that the programme can '[harness] the expertise and experience available in the Primary Native-speaking English Teacher' (ibid.: 2). For a primary school to hire a NEST under the Primary NET Scheme, it would mean joining the PLP-R (KS1), or PLP-R/W (KS 1), which includes a writing component as well – hereafter called Primary Literary Programme, or PLP – at the same time. The only way NESTs are deployed is to co-teach the PLP with a non-native-speaking Local English Teacher (usually two to four lessons per class per week), while the LETs also take care of the General English (GE) curriculum, the design of which varies from one school to another but usually involves the use of a textbook from a major publisher (e.g. Longman) and the teaching of the four language skills – namely speaking, listening, reading and writing – as well as preparing students for assessments such as Territory-wide System Assessment (TSA).

On the other hand, in the Secondary NET Scheme, expectations about the NEST enhancing the teaching and learning of English in the school come from the principal and/or the English panel head; NESTs can function in exactly the same way as their Local Teacher counterparts, teaching, for example, three English classes and preparing students for public examinations (the one at the end of secondary education is called the Hong Kong Diploma of Secondary Education, or HKDSE), or they may be asked to focus primarily on developing students' interest in the language through extracurricular activities. The current study explores how the Local English Teachers view the way NESTs in their schools are deployed (that is, the fact that NESTs in primary schools can only teach the PLP curriculum and those in secondary schools serve functions that are completely at the discretion of the management).

Relationship and interaction between NESTs and LETs

Within the Primary NET Scheme, even if the NESTs only teach one grade/form, each would be collaborating with two to five LETs regularly. In the Primary section, using the PLP, they also need to co-plan lessons with LETs at least once every three weeks for each grade. Obviously, the success of the scheme depends a great deal on the quality of the relationship and collaboration between the NESTs and their non-native-English-speaking colleagues. However, most studies on NESTs and LETs have focused on the students. They concentrate either on students' attitudes towards the two groups of teachers (e.g. Ma, 2012) or on the perceived effectiveness of the teachers. Few studies, either in HK or more widely, have examined the NET Scheme from the teachers' perspective, such as teachers' own accounts of how NESTs and LETs interact and collaborate, or their perceptions of each other's roles in the school – recent exceptions being Islam's (2011) study of NESTs and LETs in Taiwan and Shibata's (2010) study in Japan. In Hong Kong, the last official examination of the Primary NET Scheme can be dated back to the evaluation by the Education Bureau (with the help of external researching bodies) ten years ago, carried out between 2004 and 2006 (Education Bureau, 2015). The evaluation also mainly focused on change in students' English learning attitude and performance, school support and parental perceptions.

The study described in this chapter attempts to fill this gap by investigating the perception of Local HK English Teachers towards their native-speaking colleagues, particularly in aspects such as their roles in and contribution to the school and their relationship with local colleagues, as well as these LETs' actual interactions with the NESTs. It adopts a case study approach; four Local HK English Teachers (two secondary and two primary) invited through personal connection were interviewed between November 2013 and January 2014 (Rose and Vivian – pseudonyms – were personal friends, while Anna and Hannah – also pseudonyms – were colleagues of friends of mine). This purposive sampling was achieved by contacting acquaintances in my network. In this way, teachers were approached and asked who in their school worked closely with a NEST. Those who were able to help either perceived that they worked closely with NESTs and volunteered to be participants or named a colleague who was then approached. It can be said that the participating LETs were 'strategically' invited to participate for instrumental reasons (Stake, 2005) so that they could shed light on understanding LETs' perceptions of the NET Schemes and the NESTs in their schools.

The interviews were conducted in the LETs' mother tongue (Cantonese), and the recordings were transcribed and translated into English. The transcripts were then processed using Qualitative Content Analysis, which emphasises an integrated view of speech/texts and their specific contexts. It goes beyond merely counting words or extracting objective content from texts and instead examines 'the meanings, themes, patterns that may be manifest or latent in a particular text' (Zhang and Wildermuth, 2009: 1). The analysis focused on the unique themes that illustrated the range of the meanings of the phenomenon under investigation (ibid.) and the goal was to provide knowledge and better understand the phenomenon being studied (Hsieh and Shannon, 2005). In the current study, it is the interaction and relationship between the LETs and their NEST colleagues that I intend to foreground.

In terms of the particular characteristics of my research, the directive approach was adopted. This starts with a theory or relevant research findings as guidance for initial codes (ibid.). This approach to content analysis is suitable for my methodology in that most questions in my semi-structured interviews were designed from predetermined categories. First, meaningful text units in the transcripts were identified and highlighted without coding. They were then coded using preliminary codes, such as 'expectations of LET on NEST', which either came from a priori established ideas in the research questions or emerged from the data to form categories. These categories were then refined and eventually reduced to main categories, organised and presented in the following sections.

Vignettes of participating LETs who work closely with a NEST

As well as serving as a brief introduction to the case study, the following short accounts from each participating Local English Teacher provide a context for understanding the discussion that follows. Some of the themes present in these vignettes will be further explored in the later discussion.

Anna

Anna was a very experienced English teacher with more than 16 years of experience. As the English panel chair of her primary school and one of the LETs who co-taught with the NEST, she worked closely with the NEST at both teaching and administrative levels. One of the key roles she played was as a mediator between the NEST and other English panel members in disagreements over issues such as work division and involvement in co-planning. Although the NEST and other LETs did not seem to get along and there were difficulties in teaching two syllabi (PLP and GE) simultaneously, Anna still welcomed the NET Scheme and NESTs coming to Hong Kong because of their unique expertise and qualities in teaching students and resourcing LETs.

Vivian

Vivian's teaching career started with teaching adults of lower proficiencies in the USA after pursuing a Master's degree related to English Language Teaching. She had taught in her school, one of the top secondary schools in HK, for more than three years at the time of our interview. She was the 'unofficial buddy' of the NEST in her school because of seating proximity. However, in her school, there was no obvious mentorship scheme or support, particularly for NESTs. There was no co-teaching in her school either and the NEST was hired in a capacity more or less the same as that of the LETs – teaching regular English classes with a similar teaching load, acting as a class teacher and taking care of English-related extracurricular activities. Vivian also collaborated with the NEST in activities such as the school's English Newspaper and the Speech Festival.

Rose

Rose had been teaching in a high-performing primary school and been an English teacher for ten years. Like Anna, as the English panel chair of her school and one of the LETs who co-taught with the NEST, Rose needed to work closely with the NEST. However, instead of being the middleman, resolving the possible conflicts between the NEST and other English teachers like Anna did, she showed a lot of resentment towards the NEST because of her work attitude (Rose thought the NEST was unhelpful and lazy). Rose was an English teacher who had high expectations for her students and always wanted to provide them with more linguistic input (evident from her description of her ideal lesson as one in which students mastered the poem as a text type and wrote poems with rhyming words and alliteration!).

However, because there were no levels in PLP catering for the needs of students of different language abilities and because the NEST did not intend to provide the higher achievers with extra input, Rose was very frustrated; she felt the students were not able to benefit fully from the NEST as a great linguistic resource.

Hannah

After working for around seven years in a 'through-train school' (which is a school with both primary and secondary sessions, or a secondary school which can guarantee enough places for the primary school it is linked to), Hannah started teaching in a low-banding secondary school that used Chinese as the MOI and had been there for more than six years. There were quite a lot of behavioural and motivational problems among students in the lower-level classes. The current NEST was the fourth one Hannah had worked with, and each of them served in the school in very different ways, which Hannah believed was a result of the principal's changing perceptions regarding how the NEST could benefit the students the most. One taught regular English classes just like the other LETs and another was expected to make learning English really fun by organising extracurricular activities for the students, whereas the current one focused on the speaking component of the classes he taught, providing students with extra help for this skill.

Other members of the English panel were not informed of the changes over the years and there was very little communication, resulting in confusion; teachers who taught the same classes as the NEST might be providing students with very similar input, or both might be assuming that a particular topic was being taken care of by the other teacher while it was not, in fact, being covered.

Relationship between NESTs and LETs: co-workers rather than friends

According to all four participating teachers, the relationship between the NESTs in their school and other teachers, even English teachers whom they worked the most closely with, was only average and in some cases it was rather bad. The most positive situation reported was in Vivian's school, where the NEST was close to a few new teachers. Vivian suggested that this might be because the NEST was very sensitive to how LETs approached tasks and tried to conform to their practices. This NEST was actually very different from the previous one in Vivian's school, who had insisted on his own practices:

> I would say she understands the culture in Hong Kong rather well, in my opinion, and I think it's a good thing. You know different NESTs can be very different; some only care about their own cultures. Perhaps because she [the current NEST] has taught in different schools here so she knows the Hong Kong culture. (Researcher: 'What makes you think she understands the Hong Kong culture?'). Like when she realises we aren't doing certain things she would follow us and not do those either. How should I put this? Perhaps it's not because she really consciously knows that those are things we don't do but when she senses that something is going on she immediately conforms. I think as a NEST she is really sensitive to these things. Because NESTs sometimes insist on their own ways. Yes, I think the previous one would insist on his own ways more. I'm not saying the current one doesn't insist on her own ways; she has her own boundaries and principles. What I'm saying is she's more respectful of our culture, I mean our school culture, no matter whether she agrees with it or not. When she sees us do things in certain way she adjusts herself and follows us.

Still, Vivian's NEST colleague could sometimes disturb other teachers' work by engaging in too much small talk in the staffroom, even for someone like Vivian who had lived and worked abroad for years. School teachers in HK are in general very busy and not used to engaging in a lot of non-work-related conversations during work hours. Vivian sometimes had to rather bluntly tell her it was time to end the conversation.

The NEST in Hannah's school was not as fortunate in having as many close friends. In fact, Hannah noticed that he often just worked at his desk with his earphones on and looked rather lonely. Other teachers very seldom approached him and from what Hannah had gathered, it was mainly because of the language barrier and perceived cultural differences, even with other English teachers. Also, the NEST was exempted (or excluded) from all staff meetings and staff development days, which made it even harder for him to integrate into the larger school community. According to Hannah, 'We exclude him in everything we do just because he can't speak Cantonese. It's like we don't see him as part of us.'

In the two primary schools, the relationship between the NESTs and the LETs was even more negative and indeed rather problematic. Their conflicts will be detailed in the next two parts.

Disagreement over division of work and workload

The area that seemed to be causing the most conflicts was division of work and workload, although this was only a problem in the Primary NET Scheme, very likely because there was a lot of co-planning and co-teaching between the LETs and NESTs there. There was no co-planning or co-teaching in the secondary schools the participants worked in.

It is obvious from Anna and Rose's interviews that they expected the NESTs to take on more of the preparation of the PLP, since the LETs had the GE curriculum to take care of as well, which generally involved a lot of marking and lesson planning. However, at the same time, the NESTs in the two schools were already working at or even beyond their maximum number of work hours, since both primary schools were big and the NESTs would easily reach their maximum work hours just by going to classes and co-planning sessions. It can be said that the LETs felt the NESTs could do more as they only needed to take care of one syllabus, but the existence of the maximum work hours policy (enjoyed only by NESTs and not by LETs) does not allow this to happen.

Once, the NEST in Anna's school was so frustrated about LETs not contributing to co-planning sessions and expecting her to take the lead that she took the issue to the principal, Anna and the Advisory Teacher (AT) from the Education Bureau. The AT suggested each teacher took turns to facilitate the co-planning sessions, which was never actually put into practice. For a while, Anna was also invited by the NEST to sit in on all co-planning meetings to encourage especially the new teachers to contribute. While Anna understood the NEST's frustration, she also thought it was difficult for some LETs to make concrete contributions, particularly those who were asked to teach PLP for the first time but had not received any induction. As Anna explained:

> The intention was good. As I said the NEST expected each colleague to take care of one book. For each book we wanted to develop some questions for questioning when we introduced the book to students. We wanted to start developing the questions so in subsequent years colleagues could simply use those questions when reading the books. We wanted to begin doing this in that school year. But then it was the first year we extended the scheme to Primary 3 too so for all teachers it was their first time teaching that syllabus within the NET Scheme. In hindsight, it was really challenging for those colleagues; they needed to teach when everything was still so new, and on top of this the NEST was asking them to be involved in the preparation. So both [the NEST and LETs] had strong opinions. Looking back I think this was really a difference in how the two parties saw the NET Scheme. Of course, Local Teachers thought this was a scheme tailor-made for the NESTs so it would be more appropriate for them to do most of the preparation and design. Since we had GE lessons too we should be less involved in the preparation. So this resulted in what I mentioned earlier

– this person thought the other wasn't doing enough and at the same time this person thought the other wasn't engaged enough.

First, it is obvious from this state of affairs that some LETs needed to be involved in the PLP and co-teach with the NESTs, even when they had not been properly inducted. On top of this, there was clearly a difference between how much the NEST and the LET felt they and the other were expected to contribute to the PLP; while the NEST believed it was a shared responsibility among all teachers involved, the LETs expected the NEST to take on a larger share than they did.

In fact, one of the Primary Local Teachers, Rose, also expected the NEST to make modifications to the materials, to provide the higher achievers with more input, and to suggest to the school what extra materials could be bought to supplement the official ones. Interestingly, these expectations were never communicated to the NEST as Rose thought it would be asking too much of her. Still, Rose was disappointed and frustrated.

Tension exacerbated by differences in communication preferences

In the last section, I mentioned the NEST in Anna's school taking her frustration at co-planning meetings to people such as the principal and the AT. Although it is a crude generalisation, people in HK are usually considered to be members of a high-context culture, in which problems, conflicts and disagreements are resolved not through 'official channels' (e.g. voicing out problems at staff meetings and telling the principal that certain colleagues are not doing their job) but more discreetly, such as by discussing the problem privately with the colleagues concerned. The difference in communication styles further worsened the relationship, as Anna also felt:

When [the NEST] first came, we thought she's very lively and the children liked her a lot, and we were really pleased. It's only later when we started to realise that there were some cultural differences, or rather differences in the way we communicate that there began to be some misunderstanding. Gradually the emotions built up and we began to think she was too self-centred. She wants everything to be done according to her requirements and doesn't want to listen to us.

Vivian has worked with six NESTs so far (there were other native-speaking teachers in her school who were not hired under the official NET Scheme) and she felt that they were, in general, more vocal than their local counterparts, for example, at staff meetings, which could cause conflicts. As someone who had had overseas study and work experiences, she also felt she was more understanding towards the NESTs. Vivian believed that a lot more needed to be done in the area of fostering mutual understanding of each other's culture (mainly work culture and expectations) and communication preferences:

Of course there's a range but I think NESTs are in general more vocal, I mean they tend to express own opinions more. For me, I know where they're coming from because I've lived abroad and I've seen some foreigners behave that way.

I don't always feel comfortable but I understand them anyway. But then for the LETs they might find it hard to understand, and hard to accept, and then they don't know how to work with them [(the NESTs)]. So perhaps there's a need for [local] teachers to be more globalised, I mean for them to understand more about other cultures, and when they work together there might be fewer conflicts. It's mutual really. Of course the NEST can be more sensitive but then you can't expect them to give in everything since one of the greatest benefits they bring is another perspective of seeing things. Students can be exposed to various perspectives so you wouldn't want a NEST who's completely localised, would you?

Conclusion

The above discussion outlines the relationship and conflicts between the NESTs and LETs. Results of the current case study show that although the NET Scheme has been implemented in public sector secondary and primary schools in HK for almost 17 and 12 years respectively, little effort has been put into preparing the two parties to work closely together. Even in cases where induction is provided, the focus is on the contents of the curriculum that the LETs and NESTs co-teach (e.g. the PLP in primary schools), rather than on helping them develop a strong collaborative relationship. On top of pedagogical input, LETs need psychological preparation too, such as learning how to communicate their own expectations to NESTs and knowing how to resolve differences, which include cultural and work style differences. Despite the problems, all of the LETs acknowledge the unique contribution the NESTs are making, such as giving livelier lessons and teaching students correct pronunciation. As one of the LETs, Anna, suggested when asked whether she supported the continuation of NET Scheme:

I still welcome the idea of having NESTs teach in Hong Kong. I think they do possess qualities we LETs don't have. They are more willing to try new things. We also really need them in telling us if students' writings are of the right style, whether they are expressing things in a natural way. They can be our guides. It's meaningful to continue to have this NET Scheme and to have NESTs coming to Hong Kong. There's a need, but at the same time there's room for improvement.

Suggestions for improving relationships and collaboration between NESTs and LETs in Hong Kong

In view of the problems perceived by Local English Teachers regarding their relationship and collaboration with the NESTs discussed in this chapter, the following recommendations for improvement seem appropriate.

Fostering mutual understanding

First and foremost, as suggested by three out of the four LETs in the current study, mutual understanding needs to be fostered. A lot of conflicts could have been avoided if trust had been built. It would be easier for this trust to develop if the two parties had a friendship rather than merely a work relationship. Ideally, they would have time to socialise with one another and to share their own needs, as Hannah suggested:

It doesn't have to be work you talk about when you go talk to the NEST. Actually he would feel really pressured if you only talk to him about work, students, so and so from which class. Just treat him as another colleague whom you would have small talk with. 'Hey how's it going?' Casual talk. Get to know one another and communicate more. What I think. What you think. Which students are particularly disruptive and how you'd like my help in dealing with their problems. Do you want me to take them to the side? To assign them a different seating? Put them into another group? It's all about communication, isn't it?

The LETs suggest getting to know each other at the beginning of the term, through casual and relaxing activities such as taking the NEST to a Chinese restaurant. An easy way to do this is to include the social meeting as part of the school's induction programme as the school welcomes the NEST, such as an evening out after a day of orienting the NEST to work-related topics. During the year, as Hannah suggests, there can also be sharing sessions where the NESTs speak on topics which LETs are less familiar with, such as poetry, to foster a sharing culture and to encourage LETs to recognise them as rich linguistic resources.

Conducting induction that focuses more on non-pedagogical issues
In the induction organised by either the school or the Education Bureau, both NESTs and LETs would benefit from more input on understanding one another's expectations and preferred communication styles. Currently, a lot of expectations (such as the LETs expecting the NEST to play a leading role in PLP co-planning meetings) are not communicated.

Regarding communication style, it might be important for some NESTs to recognise that it is hard for many HK Chinese not to take a complaint personally, and that it is very important for them to 'save face'. At the same time, as Vivian suggests, LETs also need to understand that when some NESTs raise an issue in official meetings, it could well be because they want to find solutions, instead of wanting to attack a colleague, and LETs should therefore not take these opinions personally. These preferences and expectations can be communicated through vignettes, scenario discussions or even role plays within induction sessions where both the NESTs and LETs are present.

Creating an environment where NESTs' strengths can be put to full use
Lastly, the LETs feel that the NESTs' unique strengths and experiences are not currently being fully utilised. In the primary scheme, NESTs tend just to follow the PLP materials in classes of all proficiency levels. In high-performing schools such as Rose's, where some students find even the highest-level reading materials too easy, the English panel can perhaps free the NESTs from some of their existing workload so they can focus on tailoring and preparing extra materials. This could also ease the tension between NESTs and LETs surrounding issues such as workload.

Anna and Hannah both think that NESTs are usually more creative and livelier in presenting the materials and obviously also great resources for knowledge about the culture of their home countries. Vivian thinks the NEST in her school is really good at interpreting poems and that students see her as a language role model.

Since the Secondary NET Scheme enjoys more autonomy, perhaps NESTs should be hired to help students learn the language through extracurricular or co-curricular activities such as speech festivals, drama and Western festive celebrations, rather than teaching regular English classes and preparing students for public examinations, which is very often not what NESTs do best. As Hannah suggests, this may be because they do not grow up in the Hong Kong education system, which is very heavily examination-oriented. Actually, the NEST in Hannah's school was already very stressed even when he was only assigned to help improve students' speaking for better results in TSA, an assessment which 'aims to help schools understand students' performance in attaining basic competency' (The Government of the HKSAR, 2014: 3) in English, Chinese and Mathematics, rather than to evaluate individual students' performance for screening and selection purposes. It is not hard to imagine how challenging it would be for the NEST if he were to take on regular English classes and prepare students for examinations such as HKDSE, the results of which are crucial in determining whether a particular student can enter university.

Suggestions for future directions for research

Because of difficulties in getting access to NESTs, these findings are only the perceptions of the participating LETs. Although I think the participants tried to represent issues from the perspective of NESTs too and, on the whole, seemed to be balanced and fair in their assessments, NESTs in their schools might obviously see the problems and disagreements somewhat differently. Since some participants did not actually have very positive relationships with the NESTs, it would be inappropriate to ask them to introduce their native-speaking colleagues to the researcher for interviews. Future studies can certainly fill this gap by interviewing both the NEST(s) and LETs from the same school, perhaps by approaching the principal, so the same interactions can be studied from different angles for comparison purposes. For example, one very valuable research question would be to find out how the NESTs prefer to be deployed: to teach regular English classes or to organise English-related extracurricular activities.

Future researchers could also find out what kind of induction and support are available to the NESTs in terms of helping them understand the work culture in Hong Kong, particularly on topics such as division of work, workload, expectations of the school and colleagues, and conflict resolution, which seem to be causing the most problems in NESTs' relationships with LETs according to the participants in this study.

Acknowledgement

The author would like to thank Miss Hannah Tang for her help in the preparation of the manuscript, and the four LETs who participated in the study.

References

Census and Statistics Department, the Government of the Hong Kong Special Administrative Region (2012) *Summary results of 2011 population census announced.* Available online at: www.censtatd.gov.hk/press_release/ pressReleaseDetail.jsp?charsetID=1&pressRID=2898 (accessed 19 February 2016).

Chan, E (2002) Beyond Pedagogy: Language and identity in post-colonial Hong Kong. *British Journal of Sociology of Education* 23/2: 271–285.

Cheng, NL (2004) 'Hong Kong SAR' in Ho, WK and Wong RYL (eds) *Language Policies and Language Education – The Impact in East Asian Countries in the Next Decade, 2nd edition.* Singapore: Eastern Universities Press, 100–114.

Cheng, YC (2009) Hong Kong education reforms in the last decade: Reform syndrome and new developments. *International Journal of Educational Management* 23/1: 65–86.

Crooke, B (2000) 'Hong Kong' in Morris, P and Williamson, J (eds) *Teacher education in the Asia-Pacific Region – A comparative study.* New York: Falmer Press 33–73.

Education Bureau, the Government of the Hong Kong Special Administrative Region (2009) *Education System – Overview.* Available online at: www.edb.gov.hk/ index.aspx?nodeID=2062&langno=1 (accessed 19 February 2016).

Education Bureau, the Government of the Hong Kong Special Administrative Region (2015) *Native-speaking English Teacher (NET) Scheme.* Available online at: www.edb.gov.hk/en/curriculum-development/resource-support/net/index.html (accessed 19 February 2016).

Education Department, Hong Kong Special Administrative Region of the People's Republic of China (1997) *Information Paper – Medium of Instruction Guidance for Secondary Schools.* Available online at: www.legco.gov.hk/yr97-98/english/panels/ ed/papers/ed1508-6.htm (accessed 19 February 2016).

Ho, KO (2006) A review on the history of Hong Kong's language teaching policies and opinions on improving the standard of language teaching. *Hong Kong Teachers' Centre Journal* 5: 48–58.

Ho, WK and Wong, RYL (2004) 'Introduction: Language Policies and Language Education in East Asia' in Ho, WK and Wong, RYL (eds) *Language Policies and Language Education – The Impact in East Asian Countries in the Next Decade,* 2nd edition. Singapore: Eastern Universities Press, 1–39.

Hsieh, H and Shannon, SE (2005) Three Approaches to Qualitative Content Analysis. *Qualitative Health Research* 15/9: 1277–1288.

Islam, MN (2011) Collaboration between native and Non-native English-Speaking Teachers. *Studies in Literature and Language* 2/1: 33–41.

Leung, SW and Lee, WO (2006) 'National identity at a crossroads: The struggle between culture, language and politics in Hong Kong' in Alred, G, Byram, M and Fleming, M (eds) *Education for intercultural citizenship: Concepts and comparisons.* Clevedon: Multilingual Matters, 23–46.

Ma, LPF (2012) Advantages and disadvantages of native- and nonnative-English-speaking teachers: Student perceptions in Hong Kong. *TESOL Quarterly* 46/2: 280–305.

Shibata, M (2010) How Japanese teachers of English perceive non-native assistant English teachers. *System* 38: 124–133.

Stake, RE (1995) *The Art of Case Study Research.* London: Sage.

The Government of the Hong Kong Special Administrative Region (HKSAR) (2014) *2014 Territory-wide system assessment report.* Available online at: www.info.gov.hk/gia/general/201411/07/P201411070489.htm (accessed 19 February 2016).

Zhang, Y and Wildermuth, BM (2009) 'Qualitative analysis of content' in Wildermuth, BM (ed) *Applications of social research methods to qualitative studies in information and library.* Available online at: www.ils.unc.edu/~yanz/Content_analysis.pdf (accessed 29 February 2016).

3

Native or non-native English-speaking professionals in ELT: 'That is the question!' or 'Is that the question?'

Ali Fuad Selvi, Middle East Technical University, Northern Cyprus Campus

Introduction

Originating in the medieval era, when terms such as *natale idioma* and *lingua nativa* were used in reference to Latin (Christophersen, 1999), the term 'native speaker' (NS) – and, as a corollary, 'non-native speaker' (NNS) – is regarded as one of the most complex and controversial concepts in contemporary theoretical and applied linguistics. Situated at the heart of Chomsky's (1965: 3) formulation of the linguistic theory, which is 'concerned primarily with an ideal speaker-listener, in a completely homogeneous speech-community', the NS construct stands out as 'a common reference point for all branches of linguistics' (Coulmas, 1981: 1). More specifically, cognitively oriented mainstream second language acquisition (SLA) research, operating within the intellectual and practical parameters of native-speakerism, creates 'a monolingual bias' (Y. Kachru, 1994) and 'elevates an idealised NS above a stereotypical "nonnative" while viewing the latter as a defective communicator, limited by an underdeveloped communicative competence' (Firth and Wagner, 1997: 285). As Nayar (1994: 4) argues, 'generations of applied linguistic mythmaking in the indubitable superiority and the impregnable infallibility of the [idealised] "NS" has created stereotypes that die hard'. A byproduct of this ipso facto approach is the ideologically fused and pervasive NS/NNS dichotomy, which permeates all aspects of English language teaching (ELT). Today, 'even though a dichotomy vision of the NS–NNS discussion does not appear to be linguistically acceptable, it happens to be nonetheless socially present, and therefore, potentially meaningful as an area of research in applied linguistics' (Moussu and Llurda, 2008: 316).

Various aspects of the ELT enterprise (e.g. theory, research, methodology, publishing, instructional materials, assessment, teacher education and hiring practices) have traditionally been under the direct influence of the NS construct. What lies at the heart of the critical orientation construing these terms within ELT is the 'automatic extrapolation from competent speaker to competent teacher based on linguistic grounds alone' (Seidlhofer, 1999: 236). Thus, it creates what Phillipson (1992: 217) refers to as the 'native speaker fallacy', 'the belief that the ideal teacher of English is a native speaker' as well as what Holliday (2005: 49) refers to as 'native-speakerism', the belief that 'native-speaker teachers represent a "Western culture" from which spring the ideals both of the language and of language teaching methodology'. On a macro level, this belief manifests itself in the White, modernist, male-oriented, Western, value-laden discourses and ideology (Kubota and Lin, 2009) serving as the sword of Damocles hanging over the ELT profession(als). On a micro level, it poses a two-fold threat to ELT professionals: first, it invalidates the educational and professional investment of many Native English-Speaking Teachers (NESTs) by limiting their professional qualities and qualifications to the 'NS' construct. Second, it vitiates the professional psyche of many Non-native English-Speaking Teachers (NNESTs) by perpetuating a lack of self-confidence and low professional self-esteem and creating a schizophrenic state of mind (Medgyes, 1983) which leads to 'I-am-not-a-native-speaker syndrome' (Suárez, 2000), 'impostor syndrome' (Bernat, 2009) or 'Stockholm syndrome' (Llurda, 2009). As a result, the utilisation of the NS construct as a benchmark in learning, teaching, assessment, teacher education, material development and hiring practices creates a worldview privileging a self-selected elite of language professionals (Widdowson, 2003), thereby othering and pushing NNESTs towards marginalisation at the periphery of the ELT profession (Rajagopalan, 2005).

Despite the pervasive influence of the NS construct in ELT, the recent critical scholarship embracing the diverse uses, users and functions of English as the world's first truly global language (Crystal, 2012) has brought a set of new perspectives reconceptualising this politically driven and ideologically based NS/NNS debate. Accordingly, NNSs of English are today estimated to outnumber their NS counterparts by three to one (ibid.), the ownership of English is now distributed to all its speakers, regardless of their nativeness status (Widdowson, 1994), and about 80 per cent of ELT professionals around the globe are believed to be NNESTs (Canagarajah, 2005). This complex picture served as a powerful catalyst for the emergence of a research strand and a professional movement known as the 'NNEST movement', focusing on (1) the interrogation of the NS construct and NSist ideology, and (2) the reconceptualisation of the ownership of English, default legitimacy and expertise in ELT (Canagarajah, 1999; Leung, 2005; Widdowson, op cit).

Utilising the theoretical and practical discourses regarding the NS construct, and the scope, purpose and direction of the NNEST movement, the current chapter aims to accomplish three primary objectives: (1) provide a brief overview of the NNEST movement and research, (2) explore the commonly held myths and misconceptions about the NNEST movement and research and (3) promote a shift from 'either/or' discourse, which threatens to polarise the field, to the 'both/and' discourse. It is argued that there is a pressing need to broaden the theoretical, practical, professional and advocative knowledge base of the NNEST movement in order to establish a more democratic, participatory, professional and egalitarian future for the ELT profession.

The NNEST movement

The omnipresence of NSist ideology that permeated the various strata of ELT – as both an activity and a profession – necessitated the establishment of intellectual and transformative spaces, structures and discourses to move beyond NSism in ELT. A group of scholars founded the NNEST Caucus in TESOL International Association in 1998, which later evolved into a group with Interest Section status in 2008. Since then, the NNEST Caucus/Interest Section has served as the institutionalised home base and the intellectual space of the NNEST movement, which has the following overarching goals: (1) create a non-discriminatory professional environment for all TESOL members regardless of native language and place of birth, (2) encourage the formal and informal gatherings of NNS at TESOL and affiliate conferences, (3) encourage research and publications on the role of non-native speaker teachers in ESL and EFL contexts, and (4) promote the role of non-native speaker members in TESOL and affiliate leadership positions (NNEST-IS, 2014). The establishment of the Caucus generated a ripple effect and originated the establishment of NNEST-related entities, namely WATESOL (Washington Area TESOL) NNEST Caucus and CATESOL (California and Nevada TESOL) NNLEI (Non-native Language Educators Interest Group), both in the United States. More recently, these efforts have taken a new direction in the establishment of advocacy-orientated professional groups that are organised online and in social media (e.g. NNEST Facebook Group, TEFL Equity Advocates).

It goes without saying that these entities have been instrumental in the institutionalised advocacy efforts to establish an ELT profession defined by such qualities as equity and professionalism. To support this goal, TESOL International Association passed two resolutions entitled 'A TESOL Statement on Nonnative Speakers of English and Hiring Practices' (TESOL, 1992) and 'Position Statement against Discrimination of Nonnative Speakers of English in the Field of TESOL.' (TESOL, 2006). More recently, CATESOL and BC TEAL (British Columbia Teachers of English as an Additional Language) have issued white papers focusing on the discrimination against NNESTs (BC TEAL, 2014; CATESOL, 2013). On the one hand, these efforts are institutionalised initiatives and responses; on the other, discriminatory hiring and workplace practices are still among the grim realities of the ELT profession. This complex picture validates the existence of the NNEST movement and highlights the importance of generating new theoretical, practical and professional pathways to broaden the scope and influence of the movement. In conclusion, the accumulating intellectual legacy of the NNEST movement comes from multiple directions including (a) research efforts (books, journal articles, opinion pieces, presentations, workshops and colloquia in conferences, and MA theses and PhD dissertations), (b) policy and advocacy initiatives (establishment of the NNEST Caucus/Interest Section in TESOL International Association, NNEST-related entities in local TESOL affiliates, white papers and position statements), and (c) teaching activities (integration of NNEST issues into teacher education curricula through class discussions, activities and assignments).

Conceptual changes and misconceptions in NNEST research and the NNEST movement

Scholars around the world have been forging novel ways to move beyond contested constructs such as NS and NNS by drawing upon sociocultural, postcolonial, postmodern and post-structural theories (e.g. Norton, 2010; Pennycook, 1994; Phillipson, op cit; Widdowson, op cit). This growing trend in the field of ELT is now considered to be a 'movement' (i.e. 'the NNEST movement') (Braine, 2010; Mahboob, 2010) operationalised at theoretical, practical and professional levels. From a theoretical standpoint, it aims to redefine the intellectual parameters of the ELT profession through the reconceptualisation of the deeply inherent monolingual, monocultural and NSist approach to teaching, learning and teacher education. From a practical standpoint, it aims to establish, strengthen and sustain professional practices that form and inform ELT, as an activity and as a profession, in the light of these theoretical conversations. From a professional standpoint, it aims to reconceptualise the defining characteristics of the ELT profession by such qualities as democracy, justice, collaboration, equity and professionalism. Collectively, these overarching efforts translate as:

> the promotion of a pedagogy that is highly sensitive to diverse uses, users, functions, and contexts of English; the execution of more participatory and collaborative teaching practices; and the promotion of equity, justice, and professionalism in the workplace and hiring processes. (Selvi, 2014: 575)

While these unprecedented efforts surrounding the NNEST movement serve as a transformative catalyst spearheading change in the ELT profession, they may also be at the crux of some myths and misconceptions about the movement (ibid.). Following in the footsteps of Foucault, who argues that 'a reform is never anything but the outcome of a process in which there is conflict, confrontation, struggle, resistance ... It is a matter of making conflicts more visible' (2000: 457), the current section builds upon the emergent narrow conceptualisations about the scope, purpose and directions of the NNEST movement and its research and advocacy efforts. It is also hoped that the efforts of 'making conflicts more visible' will shed a brighter light on the past achievements, present state and future trajectories of the NNEST movement.

Myth 1: The NNEST movement is for NNESTs ('I am a NS, so I do not belong here!')

Anecdotal evidence suggests that ELT professionals, regardless of their linguistic background, may not be aware of the NNEST movement or well informed about the all-inclusive nature of the movement. They consider that the movement and the related advocacy groups (e.g. the NNEST Interest Section in TESOL International Association and NNEST entities in local TESOL affiliates) may be solely concerned with NNESTs. As a result, it is not uncommon in face-to-face or online interactions to encounter a self-described NS/NEST raising a question such as 'I am a NS/NEST. Can I join?' or offering supportive comments followed up with a remark like '... but this comes from a NS'. Along the same lines, a self-described NNS/NNEST may adopt the same hesitant attitude but from a different perspective: self-marginalisation. They may refrain from joining the movement in order to maintain a distance between themselves and a group historically marginalised on linguistic, identity and professional planes.

To some extent, the misconception about the movement may be related to the naming practices since both the movement per se and the advocacy groups in local TESOL affiliates adopt the term 'NNEST' (cf. Myth 7). As a result, 'this may inadvertently signal that the NNEST movement is stuck between being an exclusive NNEST club and preaching to the choir' (Selvi, op cit: 583). However, it should be remembered that the ELT profession has traditionally been under the decisive and destructive influence of the dominant 'either/or' discourse (i.e. NEST or NNEST), whereas one of the overarching aims of the NNEST movement is to establish a more encompassing 'both/and' discourse (i.e. NEST and NNEST) (Selvi, 2011). While, on the one hand, the movement has been and will be oriented towards raising awareness, engaging in advocacy and demonstrating activism about the issues related to NNESTs (Selvi, 2009), the establishment of cooperation and collaboration among NESTs and NNESTs will open the gateway towards a participatory future of the ELT profession. Ultimately, this roadmap for the ELT profession will inform more educationally, contextually and socially appropriate ELT opportunities (Mahboob, op cit), where language learners develop a wider sociolinguistic and intercultural repertoire for glocal interaction and participation (McKay, 2002).

Myth 2: Native speakers are from Venus, non-native speakers are from Mars ('We are two different species')

Traditionally speaking, NSs and NNSs (and therefore NESTs and NNESTs) have been distinguished on the premise that 'NESTs and non-NESTs use English differently and, therefore, teach English differently' (Medgyes, 1992: 346). As a result, NESTs and NNESTs are categorically considered 'two different species' (Medgyes, 1994), NNESTs are believed to be in a constant struggle with their own language deficiencies (Medgyes, 1986) and therefore need to adopt the teaching practices and methods of NESTs (Sheorey, 1986). In line with this pervasive ideology of categorical separation, many educational institutions around the world assign reading and grammar classes to NNESTs, and speaking, listening and writing skills to NESTs. Similarly, the term 'NNESTs' becomes a code word for insiders with absolute authority on the local, whereas the term 'NESTs' becomes a designated category for outsiders who will remain so for the rest of their professional lives.

The omnipresent divide between NS and NNS (and therefore NEST and NNEST) constructs in such a fixed, rigid and mutually exclusive manner leaves no room for contextualised negotiations of the borders of linguistic, cultural and professional identity. More importantly, adopting these oversimplified and essentialised categories perpetuates the regimes of truth in ELT and serves as a professional legitimacy benchmark defining what a teacher can/should (or cannot/should not) do, without any consideration of their linguistic and professional histories and/or negotiations of their professional identities (Menard-Warwick, 2008; Park, 2012; Rudolph, 2012). Therefore, Luk and Lin (2007: 31) called for a 'sociohistorically constructed view of NSism', which they claimed 'should not be seen as a pregiven natural identity and ability, but should be seen as being interpolated through dialogic and repeated acts of discourse in different contexts.' Along the same lines, Faez (2011) provided a forceful critique of the NS/NNS dichotomy and highlighted its inadequacy in reflecting the complexity of potential linguistic identities, suggesting that such identities therefore be deconstructed and negotiated in relation to social contexts. Consequently, the NNEST movement and research is now moving towards a direction where the accounts of teachers' sociohistorically situated negotiations of translinguistic and transcultural identity are negotiated, challenged and reconceptualised in glocalised representation of ELT (Rudolph, op cit; Rudolph et al., 2015).

Myth 3: NESTs are better teachers than NNESTs or vice versa (the 'Who's worth more?' debate)

More than two decades ago, Medgyes (1992: 440) argued that the question of 'Who's worth more: the native or the non-native?' is pointless. However, the asymmetrical power relations between NESTs and NNESTs manifested in discriminatory workplace and hiring practices (Clark and Paran, 2007; Mahboob and Golden, 2013; Selvi, 2010) are testament to the de facto validity of the argument that NESTs are better teachers than NNESTs. This understanding also influenced NNEST research and spearheaded research and advocacy endeavours focusing on what advantages were held by NESTs (e.g. procedural knowledge, knowledge of idioms, colloquialisms and culture, fluency, linguistic authenticity) and by NNESTs (e.g. declarative knowledge, successful identification of potential areas of difficulty, sharing/use of L1 when possible, provision of appropriate learning strategies, crosscultural/linguistic comparisons, greater empathy with learners).

While, on the one hand, comparing NESTS and NNESTs has been a fruitful endeavour (construing the legitimacy, making a better case for collaboration, etc.), on the other hand, it perpetuates the categorical divide between teachers and reinforces generalisations about what a teacher can or should (and cannot or should not) do in the classroom. The adoption of these loaded terms vis-à-vis predefined teacher skills and competencies overlooks the situated, historical, glocal and transformative facets of their professional identities. NEST/NNEST comparisons only essentialise these categories and widen the chasm between these teacher populations, making the professional borders more salient than ever. Most importantly, they prevent teachers from negotiating these constructs and crossing their predefined borders.

There are two inherently problematic threads running through this debate. The obvious one is the perpetuation of the NS fallacy, which grants NESTs default expertise as language users, teachers and teacher educators, thereby privileging them by birth rather than by professional training. In this scenario, 'the standard always wins, the "comparee" always loses' (Nelson, 1985: 249) and the unquestionable centrality and superiority of NSs results in 'tremendous cultural, economic and political advantages' (Y. Kachru, 2005: 160). The other problematic thread is known as the 'NNS fallacy' (Selvi, op cit), which refers to the idea that the interrogation of the NS construct and the promotion of professionalism over NS/NNS constructs do not inherently and axiomatically put NNSs (and thereby NESTs) in a more privileged and competent position. On the one hand, we try to move beyond the NS fallacy by arguing that 'people do not become qualified to teach English merely because it is their mother tongue' (Maum, 2002: 1). On the other, we need to avoid the NNS fallacy trap by contending that 'people do not become qualified to teach English merely because it is their second language' (Selvi, op cit: 589).

Myth 4: Learners prefer NESTs over NNESTs (the 'supply–demand' debate)

The ultimate argument which is often cited as a 'valid justification' for discriminatory practices in ELT is the belief that language learners and their parents often prefer NESTs over NNESTs. Referred to as an indication of a market-driven ideology in the age of neoliberalism (Mahboob and Golden, op cit; Selvi, op cit), this supply–demand approach holds some validity in the literature (Lasagabaster and Manuel Sierra, 2005; Pacek, 2005).

The narrow and oversimplified manifestations of NSist ideals suggest that students might have NNESTs in their home countries, whereas they travel abroad to be taught by NESTs (Pacek, ibid.). Furthermore, the literature also presents accounts of discriminatory practices and unfavourable attitudes directed at NNESTs and 1.5 or second-generation immigrants in the US with native-level proficiency when they return to their home country and seek employment (Hsu, 2005, as cited in Braine, op cit; Shao, 2005). These findings collectively confirm that the NS construct is also loaded with race/appearance (Amin, 1997; Kubota and Lin, op cit).

However, the scholarship examining various facets of the experiences of the NNESTs offers some evidence that not only contradicts these findings (Mahboob, 2004; Moussu, 2006; Mullock, 2010) but also necessitates taking an in-depth approach to deconstructing the 'preference' debate. Most of these studies revealed that students expressed no clear preference for NESTs over NNESTs and rather emphasised professional skills and qualities of teachers (e.g. declarative and procedural knowledge, clear and intelligible pronunciation and accent) over these terms (Liang, 2002; Mullock, op cit). Research results have also revealed that those language learners with higher levels of proficiency and those who have the opportunity of having NNESTs for extended time tend to develop more positive attitudes towards their teachers (Cheung, 2002; Moussu, op cit). As a result, researchers have called for the inclusion of both NESTs and NNESTs on the grounds that 'students do not necessarily buy into the "native speaker fallacy"' (Mahboob, 2005: 66).

Myth 5: Why the NNEST movement? ('the field of ELT is discrimination-free')

Today, the professional landscape of the ELT field is under the influence of workplace practices or hiring processes that are discriminatory on the basis of such constructs as nativeness, accent, race, gender, religion, country of origin, schooling, age, sexual orientation, physical appearance or even the passport carried (or a combination of these constructs). Propelled by native-speakerism (Holliday, op cit) and the native speaker fallacy (Phillipson, op cit), the multifaceted notion of discrimination dominating the ELT field defines the linguistic and professional qualities of NNESTs in terms of NESTs and in categorically less competent terms (Lippi-Green, 1997; Maum, op cit). Consequently, this unfounded favouritism manifests itself in discriminatory job advertisements around the world (Clark and Paran, op cit; Mahboob and Golden, op cit; Selvi, op cit; Rivers, this volume). More interestingly, NESTs from 'non-Center' countries like India and Singapore are defined as professionally less credible and instructionally less competent compared to other NESTs from the 'Center', a finding which 'legitimise[s] this dominance of Center professionals/scholars' (Canagarajah, op cit: 85).

Kumaravadivelu argued that:

> NS episteme has not loosened its grip over theoretical principles, classroom practices, the publication industry, or the job market. What is surely and sorely needed is a meaningful break from this epistemic dependency.
> (Kumaravadivelu, 2012: 15)

The NNEST movement is the 'meaningful break' at the intersection of the theoretical, practical and professional pillars with the motivation of redefining the professional landscape of the ELT field. These efforts spearheaded institutionalised responses by professional organisations towards hiring and workplace discrimination (CATESOL, op cit; TESOL, op cit). While much has been achieved on theoretical, practical and professional planes, there is clearly a very long way to go in terms of sustaining a more permanent shift in thinking about the qualities of an effective teacher (Boraie, 2013).

Myth 6: Nevertheless, we need the NS as a benchmark to define our goals in TESOL (the 'benchmark' debate)

McKay argued that:

> the teaching and learning of an international language must be based on an entirely different set of assumptions than the teaching and learning of any other second and foreign language'. (McKay, op cit: 1)

The transformation of this belief into a pedagogy that is sensitive to diverse uses, users, functions and contexts of English (McKay, ibid.; Selvi and Yazan, 2013) necessitates a critical interrogation of the idealised NS model in various aspects of ELT, such as language assessment (Firth, 2009), teacher education (Leung, op cit; Selvi, 2013) and linguistic and cultural targets for instruction (Canagarajah, 2007).

Smolder (2009) provided a forceful criticism of why the idealisation of the NS benchmark is impractical, inappropriate and unfair in many EIL (English as an International Language) teaching contexts. To begin with, considering that the great majority interaction is among NNSs, i.e. ELF (English as a Lingua Franca) situations, relying on NS norms is not found to be practical. More importantly, the ever-increasing diversity of the English(es) around the world in terms of uses, users, functions and contexts offers a strong rationale for:

> a departure from introducing a single variety to the more glocal approach of exposing and embracing multiple varieties determined by learners' contextualised needs and goals in learning the language. (Selvi, op cit: 593)

In addition, relying solely on NS norms is not an appropriate approach in most EIL contexts (Alptekin, 2002; Widdowson, op cit). Terms like 'authentic', 'target' and/or 'appropriateness' are cornerstones of the NS-as-target framework (Y. Kachru, op cit) or the standard English framework (Canagarajah, op cit; Davies, 2003), which are measured irrespective of local contextual dynamics and parameters (Canagarajah, op cit; Leung, op cit; Medgyes, op cit). Consequently, this understanding conceptualises the language as a static entity and 'place[s] it [standard variety] in a privileged, and thereby all others in an underprivileged, nonstandard, and marginalised position' (Selvi and Yazan, op cit: 5). Finally, relying solely on NS norms is not a fair practice. Traditionally, the NS benchmark has been used to define NNSs 'in terms of what they are not' (Kramsch, 1998: 28), often portraying them as perpetually incompetent, imitating or less-than-native or near-native (Valdes, 1998). This ideology is used to define NNESTs as second-class citizens in the ELT profession (Rajagopalan, op cit) and damages their professional psyche and legitimacy as users and teachers of English (Alptekin, op cit; Cook, 1999; Widdowson, op cit). As a result, the idealised NS construct has been problematised from several different angles (e.g. biodevelopmental features, identity matters, implications for language teaching, benchmarks for language learning and teaching) and redefined in many different ways (Cook, op cit; Davies, op cit; B. Kachru, 1992; Mahboob, op cit), and viewed along a continuum (Brutt-Griffler and Samimy, 1999; Liu, 1999).

Myth/Reality 7: As long as NNESTs call themselves 'NNESTs', they will perpetuate their marginalisation (the 'nomenclature' debate)
The critically oriented scholarship delineating various aspects of the NNEST movement acknowledges the complex, controversial and problematic nature of terms such as NS and NNS (and thereby NEST/NNEST) but still employs them for practical purposes or for the lack of better ones. Several scholars have proposed alternatives that might help reconceptualise the inherently problematic nomenclature of NS, including 'language expert', 'English-using fellowships', 'multicompetent speaker' and 'competent language user'. This trend was complemented with alternatives for the NNEST construct, as compiled by Brady (2009), including 'Anglophone teacher of English', 'BEST' (Bilingual English-Speaking Teacher), 'legitimate teacher of English' (adapted from 'legitimate user of English'), 'transnational English teacher', 'MEST' (Multilingual/Multicultural English-Speaking Teacher) and 'DEST' (Diverse English-Speaking Teacher). More recently, Motha et al. (2012) proposed 'translinguistic/transcultural English teachers' as an alternative for the term. While a plethora of alternatives have been proposed in the literature, none of these terms made the desired transformative impact in the ELT profession.

This brings us to one of the most controversial questions within the NNEST movement: why do we use an acronym which, by any other name, would be as confusing? (Brady, op cit). In other words, if the overarching goal of the NNEST movement is to move beyond inherently and mutually exclusive conceptualisations of the NS/NNS, why do we insist on using the term NNEST when defining the literature and the movement? Is this perpetuation of the 'non-' prefix not encapsulating prejudices, professional qualities and instructional competencies? More importantly, if we call for greater participation, collaboration, and inclusivity in the ELT profession, would calling the movement, the literature and the Interest Section after the term 'NNEST' be limiting our scope and efforts? These valid questions at the heart of the nomenclature debate are testament to the complex and multifaceted trajectories of the NNEST movement. As summarised in Table 1 overleaf, both sides of the debate have valid arguments and plausible justifications.

Table 1: Advantages and disadvantages of the NNEST label

Disadvantages of the NNEST label	Advantages of the NNEST label
Demeaning (compare with the expression 'non-White')	Making a presumed 'disadvantage' an advantage
Othering NNESTs	Valuing/acknowledging the periphery
Referring to a false standard (i.e. the NS fallacy)	Making it easy to organise against discrimination
Being a specialist acronym (not transparent to others)	Can take ownership of the term so that it becomes a positively rather than negatively loaded term
Leading others to assume that only NNESTs care about NNEST issues	Diversifies and develops leadership models
Perpetuating the link between accent and professional competencies	Using the identification already present in the research field
Self-destructing (fighting against discrimination while discriminating ourselves)	Benefiting the profession (valuing education and expertise)

(adapted from Brady, op cit, as cited in Selvi, op cit: 597)

On the one hand, it should be remembered that advocacy (the call for establishing professionalism, teacher education and equity in hiring and in workplace settings) has been and will always be at the heart of the NNEST movement. In these endeavours, the term 'NNEST' is used as a catalyst and a springboard for the exploration of biases, misconceptions and marginalisation directed at teachers around the world. On the other hand, McKay (2012: 41–42) argued that 'for too long, bilingual teachers of English, particularly in so-called Expanding-Circle countries, have been labelled and marginalised as Non-native English-Speaking Teachers' and called for 'a counter discourse that recognises and legitimises the value of proficient and qualified bilingual teachers of English'. Therefore, there is a growing recognition in the NNEST movement and literature that it is necessary to problematise (and eventually abandon) the term 'NNEST' with an intention to move beyond the asymmetrical power relations that discriminate NNSs (Kumaravadivelu, op cit), broaden the scope of the accumulating efforts and define the future roadmap of the movement.

Future directions for research, practice and professionalism

For several decades, the Kafkaesque approach manifested in the juxtaposition of teaching skills and competencies on the basis of contested and decontextualised terms (encapsulated in the decontextualised and dichotomous nature of the NS/NNS constructs) results in Orwellian perceptions and practices in the field (encapsulated in the belief that some teachers are more equal than others; Selvi, op cit). Consequently, there has been a pressing need to broaden the theoretical, practical and advocative knowledge base of ELT in order to establish a more democratic, participatory, professional and egalitarian future for the profession. From this perspective, scholars around the world push the boundaries of ELT towards new frontiers that have spearheaded the problematisation, deconstruction and reconceptualisation of the universalised, essentialised and static 'truths', 'worldviews' and 'practices' that have plagued our profession. At this critical juncture, the NNEST movement fills a major gap and serves as a catalyst for transformation in the field of ELT, which has been stuck in NSist ideas and ideals for many decades. The overarching goal of the movement may be defined as establishing such values as equity, justice, egalitarianism and professionalism as defining characteristics of the ELT profession and thereby promoting diverse uses, users, functions and contexts of English(es) around the globe.

The relatively short but immensely vibrant history of the NNEST movement offers many accomplishments that serve as a cause for celebration and inspiration for the future. While members and supporters of the NNEST movement have many valid reasons to celebrate, they should also be aware of the fact that the invisible and axiomatic nature of the NS mindset (Mahboob, op cit) is still evident in various aspects of the ELT enterprise. This understanding brings us to a point where it has become imperative to re-evaluate the overarching goals and future trajectories of the movement. What does this understanding mean for the future of the NNEST movement and research? To begin with, it necessitates 'contextualised accounts of English teachers' and users' ongoing negotiations of translinguistic and transcultural identities' (Rudolph, 2013: para. 10) as opposed to decontextualised, static, essentialised and universal regimes of truth of NSism. In other words, scholars negotiating professional and descriptive borders that exclude or include professionals need to acknowledge that the terms (NS/NNS or NESTs/NNESTs) and related experiences associated with these conceptualisations are fluid and therefore cannot be narrowed down to categorical descriptions. More specifically, critically oriented inquiries in the NNEST literature need to move beyond the traditional binary framework in order to shed brighter light on issues of privilege, marginalisation, inclusivity and (in)equity. Moreover, these accounts will provide comprehensive and multifaceted accounts regarding who these individuals are, can or should become as well as their status as learners, users and teachers of English (Rudolph, ibid.). The discussions focusing on the problematisation of the NNEST construct and the recent calls to rename the teachers, movement (and even the Interest Section in TESOL International Association) are instrumental streams of discussion forming and informing the future of the NNEST movement and research.

In conclusion, this chapter has outlined the intellectual and professional reasons for the emergence of the NNEST movement, delineated some of the commonly held myths and misconceptions embedded in this line of research and in the movement, and finally provided some directions that may serve as a roadmap for this transformatory movement within ELT. Grasping the ideas and ideals of the NNEST movement (and related research) in the light of past accomplishments, present-day realities and future trajectories is an instrumental endeavour for all stakeholders of the ELT profession. In the context of global winds of change, the NNEST movement serves as a transformatory framework and an intellectual space for 'all' ELT professionals who intend to co-construct a profession defined by such values as democracy, justice, equity, participation, inclusivity and professionalism.

References

Alptekin, C (2002) Towards intercultural communicative competence in ELT. *ELT Journal* 56/1: 57–64.

Amin, N (1997) Race and the identity of the nonnative ESL teacher. *TESOL Quarterly* 31/3: 580–583.

British Columbia Teachers of English as an Additional Language (BC TEAL) (2014) BC TEAL position statement against discrimination on the grounds of nationality, ethnicity or linguistic heritage. Available online at: https://www.bcteal.org/wp-content/uploads/2013/02/AGM-TEAL-StatementAgainstDiscrimination-passed.pdf (accessed 4 March 2016).

Bernat, E (2009) Towards a pedagogy of empowerment: The case of 'Impostor Syndrome' among pre-service non-native speaker teachers (NNSTs) of TESOL. *English Language Teacher Education and Development Journal* 11.

Boraie, D (2013, 29 July) Native English-SpeakingTeachers and trainers still idealized. [blog entry] Available online at: http://blog.tesol.org/bridging-the-gap-between-research-and-classroom-practice/ (accessed 19 February 2016).

Brady, B (2009) *What's in a name? An acronym by any other name would be as confusing.* NNEST EVO 2009. Available online at: www.slideboom.com/presentations/38883/Brock_ppt (accessed 19 February 2016).

Braine, G (2010) *Nonnative speaker English teachers: Research, pedagogy, and professional growth.* New York: Routledge.

Brutt-Griffler, J and Samimy, K (1999) Revisiting the colonial in the post-colonial: Critical praxis for nonnative English speaking teachers in a TESOL program. *TESOL Quarterly* 33/3: 413–431.

Canagarajah, AS (1999) 'Interrogating the "native speaker fallacy": Non-linguistic roots, non-pedagogical results' in Braine, G (ed) *Nonnative educators in English language teaching.* Mahwah, NJ: Lawrence Erlbaum Associates, 77–92.

Canagarajah, AS (2005) *Reclaiming the local in language policy and practice.* Mahwah, NJ: Lawrence Erlbaum Associates.

Canagarajah, AS (2007) Lingua franca English, multilingual communities, and language acquisition. *The Modern Language Journal* 91/5: 923–939.

CATESOL (California and Nevada Teachers of English to Speakers of Other Languages) (2013) *CATESOL position paper opposing discrimination against Non-Native English Speaking Teachers (NNESTs) and teachers with 'non-standard' varieties of English.* Available online at: www.catesol.org/nonnative_english_speaking_teachers.aspx (accessed 19 February 2016).

Cheung, YL (2002) *The attitude of university students in Hong Kong towards native and nonnative teachers of English.* Unpublished MA thesis, The Chinese University of Hong Kong, Hong Kong.

Chomsky, N (1965) *Aspects of the theory of syntax.* Cambridge, MA: MIT Press.

Christophersen, P (1999) *A linguist's credo: Selected papers.* Odense: Odense University Press.

Clark, E and Paran, A (2007) The employability of non-native-speaker teachers of EFL: A UK survey. *System* 35/4: 407–430.

Cook, V (1999) Going beyond the native speaker in language teaching. *TESOL Quarterly* 33/2: 185–209.

Coulmas, F (1981) 'Introduction: The concept of native speaker' in Coulmas, F (ed) *A Festchrift for native speaker.* The Hague: Mouton, 1–25.

Crystal, D (2012) *English as a global language.* Cambridge: Cambridge University Press.

Davies, A (2003) *The native speaker: Myth and reality.* Clevedon: Multilingual Matters.

Faez, F (2011) Reconceptualizing the native/nonnative speaker dichotomy. *Journal of Language, Identity and Education* 10/4: 231–249.

Firth, A (2009) The lingua franca factor. *Intercultural Pragmatics* 6/2: 147–170.

Firth, A and Wagner, J (1997) On discourse, communication, and (some) fundamental concepts in SLA research. *The Modern Language Journal* 81: 285–300.

Foucault, M (2000) 'So is it important to think?' in Faubion, JD (ed) *Power, The essential works of Michel Foucault, Vol. III.* New York: The New Press, 454–458.

Holliday, A (2005) *The struggle to teach English as an international language.* Oxford: Oxford University Press.

Hsu, H (2005, 28 November) Mainland bias against Chinese from the West. *South China Morning Post*, A16.

Kachru, B (1992) *The other tongue: English across cultures.* Chicago: University of Illinois Press.

Kachru, Y (1994) Monolingual bias in SLA research. *TESOL Quarterly* 28/4: 795–800.

Kachru, Y (2005) 'Teaching and learning of World Englishes' in Hinkel, E (ed) *Handbook of research in second language learning and teaching.* Mahwah, NJ: Lawrence Erlbaum Associates, 155–173.

Kramsch, C (1998) 'The privilege of the intercultural speaker' in Byram, M and Fleming, M (eds) *Language learning in intercultural perspective.* Cambridge: Cambridge University Press, 16–31.

Kubota, R and Lin, A (2009) *Race, culture, and identities in second language education: Exploring critically engaged practice.* New York: Routledge.

Kumaravadivelu, B (2012) *Language teacher education for a global society.* New York: Routledge.

Lasagabaster, D and Manuel Sierra, J (2005) 'What do students think about the pros and cons of having a native speaker teacher?' in Llurda, E (ed) *Non-native language teachers: Perceptions, challenges, and contributions to the profession.* New York: Springer, 217–242.

Leung, C (2005) Convivial communication: Recontextualizing communicative competence. *International Journal of Applied Linguistics* 15/2: 119–144.

Liang, KY (2002) *English as a second language (ESL) students' attitudes toward Non-native English-Speaking Teachers' (NNESTs') accentedness.* Unpublished MA thesis, California State University, Los Angeles, USA.

Lippi-Green, R (1997) *English with an accent. Language, ideology, and discrimination in the United States.* New York: Routledge.

Liu, D (1999) 'Training non-native TESOL students: Challenges for TESOL teacher education in the West' in Braine, G (ed) *Nonnative educators in English language teaching.* Mahwah, NJ: Lawrence Erlbaum Associates, 197–210.

Llurda, E (2009) 'Attitudes towards English as an International Language: The pervasiveness of native models among L2 users and teachers' in Sharifian, F (ed) *English as an international language: Perspectives and pedagogical issues.* Clevedon: Multilingual Matters, 119–134.

Luk, JCM and Lin, AMY (2007) *Classroom interactions as cross-cultural encounters: Native speakers in EFL classrooms.* Mahwah, NJ: Lawrence Erlbaum Associates.

Mahboob, A (2004) 'Native or nonnative: What do the students think?' in Kamhi-Stein, L (ed) *Learning and teaching from experience: Perspectives on nonnative English-speaking professionals.* Ann Arbor, MI: University of Michigan Press, 121–147.

Mahboob, A (2005) 'Beyond the native speaker in TESOL' in Zafar, S (ed) *Culture, context, and communication.* Abu Dhabi: Center of Excellence for Applied Research and Training & The Military Language Institute, 60–93.

Mahboob, A (ed) (2010) *The NNEST lens: Non native English speakers in TESOL.* Newcastle upon Tyne: Cambridge Scholars Publishing.

Mahboob, A and Golden, R (2013) Looking for native speakers of English: Discrimination in English language teaching job advertisements. *Voices in Asia Journal* 1/1: 72–81.

Maum, R (2002) *Nonnative-English-speaking Teachers in the English teaching profession.* CAL Digest. Washington, DC: Center for Applied Linguistics.

McKay, SL (2002) *Teaching English as an international language.* Oxford: Oxford University Press.

McKay, SL (2012) 'Principles of teaching English as an international language' in Alsagoff, L, Hu, GW, McKay, SL and Renandya, WA (eds) *Principles and practices for teaching English as an international language.* New York, NY: Routledge, 28–46.

Medgyes, P (1983) The schizophrenic teacher. *ELT Journal* 37/1: 2–6.

Medgyes, P (1986) Queries from a communicative teacher. *ELT Journal* 40/2: 107–112.

Medgyes, P (1992) Native or non-native: Who's worth more? *ELT Journal* 46/4: 340–349.

Medgyes, P (1994) *The non-native teacher.* London: Macmillan.

Menard-Warwick, J (2008) The cultural and intercultural identities of transnational English teachers: Two case studies from the Americas. TESOL Quarterly 42/4: 617–640.

Motha, S, Jain, R, and Tecle, T (2012) Translinguistic identity-as-pedagogy: Implications for language teacher education. *International Journal of Innovation in English Language Teaching* 1/1: 13–27.

Moussu, L (2006) *Native and nonnative English speaking English as a second language teachers: Student attitudes, teacher self perceptions, and intensive English program administrator beliefs and practices.* Unpublished PhD thesis, Purdue University, USA.

Moussu, L and Llurda, E (2008) Non-native English-speaking English language teachers: History and research. *Language Teaching* 41/3: 315–348.

Mullock, B (2010) 'Does a good language teacher have to be a native speaker?' in Mahboob, A (ed) *The NNEST lens: Non native English speakers in TESOL.* Newcastle upon Tyne: Cambridge Scholars Publishing, 87–113.

Nayar, PB (1994) Whose English is it? TESL-EJ 1/1. Available online at: www.tesl-ej.org/ej01/f.1.html (accessed 19 February 2016).

Nelson, CL (1985) My language, your culture: Whose communicative competence? *World Englishes* 4/2: 243–250.

Non-native English Speakers in TESOL Interest Section (NNEST-IS) (2016) *The Birth and Rise of the NNEST Movement.* Available online at http://nnest.moussu.net/history.html (accessed 4 March 2016).

Norton, B (2010) 'Language and Identity' in Hornberger, N and McKay, S (eds) *Sociolinguistics and language education.* Clevedon: Multilingual Matters, 349–369.

Pacek, D (2005) "Personality not nationality": Foreign students' perceptions of a nonnative speaker lecturer of English at a British university' in Llurda, E (ed) *Non-native language teachers. Perceptions, challenges, and contributions to the profession.* New York, NY: *Springer,* 243–262.

Park, G (2012) 'I am never afraid of being recognized as an NNES': One teacher's journey in claiming and embracing her nonnative-speaker identity. *TESOL Quarterly* 46/1: 127–151.

Pennycook, A (1994) *The cultural politics of English as an international language.* Harlow: Longman.

Phillipson, R (1992) *Linguistic imperialism.* Oxford: Oxford University Press.

Rajagopalan, K. (2005) 'Non-native speaker teachers of English and their anxieties: Ingredients for an experiment in action research' in Llurda, E (ed) *Non-native language teachers. Perceptions, challenges, and contributions to the profession.* New York, NY: Springer, 283–303.

Rudolph, N (2012) *Borderlands and border crossing: Japanese professors of English and the negotiation of translinguistic and transcultural identity.* Unpublished PhD thesis, University of Maryland, College Park, USA.

Rudolph, N (2013) Beyond binaries: Constructing and negotiating borders of identity in glocalized ELT. *NNEST Interest Section Newsletter,* 14/1. Available online at: http://newsmanager. commpartners.com/tesolnnest/issues/2013-08-27/2.html (accessed 4 March 2016).

Rudolph, N, Selvi, AF and Yazan, B (in press) Constructing and confronting native-speakerism within and beyond the NNEST movement. *Critical Inquiry in Language Studies* 12/1: 27–50.

Seidlhofer, B (1999) Double standards: Teacher education in the expanding circle. *World Englishes* 18/2: 233–245.

Selvi, AF (2009) A call to graduate students to reshape the field of English language teaching. *Essential Teacher,* 6/3–4: 49–51.

Selvi, AF (2010) 'All teachers are equal, but some teachers are more equal than others': Trend analysis of job advertisements in English language teaching. *WATESOL NNEST Caucus Annual Review,* 1: 156–181. Available online at: http://sites. google.com/site/watesolnnestcaucus/caucus-annual-review (accessed 19 February 2016).

Selvi, AF (2011) The non-native speaker teacher. *ELT Journal* 65/2: 187–189.

Selvi, AF (2013) 'Towards EIL teacher education: Exploring challenges and potentials of MATESOL programs in the United States' in Zacharias, NT and Manara, C (eds) *Contextualizing the pedagogy of English as an international language: Issues and tensions.* Cambridge: Cambridge Scholars Publishing, 42–58.

Selvi, AF (2014) Myths and misconceptions about the non-native English speakers in TESOL (NNEST) movement. *TESOL Journal* 5/3: 573–611.

Selvi, AF and Yazan, B (2013) *Teaching English as an international language.* Alexandria, VA: TESOL Press.

Shao, T (2005) Teaching English in China: NNESTs need not apply? *NNEST Newsletter,* 7/2.

Sheorey, R (1986) Error perceptions of native-speaking and non-native-speaking teachers of ESL. *ELT Journal* 40/4: 306–312.

Smolder, C (2009) ELT and the native speaker ideal: Some food for thought. *International House Journal of Education and Development,* 26/22. Available online at: http://ihjournal.com/elt-and-the-native-speaker-ideal-some-food-for-thought (accessed 19 February 2016).

Suárez, J (2000) 'Native' and 'non-native': Not only a question of terminology. *Humanizing Language Teaching,* 2/6. Available online at: http://www.hltmag.co.uk/nov00/mart1.htm (accessed 19 February 2016).

Teachers of English to Speakers of Other Languages (TESOL) International Association (1992) A TESOL statement of non-native speakers of English and hiring practices. *TESOL Quarterly* 2/4: 23.

Teachers of English to Speakers of Other Languages (TESOL) International Association (2006) *Position statement against discrimination of nonnative speakers of English in the field of TESOL.* Available online at: www.tesol.org/docs/default-source/advocacy/position-statement-against-nnest-discrimination-march-2006.pdf?sfvrsn=2 (accessed 19 February 2016).

Valdes, G (1998) The construct of the near-native speaker in the foreign language profession: Perspectives on ideologies about language. *ADFL Bulletin* 29/3: 4–8.

Widdowson, HG (1994) The ownership of English. *TESOL Quarterly* 28/2: 377–389.

Widdowson, HG (2003) *Defining issues in English language teaching.* Oxford: Oxford University Press.

4

Employment advertisements and native-speakerism in Japanese higher education

Damian J. Rivers, Future University Hakodate, Hokkaidō, Japan

As a White European male, I have undoubtedly been unfairly advantaged by my innate physical attributes when securing employment within Japanese tertiary education. However, while advantageous at the pre-recruitment stage, at the post-recruitment stage the same innate physical attributes have been instrumental in limiting the contributions I am seen to be able to make, and the scope of the roles I am expected to be able to perform. (Rivers, 2013a: 88)

Preamble

As a teacher-researcher with over 15 years' experience within the social context of Japan, I make the confessional statement above with the intention of alerting the reader to my own positioning in relation to the contents of this chapter. As someone defined by others as a native speaker of English, I have often been a reluctant beneficiary, at the pre-recruitment stage of employment, of institutional practices that assign professional value on the basis of speakerhood status[1] race, nationality and/or physical appearance. However, I have also been an equally reluctant victim, at the post-recruitment stage of employment, of institutional practices that draw from the very same criteria as a means of restricting institutional involvement, imposing conditional language policies, limiting status and denying professional development opportunities.

Drawing from research interests shaped by such contextualised experiences, this chapter examines 292 English Language Teaching (ELT) employment advertisements recruiting within the context of Japanese higher education to document the prevalence and various uses of the native-speaker criterion when listed as a qualification for employment. Based upon the data collected, this chapter then asks readers to consider whether the observed patterns of native-speaker criterion use constitute 'native-speakerism' and, if so, how and when the observed practices disadvantage potential applicants on the basis of their speakerhood status.

---

1   I have specifically referenced the term 'speakerhood status' to refer to assumptions, assessments, perceptions and/or judgements made in relation to general language background, language proficiency, language competence or any other non-formally assessed positions taken. This non-specific term is intended to avoid forced ascription to any particular ideological and/or political position as might be indicated through use of other terminology.

The resilience of the native-speaker criterion

In *A Festschrift for native speaker,* Coulmas (1981: 1) identifies the native speaker as a 'common reference point for all branches of linguistics', further asserting how 'linguists of every conceivable theoretical orientation agree that the concept of the native speaker is of fundamental importance' (ibid.). Since this time, and undoubtedly for many years prior, the native-speaker criterion has persisted as a central feature of discourse within language education and applied linguistics.

From a linguistic perspective, the longevity of the native-speaker criterion appears quite remarkable given that it has been dissected on multiple occasions in relation to its numerous theoretical shortcomings (Davies, 2013). In *The native speaker is dead!,* Paikeday (1985a: 8–10) describes the idea of the native speaker as 'a rather delicate matter and a cardinal tenet of our linguistic faith', adding how the term 'in its linguistic sense represents an ideal, a convenient fiction, or a shibboleth rather than a reality' (ibid.). During the same year, Paikeday also published an article in *TESOL Quarterly* entitled 'May I kill the native speaker?', in which, from the position of a descriptive lexicographer, he argues against the use of 'native speakers as performance models' (Paikeday, 1985b: 395).

Over a decade later, Rajagopalan (1997: 226) moves to remind us how the notion of nativity persists as 'one of the founding myths of Modern Linguistics ... not interrogated from within the disciplinary boundaries', while Pillar (2001: 121) adds further weight to calls to move away from the notion of nativity declaring that from a linguistic perspective, 'the native speaker concept is useless and should therefore be discarded.' More recently, and affirming the extent to which the native-speaker criterion continues to reside within the minds of the masses, Pederson (2012: 9) exclaims that 'the NS has no basis in reality other than as a mental representation that exists in the minds of those who believe in it or operate within social structures that rely on it'.

'Qualifying sociosemiotic associations' of the native speaker

The previous section indicates the extent to which the native-speaker criterion has resisted academic criticism and has often been excluded from the need for empirical evidence to rationalise its continued use. Today, despite definitional parameters drawing more from a supposed 'commonsensical' understanding than from empirical evidence, the native-speaker criterion remains a central component of discussions about practice, pedagogy and policy within the global linguistic marketplace of ELT (Sung-Yul Park and Wee, 2012).

Evidence suggests that, across various contexts, the native speaker has been actively commoditised through what can be termed as a plethora of 'qualifying sociosemiotic associations'. This term is intended to denote the real or imagined characteristics of an individual believed, in certain contexts and at certain times, to 'qualify' them as a legitimate or authentic native speaker of a particular language. As native-speaker status is often ascribed on the basis of criteria unconnected to actual language use (e.g. country of origin or physical appearance), such ascriptions are drawn from a particular configuration of mental representations and/or social signs (i.e. sociosemiotics) embedded within a particular context. Associations of this nature have been discussed as 'the complex baggage of "nativeness" as it is constructed in the field of English language teaching' (Stanley, 2012: 25). Furthermore, they are often deployed to further a variety of interests as they function to furnish the imaginations of eager students and other stakeholders with an idealised or prototypical image of how the native speaker should be configured (Rivers, 2011).

Through entertaining a rather superficial version of the native speaker as 'the poster child of expensive advertising campaigns' (Rajagopalan, 2015: 125) and as a central component within 'glossy university advertisements or language school brochures' (Toh, 2013: 187), the global linguistic marketplace of ELT has actively participated in the commoditisation of the native speaker via a cyclical process of mutual exchange and reinforcement. As students and other stakeholders consume the idealised or prototypical image of the native speaker – one designed to appeal to dreams, aspirations and a world of limitless possibilities – the more entrenched this ideal becomes, thus further stimulating demand and consumption (see Rivers and Ross, 2013).

In order to demonstrate some of the ways in which the native speaker is commoditised within certain contexts, outlined below are three examples of the dominant 'qualifying sociosemiotic associations' of the native speaker of English commonly referenced within Japan. These 'qualifying sociosemiotic associations' can be readily found within the literature and are often the product of various processes including, and looking beyond, financial motivations, the politics of nation-state affiliation (Bonfiglio, 2010) and sociohistorical constructions of 'linguistic identity and political membership by the way of the nation' (Hackert, 2009: 306). While some of these associations may hold universal applicability (i.e. race, colour and/or ethnicity may be contributing factors in 'qualifying' an individual as a native speaker of English within other national contexts), here the focus and supporting research evidence is framed specifically within the boundaries of the Japanese ELT context.

1   **Potential point of division and disadvantage: race, colour and/or ethnicity**
    Qualifying sociosemiotic association: legitimate native-speaker English teachers are White. For recent evidence, see Appleby, (2014); Hayes, (2013); Heimlich, (2013); Kubota and Fujimoto, (2013); Kubota and McKay, (2009); Rivers, (2011, 2013a); Rivers and Ross, (op cit).

2   **Potential point of division and disadvantage: country of origin and/or nationality**
    Qualifying sociosemiotic association: legitimate native-speaker English teachers originate from a select number of specific countries (e.g. Australia, Britain, Canada, New Zealand, the United States of America and occasionally South Africa). For recent evidence, see Hashimoto, (2011); Houghton, (2013); Rivers, (2011, 2013a); Rivers and Ross, (op cit); Seargeant, (2009).

3   **Potential point of division and disadvantage: proficiency and/or teaching ability**
    Qualifying sociosemiotic association: legitimate native-speaker English teachers possess an innate mastery of the language and are therefore the

most appropriate teachers (although often only of spoken or conversational English). For recent evidence, see Breckenridge and Erling, (2011); Rivers and Ross, (op cit); Toh, (op cit); Tsuneyoshi, (2013).

In allowing the definitional parameters of the native-speaker criterion to be shaped by such 'qualifying sociosemiotic associations', the current situation is one whereby the native speaker remains open to almost endless speculation, interpretation and manipulation – facets well suited to the market-oriented processes of commodification and consumption. Rutherford (1990: 11) touches upon these dynamics in explaining how through the 'commodification of language and culture, objects and images are torn free of their original referents and their meanings become a spectacle open to almost infinite translation'. The consequences within the domain of ELT can often be seen as a particular brand of language education which appears subservient 'to a boutique or catwalk mentality in its readiness to be part of an inner-textual network that feeds and fetes the narratives of marketization and commercial retail' (Toh, op cit: 187).

Institutional communication: the employment advertisement genre

Institutions systematically direct individual memory and channel our perceptions into forms compatible with the relations they authorize. They fix processes that are essentially dynamic, they hide their influence, and they rouse our emotions to a standardized pitch on standardized issues. (Douglas, 1986: 92)

As the above observations indicate, institutions, such as schools and universities, perform a multitude of societal roles, including the transmission and reinforcement of social categories, norms, values, attitudes and ethics. The employment advertisement, 'a genre of organizational communication' (Rafaeli and Oliver, 1998: 342), has been identified as a prominent channel through which institutions are able to transmit an array of information to a public audience. Owen (2004: 153) draws attention to how 'anyone who has studied higher education recruitment advertisements over recent years will have noticed how they reflect social trends'. Indeed, referencing how the discursive practices of higher education have been increasingly fashioned by market forces, Fairclough (1993: 143) discusses the way that institutions have 'come to increasingly operate (under government pressure) as if they were ordinary businesses competing to sell their products to consumers'. Similarly, Bhatia (1999: 149) warns how genre-mixing has resulted in 'several instances in which increasing use of promotional strategies are used in genres that are traditionally considered non-promotional in intent' (i.e. employment advertisements).

Until the early 1990s employment advertisements represented a distinct genre of institutional communication. Employment advertisements prior to this period were often print-based, impersonal, conservative and consistent in terms of linguistic content, visual format and organisational structure. Contemporary employment advertisements, in contrast, have shifted toward a promotional inter-discursive genre of institutional communication (Fairclough, 1993). Within the context of Chinese higher education, Xiong (2012: 331) details evidence of an alliance between market forces and bureaucratic elements, manifested through employment advertisements based upon 'an intertextual mix of bureaucratic/ authorless discourse and promotional discourse'. Such research points toward an uncomfortable realisation that 'we have reached a time where universities start to operate as if they were ordinary businesses' (Askehave, 2007: 725).

ELT employment advertisements and the native-speaker criterion[2]

Holliday (2005: 385) notes how the terms 'native' and 'non-native', despite their linguistic flaws, 'have very real currency within the popular discourse of ELT'. It is therefore somewhat curious to discover that published research examining the native-speaker criterion within ELT employment advertisements has been relatively sparse, often restricted to special interest publications on the margins of the mainstream. Although limited, the few studies that have been published have shown remarkable consistency in their findings across numerous local and national contexts.

Clark and Paran (2007: 407) examined ELT employability within the UK. Recruitment data collected from 90 private language schools, further education colleges and universities revealed that 41 of the 90 institutions considered the native-speaker criterion to be 'very important' when making recruitment decisions. They suggest that 'non-native-speaker teachers of English are often perceived as having a lower status than their native-speaking counterparts, and have been shown to face discriminatory attitudes when applying for teaching jobs' and conclude that a 'lack of native speaker status will be viewed as an important consideration at over 70% of the institutions in this survey' (ibid: 423–424).

In a study exploring a wide range of potentially discriminatory criteria in ELT employment advertisements, Selvi (2010: 158) highlights how 'despite the fact that there have been a number of institutionalized efforts to overcome discriminatory practices, hiring practices in English language teaching still follow a business model where stakeholders play the "native speaker card".' Following on from Selvi (ibid.), Mahboob and Golden (2013: 72) more recently contend that 'the discriminatory practices that the field has been trying to eliminate are still visible' and that 'more work needs to be carried out to make TESOL an equitable profession'. Through an analysis of 77 ELT employment advertisements recruiting in the Middle East and Asia, the authors observed that '79% of all advertisements specifically used the term native speaker' (ibid.: 76), while there was a general 'preference for native speakerness over teaching or educational qualifications' (ibid.: 78).

2 Prompted by an intervention from the author, on 12 November 2012 the British Association of Applied Linguistics (BAAL) drafted a formal policy prohibiting use of the term 'native speaker' in its online employment advertisements. This move was rationalised at the time on the basis that 'use of the term "native speaker" can be seen as discriminating against expert teachers of English for whom English is a second or other language' (BAAL draft policy dated 19 November 2012, cited in Rivers, 2013b: 37). It is interesting to note how this discourse does not offer protection to those teachers who are categorised as native speakers of English. In other words, only one group of 'teachers' are believed to be in need of protection.

Most recently, Ruecker and Ives (in press) dissect a sample of 59 ELT employment advertisements taken from a selection of teacher recruitment websites, TEFL certification websites and cultural exchange websites in China, Japan, Korea, Taiwan and Thailand. With specific reference to a recruitment website located in Korea, the authors note how 'the ideal candidate is overwhelmingly depicted as a young, White, enthusiastic native speaker of English from a stable list of Inner Circle countries' (ibid.). The authors further state that the overall message of the website is one which imposes the idea that non-native-English-speaking teachers 'from countries outside of the approved list, regardless of qualifications, need not apply' (ibid.). The data reported in the study showed that the native-speaker criterion was used within 81 per cent of employment advertisements.

Summary

Previous sections have drawn attention to a number of issues relevant to the current study. First, it has been shown that the idea of the native speaker, as linguistic benchmark, has been critically questioned for at least the past 40 years. Despite various objections being voiced concerning the linguistic reliability of the native speaker, it remains a common point of reference within language education discourse and is called upon to serve various interests. Second, the native speaker has been actively commoditised through certain 'qualifying sociosemiotic associations'. Such associations have been revealed in Japan as inclusive of elements such as race, colour and/or ethnicity, country of origin and/or nationality and additional beliefs about language proficiency and teaching ability. Third, the role of institutional communication in facilitating the establishment of categories, norms, values, attitudes and ethics within wider society has been discussed. The genre of the employment advertisement has been highlighted, with particular attention given to its evolution as a hybrid genre, often interwoven with promotional discourse intended to service the market economy. Finally, evidence has been presented from various local and national contexts showing how, within ELT employment advertisements, there exists a clear preference in the hiring of teachers based predominantly on their supposed native-speaker status.

The current study

For the current study, 292 ELT employment advertisements recruiting for full-time positions within the context of Japanese higher education covering an 18-month period (between October 2012 and April 2014) were collected. The aim was to document the prevalence and various uses of the native-speaker criterion as a qualification for employment. The employment advertisements, all written in English, were downloaded from the 'Humanities-linguistics' subsection of the Japan Research Career Information Network (JREC-IN) website.[3]

3   The JREC-IN website is operated by the Japan Science and Technology Agency (JST). Although the JST is an independent administrative institution, it is supported by government subsidies (93.6 per cent of their fiscal 2013 budget) and aims to promote policy objectives set by the Ministry of Education, Culture, Sports, Science and Technology. The discursive practices of those institutions using the JREC-IN service are not censored or regulated through an explicit anti-discrimination policy. The website only informs potential posters that JREC-IN 'shall not bear any responsibility for any of the information' (Japan Science and Technology Agency, 2014). Institutions using the JREC-IN service are requested to provide text-based information (in Japanese and/or English) using a standardised template. The template uses a selection of headers including content of work (e.g. primary duties and teaching requirements), rank (e.g. the level of the advertised position), qualifications (e.g. the explicit requirements demanded by the institution), treatments (e.g. employment terms, salary and benefits) and application materials (e.g. what potential applicants are requested to supply).

Findings and discussion

Through an initial analysis of the 292 ELT employment advertisements, a number of general observations were recorded. The mean number of qualifications requested by the recruiting institutions was 4.28 (SD=1.69) with 81 per cent (n=236) of the employment advertisements requesting that potential applicants satisfy between three and six individual requirements. Within the sample of 292 employment advertisements, 81 per cent (n=236) offered a limited-term contract position, while 19 per cent (n=56) offered a de facto tenured position with no term limit.

In terms of formal qualification requirements, 98 per cent (n=230) of the 236 limited-term contract positions required potential applicants to hold an MA-level qualification, while two per cent (n=5) required potential applicants to hold a PhD. This pattern was reversed for the 56 employment advertisements offering potential applicants a de facto tenured position with no term limit. Here, 20 per cent (n=11) of the de facto tenured positions required potential applicants to hold an MA-level qualification, while 80 per cent (n=45) required potential applicants to hold a Ph.D. This suggests that a higher level of educational achievement increases the opportunity for securing tenured employment.[4]

With reference to the primary qualification (i.e. the qualification positioned first on the list of institutional requirements), in 43.5 per cent (n=127) of all employment advertisements a formal qualification was positioned first. The most frequently desired formal qualifications were an MA in TESOL or a related area (18 per cent or n=55) and a PhD or other doctorate (17 per cent or n=50). The native-speaker criterion was listed in the primary position in 39.4 per cent (n=115) of all employment advertisements. Furthermore, 13.4 per cent (n=39) of all employment advertisements required potential applicants to hold a specified level of professional achievement, level of experience, personality characteristic or demographic status, while 3.7 per cent (n=11) of all employment advertisements demanded potential applicants to agree to some form of university mission statement, institutional belief or statement of purpose.

Looking more closely at the discursive presentation of the native-speaker criterion, the data indicate that it was specified as a qualification for employment in 63 per cent (n=184) of all employment advertisements. In 34 per cent (n=102) of the advertisements 'native speaker' was specified as the discursive header, in 15.4 per cent (n=45) of the advertisements 'native or' was specified as the discursive header, in 8.9 per cent (n=26) of the advertisements 'native' was specified as the discursive header, while in 3.8 per cent (n=11) of the advertisements the native-speaker criterion was discursively presented in some other guise. Documented below are the precise discursive forms through which the native-speaker criterion was presented within the 184 employment advertisements.

---

4 The maximum length of contracted employment offered was five years (see Rivers, 2013c, for the legal framework related to this term limit). In short, changes made to the Employment Contract Act (Act No. 128 of 5 December 2007) on 23 March 2012 through the Bill for Partial Amendment of Labour Contract Act 'allows fixed-term contract employees with contract periods of over 5 years in total to convert their employment contract to an employment contract without a definite period by requesting to their employers' (Anderson Mōri and Tomotsune, 2012: 1).

Table 1: Discursive forms through which the native-speaker criterion was presented within the employment advertisements

Discursive form	*n*
1 Native speaker	
1.1 of English of the English Language	58
1.2 of English or a person with the same competence or equivalent (level) or a person with equivalent English ability or a speaker of English with a level of proficiency equivalent to native speakers or an equivalent command of English to native speakers (TOEFL iBT 100 or above, TOEIC 950 or above, or IELTS 7.0 or above) or non-native speaker of English with native-speaker level English proficiency or one with comparable linguistic competence in English or have native-speaker English ability	13
1.3 of English irrespective of nationality regardless of nationality of any nationality who is a national of an English-speaking country	10
1.4 of English with sufficient working knowledge of Japanese with evidence to support a working knowledge of Japanese language able to work in the Japanese language for administration with a command of Japanese sufficient to fulfil administrative activities with sufficient proficiency in Japanese to deal with administrative staff without assistance with an ability to understand Japanese or a native speaker of Japanese with ability to conduct classes in English	8
1.5 of English or non-native English speakers with proficiency in English or near-native speaker ability (for non-native speakers preference will be given to those who present us with a TOEFL score report of 600 or its equivalent)	5
1.6 of Japanese who can teach courses in English	4
1.7 competence in English	3
1.8 of EU official languages	1

2 Native or _____		
2.1	near-native English ability (all nationalities welcome)	13
	near-native English-language ability	
	equivalent ability in English	
	equivalent speaker of English	
	those who have the equivalent abilities	
	possess native level fluency	
	have native-speaking ability	
2.2	near-native speaker competence in English is required and fluency in Japanese preferable	11
	near-native competence in Japanese and English	
	near-native fluency in English and Japanese	
	native-like proficiency in English with sufficient Japanese to handle administrative functions and duties or near-native speaker to conduct classes both in English and Japanese	
2.3	near-native fluency in English	8
2.4	near-native English speaker / or near-native speaker of English	5
2.5	near-native speaker of English of any nationality	3
2.6	native-like proficiency in English	2
2.7	near-native competency in English	1
2.8	near-native command of English	1
2.9	non-native English speaker who has experience teaching overseas	1
3 Native _____		
3.1	-level English proficiency	10
	-like proficiency in English	
	proficiency in English	
	English proficiency	
3.2	English speakers require proficiency in Japanese adequate for daily administrative duties	9
	English speaker with a good command of Japanese in listening, speaking and reading but not necessarily in writing	
3.3	facility in English or Japanese	3
3.4	competency in English	2
3.5	English speaker	2

4 Other		
4.1	English at native or near-native proficiency (a non-Japanese applicant must have an intermediate or above proficiency in Japanese)	2
4.2	must have (near-)native/fluent competence in both Japanese and English	1
4.3	possess native or near-native proficiency in English	1
4.4	have a very high-level (native-like) proficiency in English	1
4.5	if not a native Japanese speaker, sufficient command of Japanese is required	1
4.6	if a native speaker of English, applicants must also have a level of Japanese language ability that will allow him/her to partake fully in any assigned administrative duties	1
4.7	non-Japanese applicants should have native speaker fluency of Japanese	1
4.8	Japanese native fluent English speaker able to conduct lessons in Japanese	1
4.9	fluency in English (native speaker level)	1
4.10	applicant's native language should be English	1

As the data presented in section 1.1 of Table 1 show, on 58 individual occasions the native-speaker criterion was discursively presented in its most simplified form. This particular pattern of discursive reference impacts upon potential applicants, and indeed the wider readership, in a variety of ways. First, this simplified discursive reference implies that the native-speaker criterion requires no additional description, definition or clarification, thus working to further domesticate a profoundly illegitimate point of linguistic reference. The absence of descriptive information defining the term reflects the position that 'the more that an item of behavior is predictable, the less information it carries' (Douglas, op cit: 47). A practical consequence of this dynamic is that many institutions are 'unable or unwilling to define the parameters of the "native-speaker" label despite making it a central criterion for employment' (Rivers, 2013a: 89), such is its assumed predictability.

The disclosure of such limited information, despite the native-speaker criterion's central position in teacher recruitment, also functions to protect the institution from potential negative feedback, appraisal or interrogation. Relevant here are Gee's (2008) observations concerning the features of discourse and discursive practice, namely that 'discourses are resistant to internal criticism and self-scrutiny, since uttering viewpoints that seriously undermine them defines one as being outside them' (ibid.: 161–162). In practical terms, this might equate to the following: if a potential applicant does not know or understand without further definition what a native speaker is, and consequently whether or not they can be classified as one, then such applicants need not apply, as they are deemed as external to the shared understanding required.

Second, the simplified discursive reference rather brutally divides all speakers of English into those who possess and those who do not possess an unstated set of preferential attributes. This essentialist approach to speakerhood status 'falls short in capturing the multifaceted nature of individuals' diverse linguistic identities' (Faez, 2011: 231) and, somewhat ironically, condemns all language learners within the recruiting institution to an inferior and inescapable category of speakerhood (i.e. the non-native-English-speaking students will always be non-native speakers and therefore never awarded equal status, or opportunity for employment, as the so-called native speakers of English, regardless of the level of proficiency attained during their lifetime). Through use of the native-speaker criterion in such a reduced form, potential applicants – in addition to many others, e.g. students – are informed 'at the very least about who is an insider and who isn't, often who is "normal" and who isn't, and often, too, many other things as well' (Gee, op cit: 161).

Beyond Section 1.1 of Table 1, it is possible to uncover discursive evidence of 'many other things as well' in the form of the previously discussed 'qualifying sociosemiotic associations' in the Japanese context. As documented within Section 1.2, on 13 individual occasions the native-speaker criterion was used as a benchmark for potential applicants to comparatively appraise their own English language competence, level, ability, command and/or proficiency. With the exception of one employment advertisement, though, potential applicants were not informed about the actual standards of English language competence, level, ability, command and/or proficiency they were expected to satisfy. This lack of detail further reflects and enforces the commonsensical belief that legitimate native-speaker English teachers, as a generic collective of linguistic equals, possess an innate mastery of the language and are therefore the most appropriate teachers. Recent discussions have revealed the absurdity of this assumption:

> Native speakers, after all, differ in terms of their proficiency; some are good speakers, some not; some good writers, some not, and so on. And if we include the whole range of native speaker, from very early childhood, then we would probably agree that the gamut runs from first learning to fully proficient performance, just as it does with second-language learners. (Davies, op cit: 27)

Slight variations upon the same theme were observable on 13 other occasions (see Section 2.1), where potential applicants were required to possess 'native or near-native' English ability, speaking equivalence and/or level of fluency. Moreover, on ten further occasions (see Section 3.1), potential applicants were required to possess 'native-level or native-like' English proficiency. While certain aspects of this discourse may appear to be moving toward more equitable recruitment practices in that potential applicants are offered scope, albeit limited, for slight variations from assumed native-speaker norms, the fact that native-speaker language ability is used as a benchmark without evidence suggests that the discursive practices of such employment advertisements are far from being equitable.

A dominant trend observed within the data was the discursive uses of the native-speaker criterion alongside requests for potential applicants to have Japanese language knowledge, command, proficiency and/or ability (34 individual references as recorded in Sections 1.4, 2.2, 3.2, 4.1, 4.2, 4.5, 4.6 and 4.7).

While the need for Japanese language proficiency may, in many cases, present as quite a sensible request given the context (i.e. confirming how the relationship between national context and language are accepted as symbiotic), it is interesting to note how the majority of such requests state that the Japanese language is needed for undertaking administrative work rather than for teaching.

Several assumptions concerning the link between language proficiency and the nationality of the potential applicant were observed within the data. For example, one advertisement read:

> If you are a non-Japanese person, certification of your Japanese ability. If you are a non-Japanese applicant; we may ask you to write a short essay in Japanese at the interview. (#D113051384)

Another wrote:

> there is no restriction on nationality but successful applicants must have a high proficiency in both English and Japanese (non-native Japanese applicants must be able to perform administrative duties and tasks in Japanese. (#D113101094)

In positioning Japanese language proficiency as a qualification for employment, although only expressed in explicit terms to non-Japanese nationals (the assumption being that all Japanese nationals will speak Japanese better than any non-Japanese nationals), employment roles, responsibilities, contracted terms and expectations are covertly drawn on the basis of the dominant 'host' language rather than the actual language being taught. This heightens the potential for Japanese linguistic imperialism to impact upon recruitment policy and institutional practice.

The idea that 'host' language proficiency, in this case Japanese, is able to function as the fulcrum for discriminatory practices in ELT recruitment related to the native-speaker criterion is rarely discussed. Usui (2000: 280) warns against the perils of sponsoring the rise of 'petit nationalism as it operates across English language education and communication studies in Japan', often under the identity-bolstering shroud of anti-English linguistic imperialism discourse. More recently, with direct reference to the Japanese context, Rudolph et al. (2015) detail how:

> the idealized NS of English is glocally constructed concomitantly with the idealized NS of Japanese. The construction of linguistic and cultural ownership extends beyond English, both within a given society and the ELT situated therein. In addition, the construction of 'us' in relation to context, may serve to both privilege and marginalize local members of a society. As borders of 'inside' and 'outside' are constructed and patrolled in terms of the idealized NS of English, so too are those of being or becoming 'Japanese'. (Rudolph et al., 2015: 39)

In such situations, one can often witness how languages and their respective histories, as well as their supposed native speakers, are positioned as being in direct conflict with each other upon a battleground for professional identity, institutional membership, ideological control and status superiority. For example, in certain employment situations within Japan, those teachers who are perceived not to be fluent in all four skills of the Japanese language (i.e. non-Japanese nationals) are contractually obliged to teach additional classes as compensation. Among the many problems associated with this practice is that assessments of Japanese language fluency are often made on the basis of nationality as implied by extracts (#D113051384) and (#D113101094).

Houghton (op cit) documents a case at a Japanese university in which a Korean national, highly fluent in all four skills of the Japanese language, was categorised by the institution alongside other non-Japanese nationals who possessed a significantly lower level of Japanese language proficiency for the purpose of allocating additional teaching duties. With links to the confessional statement presented at the start of this chapter, Houghton (ibid.) further illustrates how language requirements and regulations enforced within the workplace at the post-employment stage have the capacity to discriminate against one particular group. With reference to her own workplace, she discusses how 'the head of the English section … personally banned the use of the English language in the English section' (ibid.: 67) and how 'official documents submitted in Japanese were in principle not accepted when accompanied by short email memos written in English, and the expression of opinions and ideas in English by email was ignored' (ibid: 68). A consequence of such language-based decision-making was 'the systematic and almost complete silencing' (ibid: 68) of those employed within a category exclusively occupied by non-Japanese nationals.

As language assessments are therefore commonly linked to nationality, a final observation in the data gathered concerns the specification of or reference to the nationality of potential applicants. On ten individual occasions (see Section 1.3), potential applicants were required to be a 'native speaker of English' of any nationality and/or who is a national of an English-speaking country. Such descriptions should be approached with caution, as their practical function is intended to indicate that the advertised positions are for non-Japanese nationals only. Hashimoto (2013: 159) documents how the common view that a native speaker of English 'is a foreigner has played a crucial role in the Japanese education system, and has contributed to restrictions on the functions of NSEs within the system'. Similarly, Heimlich (op cit: 174) asserts that 'there are in Japan no Japanese workers assigned roles as native speakers of foreign languages, because the categories are mutually exclusive' (although see Yanase, this volume, for a different view).

The data in the current study support the position that the native-speaker criterion often functions as a synonym for non-Japanese nationality, and this in turn identifies potential applicants, in the majority of cases, as little more than temporary 'guest' workers. With reference to similar recruitment processes within Italian higher education, Petrie (2013) declares how:

> [d]escriptors such as 'mother tongue' and 'native speaker' are to be avoided in recruitment procedures for access to employment; these terms cannot reasonably be added to a curriculum vitae as a 'qualification'. Legislation or norms using these terms have more potential to fall foul of prohibitions on

discrimination based on nationality, since they are more likely to attract applicants who are not citizens of the host state, and indeed may even be reserved for guest workers. (Petrie, 2013: 41)

In the current study, 81 per cent (*n*=236) of the employment advertisements offered potential applicants a limited-term contract position, thus showing how institutional 'policies aim to keep cycling in new batches of foreign workers' for the purpose of maintaining 'a rite of social purification of the workplace' (Heimlich, op cit: 178). The consequences of limited-term employment in those instances where the actual position is continual (i.e. in instances where one acts as a 'guest' worker) can impact upon relationships beyond the institution.

The nomadic lifestyle that limited-term contracts tend to promote often inhibits the formation of sustainable collegial relationships, restricts workplace involvement in long-term initiatives, denies emotional attachment to a specific place (i.e. developing a sense of home or belonging) and undermines sincere dedication to one's institution, such are the demands of an almost obsessive-like quest to continually search for improved working conditions. (Rivers, 2013b: 68)

In terms of racial preference, data from the current study do not directly reveal a preference for potential applicants to be of a particular race or ethnicity, which is to be expected. It would certainly not be in the best interests of the institution to be making public proclamations, in English to an international audience, favouring one race or ethnicity over another. Discourses of racial preference and race-based discrimination are often deemed incompatible with the 'masquerade of smiley faces and perpetual pleasantness decorating the veneer of "native-speaker" English teaching' (ibid.: 75).

However, the evidence that ELT recruitment in Japan shows racial preference is compelling. Kubota and McKay (op cit: 612) suggest that 'teaching English in Japan is a raced practice with preference for White native speakers', while more recently, Kubota and Fujimoto discuss the 'complex manifestations of racial exclusion and othering' (op cit: 204) within the Japanese context. Moreover, in an empirical study investigating the teacher preferences of Japanese English students, Rivers and Ross (op cit: 334) discover a 'statistically significant preference for the White race teachers'. In terms of the current study, and although mere speculation in the absence of conclusive evidence, a more covert channel of making assessments on the basis of race and ethnicity is actually provided, as 50 per cent (*n*=146) of the 292 employment advertisements required potential applicants to submit a recent photograph.

Evidence of native-speakerism?

As outlined at the start of this chapter, the motive for the current investigation was to document the prevalence and uses of the native-speaker criterion when listed as a qualification for employment. From the data presented and discussed in previous sections, readers are now asked to consider whether the observed patterns of native-speaker criterion use constitute native-speakerism and, if so, how and when the observed practices disadvantage potential applicants on the basis of their speakerhood status. In order to answer these questions it is necessary to revisit the two primary definitions of native-speakerism current in the academic literature.

An early definition of native-speakerism was provided by Holliday (op cit: 6), who identifies it as 'an established belief that "native-speaker" teachers represent a "Western culture" from which spring the ideals of both the English language and of English language teaching methodology'. Holliday (2006: 385) later added that native-speakerism stands as 'a pervasive ideology within ELT'. For Holliday, native-speakerism is therefore cast primarily as an ideological construct influenced by political, cultural, neo-racial and imperialistic forces.

The data within the current study have shown a widespread preference for potential applicants applying for ELT positions within Japanese higher education to satisfy the native-speaker criterion. To recap, the native-speaker criterion was used, in various discursive forms, within 63 per cent (n=184) of all employment advertisements as a qualification for employment. While such discursive uses might tempt the reader into concluding that these institutions have subscribed to 'an established belief that "native-speaker" teachers represent a "Western culture" from which spring the ideals of both the English language and of English language teaching methodology' (Holliday, 2005: 6), and are therefore native-speakerist, there is no conclusive evidence that this is the case.

To expand, within the data in the current study there is insufficient information available to explain exactly why 184 employment advertisements referenced the native-speaker criterion as a qualification for employment. Given this lack of information concerning institutional motive, and indeed the lack of background information found generally within the employment advertisement genre of discourse, the definition of native-speakerism proposed by Holliday (2005) does not allow us to determine whether the observed uses are indeed examples of native-speakerism. The reason for this shortcoming is that native-speakerism cannot be accurately accounted for when primarily defined as an ideological construct. While it might well be reasonable to speculate that the widespread use of the native-speaker criterion as a qualification for employment is the product of native-speakerist ideology, speculation does not provide stable ground for challenging practices, pedagogies and policies that potentially discriminate against certain individuals on the basis of their speakerhood status, a point I have made elsewhere.

While Holliday's (2005) definition has been useful in providing a foundation for new theoretical direction through which to forward explorations of issues concerning the dimensions of native-speakerism in foreign language education, we now see this definition as being limited in its ability to capture the multitude of intricate ways that native-speakerism, embedded within the fabric of the TESOL industry, is reflected through daily pedagogical practice, institutional and national policy, as well as legal frameworks which centre around issues of prejudice, stereotyping and/or discrimination (Houghton & Rivers, 2013: 7).

In their work on native-speakerism in Japan, Houghton and Rivers (ibid.) attempt to facilitate a shift away from ideological influence by moving the definition of native-speakerism toward configuration as a contemporary social problem. While certainly not seeking to deny or underestimate the influence of various ideologies, the definition of native-speakerism proposed below is intended to bring greater attention to the ways in which a wider range of practices, including many of those documented within the current study, essentially share a common foundation in stereotyping and in-group/out-group classification dynamics.

> *Native-speakerism is prejudice, stereotyping and/or discrimination, typically by or against foreign language teachers, on the basis of either being or not being perceived and categorised as a native speaker of a particular language...Its endorsement positions individuals from certain language groups as being innately superior to individuals from other language groups. Therefore native-speakerist policies and practices represent a fundamental breach of one's basic human rights.* (Houghton and Rivers, op cit: 14)

In choosing to approach native-speakerism primarily as a contemporary social problem rather than as an ideological construct, Houghton and Rivers (ibid.: 2) contend that interpreting native-speakerism 'primarily in terms of imperialism or colonialism, and thus ideology' places significant limits upon 'the analysis in ways that obscure the complexity of native-speakerism as a global, and very contemporary, social phenomenon' (ibid.). One such limit is the view that native speakers, as static ideological aggressors, are often the exclusive beneficiaries of native-speakerist practices and are therefore not in need of protection from potentially discriminatory practice. As the confessional statement at the beginning of this chapter reveals, the lines of aggression and victimhood cannot be so easily drawn. The definition of native-speakerism above thus attempts to counter the dominant unidirectional conceptualisation of perpetrator–victim discourse, as insisted upon by ideological appraisals of power and status in language education, in order to offer protection to all potential victims of questionable in-group/out-group classification dynamics.

With implications for moving the discussion forward, the definition of native-speakerism proposed by Houghton and Rivers (ibid.) further refrains from imposing ideological responsibility, shame and/or guilt (see Bueno and Caesar, 2003) upon contemporary teaching professionals of all backgrounds. As they argue:

> *When using pre-determined terminology to discuss different kinds of prejudices, the perpetrators and the victims may or may not be implied by the terms themselves, with the obvious danger being that the mere use of any given term (especially terms such as orientalism, sexism, male chauvinism and feminism) may accuse a certain group by automatically suggesting in the minds of people who are the perpetrators (in need of challenge) and who are the victims (in need of protection). And the same can be said of native-speakerism, a term which, within its present (albeit rather recently coined definition) primarily casts 'native speakers' from the English-speaking West as the perpetrators of native-speakerism (the subjects of the verb) and 'non-native speakers' from the English-speaking West as the victims (the objects of the verb).* (Houghton and Rivers, op cit: 3)

Given the definition of native-speakerism proposed by Houghton and Rivers (op cit), an evidence-based appraisal of the data in the current study allows the reader to conclude that the uses of the native-speaker criterion shown in the 184 employment advertisements constitute a clear-cut example of native-speakerism. In drawing this conclusion, it is not necessary to uncover the motives underpinning the institutional decision-making. The crucial points of focus are the institutional actions and the consequences of such actions. Simply put, once the recruiting institution chooses to reference the native-speaker criterion as a qualification for employment, they are engaging in native-speakerist practice. This conclusion is directly informed by the fact that potential applicants wishing to apply for one of the 184 positions referencing the native-speaker criterion in the current study are deemed to be qualified 'on the basis of either being or not being perceived and categorized as a native speaker of a particular language' (Houghton and Rivers, op cit: 14). Institutional decisions such as these are discriminatory against potential applicants who are not defined by the recruiting institution, or who choose not to define themselves, as native speakers of a particular language.

Future research

False dichotomies such as the native/non-native speaker have impacted upon language education practices, pedagogies and policies in various ways for an extended period of time. The depth of their entrenchment within contemporary ELT discourse remains such that there exists significant scope for future research initiatives aimed toward further revealing their inadequacy when assessed in relation to the complexity and fluidity of the individual.

Demand is growing for multidisciplinary research that advances many of the 'compelling arguments for re-evaluating the validity of the construct of the native speaker' (Sayer, 2012: 152). In terms of how native speakers – and also non-native speakers – of different languages are commoditised through mental representation, symbols and other imagery, it would be interesting to explore how their respective 'qualifying sociosemiotic associations' change across context and between languages. This kind of research, which would also be inclusive of explorations of professional identity, could take as its point of departure Toh's (op cit: 183–184) call to 'distinguish between native speaker as the socio-discursive and socio-semiotic construct that it is, and native speakers as the unique individuals (and indeed professionals) encountered in daily life and/or the workplace'.

In addition to various potential research initiatives, individual teacher-researchers may wish to engage in professional activism within and against the institution in an attempt to counter its authoritative role in the transmission and reinforcement of social categories, norms, values, attitudes and ethics. The data from the current study suggest that recruiting institutions should be challenged more frequently to define exactly what is being referenced through the native-speaker criterion. Douglas (op cit: 91) cautions that 'when the institutions make classifications for us, we seem to lose some independence that we might conceivably have otherwise had. This thought is one that we have ever reason, as individuals, to resist'. It is therefore not unreasonable for potential applicants or serving employees to ask institutional authorities for evidence showing how the native-speaker criterion qualifies potential applicants for certain positions. Other teacher-researchers seeking employment within Japanese higher education may alternatively choose not to apply to those institutions that cite the native-speaker criterion as a qualification for employment.

From my own subjective experience researching the topics discussed within this chapter, I sincerely believe that a positive change is on the horizon. As other teacher-researchers begin to speak more openly about their employment experiences, publish their research efforts and engage, without fear, in various forms of professional activism and/or resistance (see Rivers, 2015, and contributions to this collection), institutions, administrators, colleagues and other stakeholders are facing increased demands for accountability when using the native-speaker criterion as a conditional variable within the workplace. This chapter is therefore optimistic that, in the near future, institutions within the Japanese context will demonstrate greater sensitivity or restraint when contemplating using the native-speaker criterion as a qualification for employment. This shift, when it arrives, can only lead to an increase in the kind of equitable practices for which the global domain of ELT continues to search.

Acknowledgement

Sincere gratitude is offered to the volume editors and anonymous reviewers for their constructive guidance and support. This work was partially funded by a KAKENHI Grant-in-Aid for Scientific Research (No: 24520627) awarded by the Japan Society for the Promotion of Science.

References

Anderson Mōri and Tomotsune Law Firm (2012, September) *Labor and Employment Law Bulletin,* 30. Available online at: https://www.amt-law.com/en/pdf/bulletins7_pdf/LELB30.pdf (accessed 26 February 2016).

Appleby, R (2014) White Western male teachers constructing academic identities in Japanese higher education. *Gender and Education* 26/7: 776–793.

Askehave, I (2010) Communicating leadership: A discourse analytical perspective on the job advertisement. *Journal of Business Communication* 47/3: 313–345.

Bhatia, VK (1999) 'Genres in conflict' in Trosborg, A (ed) *Analysing professional genres.* Amsterdam: John Benjamins,147–161.

Bonfiglio, TP (2010) *Mother tongues and nations: The invention of the native speaker.* New York, NY: Walter de Gruyter.

Breckenridge, Y and Erling, E (2011) 'The native speaker English teacher and the politics of globalization in Japan' in Seargeant, P (ed) *English in Japan in the era of globalization.* Houndmills: Palgrave Macmillan, 80–100.

Bueno, EP and Caesar, T (2003) *I wouldn't want anybody to know: Native English teaching in Japan.* Tokyo: JPGS Press.

Clark, E and Paran, A (2007) The employability of non-native-speaker teachers of EFL: A UK survey. *System* 35/4: 407–430.

Coulmas, F (1981) 'Introduction: The concept of the native speaker' in Coulmas, F (ed) *A Festschrift for native speaker.* The Hague: Mouton, 1–28.

Davies, A (2013) *Native speakers and native users.* Cambridge: Cambridge University Press.

Douglas, M (1986) *How institutions think.* New York, NY: Syracuse University Press.

Faez, F (2011) Reconceptualizing the native/nonnative speaker dichotomy. *Journal of Language, Identity, and Education* 10/4: 231–249.

Fairclough, N (1993) Critical discourse analysis and the marketisation of public discourse: The universities. *Discourse and Society* 4/2: 133–168.

Gee, JP (2008) *Social linguistics and literacies: Ideology in discourse.* London: Routledge.

Hackert, S (2009) Linguistic nationalism and the emergence of the English native speaker. *European Journal of English Studies* 13/3: 305–317.

Hashimoto, K (2011) Compulsory 'foreign language activities' in Japanese primary schools. *Current Issues in Language Planning* 12/2: 167–184.

Hashimoto, K (2013) 'The construction of the "native speaker" in Japan's educational policies for TEFL' in Houghton, SA and Rivers, DJ (eds) *Native-speakerism in Japan: Intergroup dynamics in foreign language education.* Bristol: Multilingual Matters,159–168.

Hayes, B (2013) 'Hiring criteria for Japanese university English-teaching faculty' in Houghton, SA and Rivers, DJ (eds) *Native-speakerism in Japan: Intergroup dynamics in foreign language education.* Bristol: Multilingual Matters,132–146.

Heimlich, E (2013) 'The meaning of Japan's role of professional foreigner' in Houghton, SA and Rivers, DJ (eds) *Native-speakerism in Japan: Intergroup dynamics in foreign language education.* Bristol: Multilingual Matters, 169–179.

Holliday, A (2005) *The struggle to teach English as an international language.* Oxford: Oxford University Press.

Holliday, A (2006) Native-speakerism. *ELT Journal* 60/4: 385–387.

Houghton, SA (2013) 'The overthrow of the foreign lecturer position, and its aftermath' in Houghton, SA and Rivers, DJ (eds) *Native-speakerism in Japan: Intergroup dynamics in foreign language education.* Bristol: Multilingual Matters, 60–74.

Houghton, SA and Rivers, DJ (eds) (2013) *Native-speakerism in Japan: Intergroup dynamics in foreign language education.* Bristol: Multilingual Matters.

Japan Science and Technology Agency (2014). *Usage Notice.* Available online at: https://jrecin.jst.go.jp/seek/SeekDescription?id=002&ln=1. (accessed 22 February 2016).

Kubota, R and Fujimoto, D (2013) 'Racialized native speakers: Voices of Japanese American English language professional' in Houghton, SA and Rivers, DJ (eds) *Native-speakerism in Japan: Intergroup dynamics in foreign language education.* Bristol: Multilingual Matters, 196–206.

Kubota, R and McKay, S (2009) Globalization and language learning in rural Japan: The role of English in the local linguistic ecology. *TESOL Quarterly* 43/4: 593–619.

Mahboob, A and Golden, R (2013) Looking for native speakers of English: Discrimination in English language teaching job advertisements. *Voices in Asia Journal,* 1/1: 72–81.

Owen, CR (2004) University recruitment advertisements and textual shelf-life. *Critical Discourse Studies* 1/1: 149–157.

Paikeday, TM (1985a) *The native speaker is dead!* Toronto: Paikeday Publishing.

Paikeday, TM (1985b) May I kill the native speaker? *TESOL Quarterly* 19/2: 390–395.

Pederson, R (2012) 'Representation, globalization, and the native speaker: Dialectics of language ideology, and power' in Sung, K and Pederson, R (eds) *Critical ELT Practices in Asia.* Rotterdam: Sense Publishers,1–22.

Petrie, D (2013) '(Dis)integration of mother tongue teachers in Italian universities: Human rights abuses and the quest for equal treatment in the European single market' in Houghton, SA and Rivers, DJ (eds) *Native-speakerism in Japan: Intergroup dynamics in foreign language education.* Bristol: Multilingual Matters, 29–41.

Pillar, I (2001) Who, if anyone, is a native speaker? *Anglistik* 12/2: 109–121.

Rafaeli, A and Oliver, AL (1998) Employment ads: A configurational research agenda. *Journal of Management Inquiry*, 7/4: 342–358.

Rajagopalan, K (1997) Linguistics and the myth of nativity: Comments on the controversy over 'new/non-native' Englishes. *Journal of Pragmatics* 27/2: 225–231.

Rajagopalan, K (2015) 'On the challenge of teaching English in Latin America with special emphasis on Brazil' in Rivers, DJ (ed) *Resistance to the known: Counter-conduct in language education.* Houndmills: Palgrave Macmillan, 121–143.

Rivers, DJ (2011) Evaluating the self and the other: Imagined intercultural contact within a native-speaker dependent foreign language context. *International Journal of Intercultural Relations*, 35/6: 842–852.

Rivers, DJ (2013a) 'Institutionalized native-speakerism: Voices of dissent and acts of resistance' in Houghton, SA and Rivers, DJ (eds) *Native-speakerism in Japan: Intergroup dynamics in foreign language education.* Bristol: Multilingual Matters, 75–91.

Rivers, DJ (2013b) 'Implications for identity: Inhabiting the "native-speaker" English teacher location in the Japanese sociocultural context' in Rivers, DJ and Houghton, SA (eds) *Social identities and multiple selves in foreign language education.* London: Bloomsbury, 33–55.

Rivers, DJ (2013c) Labour contract law amendments: Recruitment indicative of change? *The Language Teacher* 37/1: 68–71.

Rivers, DJ (ed) (2015) *Resistance to the known: Counter-conduct in language education.* Houndmills: Palgrave Macmillan.

Rivers, DJ and Ross, AS (2013) Idealized English teachers: The implicit influence of race in Japan. *Journal of Language, Identity, and Education* 12/5: 321–339.

Rudolph, N, Selvi, AF and Yazan, B (2015) Conceptualizing and confronting inequity: Approaches within and new directions for the 'NNEST Movement'. *Critical Inquiry in Language Studies* 12/1: 27–50.

Ruecker, T and Ives, L (in press) White native English speaker needed: The rhetorical construction of privilege in online teacher recruitment spaces. *TESOL Quarterly.* doi: 10.1002/tesq.195.

Rutherford, J (1990) 'A place called home: Identity and the cultural politics of difference' in Rutherford, J (ed) *Identity, community, culture and difference.* London: Lawrence and Wishart, 9–27.

Sayer, M (2012) *Ambiguities and tensions in English language teaching*. New York: Routledge.

Seargeant, P (2009) *The idea of English in Japan: Ideology and the evolution of a global language*. Bristol: Multilingual Matters.

Selvi, AF (2010) All teachers are equal, but some teachers are more equal than others: Trend analysis of job advertisements in English language teaching. *WATESOL NNEST Caucus Annual Review*, 1: 156–181.

Stanley, P (2012) *A critical ethnography of 'Westerners' teaching in China: Shanghaied in Shanghai*. New York, NY: Routledge.

Sung-Yul Park, J and Wee, L (2012) *Markets of English: Linguistic capital and language policy in a globalizing world*. London: Routledge.

Toh, G (2013) 'Scrutinizing the native speaker as referent, entity and project' in Houghton, SA and Rivers, DJ (eds) *Native-speakerism in Japan: Intergroup dynamics in foreign language education*. Bristol: Multilingual Matters, 183–195.

Tsuneyoshi, R (2013) Communicative English in Japan and "native speakers" of English' in Houghton, SA and Rivers, DJ (eds) *Native-speakerism in Japan: Intergroup dynamics in foreign language education*. Bristol: Multilingual Matters, 119–131.

Usui, N (2000) The anti-English linguistic imperialism movement: Savior of Japanese identity or harbinger of petit nationalism? *Educational Studies* 42: 277–303.

Xiong, T (2012) Discourse and marketization of higher education in China: The genre of advertisements for academic posts. *Discourse and Society* 23/3: 318–337.

5

Bilingualism and globalisation in Latin America: fertile ground for native-speakerism

Adriana González, Universidad de Antioquia, Medellín, Colombia
Enric Llurda, Universitat de Lleida, Spain

Introduction

Ideologies surrounding the promotion of second language competence, especially in the context of globalisation, are strongly mediated by the pervasive myth of the monolingual native speaker as the single bearer of linguistic legitimacy. Several authors have helped uncover how the native speaker myth acts on language policy and language teaching decisions (Phillipson, 1992; Davies, 2003), and Holliday's (2005) notion of 'native-speakerism' clearly establishes the deep meaning and discriminatory practices that have developed out of such an ideology.

Latin America is not unlike many other geographical contexts in that it tries to adapt to globalisation by incorporating the dominant lingua franca in international business and communication. Several governments in the region are developing and implementing policies aimed at increasing English competence among its citizens, and especially among primary and secondary school students. Such policies have been labelled with a diversity of names, all pointing to the ultimate goal of enabling young people in the country to become proficient in English, along with the national language. Usually identified as educational agendas for bilingualism, some countries have added the adjective 'bilingual' to their names, officially or colloquially, ignoring the linguistic diversity of the Latin American nations and adhering to the pervasive view that true bilingualism is only that which includes access to the language of an economic empire. De Mejía (2002) calls this approach 'elite bilingualism'. For instance, the slogan *Colombia Bilingüe* ('Bilingual Colombia') has been the flagship of the official language policy of the Colombian government in the last ten years, with the openly declared goal of promoting English competence among Colombian citizens in the whole educational system. We should first note that using the term 'bilingual' does de facto ignore the existence of many Colombians who are already bilingual and who, on a daily basis, speak a/some language(s) other than Spanish. The main implication of the *Colombia Bilingüe* slogan and others like it is the need to incorporate English as an international language, as a means to bring Colombia into the league of countries that have a significant role on the international scene. This view challenges more dynamic notions of bilingualism, such as the ones proposed by Cook (1992) and Grosjean (2010).

In this chapter, we will analyse the discourses that are constructed around such policies in the leading newspapers of Chile, Colombia, Ecuador and Mexico, with a special emphasis on how these publications deal with the native speaker myth. We attempt to show that the countries portrayed are a fertile ground for the promotion of native-speakerism, a phenomenon that is spreading in the language education agendas in Latin America. We hope to contribute to the discussion on the topic, shedding some light upon native-speakerism, a phenomenon scarcely explored in the Latin American context.

Native and non-native teachers

Applied and educational linguists have been challenging the dichotomy between native and non-native speakers for the last thirty years, with a growing consensus on the need to move away from associating nativeness with a series of characteristics naturally belonging to a specific group of speakers of a language (Phillipson, op cit; Davies, op cit). Particularly, in the case of English, the fact that it is so widely spoken by people from all over the world, and the fact that it is spoken by more people who learned it as a second or additional language than by people who learned it as their first language, makes it very difficult to associate specifying traits to a given sub-group of its speakers, namely, native speakers. In other words, English has become such an international language that it makes no sense to try to teach it in connection to a particular community, be it either real or imagined (Llurda, 2004). According to Davies (op cit), native and non-native speakers do not have separate sets of defining characteristics; rather, alignment with one group or the other is generally based on self-ascription to a group and actual acceptance by other members of that same group. People are native speakers of a language if they choose to call themselves native speakers and other speakers of the same language accept them as members of the group. Order of language acquisition, place of birth and so on are characteristics that can be found in either category, and only self-ascription and acceptance determines the group to which somebody belongs.

With regard to language teachers, non-native speakers (often referred to as NNESTs, or Non-native English Speaking Teachers, as opposed to NESTs, their native counterparts) have been responsible for teaching English in many countries of the world. In the case of Latin American countries, as in many other countries of the Expanding Circle (Kachru, 1992), few NESTs were available to teach English. In addition, the perceived superiority of native speakers raised the status of NESTs and led many people to conclude that the quality of English language education in Expanding Circle countries would only increase if more NESTs were employed in Latin American schools. Such an approach was taken several years ago by different Asian countries. Japan and Korea, for instance, have respectively operated the JET (Japanese Exchange and Teaching Programme) and EPIK (English Program in Korea) for many years, and now similar programmes are being introduced in the Latin American countries that constitute the focus of this study (Chile, Colombia, Ecuador and Mexico).

Research on native and non-native teachers has so far produced some relevant findings that need to be briefly reviewed to provide the foundation for the subsequent analysis of data. One of the main outcomes of teacher research is that good language teaching must be understood as the result of a combination of factors that include training, personality and environmental conditions. Thus, place of birth or native/non-native status cannot be considered determining factors in the quality of teaching. However, discriminatory practices – ranging from lower salaries for NNESTs to requiring native-speaker status in job advertisements – continue to exist (Selvi, 2010). Such practices are based on the fact that many students often prefer to have NESTs and on the fact that employers, rather than considering what is best for students, simply meet the demands of the market. Whereas it is true that students often approach their English education with a set of prejudices and uncritical ideas which include the notion of the native speaker as the ideal teacher, empirical studies have shown that after having experienced both NESTs and NNESTs, students tend to value individual teachers' qualities and are less prone to generalised prejudices against NNESTs (Lasagabaster and Sierra, 2005; Moussu, 2010). In a time in which a majority of language learners choose English due to its international status and its lingua franca uses, it seems anachronistic to maintain an inextricable connection between the language and Inner Circle countries. Llurda (op cit) emphasised the inadequacy of restricting teaching to native speaker models when dealing with a language that is spoken worldwide among people of all origins and language backgrounds. The international status of English leads us to conclude that it is a truly intercultural language which may be used in a variety of contexts for a variety of purposes. Therefore, no one can claim ownership over it (Widdowson, 1994) and, conversely, many individuals can develop an appropriate level of intercultural communicative competence (Byram, 1997).

Such an intercultural dimension is not so visible when the focus of attention is on pronunciation. Some people still pursue a 'native accent' in their second language learning endeavours, regardless of repeated evidence against such a futile goal (Levis, 2005; Lippi-Green, 1997). Jenkins (2002) and Derwing and Munro (2009) argue that pronunciation instruction is most effective if intelligibility is the central element of focus. If a native-like accent ceases to be a goal in language education, NESTs clearly lose their advantage over NNESTs. Yet prejudices against the latter persist, and, surprisingly enough, non-native teachers are strong prejudice-bearers, still believing in the need to imitate native-speaker models and believing that they would be better teachers if they spoke like native speakers (Llurda, 2009). Such self-deprecatory prejudices only disappear with increased contact with different speakers of the language (Llurda, 2008), which indicates that frequent use of the language empowers second language (L2) speakers and sets them free from the inferiority complex that often accompanies them (Medgyes, 1994). In this respect, NNESTs who are educated in Inner Circle countries constitute a kind of hybrid group between local (non-mobile) NNESTs and NESTs. They are in a third space (Bhabha, 1994), neither being part of the privileged native speaker group (Berger, 2014) nor being fully local, as they no longer retain their original identity, skills and world vision after going abroad to further their education. Furthermore, these teachers may enjoy a certain prestige in their local community and be perceived as closer to the idealised native speaker. In fact, research shows how teachers educated abroad have an increased sense of being L2 users (Cook, 2005) and do not rely on the native speaker myth as heavily as teachers who have never left their home country (Llurda, 2008). Thus, being educated abroad appears to have a double value: it increases the teacher's self-confidence as a legitimate user of the L2 and it additionally improves their status among their local community.

Overall, the main problem faced by NNESTs is that of overgeneralisation. Namely, it is an unhappy reality that a certain number of teachers of English working in different parts of the world are below the threshold level of language and intercultural skills that would be generally desirable (Medgyes, 1999). Unfortunately, the existence of such a group of NNESTs may have contributed to extend the suspicion over the teaching capacity of the whole NNEST community. This is clearly unfair, as no other group of teachers suffers from such a generalisation due to the weaknesses or lack of skills of some of the members of the group. Yet this is the case with language teachers, as this professional group is unlike any other group of teachers in terms of the nature of the subject, the content and methodology of teaching and the duality of native and non-native (Borg, 2006). The following analysis will show to what extent this duality appears in many debates on language policies aimed at increasing the level of English competence among school students and it further shows how the suspicion of incompetence is extended over the whole category of NNESTs, thus projecting NESTs as superior, without further questioning of their preparation, qualifications or teaching skills.

In a number of countries, NESTs with lower academic qualifications than local teachers are paid more and are assigned to challenging advanced courses. NNESTs are usually confined to basic courses and often feel discriminated against, receiving lower salaries, as stated by Corcoran (2011) for the Brazilian context. The exemption or reduction of qualifications or teaching experience for NESTs constitutes a form of labour discrimination against NNESTs. On this discrimination, (Medgyes, 2001: 432) states that:

> their [NNESTs'] complaint is mainly levelled at unequal job opportunities: teaching applications from even highly qualified and experienced NNESTs often get turned down in favour of NESTs with no such credentials.

A stronger view of the differences in status between NESTs and NNESTs is provided by Rajagopalan (2005: 283):

> Non-native English-Speaking Teachers are typically treated as second class citizens in the world of language teaching. The problem is especially acute in the realm of teaching EFL.

Language education policies in Latin America: the case of Chile, Colombia, Ecuador and Mexico

Language education policy (LEP) is defined by Shohamy (2006: 76) as a 'mechanism used to create de facto language practices in institutions, especially in centralised educational systems'. The author states that LEPs are usually imposed by political authorities on those in charge of their implementation and, for that reason, they are determined by political, social and economic dimensions. LEP refers to the uses of home, foreign or global languages in specific contexts of education (ibid.: 77). Created as political acts, LEP makers exclude teachers from their analysis and confine them to being passive implementers (ibid.: 80).

In this section, we will briefly describe the major components of the national LEPs developed in the period 2000–2015 in Chile, Colombia, Ecuador and Mexico to present a general background to the specific actions that encourage native-speakerism in the region. We will focus our analysis on four countries that share the following features: they have Spanish as the major national language; they are home to various minority indigenous languages, many of which are endangered (Nettle and Romaine, 2000) and have speakers who are usually impoverished and marginalised (CEPAL, 2014); and they are experiencing a growth in their economies (International Monetary Fund, 2014; World Bank, 2015). Additionally, the British Council views such Latin American countries with special interest with regard to developing the programmes in its corporate plan for 2014–2016. They highlight the good prospects for Mexico and Colombia, but include Chile as a priority too:

> *Strong economic growth, an emerging middle class, democratic political stability and a growing voice on the world stage all characterise the major economies in Latin America. The importance of Brazil, Mexico and other high growth economies such as Colombia for global trade and dialogue is increasing through stronger international outlooks. The demand for integrated English, education and training services is growing everywhere.* (British Council, 2014: 30)

Chile
In 2004, the Chilean government launched a national English policy called *El inglés abre puertas* ('English opens doors'). Its main purpose was to promote English–Spanish bilingualism and increase the quality of ELT. The major actions that supported the development of the plan included professional development for teachers, improved measures of English learning and a direct intervention in the educational system. The last strategy had major components such as the National Centre for English-Speaking Volunteers, English summer and winter camps, public speaking tournaments and scholarships for undergraduates in English teacher education programmes to spend a semester in an English-speaking country. A second version of the national English policy was *Chile habla inglés* ('Chile speaks English'). The policy was introduced in 2009 as a joint initiative of the Ministry of Education, some mass media, the American Embassy and a private group of journalists and bloggers that produce content in English for the webpage *I love Chile*.

Colombia
The national policy promoting English–Spanish bilingualism for the educational system was introduced in 2004. Under the name of *Colombia Bilingüe* ('Bilingual Colombia'), this LEP included the publication of national standards for English teaching and learning; the mass administration of English proficiency tests to English teachers; the promotion of international teaching certificates; an increase

in teacher training programmes; and the establishment of academic regulations for the teaching of English in private language centres. Policy makers proposed the year 2019 as the deadline to achieve their major language proficiency objectives: all Colombian students should attain the B1 level of the Common European Framework of Reference (CEFR) at the end of secondary education and all teachers of English should demonstrate B2 level. The aforementioned initiatives generated some controversy inside the local academic community (González, 2010), especially the reduced view of bilingualism. Partly in response to the last issue, the Ministry of Education changed the name of the policy to *Programa de fortalecimiento para el desarrollo de las competencias en lengua extranjera* ('Programme for the strengthening of the development of competences in foreign language') and decided to put into action additional measures such as the academic intervention in university-based teacher education programmes to raise the standards of English proficiency of future teachers. In 2014, the programme changed its name to *Programa Nacional de Inglés: Colombia, Very Well* ('National English Programme: Colombia Very Well'). The latest measure comprised new strategies such as the publication of English textbooks to be used in public schools and the hiring of native speakers of English as teachers in public schools as well. Although they are presented as 'volunteers', they are employed by a private organisation presented by the Ministry of Education as a strategic ally in the development of bilingualism. The deadline to achieve these goals has been postponed to 2025.

Ecuador

Unlike other Latin American countries, Ecuador does not assign English–Spanish bilingualism a major role in the national development plan (Secretaría Nacional de Planificación y Desarrollo, 2013). The socialist government has proposed the improvement of the living conditions of its citizens and, according to the government documents, education is a priority. Under a national programme that promotes bilingual intercultural education, the government has advertised an investment of about $ US 200,000,000 (Ministerio de Educación del Ecuador, 2015). The achievement of better teaching standards in English has been based on the strengthening of the linguistic and pedagogical competence of teachers to impact the quality of general education. One of the major strategies to achieve this target has been sending teachers to universities in the USA to study for a semester to obtain a TESOL certificate. The Department of Higher Education, Science, Technology and Innovation (Secretaría de Educación Superior, Ciencia, Tecnología e Innovación, SENESCYT) has signed agreements with American universities to cover a population of about 5,000 teachers. They are selected if they have a university-based ELT degree, a minimum of a year's teaching experience and a B2 level of proficiency according to the CEFR (Common European Framework of Reference for Languages: Learning, Teaching, Assessment). Additionally, the Fulbright Commission webpage in Ecuador advertises the programme Study of the United States, which offers teachers the opportunity to attend a summer institute in order to develop their knowledge about the USA (Fulbright Ecuador, 2016). All expenses are covered by the Ministry of Education and the Fulbright foundation.

Mexico

Conceived as part of the National Development Plan 2007–2012, and in response to the recommendations of UNESCO and the Organisation for Economic Cooperation and Development (OECD) to have bilingual citizens, the Secretariat of Public Education (*Secretaría de Educación Pública*, SEP) promoted the introduction of English into the preschool and elementary curricula. In 2007, the Mexican government launched the *Plan Nacional de Inglés para la Educación Básica* or PNIEB (English National Plan for Elementary Education). Its major aim was to increase the quality of education and general wellbeing of Mexicans, as well as to contribute to the country's development. Some of the actions proposed in the plan include having a more homogeneous development of the teaching of the language across the nation, creating guidelines and teaching materials, and proposing teacher training programmes.

Table 1 presents the English LEPs for Chile, Colombia, Ecuador and Mexico for the period 2004–15, together with the webpages of the education ministries and specific links to papers or reports about their implementation.

Table 1: Summary of English LEPs

Country	LEP	Year of launch
Chile	El inglés abre puertas	2004
	Chile habla inglés www.ingles.mineduc.cl	2009
Colombia	Programa Nacional de Bilingüismo www.mineducacion.gov.co/1621/article-97495.html www.mineducacion.gov.co/1621/articles-132560_recurso_pdf_programa_nacional_bilinguismo.pdf	2005
	Programa de Fortalecimiento para el Desarrollo de Competencias en Lenguas Extranjera www.colombiaaprende.edu.co/html/micrositios/1752/articles-318173_recurso_3.pdf	2013
	Programa Nacional de Inglés Colombia, Very Well www.mineducacion.gov.co/cvn/1665/w3-article-343476.html	2014
Equador	Programa Inglés Ecuador	2007
	Proyecto de Fortalecimiento de la Enseñanza de Inglés como Lengua Extranjera http://educacion.gob.ec/fortalecimiento-del-ingles/	2013
Mexico	Programa Nacional de Inglés en Educación Básica www.pnieb.net/inicio.html	2007

These policies are interconnected. The initial proposals for the LEPs of Colombia and Mexico both cite Chile as an exemplary case to follow. Ecuador highlights the importance of the LEPs of Chile and Colombia. In the remainder of this paper, we will uncover the presence of an overarching native-speakerist perspective in the media coverage of such policies.

Exploring native-speakerism

The study on which this chapter reports is part of a larger qualitative case study (Merriam, 1998; Yin, 2003) investigating the discourses of the Spanish-speaking Latin American press about NNESTs (González et al., 2013). These discourses are analysed as part of the national agendas for globalisation and bilingualism. As a subset of the larger project, here we report a study on how Latin America, especially the four countries mentioned above, has become fertile ground for native-speakerism.

Our data come from two major sources: news articles and official documents that describe the LEPs in Chile, Colombia, Ecuador and Mexico. We selected articles published between 2009 and 2015 in online versions of the major newspapers of each country. The criterion used to define this was the international newspaper ranking based on metrics that include number of digital readers, digital page rank and web traffic (Riveros, 2014; 4International Media & Newspapers, 2016). We chose online versions of the papers to access the archives. The keywords for searching the news included 'English teaching', 'English learning', 'English teachers', 'English language policy', 'native speakers' and 'bilingualism'. In Table 2 we present the information about the newspapers, and the types and number of articles analysed. Chile has the greatest number of news analysed. Colombia and Mexico have nearly half of this number and Ecuador about one third.

Table 2: Information about newspapers consulted

Country	Newspaper	Website	Number of articles analysed	
			Total	On native-speakerism
Chile	El Mercurio	www.emol.com	25	5
Colombia	El Tiempo	www.eltiempo.com	13	4
Ecuador	El Universo	www.eluniverso.com	9	3
Mexico	El Universal	www.eluniversal.com.mx	13	4

Findings: the various forms of native-speakerism

The content analysis of the news articles allowed us to find strong evidence of the growing presence of native-speakerism in Latin America in the current state of the language education policies for English in Chile, Colombia, Ecuador and Mexico. In addition to the traditional portrayal of NESTs as the best possible English teachers, we found governmental educational actions that openly favour native speakers of English and advocate English-speaking settings as one of the most suitable solutions to increasing English proficiency in the four countries.

Below we describe the governmental strategies introduced as part of the implementation of the LEP in Chile, Colombia, Ecuador and Mexico, and how they are represented in the written digital media that were analysed. Although these strategies are often introduced as valuable means to raising the quality of English teaching and learning, we contend that they do, in fact, support the dominant native-speakerist ideology. In the following three sections, we will define the governmental strategies and how they are dealt with in newspaper articles that report on their implementation.

a The advocacy of NESTs as excellent English teachers

This strategy presents NESTs as outstanding representatives of the ELT activity and it materialises in two different trends: i) the presence of NESTs in private schools and ii) the hiring of NESTs as volunteer teachers in NGOs and public education. From the analysed articles, it becomes clear that NESTs are widely promoted for two reasons: one, as a quality factor that guarantees access to the original or the best language and culture content for students; and two, as a response to the alleged insufficient language proficiency of local NNESTs. As an example of this view, the Colombian Ministry of Education declared that having native speakers of English as teachers in public education 'will be vital to achieve President Santos's target of making Colombia the most educated country in the region in 2015' [own translation] (*El Tiempo,* 20 January 2015).

i The presence of NESTs in private schools

Traditionally, elite schools in Latin America have hired NESTs to provide bilingual education to middle- and upper-class students. The schools stress content-based instruction in English, promote stays in English-speaking countries, offer international language proficiency certificates or award high school diplomas that are valid locally and internationally. After the promotion of the LEP, NESTs have been hired more often in private institutions, which often have less strict employment regulations than the public sector (Clark and Paran, 2007; Corcoran, 2011). Private schools use NEST faculty as a valuable plus to advertise the quality of the educational services they offer. In an article published in *El Universal,* a Mexican teacher asserts the need to remove from the education system those teachers who do not possess the level of proficiency required to teach their classes. For English teachers, he suggests:

> *If it is necessary to bring teachers from other places to substitute them, even from countries with better educational levels, there should be no doubts. In South Korea parents demand that their children's teachers be native speakers from English speaking countries* [own translation]. (*El Universal,* 17 April 2013)

Another example of the value assigned to the presence of native speakers as a quality factor is observed in Chile. The following excerpt stresses the presence of native speakers as part of the academic success of students from elite private schools in the national standardised tests administered to Chilean students:

> *To achieve it, there are two recurrent tendencies among those successful institutions: they hire English native speakers as part of their faculty, and for local [teachers] they demand certifications of language proficiency that go beyond the teaching degree awarded by a Chilean University* [own translation]. (*El Mercurio,* 4 June 2013)

The coordinator of a private school explains that the school's success stems from the fact that the institution hires British or American English teachers for high school. He says that this 'allows students to practice and differentiate different accents' [own translation] (El Mercurio, 4 June 2013). It is important to highlight that this limited view of English assigns value only to accents that belong to the most traditional representations of ownership of English in the Inner Circle, the United Kingdom and the United States, leaving outside of this privileged space the wider territory of World Englishes.

In the same article, the English coordinator of another school explains that Chilean teachers who are not native speakers must take the Cambridge Advanced English examination. She states that:

> it certifies that the person who passes it can understand long, complex texts in English and can make flexible and effective use of the language for social, academic, professional or educational purposes [own translation]. (El Mercurio, 4 June 2013)

This means that the language training that local teachers have had in their teacher education undergraduate programme is not enough or reliable, and, therefore, that it needs the quality endorsement of the University of Cambridge through the British Council.

Another explanation for the success of some schools in the national English tests includes the introduction of English in early education, increased hours of instruction, content courses conducted in English and the presence of native-speaker teachers. The coordinator of an exclusive school describes their successful strategy:

> Students who come to the school face English from the moment they go to the playground. Their classes are taught 100 per cent in English by certified native-speaker teachers. There is a special emphasis on the promotion of logical thinking in that language [own translation]. (El Mercurio, 8 June 2013)

A thought-provoking argument for having NESTs is the benefits they may bring to the education and professional development of local NNESTs. According to Veronica Stronach, representative of the Chile English Speaking Union (ESU), it is of paramount importance to develop joint initiatives with English-speaking countries to 'facilitate scholarships, student exchange programmes, contacts with universities and international programmes to hire English speakers that support the education of every English teacher in Chile' [own translation] (El Mercurio, 8 June 2013). Her opinion questions the capacity of the country's teacher education programmes to fulfil their objective of providing future teachers with the language required to teach. She suggests the presence of NESTs as an assurance of appropriate linguistic training.

ii The hiring of NESTs as volunteer teachers in NGOs and public education
The number of private and government initiatives that invite native speakers of English to travel to Latin America as volunteers to teach English is increasing. These volunteers are usually motivated by a desire to make an impact on poor communities where they can change the lives of underprivileged children or teenagers though the work of NGOs. Additionally, contact agencies present them

with the benefits of travelling to exotic places, meeting new people and learning Spanish. These are the usual benefits that 'backpacker' EFL teachers expect from their teaching experience (Lengeling and Mora Pablo, 2012).

This strategy has recently moved from being applied to non-formal education to also being implemented in public education with the explicit approval of governments. One example of this joint action is the contract signed between the Colombian Ministry of Education and the volunteer programme Heart for Change. Two major lines of action are currently in place: the Teach English Colombia (TEC) programme and the English Teaching Fellowship Program (ETF). Both programmes provide volunteer teachers for public education settings. These volunteers are expected to teach English classes or to team teach with trained NNESTs, in a rather similar way to what has been done in Japan since 1987 with the JET programme and in Korea since 1995 with the EPIK programme. The webpage of Heart for Change includes the motto 'We dream about a bilingual Colombia'.

The presence of native speakers as instructors of English is considered significant not only by the government but also by important public figures. In Chile, for example, David Gallagher, the chairman of Asset Investment Bank, highlights the unequal opportunities within the Chilean educational system. As a solution to the problem, he proposes that:

> [i]t is possible to have some experiences with young people taking advantage of the differences in the vacations periods for the north and the south hemispheres. I believe that there must be thousands of young Americans or British that would be happy to spend their summer, the Chilean winter, doing intensive courses for our students and teachers. (El Mercurio, 27 March 2011)

The presence of 'backpacker' EFL teachers has been highlighted as one of the contradictions of the ELT profession by Lengeling and Mora Pablo (op cit). The authors stress the fact that in many school settings there is a peculiar coexistence of highly prepared local NNESTs and untrained NESTs. In some cases, it is less-qualified teachers, visiting a country as tourists, who obtain better work benefits and more social recognition just because they speak English as their native language. Nativespeakerhood is openly defended in this excerpt as a major resource for improving the quality of English teaching in Chile. This idea disregards the lack of pedagogical training of these NESTs and devalues the competences, both pedagogical and linguistic, of well-trained local NNESTs.

b The need for NNESTs to spend time in English-speaking countries to improve their language proficiency and to legitimise their teaching credentials

In general, time spent abroad appears to be considered as highly beneficial for the development of teachers' language proficiency and intercultural competence. It is used as an indication of quality in the teacher training process or as an academic enhancement, earning teachers prestige and credibility. Some institutions propose a complete package that includes language improvement, teaching training and a teaching certification.

Experts are sometimes quoted as stressing the need for teachers of English to live in the countries where the language they teach is spoken. Applied linguist Anna Uhl-Chamot suggested that spending time abroad is needed in order to

> study and be used to having a conversation. Because we also have [in the US] the problem of teachers of Spanish or French who do not know the language. They teach grammar and vocabulary, but do not teach speaking' (El Mercurio, 8 August 2011).

She recommends three to four months for advanced teachers and between one semester and a year for teachers with an intermediate level of proficiency.

Successful learning by students, reflected in the good scores obtained by students from private schools in the national tests in Chile, is explained as the result of English teacher selection:

> Regarding the training of teachers that work in those schools, many are native speakers of English, have international certifications and have academic or work experience in countries such as the United States, Canada or England. (El Mercurio, 8 June 2013)

The first government of Chilean President Michelle Bachelet (2006–2010) considered the experience of spending time in an English-speaking country as a key measure for improving the quality of teachers and tackling low student performance. The Ministry of Education created:

> an exchange program so that more teachers from English-speaking countries work in Chile. Besides, all undergraduate students from teacher education programs will study a semester in an English-speaking country. They will receive state financing, and later, they will work in underprivileged schools for two years. (El Mercurio, 26 October 2006)

Colombia presents a similar case in terms of the perceived need to send local NNESTs to an English-speaking country. In a visit to the country, Clara Amador Watson, presented in the newspaper as an expert in bilingualism, questioned the English proficiency of Colombian teachers. She was asked to express her opinion about the benefits of providing local NNESTs with professional development or bringing NESTs to the country. She responded,

> it is necessary to train and educate Colombian teachers within binational exchange programs so that they are immersed in English. (El Tiempo, 1 April 2011)

We also found the same governmental approach to improving the language proficiency and teaching skills of local NNESTs in Ecuador. The government of President Rafael Correa (2006–2017) launched the programme Teacher Go, a medium-term initiative seeking to support the national aim of decreasing the shortage of qualified teachers. The Vice-Minister of Education states the need to assess the teachers' competences, adding that:

[the Ministry] makes adjustments. We have a teacher training process here and abroad. We launched the project 'Go Teacher' to send the English teachers to pursue their master's degrees and specializations [in ELT]. (*El Universo*, 25 March 2014)

This belief in the importance of Mexican teachers spending time in an English-speaking country echoes the articles reported above in relation to Chile, Colombia and Ecuador. In an analysis of good practices for foreign language teaching in Europe, *El Universal* cites a study reported by the European Commission, highlighting the fact that:

Spain is one of few countries where future teachers of English have some previous [language] immersion abroad … 79.7% of teachers in Spain have spent more than a month studying the language they have chosen to teach in a country where it is spoken. (*El Universal,* 21 September 2012)

We also found in Mexico similar endorsement of the government's strategy of sending teachers to the United States to acquire or improve the language skills required to teach English. As part of the national educational policy that introduces English in Pre-K education as a mandatory subject, *El Universal* reports that '20 teachers, out of the 63 selected in indigenous communities, received a scholarship to be trained in Georgetown University in programs lasting from 5 months to 2 years' (*El Universal,* 14 July 2011). The article emphasises the importance of time abroad in contributing to the qualifications of those teachers who have not met the national standards.

We do believe that spending some time in an English-speaking country may have a positive impact on the lives of NNESTs. We acknowledge that linguistic, intercultural and personal growth may occur, but we question the governments' overemphasis of the effects of such experiences on teachers' language competence and pedagogical improvement. If teachers have access to pertinent and sustained professional development in their own countries, there will be positive changes in their work. Moreover, magnifying linguistic gains betrays the inaccurate belief that language competence is the only skill required to teach the language successfully (Clark and Paran, 2007: 409).

c Evident differences in requirements for teaching for NESTs and NNESTs

Hiring policies tend to demand fewer requirements or lower credentials of NESTs than they do of NNESTs. Usually, native speakers are not required to have any teaching certification or formal academic training because for many employers the fact of their being native speakers of English guarantees the quality of their work. An article published in *El Tiempo* (2002) provides a very clear depiction of this view. Although it was published some years before the time slot determined for our data, it reflects the situation in many English centres. In a discussion about the advantages and disadvantages of employing a native speaker of English as a teacher, the article reports the case of a private language centre in Bogotá. The centre employs only native speakers of English, and the director shares the idea that academic qualifications are not necessary. According to an advertisement on its website, *those who are interested in teaching in this school must have more than a diploma in TEFL, be energetic, have an open attitude,* conversation and listening skills, enthusiasm and patience [our emphasis; own translation]. (*El Tiempo,* 6 October 2002)

These requirements are consistent with what Ramírez (2015) called the 'X factor' held by teachers who do not have a teaching degree but demonstrate a high language proficiency or a native-like level of English. This distinctive feature is easily identifiable, but not clearly defined by the participants in her study. It was a *je ne sais quoi* that included good looks, a modern style of dress and an outgoing personality.

Since 2004, it has been recommended or desired that teachers of English in Latin America hold a teaching certificate such as the Teaching Knowledge Test (TKT) or the In-service Certificate in English Language Teaching (ICELT). This kind of endorsement is considered equal to or preferred over a university-based teaching degree. NNESTs holding a degree from a university-based teacher education programme are requested to obtain additional certificates of English proficiency and teaching skills. Teachers are asked to take international standardised tests and/or obtain international teaching certifications that endorse their language proficiency and teaching skills. The language proficiency and teaching endorsements are granted by the British Council or universities in the USA. This phenomenon is more frequent in private schools or language centres. NESTs are not usually asked to demonstrate either their language knowledge or their teaching training.

In the case of Colombia, technical standards were issued in 2007 establishing the requirements for the offer of foreign language courses in language centres. Concerning teaching, professionals who are 'teachers, trainers, tutors or facilitators' must demonstrate 'professional pedagogical and disciplinary training in foreign languages, or demonstrate having taken courses that certify their pedagogical and disciplinary competence' (ICONTEC, 2007: 10). Those teachers who do not have a university-based teacher education diploma in ELT may also have two years of teaching experience. Additionally, 80 per cent of the teaching staff must demonstrate a C1 level of proficiency in the CEFR as determined by an international standardised test. An open preference for teachers who are native speakers of English, or who grew up or have lived in an English-speaking country, was reported by Ramírez (op cit). Her study showed that private language centres tend to hire more teachers who comply with any of these requirements because their language proficiency and accent play a very important role in the way they are assessed. These features are preferred to local ELT training. González (2009) reported that some private schools require Colombian teachers with university-based ELT diplomas to hold an additional teaching certification such as the TKT or the ICELT. It seems that their five-year professional education is deemed inadequate without the endorsement of an international agency, promoting what González (2007) calls academic colonialism.

Although teaching certificates are recommended for those teachers with no teacher education background, native speakers may be hired even if they do not have teaching qualifications. In Colombia, the programmes for volunteers who teach English in underprivileged regions do not demand teacher education backgrounds for those who come. As an example, the American citizens who participate in the programme Volunteers for Colombia are represented in the following way:

> All are professionals, with experience in teaching and humanities. They were recruited by the World Teach Foundation, in partnership with Harvard University and in association with Volunteers for Colombia and the Ministry of Education.' [own translation] (El Tiempo, 13 January 2012)

Although it is stated that they are experienced professionals, teacher education in ELT is not mandatory or even desirable.

Conclusions and implications

Although this study focused on the analysis of articles published in major newspapers in Chile, Colombia, Ecuador and Mexico, the findings may well have a bearing on the analysis of the status of NESTs in many other countries. Overall, evidence from the study reported in this chapter indicates that the myth of the superiority of the native speaker is still strong. We can conclude that Latin America is definitely fertile ground for native-speakerism. In the findings, we identified three issues that characterise Latin American media treatment of English LEPs and the role of native and non-native speakers in implementing them. The first finding was the governments' advocacy of NESTs as English teachers. We showed how the newspapers reflect the position of educational authorities and policy makers concerning the benefits of recruiting and employing NESTs in private and public education. In particular, the increasing number of NESTs hired as volunteer teachers in NGOs and public education is claimed to compensate for problems such as the shortage of and low language proficiency of local NNESTs, but the increase underlines the benefits awarded to foreign teachers. The second finding concerns the need for NNESTs to spend time in English-speaking countries to improve their language proficiency and to legitimise their teaching credentials. We are aware of several beneficial outcomes of long stays in English-speaking countries, but we have provided evidence of the derogative view of local teacher education programmes and the magnification of the impact of the stay in an English-speaking country on the linguistic and pedagogical qualifications of local NNESTs, which we argue is another manifestation of native-speakerism. The third finding was the evident differences in terms of teaching requirements for NESTs and NNESTs. Our analysis revealed that loffering special dispensations to NESTs is a form of labour discrimination against local NNESTs. Language nativeness often motivates inequalities in salaries and in opportunities for career progression. It also overshadows the professional training that NNESTs receive in university-based teacher education programmes.

The promotion of native-speakerism in the LEPs in Latin America has various implications for the future of ELT and for local teachers. We believe that the opinions and discourses about NNESTs will remain and will contribute to the increasing loss of public trust in local teachers and in university-based programmes that train English teachers. Derived from this mistrust, we anticipate changes to educational systems that include demands for greater accountability and the increased surveillance of teachers (Day and Sachs, 2004). A third issue emerging from inequitable initiatives that promote native-speakerism is the possible reluctance of governments to invest public money in tackling fundamental problems in education and English teaching. Governments will continue to hold teachers largely responsible for obstacles in meeting national targets for English learning and will replace teachers with unqualified or poorly qualified instructors, thus failing to face the complexity of the problems in their respective educational systems.

Several questions remain unanswered in our study. Further studies on this topic are therefore recommended. In future investigations, it is advisable to explore the actual performance of NESTs in classrooms and the real outcomes of their presence in Latin American contexts. Although we know that the language proficiency of NNESTs is an issue, we are convinced that they represent an important component of the LEPs' success. By raising awareness of the inequalities underlying the promotion of native-speakerism in Latin America, we hope to have contributed to its analysis in the field of ELT and applied linguistics and, by extension, to future educational changes in the region that treat local NNESTs fairly and value their roles and professional expertise.

References

4International Media & Newspapers (2016) Available online at: www.4imn.com/topLatin-America/ (accessed 22 February 2016).

Aravena, P and Rodríguez, C (2006, 26 October) El panorama dark del inglés en las aulas chilenas. Retrieved from http://diario.elmercurio.com/detalle/index. asp?id={fa78c9ff-396c-4c19-bcd7-0d44a9035a78} (accessed 23 January 23).

Avila, A (2014, 25 March) Freddy Peñafiel, Ministro Subrogante de Educación: 'En 2017 se normalizará estudio de Inglés'. El Universo. Retrieved from http://www.eluniverso.com/noticias/2014/03/25/nota/2459956/freddy-penafiel-ministro-subrogante-educacion-2017-se-normalizara (accessed 23 January 23).

Berger, K (2014) Reflecting on native speaker privilege. The CATESOL Journal 26/1: 37–49.

Bhabha, H (1994) The location of culture. London: Routledge.

Borg, S (2006) The distinctive characteristics of foreign language teachers. Language Teaching Research 10/1: 3–31.

British Council (2014) Corporate Plan 2014–2016. Available online at: www.britishcouncil.org/sites/britishcouncil.uk2/files/corporate-plan-2014-16.pdf (accessed 22 February 2016).

Byram, M (1997) Teaching and assessing intercultural communicative competence. Clevedon: Multilingual Matters.

Carbonell, M (2013, 17 April) De profesor a profesor. El Universal. Available at http://www.eluniversalmas.com.mx/editoriales/2013/04/64082.php (accessed 18 January 2016).

Clark, E and Paran, A (2007) The employability of non-native-speaker teachers of EFL: A UK survey. *System* 35: 407–430.

Comisión Económica para América Latina y el Caribe (CEPAL) (2014) *Los pueblos indígenas de América Latina. Avances en el último decenio y retos pendientes para la garantía de sus derechos.* Chile: Naciones Unidas. Available online at: http://repositorio.cepal.org/bitstream/handle/11362/37222/S1420521_es. pdf?sequence=1. (accessed 22 February 2016).

Cook, V (1992) Evidence for multi-competence. *Language Learning* 42: 557–591.

Cook, V (2005) 'Basing teaching on the L2 user' in Llurda, E (ed) *Non-native language teachers. Perceptions, challenges and contributions to the profession.* New York: Springer, 47–61.

Corcoran, J (2011) Power relations in Brazilian English language teaching. *International Journal of Language Studies* 5/2: 1–26.

Davies, A (2003) *The native speaker: Myth and reality.* Clevedon: Multilingual Matters.

Day, C and Sachs, J (2004) 'Professionalism, performativity and empowerment: Discourses in the politics, policies and purposes of continuing professional development' in Day, C and Sachs, J (eds) *International Handbook on the Continuing Professional Development of Teachers.* Glasgow: Open University Press, 3–32.

De Mejía, AM (2002) *Power, prestige and bilingualism.* Clevedon, Multilingual Matters.

Derwing, TM and Munro MJ (2009) Putting accent in its place: Rethinking obstacles to communication. *Language Teaching* 42/4: 476–490.

El Mercurio (2013, 8 June) El 60% de los alumnos de colegios privados estudia más horas de inglés que lo establecido. Available online at: http://diario.elmercurio. com/detalle/index.asp?id={c45ac3c3-26a3-44e5-9a6c-b669f516e0f0}

El Mercurio (2013, 4 June) 36 planteles dictan casi 100 pedagogías en Inglés: la mayoría tiene baja acreditación. Available online at: http://diario.elmercurio.com/ detalle/index.asp?id={388385dc-4f55-49cd-9fce-3abe2442caa3}

El Mercurio (2011, 27 March) David Gallagher: Es una tremenda a estar en colegios injusticia que haya niños destinados de los que saldrán sin hablar inglés. Available online at: http://diario.elmercurio.com/detalle/index.asp?id={9253e48e-059b-42fc-9028-e237c8f6ff75}

El Mercurio (2011, 8 August) Anna Chamot, especialista en enseñanza de segundo idioma: Un profesor de inglés debe vivir un tiempo en un país angloparlante. Available online at: http://diario.elmercurio.com/detalle/index.asp?id={fda4b73d-bac6-4c13-a017-ae248411176c}

El Tiempo (2012, 13 January) Gringos dictarán inglés en instituciones pobres. Available online at: http://www.eltiempo.com/archivo/documento/MAM-5084495

El Tiempo (2015, 20 January) Llegaron a Colombia los primeros voluntarios para enseñar inglés. Available online at: http://www.eltiempo.com/estilo-de-vida/educacion/formadores-nativos-extranjeros-llegaron-a-colombia-para-ensenar-ingles/15125319

Fernández, A (2002, 6 October) Gringo varado dicta inglés. *El Tiempo*. Retrieved from http://www.eltiempo.com/archivo/documento/MAM-1314880 (accessed 21 January 2016).

Fulbright Ecuador (2016) Available online at: www.fulbright.org.ec/web/pag.php?c=625 (accessed 22 February 2016).

Gómez Quintero, N (2012, 21 September) Educación, problema de todos, afirma Narro. *El Universal*. Retrieved from http://archivo.eluniversal.com.mx/nacion/200171.html (accessed 23 January 2016).

González, A (2007) The professional development of Colombian EFL teachers: between local and colonial practices. *IKALA, Revista de Lenguaje y Cultura*, 12/18: 309–332.

González, A (2009) On alternative and additional certifications in English language teaching: The case of Colombian EFL teachers' professional development. *IKALA, Revista de Lenguaje y Cultura* 14/22: 183–209.

González, A (2010) 'English and English Teaching in Colombia: Tensions and Possibilities in the Expanding Circle' in Kirkpatrick, A (ed) *The Routledge handbook of world Englishes*. London: Routledge, 332–351.

González, A, Correa, D and Llurda, E (2013) *Bilingualism, globalization, non-native speaker English teachers, and the media: the case of Latin America*. Unpublished research proposal. Universidad de Antioquia.

Grosjean, F (2010) *Bilingual: Life and reality*. Harvard: Harvard University Press.

Holliday, A (2005) *The struggle to teach English as an international language*. Oxford: Oxford University Press.

Instituto Colombiano de Normas Técnicas (ICONTEC) (2007) *Norma técnica colombiana NTC 5580. Programas de formación para el Trabajo en el área de idiomas*. Available online at: http://www.mineducacion.gov.co/1759/articles-157089_archivo_pdf_NTC_5580.pdf (accessed 20 February 2016).

International Monetary Fund (2014) Regional Economic Outlook Update: Western Hemisphere. Available online at: www.imf.org/external/pubs/ft/reo/2014/whd/eng/wreo1014.htm. (accessed 22 February 2016).

Jenkins, J (2002) A sociolinguistically-based, empirically-researched pronunciation syllabus for English as an International Language. *Applied Linguistics* 23/1: 83–103.

Kachru, B (ed) (1992) *The other tongue: English across cultures, 2nd edition*. Chicago: University of Illinois Press.

Lasagabaster, D and Sierra JM (2005) 'What do students think about the pros and cons of having a native speaker teacher?' in Llurda (ed) *Non-native language teachers. Perceptions, challenges and contributions to the profession.* New York: Springer, 217–242.

Lengeling, M and Mora Pablo, I (2012) 'A critical discourse analysis of advertisements: Inconsistencies in our EFL profession' in Roux, R, Mora Vázquez, A and Trejo Guzmán, NP (eds) *Research in language teaching: Mexican perspectives.* Bloomington: Palibrio, 91–105.

Levis, JM (2005) Changing contexts and shifting paradigms in pronunciation teaching. *TESOL Quarterly* 39/3: 369–377.

Linares, A (2011, 1 April) El inglés se enseña todavía de forma muy arcaica. *El Tiempo.* Retrieved from http://www.eltiempo.com/archivo/documento/MAM-4479844 (accessed 20 January 2016).

Lippi-Green, R (1997) *English with an accent.* New York: Routledge.

Llurda, E (2004) Non-native-speaker teachers and English as an international language. *International Journal of Applied Linguistics* 14/ 3: 314–323.

Llurda, E (2008) 'The effects of stays abroad on self-perceptions of non-native EFL teachers' in Dogancay-Aktuna, S and Hardman, J (eds) *Global English teaching and teacher education: Praxis and possibility.* Alexandria, VA: TESOL, 99–111.

Llurda, E (2009) 'Attitudes towards English as an international language: The pervasiveness of native models among L2 users and teachers' in Sharifian, F (ed) *English as an international language: Perspectives and pedagogical issues.* Clevedon: Multilingual Matters, 119–134.

Martínez Carballo, N (2011, 14 July). Impartirán inglés en tercer año de preescolar. *El Universal.* Retrieved from http://archivo.eluniversal.com.mx/notas/779342.html (accessed 23 January 2016).

Medgyes, P (1994) *The non-native teacher.* London: Macmillan.

Medgyes, P (1999) 'Language training: A neglected area in teacher education'. In Braine, G (ed) *Non-native educators in English language teaching.* Mahwah, NJ: Lawrence Erlbaum Associates, 179–198.

Medgyes, P (2001) 'When the teacher Is a non-native speaker' in Celce-Murcia, M (2001) (ed) *Teaching English as a second or foreign language.* Boston: Heinle & Heinle, 429–442.

Merriam, S (1998) *Qualitative research and case study applications in education.* San Francisco, CA: Jossey-Bass.

Ministerio de Educación del Ecuador (2015) *Inversión en Educación Intercultural Bilingüe supera los 200 millones de dólares.* Available online at: http://educacion.gob.ec/inversion-en-educacion-intercultural-bilingue-supera-los-200-millones-de-dolares/ (accessed 22 February 2016).

Moussu, L (2010) Influence of teacher-contact time and other variables on ESL students' attitudes towards native- and nonnative-English-speaking teachers. *TESOL Quarterly* 44/4: 746–768.

Nettle, D and Romaine S (2000) *Vanishing voices: The extinction of the world's languages.* New York, NY: Oxford University Press.

Phillipson, R (1992) *Linguistic imperialism.* Oxford: Oxford University Press.

Rajagopalan K (2005) Non-native speaker teachers of English and their anxieties: Ingredients for an experiment in action research. In Llurda E (ed) *Nonnative language teachers: Perceptions, challenges and contributions to the profession.* New York, NY: Springer 283–303

Ramírez, C (2015) *Why is the number of EFL teachers with no English teaching degree increasing in the profession? A critical study.* Unpublished MA thesis. Universidad de Antioquia, Medellín, Colombia.

Riveros, E (2014, January 20) Ranking: Diarios impresos más influyentes de América Latina en su versión 2.0. *The Huffington Post.* Available online at: http://voces.huffingtonpost.com/eduardo-riveros/ranking-diarios-impresos-america-latina_b_4632454.html?utm_hp_ref=tw (accessed 22 February 2016).

Secretaría Nacional de Planificación y Desarrollo (SENPLADES) (2013) *Plan nacional para el buen vivir, 2013–2017.* Quito: SENPLADES.

Selvi, AF (2010) All teachers are equal, but some teachers are more equal than others: trend analysis of job advertisements in English language teaching'. *WATESOLNNEST Caucus Annual Review* 1: 156–181.

Shohamy, E (2006) *Language policies: Hidden agendas and new approaches.* New York: Routledge.

Widdowson, HG (1994) The ownership of English. *TESOL Quarterly*, 28/2: 377–389.

World Bank (2015) Global economic prospects. *Chapter 2 Latin America and the Caribbean.* Available online at: https://www.worldbank.org/content/dam/Worldbank/GEP/GEP2016a/Global-Economic-Prospects-January-2016-Latin-America-and-Caribbean-analysis.pdf (accessed 20 February 2016).

Yin, RK (2003) *Case study research: Design and methods, 3rd edition.* Thousand Oaks, CA: Sage Publications.

6

Native teachers' perspectives on co-teaching with Korean English teachers in an EFL context

Sung-Yeon Kim, Hanyang University, Seoul, Korea

Twenty-two hours is required of us. Out of the 22 hours, whether you have one other co-teacher or seven other co-teachers, which is, in my case, I have seven other teachers. [...] it would be quite ambitious to meet with every teacher beforehand and work out a lesson plan, become an oiled machine [...] That's almost impossible, as well as getting the cooperation of other co-teachers as well as for myself, it would be difficult. So most of co-teaching, it is expected to be kind of on the fly or just slowly learn about each other.
(Bob, middle school teacher)

Introduction

Since 1995, the Korean Ministry of Education, Science and Technology (MEST) has implemented the English Program in Korea (EPIK) with Native English-Speaking Teachers (NESTs) in all public schools. The programme initially began with 59 NESTs from six English-speaking countries: Australia, Canada, Ireland, New Zealand, the UK and the US, and has steadily grown to more than 9,000 teachers in 2011 (Ministry of Education, Science and Technology, 2011). The primary goal of the EPIK is to provide Korean students with increased opportunities to interact with native speakers of English while developing their cross-cultural understanding of English-speaking countries (Jeon, 2010; Kim, 2010). This programme has recruited a substantial number of NESTs into public schools, the majority of whom do not have adequate training or teaching experience (Choi, 2001; Jeon, op cit; Kim, op cit). While their lack of professional qualifications has created a host of problems, more serious problems lie in the fact that their teaching methods do not match with the goals and procedures of the national curriculum that most Korean teachers are required to follow. As a result, the NESTs' practices are often disconnected from the curriculum and their status remains ambiguous.

In order to address this problem, the EPIK has encouraged each school to implement collaborative teaching between NESTs and Korean teachers of English. Co-teaching can take many forms, according to different contextual or situational demands. Successful co-teaching, however, requires purposeful, regular and cooperative engagement among co-teachers (Buckely, 2000). As co-teaching has spread in ESL contexts (Honigsfeld and Dove, 2008), there has been a professional effort to foster a more productive relationship between NESTs and NNESTs (Carless, 2006; Medgyes, 1992, 1994). The idea was that NESTs can help learners acquire authentic language input and cultural knowledge, and that their presence can help to boost learner motivation. NNESTS, on the other hand, can better accommodate learner needs and thus better facilitate their learning since they, themselves, have experienced the language learning process and thus understand learners better (Árva and Medgyes, 2000; Nemtchinova, 2005; Phillipson, 1992; Tsai, 2007). When done expertly, co-teaching between NESTs and NNESTs can open up a number of important possibilities. For example, co-teaching can become an opportunity for professional growth for both parties.

In the Korean context, co-teaching seems to be an inevitable choice because the majority of NESTs do not have teaching experience or professional training. Despite the rapid growth in the number of teachers, empirical studies on the EPIK have noted that the roles of native teachers are not clear in schools (Chung et al., 1999; Park, 2010). With 20 years having now passed since the inception of the EPIK programme, it seems an appropriate juncture for a close examination of the programme's successes and problems.

Unfortunately, there is a lack of research that closely examines these issues, making it difficult to identify what types of co-teaching approaches are practised and what challenges exist. What is therefore needed is a better understanding of co-teaching practices from NESTs' perspectives. This chapter reports on a study that was designed to identify co-teaching practices between NESTs and NNESTs in their school context through close observation of classroom practices and in-depth interviews with NESTs. Particular attention is paid to identifying NESTs' views on co-teaching because they seem to take a leading role in co-teaching practices, from lesson planning to actual teaching.

Background

Co-teaching practice originated from concerted efforts to bring about collaboration between general and special education teachers to support students with disabilities (Gately and Gately, 2001). This practice was expanded to accommodate ESL teachers in their efforts to collaborate with mainstream teachers in the US (Dove and Honigsfeld, 2010; Wertheimer and Honigsfeld, 2000). Through this collaboration, ESL students could gain additional academic support to keep up with their classmates in their mainstream classes (Dieker and Barnett, 1996). Successful cases of collaboration have been documented in a number of studies (see, for example, Pardini, 2006). Based on some success in co-teaching in ESL contexts, there has been some effort to apply co-teaching to EFL contexts. Carless and Walker (2006) suggested that collaboration between NESTs and Local English Teachers (LETs) should become a viable option for EFL contexts. This is because NESTs can provide target language input for learners and boost student willingness to communicate. In addition, as messengers of the target culture, they can help learners acquire cultural knowledge (Carless, op cit; Carless and Walker, 2006; Liu, 2009).

However, the presence of LETs is also valuable, since teachers with the same language and cultural background can better identify learner needs and have a better understanding of the school curriculum and the local teaching context (Carless, op cit; Kim, op cit; Medgyes, 1992, 1994). These strengths of native and local teachers, when maximised and well balanced, can lead to successful classroom instruction (Matsuda and Matsuda, 2001; Medgyes, 1992, 1994). A number of previous studies have reported the positive effects of co-teaching, for example, lowering anxiety for students (Kim and Lee, 2005); enhancing learner intercultural understanding (Park et al., 2010; Park, 2010); raising student willingness to communicate with native speakers (Carless, op cit; Kim and Im, 2008); improving student speaking skills (Chung et al., op cit; Park and Kim, 2000); and facilitating the professional development of LETs (Jeon, op cit). The steady influx of native speakers of English into public school settings has made co-teaching a viable option in Korea.

However, co-teaching is not without problems. First of all, some NESTs are either unqualified or inexperienced (Carless, op cit). Such teachers are recruited into the public schools as long as they are native speakers with a college degree. With the standards for qualifications set so low, the recruitment of unqualified NESTs has created a number of academic and social problems; some cases have even included sexual offenders, drug users and other criminal cases that have appeared in the headlines in the Korean media. Even NESTs with good intentions and motivation are often without adequate pedagogical and professional resources; they are in dire need of guidance or training. Many NESTs themselves express a preference for co-teaching rather than independent teaching (Kim, op cit).

In theory, trained LETs should be able to help NESTs with their pedagogical content knowledge. NESTs, in turn, can provide language support for LETs to improve their English proficiency (Carless, op cit). While this relationship sounds plausible, this is not always the practice for a number of reasons. First, the limited English proficiency of LETs works as a barrier to communication between the two groups (Árva and Medgyes, op cit). In addition, collaboration seems to be influenced by various institutional contexts (Jeon, op cit). For example, primary school teachers were found to collaborate more often than their secondary school counterparts, probably because primary school English education places more focus on spoken language development than secondary school education. Ideally, NESTs and LETs are expected to collaborate throughout the entire process, from planning to instruction and then to evaluation. In reality, however, the collaboration seems to be very limited and is rarely carried out (Chung et al., op cit; Kim, op cit). In fact, NESTs and LETs may not communicate sufficiently (Kwon and Kellogg, 2005; Park, op cit). Other researchers have ascribed the problems to such issues as cultural conflicts, inadequate resources, unclear understanding of what to do in classes or a mismatch between teaching and testing (Chung et al., op cit; Kwon and Kellogg, op cit; Park et al., 2010). Chung et al. (op cit) observe that NESTs and LETs also have different expectations for their co-teaching roles, reporting that only 14 per cent of NESTs and LETs planned a lesson together as a team.

Previous informative studies on co-teaching have been based primarily on written surveys that examine the perceptions of these native and non-native teachers, eliciting a retrospective understanding of the collaboration between NESTs and

NNESTs. However, their data were not supported by qualitative research methods to examine the NESTs' perspectives based on concrete details of the co-teaching practices. What we need is to connect in-depth interviews to classroom practices so that the analysis can pinpoint the issues that make co-teaching successful or challenging. To support this goal, this chapter reports on a qualitative inquiry into co-teaching practices by examining NESTs' perspectives in reference to co-teaching practices. In order to provide an in-depth understanding of this issue, the researcher visited school sites where NESTs worked and observed their co-teaching practices before conducting in-depth interviews. The findings, therefore, offer concrete and informative details about why co-teaching between NESTs and NNESTS is challenging in Korean contexts.

Participants

Data for the study reported here were collected at nine secondary schools across Seoul, Korea. The participants in the study comprised nine native teachers of English teaching in secondary schools: five teaching in high school settings and four in middle school settings. The schools they worked in represented different socioeconomic status groups, as presented in Table 1.

Table 1: Demographic information about the participants

Pseudonym	School level	Gender	Origin	Teaching experience in Korea	Education (BA subject)	Age	School district SES
Wilson	high	M	US	1.5 years	other	30s	low
Anthony	high	M	US	Just started	English	20s	low
Charles	high	M	US	Just started	other	20s	mid
Gabriel	high	M	US	2 years (9 years in total in the US, the UK, Sweden and Korea)	Education	30s	high
Angela	high	F	US	1.5 years	English	20s	high
Clara	middle	F	Austria	Just started	other (+ TESOL certificate)	20s	low
Kristine	middle	F	Canada	Just started (5 years in Canada)	Education	20s	high
Bob	middle	M	US	2 years	other	20s	mid
Neil	middle	M	US	Just started	other	20s	low

Among the nine NESTs, seven teachers were from the US, one was from Canada and the other was an Austrian-American who grew up in Europe and had lived in the UK. There were six male and three female teachers. With regard to teaching experience, four of them had taught in Korea for more than a year, and five others had just started their public school teaching in Korea at the time of data collection. Two of the teachers, Gabriel and Kristine, were highly experienced teachers and thus very competent and confident. Gabriel had nine years of teaching experience in secondary school settings, including six years of overseas teaching experience in Korea, the UK and Sweden. Kristine had taught in elementary school settings in Canada for five years.

In terms of age, most of them (n=7) were in their twenties and only two male teachers were in their thirties. With regard to education, two teachers had a BA in Education, while two others had obtained a BA in English. More than half of the participants had obtained degrees from fields other than English or Education. One of them with a BA from another field of study had a TESOL certificate. It can be inferred from the teachers' demographic information that most of the NESTs did not have sufficient overseas teaching experience or ELT training.

Data collection

The findings reported here are part of a wider study which drew on classroom observations and interviews with both native and non-native teachers. A total of nine classes were observed and videotaped. Each class session lasted about 45 minutes (in the middle schools) or 50 minutes (in the high schools). The observation data was used to identify and confirm what NESTs reported about their co-teaching practices.

The interviews were conducted in English with the native teachers and in Korean with the non-native teachers. It took between 50 minutes and an hour to conduct each interview. All the data were transcribed and analysed according to Denzin and Lincoln's (2011) qualitative protocol. Particular emphasis was placed on examining how collaborative teaching was conducted and viewed by native and non-native teachers of English in reference to the expectations of the EPIK.

Interview data was examined to identify some common characteristics of co-teaching or collaborative efforts between the NESTs and their Korean counterparts. This included the planning stage as well as actual teaching episodes. Following the coding procedures in the qualitative research protocol (Glesne and Peshkin, 1999), the common themes and various opinions within them were pulled into the thematic categories that are reported here. The following sections are selected to illustrate the main concerns the NESTs had about preparing and conducting their co-teaching practices.

What the NESTs say about their co-teaching experience
Influence of institutional and instructional context
Since all the nine NESTs in the study were from different schools, they worked in different instructional and institutional contexts. These teachers seemed to be well informed of the possible variance when they received orientation training organised by EPIK officials, as seen in the following comments.

> When we had EPIK orientation, I think they did a little bit of a good job of telling us that everyone is gonna be in a different situation. And you might get to do whatever you want in the class. You might have a co-teacher that really is

helpful or you might have a co-teacher that never comes to class, so be prepared for the variance in that. And so I was expecting a little bit of variance between different schools. (Kristine, middle school teacher)

The interviews with the NESTs revealed that they were expected to collaborate with five to eight non-native teachers of English at their schools. In one particular case, the NEST had to work with two Korean co-teachers simultaneously in a class. All the NESTs in the study were contracted to teach 22 hours per week, and yet there was a great deal of variation between institutional contexts in how these 22 hours were used . What was common across the schools, however, was that only one NEST was assigned to each school. This indicates that the students did not have a sufficient number of English classes taught by their NEST. From the students' perspectives, they met their native teacher only once a week or once every other week – or even not at all.

The teaching schedules of the NESTs were also influenced by the grade level of the students. Many high schools did not let the NESTs teach their senior students since these students were supposed to prepare for the college entrance examination that focuses more on reading and grammar in English. As a result, the NESTs were primarily assigned to freshmen or junior students in high schools. In the middle school setting, however, the NESTs rarely taught first-year students and instead taught mostly second- and third-year students. The rationale behind this organisation was that freshmen at middle school levels were not ready for classes taught by native teachers because of their low proficiency. As in the high schools, however, NEST instruction for these courses was limited to once a week or once every other week. This seemed to be an administrative decision made by school officials given the set number of courses NESTs were contracted to teach.

In general, therefore, there seemed to be only a weekly or biweekly English lesson taught by a NEST among the schools examined in the study. Considering that an instructional session for each class lasted only 45 minutes (in middle schools) or 50 minutes (in high schools), the number of hours or the frequency of class meetings was far below the basic requirements for any substantial difference in language proficiency development to be made. This was problematic considering that the purpose of the EPIK was to expose students to the authentic language input that native teachers can provide. That is to say, the frequency and the intensity of input did not seem to meet the threshold level required for proficiency development or language exposure.

The curricular decision-making process and its problems

With regard to determining what to teach, the NESTs seemed to make the decision by themselves. Indeed, none of the NESTs reported that they planned their lesson together with their co-teachers ahead of their classes. None of them experienced any type of meetings arranged for lesson planning, whether formal or informal. The lack of involvement in these curricular decisions was well expressed in the following remarks by a NEST at a high school.

I was just under the impression that it was all my responsibility to develop materials and I can check with them, and I did to see how coherent the lessons were or if they were appropriate for the levels of the students. But, as far as collaboration is concerned, it didn't really exist much unless I asked for it. They didn't know how to help me or they weren't too concerned about helping me. (Angela, high school teacher)

In the absence of any collaborative effort, NESTs were, in most cases, left to determine what to do on their own. Among the nine NESTs, five covered the listening or the speaking sections of the textbook while four of them developed their own teaching materials, including PowerPoint slides or student worksheets. That is to say, the NESTs became accustomed to, or even preferred, working alone to prepare their lessons. One of the NESTs considered himself to be a competent teacher, and he believed that his independent lesson planning would be sufficient. He had a BA in Education and nine years of teaching experience in public school settings in different countries including the US, the UK, Sweden and Korea. Another case was a Korean-American teacher named Bob, who had to prepare his lesson, including instructional materials, without any feedback from his co-teachers.

However, this does not mean that there was no communication at all. Some Korean co-teachers seemed to be involved, albeit at a minimum level, in checking and monitoring the adequacy of the lessons designed by the NESTs; some schools, in fact, required NESTs to share their course materials with their co-teachers. Unfortunately, most NESTs reported that they did not receive any detailed feedback from their co-teachers. Instead, they received feedback in the form of a brief or casual remark, and it seems clear that most curricular decisions about what to teach and how to teach were left to the NESTs.

One problem with the lack of guidance from co-teachers was that some classes by the NESTs were not run in a way the EPIK had envisaged. This was potentially problematic when some NESTs resorted to teaching styles that were not encouraged in the EPIK. This was more often the case with those NESTs who did not have any training in TESOL or education. Not being knowledgeable about language learning principles or teaching methods, these NESTs simply relied on their personal experience in devising their teaching plans. The following illustrated a case in point as the teacher expressed his belief in repetitions and drills.

What's interesting is, what's most creative for me, what's most interesting to me is not necessarily what's best for students. They like repetition; they need repetition. I think it's important when you learn a language, to get that structure in repetition. I see it from their perspectives. They gain more from that. When I was learning Spanish in high school, I really appreciated the repetition. (Wilson, high school teacher)

This teacher spent the entire class time having students repeat and drill the dialogues taken from the textbook. When he did a role play with each student in the class, using the dialogue in the textbook, other students waited their turn. Although repetition and drills may be necessary to some extent, the excessive focus on them did not achieve the goal of interactional exchange between native teachers and non-native students that the EPIK programme sought to promote. There were other teachers who spent the entire instructional time lecturing about course content presented in the textbook. Regardless of the topics these lectures were developed from, they did not generate enough language interaction for the students.

The lack of teaching experience or training often produced some extreme cases of ineffective teaching. One teacher named Neil took on the role of a grammar drill sergeant who did not tolerate any grammatical mistakes his students made. His strict attitude toward grammatical accuracy had to do with his past work experience in the military. When he was doing listening exercises, he started to speak louder when the students did not respond to him. Naturally, the students in the class showed minimal interest and involvement, which, in turn, made the teacher feel more frustrated and prompted him to speak even louder.

In summary, there seemed to be a lack of collaborative effort in making curricular decisions for the classes taught by the NESTs. Due to this absence of concrete guidelines, the NESTs were largely left alone in planning their courses. This is partly attributed to the fact that NESTs' courses were considered independent of, and thus deviated from, the mainstream English instruction in Korea that is more focused on reading and grammar. With minimum involvement of LETs in co-teaching, NESTs' courses are likely to remain disconnected from other English courses and the quality of teaching is then largely up to each NEST's individual propensity and ability. The following section addresses the issue of how the NESTs' courses were carried out in the presence of their co-teachers.

Collaboration in classroom teaching

Unlike the scarce interaction in the planning stage, there seemed to be some degree of collaborative involvement in classroom teaching. Among the various co-teaching styles, the NESTs in the present study mostly adopted the supportive teaching model (Villa et al., 2008), in which one teacher leads the class while the other assists students. The participants reported that, in the majority of cases, the NESTs took the role of the lead teacher who directed the classroom teaching, while their Korean co-teacher assisted the process. The Korean co-teachers often remained either silently seated at the back or moved around to discipline or assist their students while their native counterpart was teaching.

Considering that most teaching plans were constructed by the NEST, this was understandable. Indeed, some NESTs did not even see this setting as co-teaching, as shown by the following remarks by a NEST:

> Here I don't have a textbook I go out of, so lessons I make usually are led by me. And the co-teacher who will usually find their own role into the class depending on their own personality [...] The co-teaching really doesn't happen here. It's mostly just me leading the class and the co-teacher helping wherever they can. So if there was more of a set formula, that would be nice.
> (Bob, middle school teacher)

The absence of active involvement by the LETs seemed to make it difficult to conduct any type of task collaboratively during the class period, even if the NEST wanted to. This was particularly so when the LET remained quite passive during the classroom instruction, even when the NEST had wanted help, as the following comments showed:

I guess there are some situations where it doesn't seem like the co-teachers are really involved at all. It's kind of view of [...] they view their own classes as their classes and they view my classes that I teach as my classes and view them very separately. And so when it comes to the class I'm teaching, they're like, okay, this is your class or I'll just let you do your thing. I'll sit at the back and you know if I hear that you need some help, for sure I'll help. Otherwise I'll just do my own thing, mark, or do whatever I need to do, and kind of it's all up to you, which is fine sometimes if the classes are running really well. But then in some cases when it's not, and I do need help, then it becomes maybe a problem.
(Kristine, middle school teacher)

Even the seasoned NESTs seemed to hope for some involvement from their co-teachers. They wanted feedback on more specific and concrete issues as each new setting presented a new set of tasks. The following is extracted from the interview with one of the more experienced teachers, Kristine. Although she had taught at an elementary school in Canada for five years, she was new to the secondary school context in Korea.

I like that freedom a little bit because I feel like I have lots of experience planning lessons and so I'm able to come up with ideas on my own and I kind of think, I guess, I would appreciate maybe a little bit more consistency with co-teachers because it's hard to work with some, the really different ones [...] I feel like I would love to have a little bit more of their feedback or help. I don't get that. (Kristine, middle school teacher)

To some extent, the lack of involvement was inevitable because of the cultural or systemic differences among those involved. This worked as an obstacle that prevented the LETs from becoming actively involved in co-teaching practice, as shown in the responses from one of the NESTs.

I think I have six, I mainly work with three of them. I feel like I collaborate with them well. They all have different vibes and different things that they provide in terms of instructions [...] A thing that can be most frustrating is, not even to name anybody, but some of the older teachers because of the cultural differences and historical things they were educated in Korea in English when there weren't even any English speaking teachers [...] so sometimes I think their translation gets lost [...] (Anthony, high school teacher)

However, not all co-teachers remained passive during the collaboration. Some Korean teachers deliberately did not get involved, thinking that this would create more opportunities for their students to interact with their native counterpart. Other teachers were actively involved in seeking ways to help. Without a pre-arranged consensus as to what co-teachers were supposed to do, however, some of the co-teacher's actions created problems for the NEST.

One area which brought differences in language teaching philosophy to the fore was the practice by Korean co-teachers of translating the NEST's talk. When the details of whether and how translation was to be done had not been agreed, this issue tended to become problematic. At one middle school, the Korean teacher translated every single sentence the NEST produced during her instruction. While the Korean teacher meant to help those students with comprehension problems, the native teacher considered the practice to be a nuisance, disrupting the flow of the class. The following remarks from the NEST demonstrate how this translation issue became a matter of second language learning philosophy:

> At the beginning when I first met them, there's 'Again' or 'What?' You know, if you keep asking them 'What is this?' 'What is this?' 'What is this?' 'What is this?' 'What is this?' 'What is this?' kind of, then, they learn like, 'Oh, that means …' […] even though they may not learn but then a lot of time immediately after I say something, she will be like 'blah blah blah' in Korean and I don't really, you know, where they have to learn English, just translating into Korean is not going to help them learn English. (Clara, middle school teacher)

This type of difference is understandable considering that the Korean co-teachers were rarely involved in teaching decisions. This can also be ascribed to a lack of discussion as to what role the co-teacher should play during the actual classroom interaction. Without prior consensus on what to do and how to do it, technical differences like providing translation became a source of tension between the NESTs and their co-teachers.

Not all collaborations were ineffective or considered a nuisance, however. There were some areas of teaching in which many NESTs considered their co-teachers' involvement indispensable. The presence of Korean teachers was essential for classroom management according to many NESTs. Some students seemed not to get involved in what went on during the classroom instruction because of their lack of language proficiency or motivation. In these cases, the Korean teachers helped to keep the students attentive during instruction. Some NESTs mentioned that their students would not have paid attention in class without the presence of their Korean co-teachers.

> I think that there's lots of advantages. They know the students a lot better than I do because they have seen many students, and they see that class of students more often than I do, so they have a lot more closer relationship with them and know them, and in terms of classroom management, therefore, they know their names, they know what students could be a problem to help and also especially with lower level students that tend to often be the ones who have behavior problems. (Kristine, middle school teacher)

To sum up, many NESTs expressed the opinion that Korean co-teachers could help maintain the order of the classroom so that the main classroom activities could run smoothly. One of the NESTs, Neil, attributed his students' lack of attention and interest to the fact that he did not have the power to conduct classroom assessment. He believed that reading- and grammar-oriented classroom assessment had a negative backwash effect on his class because the students did not see the point of paying attention to his instruction. Some students actually looked distracted and displayed undesirable behaviours in class, such as chatting, sleeping, texting or doodling. For this reason, the native teachers required the

NNESTs' contributions to classroom management, however minimal their roles in the class itself.

The NESTs also requested LETs when they had to deal with those who had limited proficiency. Some students in the NESTs' classes had a low comprehension level, and thus NESTs had to receive some support from their Korean counterparts. Translation assistance from LETs was valued highly by some NESTs, as shown in the following comments:

> Oh, it is imperative (to have a non-native teacher). It really is important for this size of class. If you're dealing with 35, 40 students, that they really wouldn't be much. Well, there would be benefit for all the reasons I stated: the cultural, seeing a, hearing different voices, getting a specific understanding of an English speaker, but they wouldn't be, in terms of pedagogy, in terms of actual learning, they would be less, far less, if there is no Korean teacher present because that translation is pivotal to them to understand what's, what's, what's going on. Try to minimize some of the translation but if they don't have that, then there's no, you know, there's no grasp of what I'm saying, so that really is important. So I do see this pivotal in the high school, public high school system. (Wilson, high school teacher)

In this context, students would get additional help by interacting with their co-teachers with regard to what was going on during the classroom instruction. Given the individual and contextual differences, it is understandable that co-teaching between native and non-native teachers was difficult to accomplish. Nonetheless, there seemed to be some areas where co-teaching was effective or even necessary. These are discussed in more detail below.

Discussion and conclusion

The point of departure for this chapter was the assumption that teacher collaboration is a necessary element for improved student achievement and ongoing school success (DelliCarpini, 2008). Through a detailed qualitative analysis of nine different school settings (four middle schools and five high schools), the study probed the NEST's perspective by conducting in-depth interviews and classroom observations in each setting.

One important finding is that these NESTs were professionally isolated from the rest of the Korean teaching staff. None of the NESTs interviewed for the study reported having had formal or informal meetings with Korean teachers of English in planning their classes. Occasionally, there was some quick and impromptu consultation right before or after classes, as Korean English teachers were often required to accompany their NEST counterparts. As a result, the NESTs planned their lessons and prepared learning materials by themselves. While this arrangement seemed to work for some NESTs, others struggled, resorting to their own personal experience or textbook instructions. The novice NESTS expressed a need for professional feedback from their Korean colleagues.

The paucity of communication can be attributed to a number of factors. Korean teachers are usually loaded with several administrative duties. In addition, some

Korean teachers are not proficient enough to communicate with the NESTs; therefore, they may respond reluctantly or passively to attempts at collaboration. In contrast, those who were comfortable speaking in English were found to communicate more often with their counterparts and thus supported them with their pedagogical content knowledge and skills. The lack of communication between co-teachers was particularly problematic when the NESTs were either inexperienced or lacked qualifications. Novice NESTs sought professional help in terms of content knowledge and classroom management. Unfortunately, there was no adequate support for those NESTs, especially in the planning stages, and they were generally left to plan everything from scratch.

Korean co-teachers were required to be present in the NESTs' classes in order to support their counterparts. Since the lesson planning was done by NESTs, however, most Korean co-teachers played passive roles in class, simply monitoring the students' behaviour or, on some occasions, just sitting at the back. Even though the NESTs took the lead role in classroom teaching, their position and status remained unclear. This was partially because student performance in their classes did not affect the students' records. As a result, these NESTs did not have firm control or authority when their students were not interested in learning or displayed behavioural problems.

What, then, would be the ideal mode of co-teaching in these classes? Carless (op cit) argues that the presence of two teachers can be a waste of time if one dominates and the other simply plays the role of a spectator or a disciplinarian. Some Korean co-teachers in the study tried to do more than that by providing language support. For instance, they tried to translate what the NESTs were saying for low-level students, even when the NESTs' views on this matter were mixed. One novice NEST expressed a strong need for his co-teacher to translate for low-level students; he frequently expressed frustration when the LETs were not readily available to provide translation in a low-level class. In contrast, experienced and competent NESTs were able to accommodate both high- and low-level students in their classroom teaching. Interestingly, one experienced NEST considered her co-teacher's excessive translation to be a nuisance, interrupting the flow of interaction. The clash on this matter can often be ascribed to broad differences in teaching philosophy. With regard to translation practice, the experienced NEST criticised her co-teacher for underestimating the students' potential and limiting their development by 'spoon-feeding' them. This confirms the finding by Moote (2003), who noted communication problems and clashes of teaching style as two common barriers to collaboration.

To sum up, the success of the EPIK may depend on the professional quality of NESTs in terms of teaching experience and content training. In the case of the more competent teachers, their classroom instruction differed in many respects. They demonstrated professional competence in class and knew how to communicate with LETs. They were also more competent and confident about instructional choices they made for their classroom teaching. The NESTs with an ELT-related background were confident enough to design tasks or activities that could facilitate their students' speaking practice.

On the other hand, those who lacked relevant knowledge and skills taught classes based on their own learning experiences. Recalling drill-based language learning experiences, they typically used mechanical drills or repetition in their classroom instruction. This indicates that teachers' professional qualifications weigh more than other background variables. In other words, being a native speaker did not guarantee that they would automatically become competent and confident teachers. Although the NESTs without so much training in language education expressed demands for collaboration and communication, the system at schools and EPIK did not provide sufficient professional and material support. Given the lack of adequate and extensive training within the EPIK programme, its success depends mostly on the types of teachers that are recruited.

In recent years, co-teaching as an instructional strategy has declined with a change in government policy. In 2012, the Ministry of Education announced a gradual reduction in the size of the EPIK and thus in the number of native teachers. NESTs may be phased out in secondary schools over the next few years, although they will still be in elementary school settings. This change reflects the government-led evaluation of the programme in general. It is not certain, however, whether this decision was based on a close examination of the school contexts and working environments NESTs were placed in. If the decision was made ad hoc, the remaining EPIK programs are likely to suffer a similar fate.

The following suggestions can be made on the basis of the findings of this study. First of all, there needs to be a more rigorous system for recruiting and training NESTs if they are placed into the educational system in EFL contexts. The present research has demonstrated that teaching experience and content knowledge is much more important than the candidate's other qualifications. With this qualification, NESTs would be better prepared for the demands that are made of them in school contexts. However, regardless of professional qualifications, all NESTs need more rigorous training once they are in the system. This training needs to include not only content knowledge but also cultural training that informs them of the distinctive institutional and instructional features the Korean educational system is based on. In addition to this formal training, there should be more customised and individualised training that helps NESTs adjust to each individual school context. For this adjustment, Korean teachers should be more involved in the form of collaboration or co-teaching. Given that Korean teachers are loaded with other administrative tasks, the collaboration has to be incorporated into a professional development programme.

One way to achieve this is to run a learning community or teachers' workshop through which the two groups of teachers should meet on a regular basis. Once NESTs and LETs get used to ongoing, regularly scheduled meetings, they should be encouraged to collaboratively plan their lessons. According to Dove and Honigsfeld (2010), sustained collaborative practices not only create a model of teacher support for novices but also lead to teacher leadership development for more experienced teachers. Therefore, time must be built into the regular school day to accommodate professional conversations among teachers in collaboration with one another (ibid.).

The findings also suggest that this collaborative effort should begin with curricular decisions. Once co-teachers are involved in planning, it may make it easier for both groups of teachers to share the responsibility of taking the lead in class. This type of collaboration would give Korean co-teachers more opportunities to share their professional expertise with NESTs. It is imperative that both NESTs and LETs develop communication strategies that consistently keep all parties informed and allow for shared decision-making.

Shared decision-making also needs to be expanded to assessment. Each school needs to find a way to make the student performance in NESTs' classes count, as this would allow NESTs to have much more authority and influence over the learning process. Therefore, they should be allowed to test their students based on what they have covered in class; otherwise, the students are unlikely to be active in the NESTs' classes. Moreover, to raise the effectiveness of the EPIK, the NESTs should be asked to take on more instructional hours in order to be able to teach more students, and be compensated accordingly.

Most importantly, perhaps, we should revisit the role of non-native teachers in an EFL context. While the presence of native teachers works as a motivating factor (Árva and Medgyes, op cit), they may not always be the best candidates for teaching. As Seidhofer (1999: 238) explains, 'native speakers know the destination, but not the terrain that has to be crossed to get there; they themselves have not travelled the same route.' Non-native teachers may be as good as NESTs because they can better understand the learning needs of their students, predict their learning difficulties and teach effective learning strategies accordingly.

References

Árva, V and Medgyes, P (2000) Native and non-native teachers in the classroom. *System* 28: 355–372.

Buckely, FJ (2000) *Team teaching: What, why, and how?* Thousand Oaks, CA: Sage.

Carless, D (2006) Good practices in team teaching in Japan, Korea, and Hong Kong. *System* 34/4: 341–351.

Carless, D and Walker, E (2006) Effective team teaching between local and native-speaking English teachers. *Language and Education* 20/6: 463–477.

Choi, Y (2001) Suggestions for the re-organisation of English teaching program by native speakers in Korea. *English Teaching* 56: 101–122.

Chung, GJ, Min, CK and Park, MR (1999) A study of team teaching for the utility of the native English teacher in the elementary and secondary school. *English Teaching* 54/2: 210–227.

DelliCarpini, M (2008) Teacher collaboration for ESL/EFL academic success. *Internet TESL Journal* 14/8. Available online at: http://iteslj.org/Techniques/DelliCarpini-TeacherCollaboration.html (accessed 22 February 2016).

Denzin, N and Lincoln, Y (eds) (2011) *The Sage handbook of qualitative research.* Thousand Oaks, CA: Sage.

Dieker, LA and Barnett, CA (1996) Effective co-teaching. *Teaching Exceptional Children* 29/1: 5–7.

Dove, M and Honigsfeld, A (2010) *ESL co-teaching and collaboration: Opportunities to develop teacher leadership and enhance student learning.* Available online at: www.academia.edu/1555511/ESL_Coteaching_and_Collaboration_Opportunities_to_Develop_Teacher_Leadership_and_Enhance_Student_Learning (accessed 22 February 2016).

Gately, S and Gately, F (2001) Understanding co-teaching components. *Teaching Exceptional Children* 33/4: 40–47.

Glesne, C and Peshkin, A (1999) *Becoming qualitative researchers: An introduction.* New York, NY: Longman.

Honigsfeld, A and Dove, M (2008) Co-teaching in the ESL classroom. *Delta Kappa Gamma Bulletin* 74/2: 8–14.

Jeon, I (2010) Exploring the co-teaching practice of native and non-native English teachers in Korea. *English Teaching* 65/3: 43–67.

Kim, JO and Im, BB (2008) A guide to improving team teaching in Korean middle schools. *Modern English Education* 9/2: 71–94.

Kim, K and Lee, C (2005) The effects of team teaching on elementary school students' affective domains and the directions for effective team teaching. *Primary English Education* 11/2: 133–171.

Kim, M (2010) How do Native English-Speaking Teachers perceive co-teaching? *Korean Journal of Applied Linguistics* 26/4: 213–249.

Kwon, M and Kellogg, D (2005) Teaching talk as a game of catch. *The Canadian Modern Language Review* 62/2: 335–348.

Liu, T (2009) *Teachers' narrative understanding of the Taiwanese foreign English teachers recruitment project.* Unpublished PhD thesis, University of Manchester, UK.

Matsuda, A and Matsuda, PK (2001) Autonomy and collaboration in teacher education: Journal sharing among native and non-native English-speaking teachers. *CATESOL Journal* 13/1: 109–121.

Medgyes, P (1992) Native or non-native: Who's worth more? *English Language Teaching Journal* 46/4: 340–349.

Medgyes, P (1994) *The non-native teacher.* London: Macmillan.

Ministry of Education, Science, and Technology (2011) *Statistics of native English speaking teachers in Korea.* Updated on April 30, 2011. Government of Republic of Korea.

Moote, S (2003) Insights into team teaching. *The English Teacher: An International Journal* 6/3: 328–334.

Nemtchinova, E (2005) Host teachers' evaluations of nonnative-English-speaking teacher trainees: A perspective from the classroom. *TESOL Quarterly* 39/2: 235–262.

Pardini, P (2006) In one voice: Mainstream and ELL teachers work side-by-side in the classroom teaching language through content. *Journal of Staff Development* 27/4: 20–25.

Park, HY (2010) An analysis of native and nonnative English teachers' perception on their role in elementary school settings of co-teaching. *English Language Teaching* 22/4: 133–163.

Park, JE, Choi, H, Choi, C and Yoon, E (2010) Issues on selection and support systems of native English speaker teachers and suggestions for the improvement of the systems. *Foreign Languages Education* 17/2: 229–255.

Park, JS and Kim, DJ (2000) Pedagogical effects of team teaching with native speakers: An experiment to compare alternative teaching models. *Foreign Languages Education* 7/1: 97–121.

Phillipson, R (1992) *Linguistic imperialism*. Oxford: Oxford University Press.

Seidhofer, B (1999) Double standards: Teacher education in the expanding circle. *World Englishes* 18/2: 233–245.

Tsai, JM (2007) *Team teaching and teachers' professional learning: Case studies of collaboration between foreign and Taiwanese English teachers in Taiwanese elementary schools*. Unpublished PhD thesis, The Ohio State University, USA.

Villa, TA, Thousand, JS and Nevin, AI (2008) *A guide to co-teaching: Practical tips for facilitating student learning*. Thousand Oaks, CA: Corwin.

Wertheimer, C and Honigsfeld, A (2000) Preparing ESL students to meet the new standards. *TESOL Journal* 9/1: 23–28.

7

NEST schemes and their role in English language teaching: a management perspective

Greg Keaney, CfBT Education Services, Brunei Darussalam

Introduction

In the seven decades since the end of the Second World War, English has become not only an international language but the global language – a language of immense economic, social and political importance (McCrum, 2010). The situation of global English is unique – never before has a language been so widely spoken or desired (Crystal, 2003). Of course, along with 'the rise and rise of English' ('Top dog', 2010) has come the rise and rise NEST (Native English-Speaking Teacher) schemes and projects in a diverse array of geographical locations and social, political and economic circumstances.

This chapter discusses NEST schemes and their effective management. It commences with a brief look at the emergence of NEST schemes in Europe and Asia, particularly those partnered by the author's organisation, CfBT. It proceeds to analyse the traditional client view of Local Teachers and NESTs. The chapter then examines ways to ensure that NEST schemes can better achieve their aims, proposing a management model for such schemes before discussing some of the opportunities and threats for the future of NEST and EEST (Expert English Speaking Teacher) schemes.

In 1984, as a young, freshly graduated high school English teacher from the 'Inner Circle' (Kachru, 1985) – traditional native speaker countries, especially the UK and the US but also Australia, Canada, New Zealand and Ireland – I 'hit the road' in South-East Asia. Like many such travelling teacher contemporaries, I have now spent more than three decades of my professional life teaching and managing a range of NEST projects and schemes across East and South-East Asia.

I started as a 'backpacker' teacher in Bandung, Indonesia before working in an educational administration role for a large English conversation school chain in Japan that employed hundreds of NESTs. I then worked as the Assistant Director of ESL for a US university-twinning programme (80 NESTs), also in Tokyo. Later, I was the Head of English of a large Australian university-twinning consortium in Trolak, Malaysia, with a mix of 20 NESTs and Local Teachers in the department. I am now the programme director for one of the world's largest NEST schemes in Brunei Darussalam, managing nearly 300 NESTs. In all of these organisations, a key prerequisite for employment was being a 'native speaker' of English. In these various professional contexts, I have seen the positive impacts of such schemes as well as their many pitfalls and potential areas for improvement.

NEST schemes and their role in ELT

ELT is undoubtedly a serious business. Far from shrinking in importance, English has grown its dominance in the international communication space in recent years. Indeed, it is possible to make the case, at least from an international economic perspective, that English is moving from having been 'a marker of the elite' in years past to becoming 'a basic skill needed for the entire workforce, in the same way that literacy has been transformed in the last two centuries from an elite privilege into a basic requirement for informed citizenship' (Clark, 2012).

By the end of the 1960s, ELT was already well established as a recognised professional discipline, complete with a supportive framework of academic courses and qualifications as well as associated publications and periodicals. While issues of theory remain in dispute and there have been shifts of emphasis in areas such as syllabus design and language learning psychology, ELT practitioners around the world recognise an essential unity in their field (Williams and Williams, 2007). Academic study in the area, particularly in Inner Circle countries, has tended to be sited in departments of applied linguistics rather than education – a fact that can have a range of consequences for the teaching of English at school level in non-native-speaker countries. Most importantly, this includes a focus on the more micro level (the language, the tasks and the classroom interaction) rather than a broader social and political examination of the learning context and the socioeconomic status of the participants. Pennycook (2001) notes that classrooms in much of applied linguistics are constructed as relatively neutral pedagogical transaction sites, thus ignoring dynamics of power and inequality that have been a central concern of writing on education since at least the 1970s (see Freire, 1973, 1974).

The role of native-speaker teachers in language acquisition, disputes about their impact and worries about their possible influence on local values are almost as old as language learning. Romans more than 2,000 years ago were as ambivalent about their native Greek-speaking teachers as many in similar positions today may feel about their NESTs (Johnston, 2003). The Roman Senate was so concerned about the power of foreign teachers to shape the minds of young people and encourage disobedience that in 161 BCE, and again in 91 BCE, they expelled all such teachers (Lamaoureux, 2009). Such concerns are not so far away from contemporary accounts of the 'dangers' of teachers from overseas (see, for example, Al-Seghayer, 2013; Ford, 2005).

ELT theoreticians and practitioners from Kachru's (op cit) Inner Circle have tended to favour learner-centred approaches to teaching and learning. Jack Richards (2002) outlines a list of ELT practices (based on the work of Brown, 2000) that are reasonably indicative of core pedagogical styles and beliefs promoted by the Inner Circle. These include lowering inhibitions; encouraging risk-taking; building students' self-confidence; developing students' intrinsic motivation; promoting cooperative learning; and getting students to use their mistakes to develop. In addition, unlike the teaching of most other 'modern foreign languages', which has tended to favour bilingual approaches, it is noticeable that ELT has tended to utilise a monolingual approach, avoiding translation and promoting the sole use of English for instruction and explanation in class.

While each of these practices and pedagogies may be valuable in its own right, in sum these core styles and beliefs can work to empower native-speaker teachers of English and to disempower non-native-speaker teachers. In particular, the very strongly promoted tenet that bilingual teaching and code-switching is more of a liability than an asset is an area of concern. See Swan (1985) and Auerbach (1993) as well as a wide range of articles and discussions in the TESOL NNEST Interest Section (NNEST-IS, 2015).

NESTs and Local English Teachers

It has been estimated that about 80 per cent of the world's English teachers are non-native English speakers (Braine, 2010). In very broad terms, we might divide these non-native English speaker teachers into those who have been well trained and accredited in accordance with the requirements of their respective countries and those who lack such training or skills. Most well-trained Local English Teachers (LETs) are what I will call in this chapter the 'pillars' of the ELT world, developing learners across the globe and helping billions in their entry-level steps into English.

Because of the explosive demand for English, however, there are also many non-native teachers who are working as English teachers without sufficient training or knowledge of the language, whom I will call the 'toilers'. This group of LETs clearly struggle with the demands of the job and should ideally be engaged in training and professional development activities that work to improve pedagogical skills. Indeed, capacity-building in this area is a feature of many current aid and educational improvement projects (see, for example, CfBT, 2003, on work in Vietnam, CfBT, 2004, in relation to Afghanistan and CfBT, 2013, on work in Singapore).

The ratio of pillars to toilers varies across different education systems. Few accurate data exist on the English proficiency of LETs globally and it is likely that, for many, proficiency remains a very real problem. Two South-East Asian examples give an insight into the scale of the issue. Malaysia, an Outer Circle country with a reasonably strong tradition of English-medium education, conducted national testing of all of its English language teachers. These proficiency tests were calibrated to the CEFR scale (Common European Framework of Reference for Languages: Learning, Teaching, Assessment) and indicated that approximately half of Malaysia's Local Teachers had B1 or B2 (intermediate) proficiency in English. Approximately 25 per cent were proficient users (C1 or C2) and 25 per cent were basic speakers (A1 or A2), (Ministry of Education, Malaysia, 2013).

The Philippines, another Outer Circle country with a strong tradition of English-medium and bilingual education, has long been put forward as a price-competitive location to source English language teachers (McGeown, 2012). However a self-assessment test conducted by the Department of Education showed that only one out of every five public high school teachers was proficient in English language; of the 53,000 teachers who took the exam, only 19 per cent or 10,070, scored at least 75 per cent, the passing grade (Bonabente, 2007; Wa-Mbaleka, 2014).

It is this very real 'proficiency gap' that explains much of the global demand for NESTs. While it may seem unfair, there is a widely held intuitive sense (particularly among those paying for language tuition) that native speakers are experts in their own language. In addition to this, in many places, 'parents who pay the high prices for lessons don't speak English themselves, making it difficult to track the progress of their child or gauge the talent of his or her teachers' (Hartley and Walker, 2014: no page number).

The issues around linguistic expertise have meant that the concept of a 'NEST' has come to be seen as an integral part of global ELT and from a managerial perspective it would seem likely that NESTs will play an important role in ELT for many years to come.

It is probable that the (vast?) majority of native-speaker teachers working outside their countries of origin might be labelled 'backpacker teachers'. Precise numbers or percentages are difficult to pin down, as many backpacker teachers are working without official visas or even employment status. The situation is particularly noticeable in North-East and South-East Asia. Clark (op cit), for example, estimates that there are 100,000 NESTs in China alone, most of whom would have minimal or no teaching qualifications. All of the most highly populated nations in the region including China, Japan, Korea, Taiwan, Thailand, Vietnam and Indonesia have visa regimes that only specify the holding of a degree as a basic requirement for a long-term visa to teach English. Mostly, these NESTs are teaching either as novices or as an incidental occupation to their desire to travel or to live in a particular country. It may be worth noting in passing that while backpackers are often referred to disparagingly throughout the ELT literature (see, for example, Sung, 2012), many current professional NESTs, applied linguistics academics and significant figures in the ELT field commenced their careers as volunteers or backpacker travelling teachers.

A far smaller group of native speakers are, from a client and commercial perspective, the ELT stars. These are the small group with internationally recognised teaching qualifications and sufficient knowledge and experience to be able to deliver effective English language training. For want of a better term, the matrix in Figure 1 labels this group 'the prima donnas', mindful of both the positive and the negative connotations of the label. Terms and conditions for these 'prima donnas' are generally very good by the standards of other members of the profession.

While for many LETs the key issue is proficiency, for native-speaker teachers of English it is pedagogy – both knowledge and skills. Traditionally, English language teaching in its 'NEST' strand has been one of the least regulated areas of education globally. Many native speakers are working as 'teachers' without any particular training or experience. In many locations, those with a 'four-week certificate' are held to be not only 'classroom-ready' but particularly well trained. This is a quandary for all of us involved at the chalkface of NEST schemes. That a proportion of NESTs who come into the profession untrained or inexperienced nevertheless do a reasonably satisfactory job, particularly if they are working with motivated or more academically able learners, should not disguise the immense variability in performance.

At the risk of oversimplification, therefore, the matrix below (Figure 1) illustrates these four broad groups of teachers working in ELT. While one must be mindful of the generalisations involved, there is value in being able to identify four such 'types' of English language teachers. NEST schemes have usually been set up in response to political pressures and so 'proficiency' is generally viewed through a non-expert lens. It is important to underline that the 'proficiency' dichotomy can often be one of client or public perception rather than fact. Anyone who has worked closely with 'backpacker' English language teachers knows that the assumption that 'native speaker' necessarily correlates with language proficiency is frequently untrue!

Figure 1: The English language teacher matrix

Less likely to improve student outcomes	More likely to improve student outcomes	
Backpackers	**Prima donnas**	More likely to be a native speaker
+ proficiency (?)	+ proficiency	
- pedagogy	+ pedagogy	
- sociocultural awareness	- sociocultural awareness (?)	
Toilers	**Pillars**	More likely to be a non-native speaker
- proficiency	- proficiency (?)	
- pedagogy	+ pedagogy	
+ sociocultural awareness	+ sociocultural awareness	

NEST schemes at their design stage usually hope to recruit native-speaker prima donnas. Their choices, though, constrained either by resourcing or political circumstances, mean that many have to recruit their native speakers from close to, or within, the 'backpacker' quadrant. This means that much of the tension between NESTs and LETs occurs between the LET professionals in the 'pillar' quadrant and the NEST amateurs in the 'backpacker' quadrant. Piller and Takahashi's (2006) analysis of advertisements from four major English language schools in Japan found that photographs in the advertisements all showed smiling White men (see also Rivers, this volume). The accompanying text elaborated on the teachers' personal lives, not their teaching credentials, and implied that a female student would learn English quickly because she would be 'anxious to see her good-looking White male teacher again soon' (Piller and Takahashi, op cit: 65). Insulting and offensive on so many levels.

Considerable tension may also exist where highly effective LET pillars doing similar or even more difficult work in schools and settings are paid less than NEST prima donnas. This may not only be in matters of salary but also in areas such as accommodation allowances, schooling and flight allowances or other expatriate benefits. Indeed, it has been frequently noted that the very notion of an expatriate is racially loaded (see Antropologi, 2011).

There are currently about 320,000 teachers working in international schools and NEST projects globally, and this figure is likely to double in less than a decade (Hayden and Thompson, 2011). The impact on traditional NEST recruitment is likely to be immense. Demand and price pressures will clearly force changes to the current supply model of NESTs, although how this will play out internationally is not yet known.

Demonstrating the probability that *effective* Outer Circle LETs would have a greater positive impact on learning outcomes than *ineffective* Inner Circle ones is probably the key management challenge for those of us involved with NEST schemes. The question should not be 'NEST or LET?' but rather 'effective or ineffective?'.

Types of NEST schemes

The definition of a NEST scheme is somewhat similar to that of Supreme Court Justice Potter Stewart's threshold test for obscenity: 'no one can precisely define what it is but we know what it is when we see it' (Lattman, 2014). The Foreign Expert (FE) scheme in China, the Native English Teacher (NET) scheme in Hong Kong and the Japan Exchange and Teaching (JET) scheme in Japan (Jeon and Lee, 2006) are all cited by Choi (2007) in his discussion of a further NEST scheme, EPIK (the English Programme in Korea), as some of the best-known examples (see Copland et al., 2015, for a full discussion). There are also numerous aid schemes and government-to-government projects, including volunteer teach-abroad programmes, which have large numbers of participants. These include government-sponsored schemes such as those run through or organised by the Peace Corps and VSO (Voluntary Service Overseas) (Snow, 1996), which continue to play an important role in the early career development of many native English teachers. My own organisation, CfBT (formerly the Centre for British Teachers, now CfBT Education Trust), has been particularly prominent as an organiser and intermediary in the development of many of the largest public-private partnership (PPP) schemes since the mid 1960s.

There are, of course, significant differences between NEST schemes, and these tend to account for the types of NESTs they can and do attract. There are also significant distinctions in aims, purposes and outcomes of the schemes; in the quality, skills and experience of the NESTs recruited; in the terms and conditions the NESTS are contracted to; and in the resourcing, management and quality of the programmes themselves (Neilson, 2009).

The working life of many NESTs is probably not too dissimilar to my own. It moves from work as a backpacker teacher with minimal qualifications or experience in a relatively low-paid position to better-paid work, often in a newly opened, rapidly expanding, challenging or struggling setting. After further experience and perhaps additional qualifications, there is a move either to entry-level school, college or university teaching positions or to traditional language school positions with better-known organisations such as the British Council or International House.

Well-remunerated work on professional NEST schemes or at universities sit near the apex of this progression, while NEST schemes can be positioned at any point along it. The Hong Kong NET scheme and the CfBT project in Brunei, for example, are career positions with substantial salary and professional benefits, while the JET and EPIK programmes are designed for early-career or non-career teachers.

CfBT's role in NEST schemes

With the possible exception of the British Council, the UK-based organisation that has been most heavily involved in professional NEST schemes is CfBT. Since the 1960s CfBT has been involved in the management and administration of NEST schemes in Europe, North Africa, the Middle East and South-East Asia, and it continues to run one of the world's largest NEST schemes in Brunei among a broad range of school improvement, school ownership and management, international development and other educational activities.

In the 1950s, Tony Abrahams, the founder of CfBT, began to appreciate two important facts about English language teaching: firstly, that there was significant and growing demand for native-speaker teachers of the language and, secondly, that teachers working overseas faced considerable practical challenges that made their professional lives difficult (Taylor, 2009). In the mid 1960s, Abrahams was on holiday in Bavaria, where a local mayor explained that schools in the area needed teachers of English. With Tony's support, 13 teachers from the UK were recruited. Soon other districts in Germany started to display similar interest and, by 1968, 32 graduate teachers of English were recruited and began work. By 1974, there were more than 500 CfBT NESTs serving in a range of schools in Germany.

This first CfBT NEST scheme contained many similarities with such schemes today. British teachers could work tax-free in Germany for a maximum of two years. CfBT employed the teachers and paid them the same as a typical German counterpart received net of tax. The CfBT scheme relieved the local ministries of responsibilities such as engaging in complex recruitment exercises, validating qualifications, administering salaries and supervising performance.

Another of the project's similarities with today's schemes was that it grew from needs and demands that defied easy solutions. It presented huge advantages for the German Ministries of Education, who were desperate to find teachers of English for their secondary schools because English had recently officially replaced French as the first foreign language (policy and/or reality overtaking capacity is a regular theme worldwide in English language teaching). Ultimately, any large-scale recruitment of expatriate teachers is immensely difficult unless it is done at scale, due to the complexities of the recruitment exercise itself, the validation of the prospective teachers' qualifications and the difficulties faced by local authorities in the unfamiliar task of the administration of 'foreigners' (Taylor, op cit).

CfBT built on the experience gained in Germany to establish similar projects in Eastern Europe, Morocco, Oman and Malaysia in the 1970s. These were all public-private partnerships, with the funds for the schemes being provided by the host government but all of the educational and administrative activities handled by CfBT.

CfBT Brunei

CfBT signed its initial contracts to operate in Brunei in October 1984, making the scheme the longest-running and one of the largest PPP NEST schemes in the world. CfBT in Brunei works to increase the proficiency and attainment levels of Bruneian students; to improve the delivery of high-impact teaching and learning which promotes student involvement; and to build the capacity of CfBT and Bruneian English teachers. CfBT currently places 267 teachers into government schools in Brunei, with 192 in secondary schools and sixth-form colleges and 75 in lower primary. CfBT recruits and manages all 267 expatriate teachers, placing each into Bruneian government schools as well as delivering a broad range of capacity-building initiatives. The author is the current programme director of this scheme.

An independent research investigation conducted in 2012 by Professor Pam Sammons and a team from Oxford University identified five evolutionary paths in the project over its 30-year lifespan within an overarching theme of system-wide improvement in Brunei. These paths were:

1. **Bilingual policy,** which has evolved from the uncertain period of the 1990s and the pressures of 'critical TESOL' to a confident 'sustained commitment to promoting both English and Malay and recognition as one of the leading nations in English achievement in the ASEAN region.'

2. **Education system,** which has moved from a 'more teacher-centred focus' to 'more student-centred learning and stronger outcomes focus'.

3. **The Ministry of Education–CfBT relationship,** which has moved from being a recruitment link to being a bilingual education partnership.

4. **Student programmes,** which have evolved from pockets of good practice to national-level reach with context-specific strategies.

5. **Teacher development,** which has also evolved from a state of 'recruitment plus capacity-provision' to genuine capacity-building.

(Sammons et al., 2014: 8)

The journey of the CfBT Brunei scheme provides many lessons in improving the management of NEST schemes more broadly and enabling such schemes to play their desired role in more general improvement in the host nation's educational system. It is, therefore, to the management of NEST schemes and the way that they may more efficiently and effectively improve the English language skills of their beneficiaries that we now turn.

NEST scheme management

The core task of NEST scheme managers is to take responsibility for the ongoing health and success of their project and its impact on the host society. NEST managers need to ensure that there is significant educational impact for the student beneficiaries of the scheme as well as demonstrable return on (very significant) investment value in the project for the host country or institution. The CfBT project in Brunei, for example, consumes more than three per cent of the country's annual direct expenditure (including salaries) on school-level education. Hong Kong government figures suggest that the Hong Kong NET scheme consumes a similar percentage there (Hong Kong Education Bureau, 2014).

Most large NEST schemes, however, suffer from immense variability in the quality of the teachers within them (see Legislative Council Panel on Education, 2005, for some of the issues faced by the NET or Native English Teacher scheme in Hong Kong; Asiapundits.com (2011) on the Seoul Municipal Government Programme; and Constantine (2013) on the JET programme in Japan). Despite this, NEST 'prima donnas' remain in high demand globally, as anyone who conducts employment searches on popular websites such as www.tefl.com (usually about 10,000 jobs available on any particular day) or www.daveseslcafe.com quickly realises. Qualified, experienced native-English-speaker teachers with sound cross-cultural skills are in short supply and can command salaries and employment conditions accordingly. Furthermore, even in NEST schemes that pay full expatriate benefits, very few applicants have the necessary qualifications, experience and temperament to be employed. In the CfBT scheme in Brunei, for example, only five per cent of applicants are assessed as being suitable for interview, with only two per cent ultimately being successful.

Management of NEST schemes also suffer from variations in effectiveness. Government-run schemes often lack the organisational focus necessary to deal with the variability in pedagogical skill level of their teachers. Such schemes tend to rely solely on metrics such as qualifications and experience, even though Hattie (2009), in his synthesis of more than 800 meta-analyses in this area, convincingly shows not only that good teachers are so much more effective than bad teachers but also, perhaps surprisingly, that 'neither teacher experience nor teacher qualifications explain much of the variance in teacher effects' (Hattie, op cit: 108).

Some schemes leave almost all educational decisions in the hands of individual NESTS, presuming that along with 'native-speakerness' goes an understanding of effective pedagogy. In reality, many NESTs are ill equipped for this level of autonomy, especially in a culture and a teaching environment 'far from home'.

The longevity of many NEST schemes, particularly in East Asia, suggests that most NEST schemes provide service within a zone of tolerance – not as good as 'hoped for' but not (yet) below the 'minimum acceptable'. Increasing pressure from LETs and from the wider public, however, means that 'satisficing' is a very poor strategy (see, for example, 'Linguistic lust for the world's adulation–"OMG!"', 2014). For NEST schemes to continue to be promoted as a 'solution', much more work needs to be done on ensuring that they provide real value to their beneficiaries and host communities.

Liz Thomson (2009), in *The Personal Touch*, outlined a range of principles that led to CfBT's success in managing the large NEST scheme in Germany and underpinned the management of subsequent NEST schemes around the world.

These included: effective recruitment and selection processes; a systematic approach to staff induction; standardised personnel procedures; support for professional and career development; and developing the culture of a learning organisation and leadership that supports development (Thomson, op cit: 5).

The 5P's Quality Management Model of Pryor et al. (2007) describes five elements that an organisation needs to be successful. The five elements are purpose, principles, processes, people and performance. Thomson's areas can be subsumed into this model to provide a useful tool for the management of NEST schemes, where each of the original five 'P' elements has a matching educational focus (see Figure 2).

For most NEST schemes sitting within a host country's education system, the purpose is very much one of partnership. The key principle of the scheme is that the expert language skills of the NESTs will, in turn, improve the proficiency of beneficiaries (and, indeed, the success of the scheme should be largely measured against this). The NEST scheme's processes should aid NEST productivity, while ongoing professional development of its people should increase NEST professionalism. Finally, NEST scheme performance needs to be largely focused on the quality of the teaching provided both by the individual teachers within the scheme and by the scheme overall.

Figure 2: The 5P Model for NEST schemes

Pryor et al. (2007)		NEST scheme focus
Purpose	→	Partnership
Principles	→	Proficiency
Processes	→	Productivity
People	→	Personality
Performance	→	Pedagogy

Let us now briefly examine each of these elements and their implications for NEST scheme management.

Purpose and partnership

By definition, NEST schemes are bringing teachers into very different social and learning contexts. For such schemes to be successful, it is vital that a strong sense of partnership develops and that the NESTs, the scheme's academic and administrative managers, LETs and the host societies all have plenty of 'skin in the game'.

The desire of education ministries to improve English language performance quickly is clear. LETs working effectively with competent NESTs can probably develop more effectively than through many other methods of teacher development. This was noted even in CfBT's early work in Germany nearly 50 years ago:

To penetrate the sophisticated German school system in this way was … a miracle. Gradually we all came to realise that a new and beneficent organisation had been injected into the Germans' educational bloodstream. (Taylor, op cit: 13)

In the Brunei NEST scheme today, the implications for system-wide improvement offered by Brunei's continued partnership with CfBT, and for the infrastructure that has been built thus far, are significant. Initiatives and programmes put in place by the NEST scheme are underpinned by the supportive bilingual policy context of the country. The collective range of cooperative interventions in the English language subject area by CfBT and the Ministry of Education continue to influence educational experiences at whole-school level and across the different stages of schooling.

Such partnerships take time to become highly effective, though. Trust needs to be built in stages. The relationship in Brunei evolved from one based mostly around the recruitment of good-quality teaching professionals to more of a partnership in supporting and enhancing bilingual education. This process was characterised by an attitude of 'learning the lessons together'; Sammons et al. (op cit: 49) noted that CfBT's work with the Brunei Ministry of Education could be viewed as a 'textbook partnership', with iterative learning and improvement cycles.

With partnership, however, comes responsibility. As noted above, traditional Inner Circle sources to recruit effective teachers for NEST schemes will be insufficient to match the increasing global demand. This means that there is a growing need to source teachers from Outer Circle nations, such as India, Nigeria, the Philippines, Malaysia, Tanzania and Kenya among others. Movement in this area can already be observed in increasing English language student flows into the Philippines, for example, as well as in the use of a broad range of teachers from non-traditional sources in NEST projects in Thailand and the Middle East. This trend should both increase the political and ideological acceptance of NEST schemes and reduce their cost sufficiently to allow their greater use in large emerging nations such as China, Brazil, Thailand, Indonesia and Vietnam. Cost reductions would occur not only through salary differentials but also through factors such as lower hiring costs, lower airfares and expatriation costs, higher retention rates/lower turnover and lower schooling costs for dependent children.

In order for a broader range of teachers to be working in NEST schemes there will need to be a range of capacity-building and quality assurance work to support transition to NEST-like schemes using teachers from non-traditional Outer Circle countries. Demand for NESTs, NEST schemes and NEST-like schemes is likely to remain an important component of global ELT but capacity constraints and price pressures are likely to lead to a far greater diversity of NESTs (and a change of terminology, perhaps to EESTs!) in the years ahead.

The purpose of a well-designed NEST scheme is to provide maximum benefit to beneficiaries. A successful blend of evidence-based improvements at the teacher and classroom level alongside effective, cooperative capacity-building for both NESTs and LETs need to be core goals.

Implication(s) for NEST scheme management:
Effective partnerships will deliver superior results.

Principles and proficiency

The underpinning intellectual principle of NEST schemes would seem to be the assumption that proficient users of a language make better teachers of that language than less proficient users, and that therefore, by extension, native-speaker teachers should be the best of all.

The modernist idealisation of the 'native speaker' permeated the academic disciplines of anthropology and linguistics well before the dominance of English in the post-World War Two world. The quote below, from an American anthropologist (referring to her Spanish), accurately summates the experience and frustration of the 'near-native speaker'.

> *being near-native is a little like being a number approaching infinity – no matter how far I go or how near I get, I'm never going to lose that tell-tale little thing that sets me ever-so-slightly apart.* (Babel, 2014)

Fortunately or unfortunately, language expertise is far more transparent than most other school subjects. The mathematics teacher who is weak in differential calculus rarely gets caught out, whereas the Local English Teacher who struggles with the past perfect continuous or the latest idiom in a popular song may be more readily noticed. For this reason, the 'native speaker' label has seemed to be a convenient attribute to ensure competence. In addition, it is a reasonable assumption that the language proficiency of any group of native speakers of a language *as a cohort* could reliably be expected to exceed that of a matched group of non-native speakers.

Furthermore, there is no doubt that some aspects of language are difficult to acquire as an adult, particularly in the areas of idiomatic usage, 'new' language and complex pronunciation and prosody variables. The extent to which these are important in teaching contexts, however, is debatable. From a practical viewpoint, new models of proficiency, particularly from a classroom perspective, will need to be developed in regions where there is particular demand for English language teachers who are proficient both in the language and in the classroom. Increasingly, organisations such as CfBT and the British Council, which have long been identified as NEST providers, are using their influence to 'move the goalposts' in this area. In definitions of required qualifications and experience, there has been a move from 'native' to 'native-like', and it is hoped that this positive trend will continue and, indeed, accelerate.

The link between ELT teacher proficiency and pedagogical skill is, at the very least, tenuous. While LETs with higher levels of English proficiency tend to be more effective than LETs with lower levels of English proficiency, it does not follow that NESTs are therefore better teachers than their local colleagues (see, for example, Oga-Baldwin and Nakata, 2013). In fact, given the lack of formal effort required to learn a language in childhood, it is not difficult to make the case that a near-native

LET would, in most cases, outperform a monolingual NEST, especially in the LET's own context.

Clearly, a more nuanced approach needs to be adopted. Examining education systems to ensure the appropriate level of proficiency for particular levels of students is an effective method of 'human resource allocation'. We currently do not expect primary school maths teachers to be rocket scientists, but many nations hold that all their English teachers should have perfect English. It is extremely unlikely, from a pedagogical viewpoint, however, that language teachers need to be more than one CEFR grade of fluency higher than their students.

Sparks (2004) showed that teachers trained in the field they are teaching in were more effective than those not so trained. CfBT's own teacher training practice in projects involving LETs in this area has always been to improve teachers' English language *proficiency* through *pedagogy*. That is, even where the stated goal of a programme is to improve LETs' English language 'proficiency', course content and objectives focus on improvements in 'pedagogic' skills.

Obviously, training programmes that aim to raise teacher skills in the 'content' of their specialist subject are more likely to demotivate, as they are perceived as a 'deficiency' or 'remedial' model (activating 'protection' mental models), whereas those that focus on pedagogy are seen as promotion-focused and hence more likely to be inspirational (Halvorson and Tory Higgins, 2013).

The continuing demand for English language education globally will lead to a concomitant demand for ELT improvement schemes. While these have traditionally been designed as NEST schemes, there needs to be increasing effort to ensure that NESTs and LETs are deployed where they can be most effective.

Implication(s) for NEST scheme management:
Native-speaker involvement in ELT springs from the importance of English as a global language. While proficient users of a language may make better teachers of that language than less proficient users, it is unlikely that language teachers need to be more than one CEFR grade of fluency higher than their students.

Processes and productivity

Another key variable in the effectiveness of any educational innovation is its leadership and management. CfBT, in its work in this area over the past 50 years, has learned and relearned that the quality of management and leadership in a NEST scheme is closely tied to the sustainability and impact of the programme. Weak management and leadership frequently lead to poor programme outcomes. NEST schemes are far less likely to succeed when NESTs are recruited and then left to their own devices. Simply putting a native-speaker teacher or mentor in every target school or classroom is unlikely to lead to anything other than sporadic and incidental improvements in English language performance.

Teacher quality control and performance management should be key features of the ongoing management of a NEST scheme. CfBT Brunei commits to incorporating its values of excellence, integrity, accountability and collaboration into the day-to-day work that it undertakes in Brunei. A rigorous and supportive performance management process ultimately upholds these four values in all domains of the work.

NESTs in the CfBT Brunei scheme have individually tailored Performance Reviews and Professional Action Plans that not only encourage honest and critical self-reflection and the opportunity to define professional goals with clear outcomes and success criteria but are also closely linked to the aims of the scheme itself. The reviews cover not only classroom performance but also broader school duties and additional contributions as well as national-level CfBT and Education Ministry ones. Action plans set professional SMART (Specific, Measurable, Achievable, Relevant and Time-bound) targets and include professional pathway discussions.

All NEST schemes need to pay particular attention to the management of their inputs and outcomes. Teachers in NEST schemes need to be professionally managed and scrutinised. The effectiveness of the scheme and of the teachers within it needs to be judged primarily on evidence derived from beneficiary impact.

Implication(s) for NEST scheme management:
Managed teachers, that is, those with a clear sense of organisational/institutional focus, tend to perform more effectively and have a stronger impact on student learning outcomes than unmanaged or unfocused ones. The correct balance needs to be found between professional autonomy and consistent quality across settings.

People and personality

NESTs are often seen to be a motivating influence for learners. The challenge of disentangling the multiple variables in this area, however, makes this enormously difficult to either prove or disprove. Indeed, attempting to link teaching impact and success with particular personal or personality attributes is dangerously complex. On the other hand, anyone who spends time examining NEST recruitment sites will observe that everyday personality traits such as 'warmth, flexibility, resilience and enthusiasm' pervade advertising for NESTs and do play a role in their professional performance.

Intrinsic motivation to learn a foreign language has been shown to be an important indicator of success. While immersion in a foreign (target) language environment is rarely a realistic option for most learners of English, encounters with native speakers may, at the margins, provided enhanced motivation for some learners.

Howatt and Smith (2014) label the period since 1970 the 'Communicative Period' and suggest that the aim of 'real-life communication' is its core concern. It is easy to see how this can become associated with a preference for NESTs. There may be some correlation between Inner Circle teacher styles in general and those advocated by Communicative Language Teaching (CLT). Correctly or incorrectly, the notion of CLT has become the dominant pedagogical framework in ELT and there appear to be many links between CLT and the beliefs and activities commonly found in the educational experiences of those from Inner Circle countries. From a very broad view, accompanying notions of learner-centredness, individuation and differentiation, experiential learning and task-based 'hands-on' student learning activities are also more prominent features of Inner Circle education compared to most non-Western Outer and Expanding Circle education systems. The feeling that 'traditionalism' in language teaching is less effective (see the distinctions tabled by Lamb and Nunan, 2001) may account for some of the preference for NESTs in ELT.

On the other hand, the relationships that teachers form with students plays a key role in education. Hattie (2009) observes that:

> when students, parents, principals, and teachers were asked about what influences students' achievement, all but the teachers emphasized the relationships between the teachers and the students. (Hattie: 2009: 118)

Cornelius-White (2007, cited in Hattie, 2009: 118) located 119 studies from 355,325 students, 14,851 teachers and 2,439 schools and found a significant correlation across all person-centred teacher variables and student outcomes, particularly in the areas of creative/critical thinking and verbal skills. It is likely, therefore, that managers of NEST schemes need to monitor and measure not only 'in-classroom' teaching attributes but also the success of teachers in building appropriate relationships with their students and the wider community. Effective LETs clearly have advantages in this area as they already share culture and language with their students.

While NESTs may provide some increased motivation for their learners and may have some advantages in teaching communicatively, LETs' abilities to build relationships with their students can easily balance or outperform these advantages. It is likely that focusing on the best teachers for the context is, as always, the best hiring policy.

Greater explication of the character traits and personal attributes of effective English language teachers is needed. Equating 'native-speakerness' with particular personality traits or teaching styles, however, is a flawed approach.

Implication(s) for NEST scheme management:
Interaction skills and enthusiasm play an important role in motivating learners and in improving language performance outcomes.

Performance and pedagogy

The processes of teaching and learning are immensely important. While Hattie's (2009: 108) data indicate that 'neither teacher experience nor teacher qualifications explain much of the variance in teacher effects', it is likely that teacher training and appropriate ongoing professional development play an important role in teachers' classroom performance and effectiveness.

Effective pedagogy has to be mapped to teacher standards with clear performance rubrics; it should involve sound assessment of learning principles, including the use of data in curriculum choices and decision-making as well as differentiation techniques. In short, effective pedagogy in ELT is (no surprise) quite similar to effective pedagogy across the curriculum. ELT may have a more important focus on learner activity and it is here that LETs' performance is occasionally less strong – especially if they come from more teacher-centred backgrounds or hold closely to such beliefs (Watkins, 2000).

The typical model for CfBT school-level programmes has been to select native-speaker teachers possessing experience (usually three or more years) as well as QTS (qualified teacher status) to be English teachers (for secondary) or primary (for younger learners) in their countries of origin. Such qualifications generally include an undergraduate university degree and a one-year postgraduate teacher qualification such as a Postgraduate Certificate of Education or a Diploma of Education or equivalent. These teachers typically have sufficient skills in most areas of school-level teaching and learning, including classroom management, learner administration and language development and enrichment.

Recruited teachers are then offered free or heavily subsidised training in specific ELT qualifications such as Master's degrees in Applied Linguistics, Cambridge ELT Diplomas and Certificates or qualifications for the teaching of English in primary school, which were developed in Brunei. It has become increasingly difficult to use 'off the shelf' courses, so a range of bespoke training programmes and certifications have also been developed.

To build employment opportunities in NEST schemes for Outer Circle teachers there is a need to create a framework of competencies that such teachers must have and, ideally, a series of independent organisations for certification of achievement in these areas. An ideal starting point would be international teaching academies located in particular regions and managed at a regional level (for example, ASEAN for South-East Asia) that would be able to train and certify teachers of English as being of a 'NEST' level in proficiency (C2 CEFR) as well as in particular teaching competencies. These may include relevant knowledge of applied linguistics; ELT methods and materials; cross-cultural issues in teaching and learning; and literacy, numeracy and cognitive development across languages. Classroom management in multilingual and bilingual settings and content and language integration skills could also feature. CfBT is certainly interested in partnering on research and development in this area!

NEST schemes themselves need to broaden hiring criteria where possible to attract highly effective teachers, whatever their country of origin. They also need to ensure that capacity-building and professional pathways exist within the scheme. While native or native-like proficiency will continue to be important hiring criteria, pedagogical skills, personality and professional performance should carry an increased weight in hiring and promotion choices.

Implication(s) for NEST scheme management:
Well-trained, highly effective teachers are likely to have a stronger impact on student learning outcomes than poorly trained or ineffective teachers. Capacity-building and performance management need to be integral to NEST schemes.

Conclusion

NEST schemes have been established across the ELT spectrum, from small-scale short-term volunteer projects with untrained staff to large-scale national programmes lasting for decades. NESTs now work in almost all ELT contexts, and not only with older, specialised or more advanced learners. Age of learners, ability of learners, learner goals, cultural background, linguistic background, teacher pedagogy and a range of social, cultural and political factors all play a role in the degree of impact of any particular NEST or EEST scheme.

The question is no longer 'who is more effective: a NEST or a LET?' (and nor should it have ever been) but rather 'how can the combined resource of NESTs and LETs be best utilised to achieve maximal language and learning outcomes for our beneficiary learners and their societies?'.

Both hope and despair can be self-fulfilling prophecies (Day et al., 2010). As someone who has spent much of his professional life in NEST schemes, I remain hopeful that such schemes have added and will continue to add significant value to education systems around the world as we all struggle with the implications and importance of the growth of English as a global language.

References

Al-Seghayer, K (2013, 29 January) Teach us English but without its cultural values. *Saudi Gazette.*

Antropologi (2011) *Global apartheid: Are you expat or immigrant?* Available online at: www.antropologi.info/blog/anthropology/2011/expats-and-migrants (accessed 23 February 2016).

Asiapundits (2011) Seoul to Sack Native English Teachers; An insider's perspective. Available online at: http://www.asiapundits.com/seoul-to-sack-native-english-teachers-an-insiders-perspective (accessed 10 March 2016).

Auerbach, ER (1993) Re-examining English only in the ESL classroom *TESOL Quarterly* 27/1: 9–32.

Babel, AM (2014) On being a near-native speaker. Society for Linguistic Anthropology. Available online at: https://u.osu.edu/babel.6/files/2014/12/2014-On-Being-a-Near-Native-Speaker-15tnebs.pdf (accessed 23 February 2016).

Bonabente, CL (2007, 6 October) Teachers' English proficiency poor. *Philippine Daily Inquirer.*

Braine, G (2010) *Nonnative speaker English teachers: Research, pedagogy and professional growth.* Oxford: Routledge.

Brown, HD (2000) *Principles of language learning and teaching.* New York, NY: Longman.

CfBT (2003) *English language teacher training in Vietnam*. Available online at: www.educationdevelopmenttrust.com. Printed copies available on request from the Education Development Trust.

CfBT (2004) *Support for language teaching in Afghanistan*. Available online at: www.educationdevelopmenttrust.com. Printed copies available on request from the Education Development Trust.

CfBT (2013) Case study: *English language teaching in Singapore*. Available online at www.educationdevelopmenttrust.com. Printed copies available on request from the Education Development Trust.

Choi, KK (2007) *The language policy issues in Seoul: Hiring native speaker English teachers*. Available online at: http://www.google.com.bn/url?sa=t&rct=j&q=&esrc=s&frm=1&source=web&cd=10&cad=rja&uact=8&ved=0CFAQFjAJ&url=http%3A%2F%2Fwww2.hawaii.edu%2F~cmhiggin%2FFall%25202008%2520courses%2FChoi%2520Lang%2520Policy%2520660.doc&ei=82vcVL_KMILr8AXy-YG4Ag&usg=AFQjCNHC0Dko-IX2nfwPu-TGRnHmrWWQtg&sig2=SxDzpYLr4UJAK5XEDT2edA&bvm=bv.85761416,d.dGc (accessed 23 February 2016).

Clark, D (2012, 26 October) English, the language of global business? *Forbes Magazine*. Available online at: www.forbes.com/sites/dorieclark/2012/10/26/english-the-language-of-global-business/ (accessed 23 February 2016).

Constantine, P (2013, 29 January) Is the JET program really necessary for Japan? *Japan Today*. Available online at: http://www.japantoday.com/category/opinions/view/is-the-jet-program-really-necessary-for-japan (accessed 23 February 2016).

Copland, F, Mann, S, Garton, S with Davis, M (2015) *Investigating NEST schemes around the world: Supporting NEST/LET collaborative practices*. London: The British Council.

Crystal, D (2003) *English as a global language*. Cambridge: Cambridge University Press.

Day, L, Hanson, K, Maltby, J, Proctor, C and Wood, A (2010) Hope uniquely predicts objective academic achievement above intelligence, personality, and previous academic achievement. *Journal of Research in Personality* 44/4: 550–553.

Ford, L (2005, 24 June) S Korea 'more hostile' for foreign staff. *The Guardian*. Available online at: www.theguardian.com/education/2005/jun/24/tefl.lizford (accessed 23 February 2016).

Freire, P (1973) *Education for critical consciousness*. New York, NY: Seabury Press.

Freire, P (1974) *Pedagogy of the oppressed*. New York, NY: Seabury Press.

Halvorson, HG and Tory Higgins, E (2013, March) Do you play to win—or to not lose? *Harvard Business Review*. Available online at: https://hbr.org/2013/03/do-you-play-to-win-or-to-not-lose? (accessed 23 February 2016).

Hartley, M and Walker, C (2014, 7 January) White people with no skill sets wanted in China. *Vice*. Available online at: www.vice.com/read/lazy-and-white-go-teach-in-china (accessed 23 February 2016).

Hattie, J (2009) *Visible learning: A synthesis of over 800 meta-analyses relating to achievement*. London: Routledge.

Hayden, M and Thompson, J (2011) 'Teachers for the international school of the future' in Bates, R (ed) *Schooling internationally: Globalisation, internationalisation and the future for international schools*. Abingdon: Routledge, 83–100.

Hong Kong Education Bureau (2014) *Figures and Statistics*. Available online at: www.edb.gov.hk/en/about-edb/publications-stat/figures/index.html (accessed 23 February 2016).

Howatt, APR and Smith, R (2014) The history of English as a foreign language, from a British and European Perspective. *Language and History* 57/1: 75–95.

Jeon, M and Lee, J (2006) Hiring native-speaking English teachers in East Asian countries. *English Today* 22/4 53 – 58.

Johnston, B (2003) *Values in English language teaching*. Mahwah, NJ: Lawrence Erlbaum Associates.

Kachru, B (1985) 'Standards, codification and sociolinguistic realism: The English language in the Outer Circle' in Quirk, R and Widdowson, HG (eds) *English in the world*. Cambridge: Cambridge University Press, 11–30.

Lamaoureux, E (2009) *Rhetoric in Rome*. Available online at: http://interactivemedia.bradley.edu/ell/rinrome.html (accessed 23 February 2016).

Lamb, C and Nunan, D (2001) 'Managing the learning process' in Hall, DR and Ewings, A (eds) *Innovation in English language teaching*. New York, NY: Routledge, 27–45.

Lattman, P. (2014) The origins of Justice Stewart's 'I know it when I see it'. *Wall Street Journal Online*. Accessed 07 March 2016.

Legislative Council Panel on Education (2005) *Background brief prepared by Legislative Council Secretariat Native-speaking English Teacher Scheme*. Available online at: www.legco.gov.hk/yr04-05/english/panels/ed/papers/ed0711cb2-2167-2e.pdf (accessed 23 February 2016).

Linguistic lust for the world's adulation–'OMG!' (2014, 22 April) *The Malaysian Insider*. Available online at: www.themalaysianinsider.com/sideviews/article/linguistic-lust-for-the-worlds-adulation-omg#sthash.1yHo4ZZL.dpuf (accessed 23 February 2016).

McCrum, R (2010) *Globish: How the English Language became the world's language*. New York, NY: Norton.

McGeown, K (2012, 12 November) The Philippines: The world's budget English teacher. *BBC News*. Available online at: www.bbc.com/news/business-20066890 (accessed 23 February 2016).

Ministry of Education, Malaysia (2013) *CEFR Symposium 2013: Towards language education transformation in Malaysia*, 29–30 October 2013.

Neilson, R (2009) Travellers' tales: *The expatriate English language teacher in the new global culture*. Newcastle Upon Tyne: Cambridge Scholars Publishing.

Nonnative English Speakers in TESOL Interest Section (NNEST-IS) (2015) Available online: http://nnest.moussu.net/ (accessed 23 February 2016).

Oga-Baldwin, W and Nakata, Y (2013) Native vs. non-native teachers: Who is the real model for Japanese elementary school pupils? *The Journal of Asia TEFL* 10/2: 91–113.

Pennycook, A (2001) *Critical applied linguistics: A critical introduction*. Mahwah, NJ: Lawrence Erlbaum Associates.

Piller, I, and Takahashi, K (2006) 'A passion for English: Desire and the language market' in Pavlenko, A (ed) *Bilingual minds*. Clevedon: Multilingual Matters, 59–83.

Pryor, MG, Anderson, D, Toombs, LA and Humphreys, JH (2007) Strategic implementation as a core competency: The 5P's model. *Journal of Management Research* 7/1: 3–17.

Richards, JC (2002) *Methodology in language teaching: An anthology of current practice*. Cambridge: Cambridge University Press.

Sammons, P, Davis, S, Bakkum, L, Hessel, G and Walter, C (2014) *Bilingual education in Brunei: The evolution of the Brunei approach to bilingual education and the role of CfBT in promoting educational change*. CfBT Education Trust. Available online at: http://cdn.cfbt.com/~/media/cfbtcorporate/files/research/2014/r-brunei-full-2014.pdf (accessed 23 February 2016).

Snow, D (1996) *More than a native speaker*. Alexandria, VA: TESOL.

Sparks, D (2004) The looming danger of a two-tiered professional development system. *Phi Delta Kappan* 86/4: 304–306.

Sung, K (2012) 'Critical ELT practices in Asia: A project of possibilities in the era of World Englishes' in Sung, K and Pederson, R (eds) *Critical ELT practices in Asia: Key issues, practices, and possibilities*. Honolulu: University of Hawaii Press, 23–40.

Sutherland, S (2012) *Native and non-native English teachers in the classroom: A re-examination*. Available online at: www.academia.edu/2331022/Sutherland_2012_-_Native_and_Non-native_English_teachers_in_the_classroom (accessed 23 February 2016).

Swan, M (1985). A critical look at the communicative approach. *English Language Teaching Journal* 39/2: 95–101.

Taylor, C (2009) *Interesting Company: CfBT Education Trust since the 1960s.* Reading; CfBT.

Thomson, L (2009) *The personal touch.* Reading: CfBT.

Top dog: The world's language is globish. (2010, 27 May) *The Economist.* Available online at: http://www.economist.com/node/16213950 (accessed 23 February 2016).

Wa-Mbaleka, S (2014) Teaching English to speakers of other languages: The case of the Philippines. *International Journal of Academic Research in Progressive Education and Development* 3/3: 64–78.

Watkins, D (2000) Learning and teaching: A cross-cultural perspective. *School Leadership & Management* 20/2: 161–173.

Williams, E and Williams, A (2007) ESOL and EFL: An unhelpful distinction? A report commissioned by CfBT Education Trust. Reading: CfBT.

8

Native English-Speaking Teachers (NESTs) in Taiwan: policies and practices

Tzu-Bin Lin, Department of Education,
National Taiwan Normal University
Li-Yi Wang, National Institute of Education, Singapore

Introduction

English is the most popular and widely taught foreign language in countries in East Asia, and Taiwan is no exception. In 2003, the Taiwanese government was even planning to make English a semi-official language due to its popularity in this global era. Meanwhile, the low performance of Taiwanese students in international English proficiency tests such as IELTS, TOEFL and TOEIC became a recurring nationwide issue. As a result, the Ministry of Education (MOE) decided to initiate a programme in which NESTs would be brought in to improve the English proficiency of Taiwanese people, especially for those students in remote and disadvantaged areas, a policy that has also been pursued by other Asian countries (Wang and Lin, 2013). This chapter aims to explore the policies and practices involved in introducing NESTs to teach English in lower secondary schools, i.e. junior high schools, in Taiwan and to present NESTs' experiences of working in ELT classrooms in Taiwanese schools.

In order to map out the role played by NESTs in Taiwanese EFL classrooms, it is necessary to look both at policies and at the implementation of NEST recruitment. Based on empirical data including official policies and interviews with NESTs and Non-Native English Speaking Teachers (NNESTs), the study reported here investigated the existing mechanism of introducing NESTs into junior high schools in Taiwan as well as their roles in junior high school classrooms and their relationships with their local colleagues. Schools with NESTs were selected in New Taipei City, which is the biggest city in Taiwan and has a NEST recruitment programme at city level. A total of six cases are investigated in this chapter. This chapter hopes to offer a full picture of NEST recruitment policy and its implementation in Taiwan as well as a preliminary understanding of NESTs' roles and experiences working in the Taiwanese context.

Background

In the field of English language teaching (ELT), the socioeconomics and cultural-political effects of English as a global language have been widely discussed (Block and Cameron, 2002). As Price (2014) pointed out, improving citizens' English competency is regarded in various countries as a means of enhancing a nation's competitiveness in the global economic arena. This argument has been compelling in several East Asian countries, such as Taiwan and South Korea, and English is given a significant role in the language policies in these countries (Nunan, 2003). For example, English is the only compulsory foreign language across various levels of schooling in Taiwan (Chern, 2002). In 2003, the Taiwanese government was even planning to make English as a semi-official language due to its popularity in this global era and its crucial role in maintaining the country's international competitiveness and in serving certain political purposes of the ruling party (Price, op cit; Tsai, 2010).

In 2001, the age at which students started learning English in school was brought down from Grade 7 (ages 12–13) of junior high to Grade 5 (ages 10–11) of primary, and in 2005, it was further lowered to Grade 3 (ages 8–9). However, Taiwanese students' English proficiency subsequently fell and is in the bottom half of all Asian countries, according to the TOEFL result (Educational Testing Service, 2015). The low performance of Taiwanese students in international English proficiency tests such as IELTS, TOEFL and TOEIC became a recurring nationwide issue related to the nation's global competitiveness and domestic education equity (Kuo, 2014; Price, op cit); it has been argued that English competency is a predictor of 'success and upward social mobility' in the Taiwanese context (Chang and Su, 2010: 265). In order to respond to pressure from parents and employers to improve English proficiency among Taiwanese people, the Ministry of Education (MOE) decided to initiate a programme to bring in Native English-Speaking Teachers (NESTs), especially for those students in remote and disadvantaged areas with lower socioeconomic status.

This chapter aims to explore the policies and practices involved in recruiting NESTs to teach English in lower secondary schools, i.e. junior high school, in Taiwan and to present NESTs' experiences of working in ELT classrooms in Taiwanese schools. We place special focus on presenting their reasons for choosing Taiwan, their perceptions of ELT in Taiwan and their relationships with NNESTs. In doing so, we hope to illustrate how the NESTs adapt to a different cultural context and explore their relations with NNESTs.

The context of NEST recruitment policies at both central and local government level is introduced and then a section on data collection is provided. In the third section, interviews with NESTs are analysed based on three themes. Finally, the conclusion presents a summary of the findings and suggestions for future research.

As there are various official NEST recruitment programmes (Wang and Lin, op cit), we hope that the findings of this Taiwanese case study will enrich the literature on NESTs working in different cultural contexts such as Japan, South Korea and Hong Kong. Moreover, we hope that this chapter will be a useful reference for NESTs who would like to work in an unfamiliar cultural context.

Taiwan's NEST recruitment policy: from central to local

In December 2002, the Foreign English Teacher Recruitment Project (FETRP) was announced in accordance with the implementation of the Taiwanese government's six-year national development plan, Challenge 2008, whose major goals included upgrading people's English proficiency (Wang and Lin, op cit) and making English a semi-official language in Taiwan. Although the proposal failed during the legislative process, this did not stop other attempts to improve English proficiency among Taiwanese people. An overarching framework known as English For All now aims at improving the English proficiency for the whole Taiwanese population. Price (op cit: 572) offers a concise account of this framework, emphasising the need to 'cultivate competitive citizens with international foresight' and 'move forward into the new century' in a 'world where national boundaries are disappearing', as well as to enhance 'the international competitive advantage of higher education institutions'.

To some extent, it can be argued that the FETRP is the realisation of the Taiwanese government's attempt to introduce English For All into formal schooling. Its implementation demonstrates that the Taiwanese government wishes to build a bridge between Taiwan and the rest of the world and boost Taiwan's competitiveness by improving the English proficiency of young people (Ministry of Education, 2003). Some of the aims of this programme can be summarised as follows (Ministry of Education, n.d.):

- to offer elementary school English education in the third grade in the 2005 school year
- to give priority consideration to students in remote areas and to narrow the gap in educational equality between city and rural areas
- to promote pedagogical and cultural exchange between domestic and foreign English teachers
- to introduce the first group of Canadian English teachers at the end of 2004
- to give county/city governments powers to recruit foreign English teachers autonomously from 2005.

As a result of this programme, the first group of NESTs started working in Taiwan in 2004, and county and city governments had the power to recruit NESTs from 2005. NESTs recruited through the FETRP were expected to fulfil the following responsibilities (Ministry of Education, 2003):

- to teach English
- to conduct team teaching with Local English Teachers
- to compile ELT materials
- to offer professional development to Local English Teachers.

At the local government level, therefore, two approaches are used to introduce NESTs into local schools: one through local governments and the other through the Ministry of Education (MOE). When county and city governments would like to recruit NESTs by themselves, they have to fulfil the recruitment requirements stated in FETRP by MOE. Local governments need to handle the whole recruitment process; otherwise, local governments can request MOE assistance in NEST recruitment. Under the second method, MOE does the screening, interviewing and all the paperwork and then posts NESTs to various counties and cities. As an example, in New Taipei City, the Education Department applies the first approach. Regarding the criteria for recruiting NESTs in Taiwan, those who would like to apply for the FETRP must be Native English Speakers (NESs) from a limited group of countries identified by MOE, such as the US, the UK, Canada, Australia, New Zealand, Ireland and South Africa. These NESs should have, as a minimum, bachelor's degrees and proper teaching certificates from their native countries. Unlike in other NEST programmes, the preference for NESTs who have basic Mandarin skills is inscribed in the FETRP. Professional training in linguistics-related fields and previous teaching experience are considered a bonus but not required (Ministry of Education, 2003).

The recruitment policies of Taiwan, Japan, Korea and Hong Kong are broadly similar, and, although there are some differences in the roles of the NESTs, there are two responsibilities most schemes have in common: firstly, NESTs have to conduct team teaching with Local English Teachers and, secondly, they have to provide professional development for NNESTs (Wang and Lin, 2013).

Among the four East Asian countries mentioned above, Taiwan sets the strictest selection criteria for NESTs, while offering NESTs the lowest pay and other benefits of the four countries (Wang and Lin, op cit). For example, only native speakers from the US, the UK, Canada, Ireland, South Africa, Australia and New Zealand are accepted as applicants for the FETRP. As a result, the MOE Taiwan was not originally able to recruit enough qualified NESTs and the recruitment target was reduced from 1,000 to around 500 annually. However, this target could still not be met. This unsuccessful recruitment campaign led the MOE to consider hiring NESTs without teaching certificates and experience (Wang and Lin, op cit). The recruitment difficulties encountered by the MOE in Taiwan show that native speakers with professional training and experience are not necessarily interested in coming to Taiwan, where they might face various systematic issues such as having to team teach with local NNESTs and crosscultural adjustment (Chu and Morrison, 2011; Ohtani, 2010). Therefore, the first theme we would like to explore is the reason why NESTs choose to teach in Taiwan under the FETRP given that the criteria and conditions are the least attractive in the East Asian region. Next, we investigate NESTs' perceptions of the teaching and learning environment in Taiwan. The relationships between NESTs' and Local English Teachers (LETs) is the third theme we study. With these three themes, we attempt to map out the experiences of NESTs under the FETRP.

Rationale for choosing New Taipei City

There are two reasons for our choosing New Taipei City: first, it is one of the most populous cities in Taiwan, and, second, it adopts the first approach to NEST recruitment under the FETRP. In contrast, the capital city of Taiwan, Taipei City, has no similar programme. However, NESTS working for New Taipei City are not posted to disadvantaged areas as stated in FETRP by MOE, but to selected schools in mostly urban areas. New Taipei City does not follow the recommendations of MOE because its capacity to support NESTs and to use them effectively has not yet been fully developed. The overall and long-term aim of New Taipei City is to improve students' English proficiency but this cannot be accomplished in a short period of time. The chosen urban schools, therefore, function as pilot schools, or, in their own words, 'seed schools', in order to develop models of how NESTs might function in local schools. Meanwhile, due to the huge demand for NESTs in schools, the New Taipei City government is planning to recruit many more NESTs in the near future.

Remarks on data collection

The data analysed is from semi-structured interviews with six NESTs. The number of NESTs interviewed is one-third of the total number of NESTs working in New Taipei City schools through official recruitment in 2014. Once assigned a post by the city government, these NESTs belong to one school; in other words, they are not peripatetic. Data was collected in December 2014. The interview guidelines, consent form and questions for NESTs were developed and provided by the research team working on a British Council funded project called *Investigating NEST schemes around the world: Supporting NEST/NNEST collaborative practices.* All interviewees read an information sheet and signed the consent forms.

Each interview lasted about 40 to 60 minutes and mainly followed the guiding questions devised by the research team. Some follow-up questions were added when further clarification was needed. All interviews were conducted by Dr Tzu-Bin Lin, one of the authors of this chapter, and digital voice recorders recorded the talk. All interviews were then transcribed by a professional transcriber and verified by the interviewer. Basic information about the six NESTs is presented in Table 1.

Table 1: Basic information about the six NESTs in New Taipei City

Name*	Country of origin	Teaching qualification	Teaching experience	Mandarin skills
Adam	US	Music Education	5 years' EFL teaching in another city in Taiwan	good (can communicate in Mandarin)
Chad	US	Social Studies	6 months' EFL teaching in another city in Taiwan	beginner (understands phrases and some simple sentences)
Frank	US	ESL for elementary students	2 years in other Taiwanese cities	beginner
Brian	US	Special Education	11 years in Special need education in USA	beginner

Vicky	US	Chemistry	12 years in public school in the USA	beginner
Eric	South Africa	English Literature	4 years in other countries	beginner

* All of the NESTs are identified by pseudonyms, except Vicky, who gave consent for her real name to be used.

Reasons for coming to Taiwan

The six NESTs are certified and experienced teachers in their home countries and have different reasons for having come to Taiwan to continue their teaching careers. Interestingly, Taiwan was not the only or first country they considered when they were thinking about taking teaching jobs overseas. Among the six teachers, Adam and Chad shared the experience of having taught in other Asian countries before they came to Taiwan. Adam was initially a contracted teacher in Luoyang, China after he left the US, but decided to give up the position due to several contractual disputes. He then went to Hong Kong intending to find a teaching position but realised the cost of living was too high to maintain a good quality of life. With the help of a family friend who has lived in Taipei for more than ten years, he got acquainted with the Local English Teaching employment market in Taiwan and was offered the current teaching position via a recruiter. Chad had taught English in South Korea for three years before coming to Taiwan.

Unlike Adam and Chad, Frank did not have experience of teaching in other countries. He had once thought about teaching English in Korea or Hong Kong because of the superior payment and benefits, but eventually did not accept any offers due to lack of acquaintances and contractual issues. He later became familiar with the Taiwanese English teaching employment market through a family friend, an American citizen living in Taipei, and found his current position via a local recruiter.

For the other three NESTs, the decision to come to Taiwan was strongly affected by the attraction of an exotic culture. Because of that, Taiwan was not their only focus when they were looking for teaching jobs overseas. Many other Asian countries, such as Korea, Hong Kong and Thailand, were also on these NESTs' shortlists. Brian, for example, knew little about Taiwan before he found himself in this country:

> My initial decision to come to Taiwan really wasn't focused only on Taiwan. Actually, before I came to Taiwan, I am embarrassed to say that I knew little about Taiwan. But as an undergraduate student at Illinois State, I had a roommate from Korea, and I worked with a student in Hong Kong. And through this individual became acquainted somewhat with Asian culture, and I was very impressed with their respect for teachers in general. I also worked as a tutor for a Vietnamese student in Illinois and the student made me curious about what it would be like to teach in an Asian country. Then, about 11 years ago, I was working in a very stressful special education setting and reached the point we had to take a break. I put my resume on the internet, and was contacted by the

recruiter from Taiwan. I talked with this person at length and was interested in coming to Taiwan at that time. They referred me to a consultant for private schools and that was my first opportunity to teach in Taiwan. I accepted it and I came. (Brian)

Also pursuing cultural stimulation, Vicky was initially looking for teaching opportunities in any country with a different culture and was particularly attracted by Korea and Thailand. She eventually decided to come to Taiwan after considering several socioeconomic factors such as economic development, technology infrastructure and pay. Similarly, Eric's decision to come to Taiwan was closely related to his personal interest in language and culture. He eventually chose Taiwan because of his particular interest in Buddhism, thinking that Taiwan was probably 'the best place in the world' to study Buddhism.

Teaching and learning environments

In our interviews, the six NESTs shared positive experiences of teaching English in secondary schools in Taiwan. They also reported a number of challenges that they had encountered in the classrooms and the schools. These positive experiences and challenges were closely related to the culture of teaching and learning as well as to the operational and administrative culture of the schools.

Positive experiences of teaching English in Taiwan

Culture of appreciation for learning
Brian, Chad, Vicky and Frank all mentioned that they felt great respect and appreciation from the students in their schools. They described the students as nice, respectful, wonderful, kind, honourable and responsive learners. Brian pointed out that one thing he admired the most about teaching English in a Taiwanese school was the culture of appreciation for learning:

There is an appreciation for learning in your (Taiwanese) culture that I highly admire. Kids that local teachers consider naughty are very mild compared to experiences I have in my home country, even those naughty kids show me more respect ... The kids are amazing, and the general appreciation for learning in Taiwanese culture is inspiring to me. (Brian)

Supportive collegiality and great flexibility
Among the NESTs, Adam, Chad and Vicky all expressed appreciation for the support they received from colleagues, reporting officers and school leaders in their schools. Adam, for example, showed a high level of job satisfaction, describing his current teaching position as 'the perfect job' for him. This high satisfaction came from supportive colleagues and from the autonomy and flexibility given to him by his school:

Everybody is super lovely and helpful. All the people I work with here want me to be happy. They take the perspective like: 'How would I feel if I was in a foreign country?' You know what I mean? So they put themselves in a very empathetic, put themselves in my shoes, and they address issues cheerfully instead of like 'Oh my god, really? You need me to introduce again or something?' School is *extremely flexible and they really just bend over backwards to make sure I am happy. I do not know that it is like that in every school. I think I am just really lucky. I think I greatly fit in this school. They like my teaching style, and they give me a lot of flexibility to plan my lessons. So really it's like night and day compared to being a teacher in US.* (Adam)

Challenges of teaching English in Taiwan

The six NESTs encountered different kinds of challenges when they worked with local NNESTs, school leaders, administrators and students in their schools. Some of these challenges were related to systematic and operational regulations and others had more to do with teachers' backgrounds/training and students' abilities.

Lack of time spent discussing and collaborating with NNESTs

One big challenge, mentioned by all the NESTs except Chad, was that they always found it hard to ask their NNEST partners to make time to sit down with them to discuss or give feedback on lesson plans. This constraint has greatly restricted the assigned role of NNESTs as collaborators in English classrooms and thus the effect of co-teaching. As Adam explained:

I do not sit down with the local teachers. I do not sit down with them and say: 'Oh, what we are going do for Unit 7 today?' You know what I mean? Like next week, 'What do you think? We do this and this ...' Actually, they do not want me to because they do not have time ... So, the role in the classroom with the local teacher is bound by the restriction of time. You know what I am saying? Because of the nature of the beast, we cannot have a more collaborative role as co-teachers. (Adam)

The impact of time restriction on the roles of NNESTs as collaborators in co-teaching classes was also highlighted by Eric, who believed that co-teaching classes should involve two teachers working together on lessons plans. But he found it impossible to achieve this goal in his school because the NNESTs he collaborated with were always too busy:

When I studied collaborative teaching or team teaching for my teaching certificate, usually it involves two teachers writing a lesson plan together. I know we do not have time. I understand. We do not do that ... I am afraid that most of the Taiwanese teachers are too busy. I am sure we can make time, but actually we just do not make time. I don't want to bother them either. They have so much work. (Eric)

As discussed by Copland et al. (in press) this issue is endemic across various NEST programmes in the world. NESTs in Taiwan are facing a similar issue to their counterparts in other countries.

Heavy teaching load

Another major challenge shared by several of the NESTs, including Adam, Eric and Frank, was their heavy teaching load. In Frank's experience, although he and the NNESTs were in alignment in terms of how they wanted to approach the students in co-teaching classes, it was not possible to carry out these plans due to the classes assigned to him and his NNEST partners:

> That (doing lesson plans together) was what we decided in professional development workshop about co-teaching, and there are some teachers that I get along really well with. We agree about what we should do. But this school has a couple of naughty and low-achieving kids and we want to work with local teachers. So if I work with maybe three NNESTs, we have time to meet with each other. I know you. You know me. We can talk and agree or disagree and get plans. But I have 23 classes a week and work with maybe 15 different teachers. So even though I agree that we should plan together and we should communicate, it is simply not possible. (Frank)

Large student population

For Chad, Vicky and Frank, the large student population in public secondary schools in Taiwan was a huge shock and a challenge. Vicky mentioned that there were 4,000 students in her school and that she would not teach in a school with that kind of population in her home country because 'four thousand kids could be a zoo'. Comments made by Frank also revealed his concern about the pressure of teaching in such a populous school:

> We do not work with as many students in my home state. Maybe I worked with two hundred, or three hundred in my home state, but we know the two hundred students very well. So if we have a problem, we know who the grandmother is, who the childcare worker or policeman is. The most important things are, like, fostering a good attitude toward school, a good attitude towards learning, getting them prepared for college and so on, the things that make teaching valuable to me. I feel like I do not have time in the system with so many students. (Frank)

Obedient school culture

Coming from the US, Frank found it challenging to teach English in his school because of the obedient school culture. He mentioned that, in his school, it seemed important that everyone should follow orders given by the school leaders, which was quite different from the school culture he had been used to back in his home country:

> From a Westerner's perspective, like morally, if you have to say 'no' to your boss to do the right thing for the students, if you need to have a disagreement with other teachers to do what you think is correct, for not just your content teaching but the overall being of a child, you know, this is okay. (Frank)

Inefficient administration culture

Both Brian and Adam raised the subject of the culture shock they felt due to the inefficient administrative culture in their particular schools. The communication between them and the school administrators was slow and inefficient, and this caused them anxiety and frustration. As Adam explained:

> You got a job and you came in the beginning of August, and there was no other teacher there. So, you come in and you sit in the office and I asked them (school

administrators): 'Can I have a copy of the textbook, so I can get started here?'
They replied: 'Oh no, they are not in yet.' So they get the textbook basically the
day teachers come back to school after summer vacation, like three days
before the school week was going to start ... There seems to be this thing in
Taiwanese schools where the attitude about some pending event is, 'We will
deal that when we get to it.' You know what I mean? Or, 'We will cross that bridge
when we get to it'. You know what I mean? ... So, that is sort of challenging to
me. It is like a sort of the initial laid-back attitude about things ... That is a little
bit frustrating to me. (Adam)

Low English proficiency of NNESTs and school leaders
Low English proficiency of local school leaders and NNESTs was also perceived by
Adam, Brian, Eric and Frank as a major challenge to their teaching. According to
Eric, the most difficult thing about teaching English in his school was the language
difference: 'Maybe someone says something, and it comes out the wrong way. Or
you say something, and it is understood incorrectly.' (Eric). Low English
proficiency of school leaders and NNESTs was also identified by Brian as his
'biggest challenge'. He had once tried to give feedback to his school leaders
regarding the lack of time to work with his NNEST partners on lesson plans, but
found it hard to communicate well with the leaders because they did not speak
English. The low English proficiency of some local NNESTs had also caused
confusion and misunderstanding when he tried to collaborate with the NNEST in
the classroom:

Communication is continuing to be a challenge for me. I think that is my biggest
challenge ... There have been times the particular teacher (NNEST) ... Her
English is an obstacle. Many times I talked with her one on one trying to explain
what I am going to try and do in a particular lesson. And when we get in, she
starts translating ... And there have been times when she did that, and the kids
do something kind of contrary to what I want them to do. And the same thing
happens in the lesson plan meetings. Even though more proficient non-native
teachers are in the meeting, I tried to explain what I would like to do and it gets
misinterpreted. (Brian)

Lack of knowledge of students' L1
All the six NESTs, except Adam, said that they spoke little Mandarin. Probably for
that reason, having to communicate with students and not being able to use the
students' mother tongue was regarded by the NESTs as a challenging task for
them, although there were local NNESTs who could play the role of translators in
the classrooms. As Adam put it, 'The challenges are communicating the activity
information to the students without using any Chinese. That is a big challenge'
(Adam).

Wide range of student abilities
Another major challenge that Adam and Vicky faced in the classrooms was the
Taiwanese students' wide-ranging English proficiency. For NESTs like Adam and
Vicky, who did not receive training on differentiated instruction, giving meaningful
instruction to the students was a difficult task:

I teach eighth and ninth grade. I would say that, those students, about ten per cent of them are fairly proficient in English at the level they should be, which would be equivalent to the fourth or fifth grade level in US. And then, about 50 per cent are kind of in the middle, and the other 40 per cent are the low end. So, you have a wide range of learning abilities and styles ... So it is not easy to teach the students. (Adam)

The mixed-ability issue was recently reported by Copland et al. (2014), who point out that mixed-level teaching is a common global phenomenon with young learners. One of their findings is that 'children's knowledge of English may differ because some attend private English language classes outside school' (Copland et al., ibid.: 747). This particular finding may explain what Adam described above. In Taiwan, as in many other Eastern Asian countries, it is common for students to attend tuition centres and have private classes.

Relationships with local NNESTs

In general, the NESTs perceived the NNESTs in their schools as nice, open people and enjoyed working with them. However, while the NESTs had strong professional relationships with the NNESTs in their schools, they reported relatively weak personal relationships with them.

Professional relationships

The NESTs' perceptions of their professional relationships with NNESTs were mainly built upon the various forms of support they gained from the NNESTs inside and outside the classroom. In the classroom, this support was manifested in the different roles that NNESTs played in NEST-led classes. For Adam, Brian, Vicky and Frank, the most significant role that their NNEST partners played in their classes was as translators. For Adam and Eric, the NNESTs also served as monitors. The purpose of having NNESTs in these two roles was to ensure that the NESTs' instructions were comprehensible to the young students and to keep them on task. These two roles are illustrated in Adam's description of his typical class:

Whenever I say objectives to pupils, the local teacher will say them in Chinese. They are doing translation for me. And then, I will go over the specifics of the activity that we are going to do or whatever it is. And if it is the first time we have ever done this activity, the local teacher will give a little extra translation and make sure everybody understands what we are going to do ... And then, once I know the instruction is very good and the activity gets going, I can get up and monitor the other students, walk around. Now during this time, the local teacher (the NNEST) also monitors other students and clarifies the points and things like that. (Adam)

The NNESTs' support as monitors was also highly appreciated by Eric. He found this was important not only in giving guidance to students but also in managing their behaviour so that the lesson could run smoothly, with minimal disruption:

For me, the most important thing is when we are doing group work, it (the NNEST's role) is just to monitor the students and give them some guidance ...

Also, I have some behaviour problems in a couple of the classes. Yeah. The role of NNESTs as monitors helps a lot too. (Eric)

In addition to treating the NNESTs as translators and monitors in their classes, Adam and Vicky both mentioned that they attempted to treat them as 'co-teachers' by trying to involve them as much as possible in classroom activities: 'I will have them play the game with the students or model together with me about what we are going to do' (Adam). However, the other four NESTs did not mention involving NNESTs in classroom tasks as 'the other teacher'.

Lastly, Adam mentioned that he also saw NNESTs as 'facilitators' who were quite helpful to him when he had technical issues with the printers or computers in the office. This kind of support also contributed to Adam's perceptions about his relationships with the NNESTs:

> *I have a really good rapport with all the co-teachers that I worked with. And they will do anything that I ask them to. I will do pretty much anything for them, too. But, like, I have troubles sometimes, like getting the printer to work, my laptop. So if I email the teacher and say: 'Can you print this out for me?' They will be like: 'No problem.'* (Adam)

However, professional relationships between the NESTs and their NNEST partners were not always straightforward: tension between the two groups of teachers could occur. As mentioned earlier in this chapter, one of the major challenges the NESTs faced in the Taiwanese English teaching context was the lack of time to communicate and discuss with NNESTs about lesson plans. This challenge had, in Brian's school, created tension between him and the NNESTs in his school:

> *Last year, I worked with different teachers and we had a little more time for lesson plan meeting and we met regularly ... This year, they just gave me a handout basically that has a semester outline, and I have met some of the local teachers maybe four times since August. Four lesson plan meetings and there is really little discussion about what they'd like me to do ... I sent this year's lesson plan. They did not respond to my emails with my lesson plan ... I perceive some tension and there is little communication this year.* (Brian)

Another potential cause of tension between the NESTs and NNESTs are different beliefs about the teaching methods to be used and the 'value' of English teaching and learning. This tension was perceived by Frank to be destructive to the professional relationship between NESTs and local teachers:

> *People (the recruiter and school administrators) who want us (NESTs) to change the system from system-centred to student-centred methods never told other people (the NNESTs). So I had some difficult arguments with teachers who would say: 'We need to use this workbook.' And I think choosing A, B, C, D (multiple-choice questions) is of very little educational value ... I wish we could have a closer relationship actually.* (Frank)

Personal relationships

Comparatively, the NESTs' personal relationships with their NNEST partners were not as strong as their professional relationships. Although all the NESTs claimed that they had a great personal friendship with their NNEST partners, Adam, Brian, Vicky and Frank admitted that they did not socialise much with the NNESTs in their schools:

> We have a nice friendship. They (the NNESTs) initially helped me with some of my life problems, like getting internet access in my place that kind of thing. Little things. So, occasionally we will go out for hotpot or go to Shi-Da night market, Ler-Hua night market. And actually my girlfriend came here last Chinese New Year, she became really good friends with them ... Then, generally, occasionally, once a year, the principal will have all the teachers to lunch or dinner. Other than that, no, I do not socialize with teachers. (Adam)

Similarly, Brian, Chad and Vicky all mentioned that their personal relationships with the NNESTs in their schools were merely built upon participating in whole-school events such as the Christmas lunch. Brian and Chad shared similar experiences, saying that their personal relationships with NNESTs were limited to school events or formal teacher gatherings:

Brian:	We went to camps. We attend functions of school.
Interviewer:	Okay.
Chad:	We did [school anniversary] celebration together. And sometimes after work I play basketball [with students].
Interviewer:	And then do you socialize with non-native co-teachers outside the classes?
Chad:	I want to do it more. Really.
Brian:	But now, just formal gatherings.

Conclusion

During the interviews, we found that Taiwan was not the first choice of destination for most of the NESTs. China, Hong Kong, Japan and Korea might be more attractive to NESTs in this region. However, the quality of life, cultural elements and the friendliness of the people had enabled most of the NESTs to adapt quite well to Taiwanese society, even though not all of them were able to communicate with local people in Mandarin.

Regarding the ESL teaching and learning environment, the NESTs were highly appreciative of the learning culture among Taiwanese students and the supportive collegiality. They also reported that the flexibility of their schools was a positive experience. Meanwhile, they shared the challenges they were facing in Taiwanese schools. One of their biggest concerns was that they did not have much time to prepare lessons with Local English Teachers if they wanted to. Therefore, there was little real team teaching or collaboration between NESTs and NNESTs in the school context. The local teachers' extensive teaching and administrative duties and the NESTs' heavy teaching load might explain why it was difficult for them to meet up for lesson preparation. Mutual difficulties in communication might also contribute to the issue of lack of collaboration. Furthermore, some NESTs indicated that the English proficiency of some NNESTs and school leaders was low and that NESTs' communication with NNESTs and school leaders was negatively influenced as a result. To some extent, these issues reduce the positive effects of bringing NESTs into schools. In other words, MOE and the local government have not formulated proper contingency plans to deal with emerging issues. Bringing NESTs into schools has benefits but it does not mean that school leaders and NNESTs do not need to prepare or train NNESTs to collaborate better with NESTs. FETRP should be improved before more NESTs are recruited to teach in Taiwanese schools.

As researchers in this field, we are planning further investigations into NESTs' experiences in Taiwan and potentially to draw international comparisons with other East Asian countries. The qualitative approach used in studying NESTs' experiences in Taiwan is still in its infancy. In this chapter, we offer preliminary findings from the first phase of our study. By doing so, we hope to trigger more dialogue, both domestically and internationally.

References

Block, D and Cameron, D (eds) (2002) *Globalization and language teaching.* London: Routledge.

Chang, C and Su, Y (2010) Educational reform in Taiwan: Beliefs about EFL teaching and learning. *The International Journal of Learning* 17/2: 265–277.

Chern, C-L (2002) English language teaching in Taiwan today. *Asia Pacific Journal of Education* 22/2: 97–105.

Chu, CK and Morrison, K (2011) Cross-cultural adjustment of native-speaking English teachers (NETs) in Hong Kong: A factor in attrition and retention. *Educational Studies* 37/4: 481–501.

Copland, F, Garton, S and Burns, A (2014) Challenges in teaching English to young learners: Global perspectives and local realities. *TESOL Quarterly* 48/4: 738–762.

Copland, F, Garton, S and Mann, S (in press) *Investigating NEST schemes around the world: Supporting NEST/LET collaborative practices.* London: British Council.

Educational Testing Service (2015) *Test and score data summary for TOEFL iBT tests and TOEFL PBT tests (January 2014–December 2014 Test Data).* Available online at: www.ets.org/s/toefl/pdf/94227_unlweb.pdf (accessed 23 February 2016).

Kuo, CH (2014, 7 May) Don't downgrade high school students' basic competency. *The China Times.* Available online at: http://focustaiwan.tw/search/201405070031.aspx?q=English competency (accessed 23 February 2016).

Ministry of Education (MOE) (2003) *The report on the foreign English teacher recruitment project*. Taipei, Taiwan: MOE. Available online at: http://mail.nhu.edu.tw/~society/e-j/50/50-12.htm (accessed 23 February 2016).

Ministry of Education (MOE) (n.d.) *Recruitment of teachers of foreign nationality*. Available online at: http://english.moe.gov.tw/ct.asp?xItem=1407&ctNode=502 (accessed 23 February 2016).

Nunan, D (2003) The impact of English as a global language on education policies and practices in the Asia-Pacific region. *TESOL Quarterly* 37/4: 589–613.

Ohtani, C (2010) Problems in the assistant language teacher system and English activity at Japanese public elementary schools. *Educational Perspectives* 43/1&2: 38–45.

Price, G (2014) English for all? Neoliberalism, globalization, and language policy in Taiwan. *Language in Society* 43: 567–589.

Tsai, S-L (2010) Language skills and status attainment in Taiwan. *Journal of Language, Identity, and Education* 9: 229–249.

Wang, L-Y and Lin, T-B (2013) The representation of professionalism in Native English-Speaking Teachers recruitment policies: A comparative study of Hong Kong, Japan, Korea and Taiwan. *English Teaching: Practice and Critique* 12/3: 5–22.

Appendix

NESTs interview guide

Possible interview question	Topic and comments
How long have you been a teacher? What teaching qualifications do you have?	Experience, background and qualifications
Can you tell us about how you applied for x scheme/how you got the job?	Recruitment/application (try to find out details of recruitment criteria and qualifications). Explore why and how they applied for the scheme.
What induction or preparation did you have before you started?	Preparation/induction
Did you have any induction/preparation specifically for teaching in this context?	
What surprised you most when you first started working in this role?	
Can you describe your typical class (if not apparent, check on whether the teacher has own classes or usually team teaches)?	Working patterns (some may teach in more than one institution too)
Tell me about how you plan what is going to happen in the class.	Preparation/planning
In your teaching, what roles does each (team) teacher tend to play?	In-class interaction/roles (spend quite a bit of time probing this question in terms of who does what. Be sensitive and probe how the teacher feels about this division). Power?
Tell me about the relationship between you and the NNESTs.	
Could you describe what languages are used in the classroom and who uses them?	If a NEST – do they have access to L1? How much code-switching/translation goes on between learners and the LETs?
What is the learners' response to you both in the roles you take?	Learner response/attitudes (find out about teacher-learner interaction patterns as well as issues like engagement and discipline).
What do you think works well in the way you run your respective classes/team teaching?	What does the teacher think has been successful? This should lead naturally into the next question and is the SWOT phase of the interview.
If you could change anything about the team-teaching relationship/relationship with the NNEST, what would you change?	How might things be improved? Any changes that would be 'ideal' but perhaps not achievable for some reason? Details of any conflict.

Outside of the ELT classes, what sort of activities or roles do you play in the school?	Look for detail about clubs, contact with other teachers, materials development, talk with other local teachers.
What are the challenges of working in your context? What are the best things about working in your context? Describe your teaching in three words.	
Why do you think the government wants a NEST scheme?	
Do you have much contact with other NESTs?	Information about support and contact with other team-teachers (both NESTs and non-NESTs)
Do you have much contact with other NNESTs?	
What advice would you give to teachers considering this scheme?	A chance to pick up some extra detail about what the teacher thinks is important about managing/getting the best out of such a relationship.
What do you wish you had known before you started the job?	
Overall, how do you feel about the scheme as a whole?	Overall evaluation – pick up any issues to do with the running of the scheme, recruitment policy, support, value to participants.

9

Power, balance and identity: an insight into intercultural team teaching

Jaeyeon Heo, Chungbuk National University, Korea

Introduction

This chapter presents three cases of team teachers (Local English Teachers, or LETs, and Native English-Speaking Teachers, or NESTs) in three different Korean primary schools. All the team teachers experienced conflicts and tension arising from diverse issues, which caused stress and challenges in their working relationships. However, both teachers in each case handled the problems in a variety of ways, which also revealed different power relationships between them. This chapter aims to provide a better understanding of interpersonal relationships between LETs and NESTs, focusing particularly on issues of differences in power. The hope is that such a study might help other team teachers to develop an awareness of how to negotiate the more challenging aspects of relationship in team teaching contexts. In order to do this, I employ critical incident vignettes that incorporate the teachers' voices.

The first section summarises the contextual background in relation to Korean primary English education, EPIK and the three cases of team teachers. After that, I will present three critical incident vignettes with a focus on the perspectives and viewpoints of the team teachers. The final section discusses power and identity in these teaching partnerships in terms of professional, linguistic and contextual factors.

Context

Primary English education in Korea

English teaching was introduced in Korean primary schools for the first time in 1995 as an extracurricular subject for students above third grade (aged ten). It then became a compulsory subject for students from Grades 3–6 in 1997. According to the Ministry of Education, Science and Technology (henceforth MEST, 2009), the purpose of the English curriculum in Korean primary schools is to increase students' interest in English and foster their basic ability to understand English and express themselves in English. More specifically, the goals for learners are:

1. to acquire interest in English

2. to build confidence in the basic use of English

3. to build a foundation for basic communication in English in everyday life

4. to understand foreign customers and cultures through English education.

In addition, an official textbook was introduced to the third and fourth grades in 2001 containing a variety of learning activities and tasks aimed at achieving communicative competence, with an emphasis on developing oral and aural skills in English. However, the problem confronting primary school teachers was they had not received English language teacher training during their college studies before 1997. Consequently, they often felt a great deal of pressure having to take charge of teaching English in their schools. Moreover, while the Teaching English Through English policy has recommended that non-native primary teachers use English as a medium of instruction in the classroom (Kang, 2008; Shin, 2012), a majority of Korean teachers in primary schools were not fully prepared for English instruction in English. Indeed, this recommendation proposed by MEST frustrated many Local English Teachers, since few had the proficiency to meet the demand. In May 2005, as part of a continued effort to facilitate English education, MEST announced a Five Year Plan for English Education Revitalization aimed at facilitating students' English communication ability, strengthening teachers' English ability and constructing an infrastructure of English education. The number of English classes for the third and fourth grades of primary schools increased from one to two English classes per week in 2010, and the fifth and the sixth grades started having three English classes per week from the first semester of 2011. Due to an increase in the number of English classes per week, primary schools need more English teachers to cover these additional classes. More specifically, they planned to place a professional conversation instructor in every primary school by 2012, expand English-Only Classrooms to all schools by 2011 and promote a 'one NEST per school policy' at primary and secondary school levels. In this context, the EPIK scheme has been systematically enhanced since 2007 and its nationwide implementation has had a more significant impact on English classrooms where LETs and NESTs usually work together.

EPIK

EPIK (English Programme in Korea) is a government-funded project to recruit NESTs to teach collaboratively with LETs in Korean primary and secondary schools. It is co-sponsored by MEST and the 17 Korean Provincial (Metropolitan) Offices of Education. EPIK was launched in 1995 with the following aspects of its mission: 'Reinforcing Foreign Language Education' and 'Reinforcing Globalisation Education'. These mission statements were promoted as education reform tasks (EPIK, 2011). In 1995, the project started with 54 NESTs from six countries including Australia, Canada, Ireland, New Zealand, the UK and the US. Its nationwide implementation has been activated more systematically since 2007 and over 10,000 NESTs have successfully completed their duties and returned home. It was reported that more than 9,000 new NESTs were recruited and placed in public schools between 2009 and 2014 by the National Institute for International Education.

Three cases of team teachers

This paper focuses on three pairs of team teachers who were assigned to conduct team-taught lessons in three different Korean primary schools on a regular basis in the 2010 academic year. Individual teachers had varying professional and educational backgrounds (see Table 1) and each team experienced different teaching conditions in schools (e.g. classroom or staffroom, teaching aid facilities, allocated time for classes and the number of team teachers). In these contexts, the teachers had had a variety of experiences in terms of team teaching practice, learning, challenges and relationships with their teaching partners. Individual interviews were conducted in Korean and English for LETs and NESTs respectively, according to the participant teachers' preference. Interview data was collected for over 18 weeks and transcribed in each native language: Korean for LETs and English for NESTs. Later, the LETs' data was translated into English.

Table 1: Three cases of team teachers

Team teacher	Age	Gender	Nationality	Qualification(s) (previous teaching experience)
Case 1				
Jessica	39	F	Korea	BA in General Primary Education 1st teacher's licence in primary school MA in TESOL in Korea TEE Master (more than 15 years)
Matthew	24	M	UK	BA in Health Science in the US Online TEFL course
Case 2				
Mary	29	F	Korea	BA in Korean Language Education 2nd teacher licence in primary school (2 years)
James	29	M	USA	BA in Communication in Greece (1 year)
Case 3				
Rona	25	F	Korea	BA in General Primary Education 1st teacher licence in primary school (6 months)
Kevin	36	M	USA	BA in Management in the US ESL certificate (6 years)

As mentioned earlier, this chapter prioritises participants' voices and so concentrates on views and perspectives from the interview data. In particular, the paper features critical incidents which have been selected from the interview data. Critical incidents provide 'the way we look at the situation' and 'an interpretation of the significance of an event' ((Spencer-Oatey, 2013: 3). The following three critical incident vignettes portray not only the conflicts caused by misunderstandings, discrepancies in opinions and disagreements but also the teachers' different problem-solving processes. The reason for choosing the following three critical incidents is that giving space to a fuller description of one incident enables us to gain an understanding of complicated relationships between team teachers. In addition, the critical incidents present 'a means of enabling teachers to be more aware of the nature of their professional values and problematics' (Tripp, 2011: 17).

Misunderstanding: 'I have no intention of disgracing you.'
Jessica (LET) was a hardworking teacher and usually stayed late at school for teaching preparation. One evening, when Matthew (NEST) entered the staffroom, he saw Jessica working hard. He went over to her and yelled 'Go home!' at Jessica a couple of times. Jessica felt bad and left the room. As of the next day, Jessica did not talk to Matthew and he was confused by her cold attitude because he did not know the reason. Jessica expressed her feelings about this incident as follows:

> I was really really embarrassed and angry at Matthew and felt deeply insulted
> by him (.) how dare a young and inexperienced teacher like Matthew do this! (.)
> after I came back home (.) I felt worse and worse because there were other
> colleagues in that room, in particular (.) junior teachers (.) as I could not accept
> this situation and needed time to calm down (.) I stopped talking with him and
> even did not have any eye contact inside and outside the classroom

As Jessica had a perfectionist personality trait and took great pride in her professional practice, she found it hard to accept Matthew's behaviour towards her. As Jessica seemed to be sensitive to issues of status and competence as a senior teacher, Matthew's act was 'face-threatening' (Brown and Levinson, 1987: 60) to her; that is, she felt that she had lost face publicly, which made her more uncomfortable and embarrassed. Jessica interpreted Matthew's yelling as an insult. However, Matthew explained the reason and his feeling as follows:

> I just worried about her health (around that time, she was diagnosed with a
> serious disease) (.) I tried to make Jessica leave the school and take a rest as
> much as possible after classes (.) I did not imagine my act (yelling) made her
> angry (.) so I did not have any clue (.) why why Jessica had a cold attitude to me
> (.) later I got to know the reason (.) and I was embarrassed at her reaction (.) I
> really really felt bad

Even though his intention was to show concern for her health, Jessica identified his act as an insult and Matthew was embarrassed at the unexpected situation. What was worse, he was very offended at the way she handled this issue without any explanation of the reason. A couple of weeks later, the two teachers had time to talk with each other and solved the problem. This enabled Matthew to develop a fuller understanding of her position and some related issues embedded in Korean school culture (e.g. the hierarchical system, honour and face). Once he understood, he circulated an apology email to all colleagues in the school to gain face for Jessica. Through this conflict, they realised unintentional behaviours or words could lead to more serious misunderstandings, which could harm their relationship. Even though Matthew reflected on this incident as being 'an unpleasant memory' which had given him 'a red face', he commented that his team teaching with Jessica was positive and successful and that they will keep in touch with each other. Interestingly, his teaching performance was evaluated with good feedback in 2011. He became a head teacher to support new NESTs in the district Office of Education and won the Native Teacher of the Year award in 2013.

Discrepancy in discipline: 'Please respect me!'

Mary (LET) and James (NEST) had different perspectives on disciplining students in class. Although I did not witness this incident or argument, it was recounted vividly by each teacher the next day. The following is a composite account summarised from the description from both of the teachers. One day, James saw a girl in class who was not paying attention to him and was scribbling something on the desk with a pen. James warned the girl student not to do it, but she could not understand what he had told her. Even though James gave another warning to the girl, saying 'Don't do it', she did not recognise the seriousness of the situation and kept scribbling. Finally, James became really upset and angry: his face turned red and he yelled at the girl. She was startled by his sudden shouting; she started crying in class and the class became noisy due to this incident. Then Mary soothed the crying girl and handled the situation. After the class, Mary closed the door of an English-Only Classroom and had a big argument with James, yelling at him in anger. James was also angry with Mary, yelling back at her and then leaving the English-Only Classroom. Mary explained the situation and her reasons for being angry with James as follows:

> I was really angry at James' act (.) because we had already discussed the issues related to discipline before (.) I had already advised James not to scold one to one in class (.) especially lower level students (.) who tended to be shy and defensive under his forceful attitude or action (.) even several students in school had some physical (.) psychological or intellectual challenges in learning ability (.) that was why I had advised him to discipline students not individually but as an entire class (.) even though I believed James could have fully understood and accepted this issue (.) an unpleasant incident occurred in class (.)

As Mary thought James was unfamiliar with the primary school context (e.g. students, curriculum and policy), she did not want him to control the students in his arbitrary way. Despite her advice, James persisted with his strict disciplining style, which created problems and a breakdown in their relationship. However, James had some reasons for his strict approach to discipline due to a bad experience, which he explained as follows:

> in this school (.) I had a bad experience (.) a couple of boys the sixth grade students came to me (.) telling something in Korean with a smile (.) so I regarded it as a kind of friendly gesture (.) however (.) when I got to know that the boys

had sworn at me in Korean (.) I was really really shocked and (.) upset with their deceptive attitude towards me (.) I felt some students showed disrespect to me (.) I thought that 'if I am not strict (.) kids will take advantage of me' (.) as I would like to be respected as a teacher (.) like other Korean teachers (.) I tried to manage and control a class in stricter ways (.)

In addition, he complained about the discrepancy between Mary's approach to discipline and his own, arguing as follows:

I think (.) some students misbehave in class they should be disciplined strictly and fairly (.) otherwise it will not be good for the classroom atmosphere (.) the girl could have understood what I said to her because I gave a warning a couple of times (.) but she did not listen to me (.) I felt really bad and annoyed at her (.) and I could not understand why Mary did not intervene in discipline in that situation (.)

James considered that he was being ignored or ill-treated by the girl despite his warning, and that he was also not being respected by his partner, Mary. As Tsai (2007) points out, lack of 'professional respect' between team teachers can impact on their relationships; in the case of Mary and James, neither seemed receptive to disciplining styles different to their own. In addition, the discrepancy in disciplining issues seemed to be caused by their failure to compromise. A couple of hours later, Mary helped the girl to understand the incident, explaining what the problem was and the reason why James had got angry at her at that time. Mary encouraged the girl to apologise to James for her misbehaviour and explained that the girl really had not understood what he had said to her. When the girl apologised to him with the help of Mary's interpretation, James was pleased to receive her apology, shaking hands with the girl. After work, Mary and James had time to talk about their conflict and discussed the discipline issue more seriously. As Carless (2006: 345) points out, team teachers need to be aware of interpersonal 'sensitivity towards their viewpoints and practices, particularly when differences emerge'. Finally, they reached an agreement: Mary promised James that she would manage and control the classroom more actively and strictly than before, and James promised to discipline students as a whole class, with more attention to 'challenged' students who needed additional support. When I observed their classes, I noticed something about their disciplining styles: Mary became much stricter, controlling misbehaved students individually and even making them stand at the back of the classroom, whereas James seemed secure and comfortable, showing less involvement in discipline and simply counting numbers as a warning. After this severe conflict, Mary and James did not have any problems related to discipline and recovered from the temporary breakdown in their relationship. After learning about his bad experience, Mary could understand James' attitude better and became more sensitive to his position as a team teacher. James accepted Mary's advice and tried to find out about students who needed extra support.

Disagreement on an 'open class': 'Do it as usual!'
All novice teachers with less than three years' teaching experience should have regular supervision from senior teachers and a principal in their schools in Korea. This supervision aims to improve a novice teacher's instruction through senior

teachers' classroom observation, feedback and discussion in a face-to-face relationship with a novice teacher. As a novice teacher, Rona (LET) was being supervised for the first time. In her case, team teaching practice with Kevin (NEST) was open to observation and Rona was supervised by a principal and senior teachers. For more than a month, Rona had been stressed, nervous and worried about this open class, and she had made a great effort to prepare for it. Rona wanted to take charge of instruction more than usual and share the teaching of the open class equally with Kevin. However, Kevin did not accept her suggestion because he thought they should present their natural and usual team teaching practice to others. Rona was annoyed at Kevin's lack of consideration for her situation. When she was interviewed before the open class, she had extremely complicated emotions:

> I am extremely nervous and anxious (.) it is the first time for me to be observed and evaluated by senior teachers and a principal (.) while preparing for open class (.) I would like to lead teaching practice (.) and get support from Kevin and we divided instruction into two parts clearly (.) however (.) I got angry at him (.) he always says to me (.) 'don't worry' or 'don't be nervous' (.) 'it will be okay' but I am not okay (.) it did not make me comfortable but annoyed (.)

As she had been asked by the senior teachers and the vice-principal to take a leading position as a LET, Rona encountered a dilemma between their expectations and the actual situation in terms of their normal routines. Rona felt frustrated by Kevin's attitude, feeling that Kevin neither regarded the open class as a serious matter nor cared about Rona's challenges or anxiety. However, Kevin expressed the following principled views about the open class:

> I am not nervous (.) I am used to having one or two classes every semester (.) if you go to another school, they rehearse a lesson (.) it is like the students already know all the material, it is a show, it is not even a class (.) it is a show (.) and I really hate that (.) if I go to the open class, the students have questions and they actually do not one hundred percent understand the material (.) I am much happier because this is actually like a real class (.) if your open class is something they are already very comfortable with, they are not learning anything, they should not call it a class (.) they should call it a show (.) I cannot understand Rona's unusual preparation (.) what we need is to present our actual teaching in class (.) not a show (.)

Kevin was confident and assertive due to his wide experience and professional skills. As he had had several open classes before, he did not see it as a serious issue. In addition, he valued their natural approach to the class and disagreed with Rona's 'radical' changes. Interestingly, Kevin stuck to his principles when his teaching practice was evaluated by the education officers. When I attended their open class with the senior teachers, I was surprised at Rona's more active engagement in teaching, which had not been seen before. Even though they did not take charge of teaching equally, Rona and Kevin jointly instructed a lesson, leading activities separately and sharing roles together. Their open class was successful and both Rona and Kevin were satisfied with their performance. When

Rona was interviewed later, she appeared relaxed and comfortable but still felt sorry about Kevin's intransigent attitude towards her.

Discussion

As illustrated above, each pair of team teachers experienced interpersonal conflicts and solved them in their different ways. These problem-solving processes were closely related to their power relationships. The following section discusses power and identity in these working relationships in relation to professional, linguistic and contextual factors.

Power and identity in team teaching partnerships

Even though equal contributions are essential in team teaching partnerships, there is often inequality in their power relationships and practices (Fujimoto-Adamson, 2005; Wang, 2012). Team teachers have different roles, positions, status and responsibilities in their contexts, and unequal relationships become particularly evident when one of the teachers is less qualified, experienced or capable than the other. Yet inequality in status or in the division of roles between two teachers does not affect the relationship negatively in every case. For example, while team teachers may use forms of co-presentation (e.g. modelling or role play) in their lessons, more experienced and capable teachers are also able to direct their inexperienced team partners through intervention, guidance and support. As Korean schools tend towards a hierarchical, authority-based culture (NIIED, 2012), the power differential of such unequal relationships would usually be regarded as unproblematic. In fact, each of the three pairs of team teachers in the present study displayed different types of power relationships in professional, linguistic and contextual terms, which led not only to power differences between them but also power-sharing relationships adapted to their capabilities and contexts.

Professional power: more experience, more power

Each pair of team teachers had different professional backgrounds and qualifications, and it was largely these differences that affected their interactions and relationships, particularly in terms of the allocation of roles. The more experienced and skilful teachers took a leading position in terms of controlling the direction of lessons and lesson guidance as a whole, taking on more responsibilities than their novice partner teachers. For example, Jessica (LET) strongly encouraged Matthew (NEST) to prepare lessons fully and gave him comments or feedback after checking his lesson plans, whereupon he mostly followed her suggestions and advice. Matthew's comments on the process of creating lesson plans with Jessica are presented in the extract below:

> I give it to her (.) she goes 'I like this I like this (.) don't like this (.) like this like this' and we discuss the parts that are on that (.) that she doesn't like (.) then we quickly talk about it and make a decision what to do (.) and then I correct the lesson plan and that should be the final lesson plan (.)

Interestingly, Matthew was always seen to wear smart shirts and formal trousers, whereas the other NESTs that I met usually dressed casually in blue jeans and T-shirts. I found out the reason for this while having an interview with Jessica. After commenting on Matthew's formal attire, Jessica said the following:

on the first day in the first semester (.) I asked him to wear formal clothes except for sports days in school (.) maybe other native colleagues told him (.) 'it's too formal' (.) so he asked me the reason (.) I answered 'it's better for you' and he agreed with me (.) I think we need to be well presented to the students as a teacher (.) he looks neat and professional all the time (.) I think it is a right decision (.)

Jessica seemed proud of him, expressing satisfaction at his formal style and her decision. She played a critical role as a trainer and 'mentor', and Matthew was like a trainee or 'apprentice' in many respects (Richards and Farrell, 2005: 162). Even though Matthew felt it wasn't always easy to meet Jessica's requests, he tended to follow her decisions as much as possible. He reflected that '(.) as I did not have any teaching experience (.) it was to my advantage to look like a professional teacher'. In addition, their power relationship was clearly revealed when they encountered conflicts. As mentioned before, Matthew was likely to accept and comply with what Jessica wanted to do or decided to do. Jessica also tried to maintain a good relationship with Matthew, saying that '(.) I try to respect him as much as I can and pay much attention to saying "thank you" as he loves that expression so much'.

Kevin (NEST) was also professionally more powerful than Rona (LET) inside and outside the classroom. In addition to his professional background, Kevin had worked in that particular school longer than Rona had, so she could not help being largely reliant on him. Even though Kevin did not administer strict guidance in the way that Jessica did, he tended to push Rona to follow his instructions. Whenever they had to make a decision, and particularly when they had a disagreement, Kevin tended to insist strongly on his opinions and Rona was generally receptive to his ideas and suggestions. As described earlier in this chapter, their problem-solving process and its results reflected their unequal power relationship as well. Although there was evidence that Rona was engaging more actively in instruction in the open class than she had previously, Kevin stubbornly maintained his stance and it was Rona who backed down. After the open class, Rona received comments from a senior supervisor advising her to take more of a leading role rather than mainly supporting Kevin. The senior supervisor raised the issue of their unequal division of roles, with Kevin acting as the main teacher and Rona in an assistant-like role. However, Rona seemed unwilling to take a more dominant position, saying '(.) how can I deal with it? I am not in a position to argue my ideas with him because he is much better than I in many ways'. She seemed to believe that Kevin would make better decisions about coordinating the teaching. Due to Rona's lack of confidence as a teacher, she and Kevin had a more imbalanced power relationship than the other pairs of team teachers.

Linguistic power: English and Korean

Two of the pairs of team teachers (Jessica and Matthew, and Mary and James) usually taught every lesson in English and communicated with each other in English inside and outside the classroom. However, Rona had more difficulties in relation to English proficiency than the other LETs. Mann and Tang (2012) argue that non-native novice teachers of English face additional challenges in terms of their linguistic competence. As a novice teacher, Rona was afraid to communicate with Kevin in English, mainly due to low self-confidence resulting from low English proficiency. Whenever she had to deliver notices or information to Kevin, Rona was stressed by her limited fluency in English, admitting that '(.) whenever Kevin asks me to help his matters (.) I become nervous and need to look up unfamiliar words in a dictionary'. Moreover, Rona even felt uncomfortable when Kevin came to chat to her after class on one occasion. Rona was negatively affected by her English competence and seemed to struggle to establish a close relationship with Kevin. Kevin understood some of the challenges that LETs faced:

> a few Korean teachers enjoy teaching English but many of them really hate it (.) and I understand why (.) it's a difficult thing to teach a language you're not a hundred percent comfortable with (.) it's a difficult thing to do (.)

Through his previous working experience with other Korean primary school teachers, Kevin recognised that some Korean teachers were not willing to take charge of English subject teaching due to lack of English competence. However, Kevin emphasised the need for English teachers to have a high level of competence in English:

> some of our advanced students can speak much much better (.) now I know a couple of them actually lived in other countries and that is fine (.) English teachers must be the best speaker in the classroom (.) English teacher should be able to speak better than almost every student in the entire school

Although LETs Jessica and Mary could communicate fluently with their partners in English, they felt that their English proficiency was not high enough to allow them to express whatever they wanted without restriction. Moreover, they taught lessons in English by using code-switching when it was necessary, but they still wanted to improve their fluency in both spoken and written English. Interestingly, the NESTs stated that there was no language barrier when they communicated with their LETs in English. However, three of the LETs were neither fully satisfied with nor self-confident in their English proficiency as English teachers. Even Jessica, a veteran teacher who had a TEE (Teaching English in English) Master certificate and a Master's degree in TESOL, felt the burden of TETE (Teaching English Through English). She self-assessed her English proficiency as insufficient, saying:

> I still feel less confident in my ability to correct students' writing or to talk about diverse current affairs with Matthew (.) without a native English speaking partner I will have more challenges to teach English in English and need more preparation and time for teaching.

The comments above show the gaps between 'the English teachers' self-assessed language proficiency' and 'the desired proficiency' she believes would enable her to teach English in primary schools (Butler et al., 2004: 245). Jessica and Mary regarded the NESTs as a good linguistic resource as well as an English tutor to them. Miyazato (2009) describes LETs in Japan as being 'linguistically powerless' in the target language whereas NESTs are 'linguistically and socio-culturally powerful' in the target language. The LETs described in this chapter were often observed to receive English language support from their NESTs inside and outside the classroom (e.g. with NESTs providing unfamiliar expressions or vocabulary, correcting students' writing, proofreading and revising PowerPoint slides or official documents). Even though they did not have a strong belief in the superiority of the native speaker, the LETs' perceived deficiency in English led to a lack of confidence, which influenced their power relationship with the NESTs. Jessica mentioned that '(.) I think a native English speaking person is better than I in terms of English capability regardless of his/her background'. In addition, as Korean society has built strong public faith in 'native speakers' or 'native-speakerism' (Park 2008: 148), the LETs sometimes encountered this issue. For example, Jessica mentioned the 'Matt Effect', which had a significant impact on the students' responses and attitudes in class. Compared to her solo teaching classes, she found that the students were more active and excited in team teaching classes. With regard to parents' expectations, Mary observed their preference for NESTs as follows:

> when we organise an English camp during a vacation, we have to put a native speaking teacher's name on the name list of tutors (.) otherwise, parents and students are less interested in or insecure about the camp programmes

As for Korean, Kevin was the only NEST that could speak in Korean when explaining grammar or vocabulary or disciplining students in the classroom. Kevin stated the reasons for his speaking Korean during a lesson as follows:

> even though I don't have to speak with the students in Korean in the classroom (.) I have to learn some Korean (.) if they see that I understand the problem ... you know what they're trying to do (.) and they see what I'm trying to do (.) what they have to do and they appreciate that (.) and they behave better if I can understand some of what they say (.) it's helpful

Kevin used simple Korean to enhance students' understanding, to handle classroom management and to encourage lower-level students in the class. In particular, when some students came to chat with him before or after class, Kevin often responded to them in simple Korean, e.g. *ahni* ('no'), *bbalribbalri* ('hurry up') and *molrayo* ('I don't know'). Consequently, Kevin had a closer relationship with the students and he was relatively less reliant on the (L1) language support and classroom management provided by his Korean partner. This is undoubtedly one of the reasons why Kevin seemed more dominant and independent and needed limited help from Rona.

The EPIK scheme and policy clearly stipulate NESTs' duties and regulations, giving an overview of their roles and responsibilities. In particular, EPIK refers explicitly to a NEST as a 'GET' (Guest English Teacher) (NIIED, op cit). Like AETs (Assistant English Teachers) in the JET programme in Japan, GETs in EPIK mean NESTs are not permanent teachers but temporary ones – in other words, guests. According to Miyazato (op cit), as NESTs are treated as special guests, they remain politically weak in the educational system; that is, they have the status of foreign visitors, in contrast to LETs. Indeed, the NESTs described in this paper were on a one-year contract. As for Kevin, he had renewed a contract every year for the last four years in accordance with scheme regulations. Even though NESTs' contracts are renewed through the mutual written agreement of the school, the Metropolitan

Offices of Education and the NESTs, the renewal of working contracts is mainly decided by the Korean team teachers through performance evaluation. For instance, LETs Mary and Rona managed administrative work for their respective NEST team teachers, James and Kevin. In addition to providing living support in areas such as housing, bills, payment and visa issues, one of their important roles as LETs was to evaluate their team partners and report on their performance. Therefore, Mary and Rona were evaluators as well as team partners to James and Kevin. Mary explained that the inconsistency between the two roles could sometimes be difficult:

> sometimes I feel my role as a team teacher contradicts that of administrative work (.) when we organise a lesson, I am a co-worker to him so we need to discuss any matters with each other (.) but while doing administrative work, I am like an administrator not a team partner (.) these days I feel I become more like an administrator and James tries to read my mind (.)

As described above, Mary felt uncomfortable about having two different roles with regard to James. Tsai (op cit) points out that LETs taking charge of evaluating their native team teachers creates a critical hindrance to the development of desirable relationships. That is because they do not have a team teacher relationship but rather an evaluator–evaluatee relationship, which highlights the inequality between them.

Rona submitted her reference and evaluative report on Kevin's teaching performance to the district office of education and, as a result, Kevin was recognised as an excellent NEST and awarded a prize for successful teaching performance, largely on the strength of Rona's supportive letter. Positive evaluative reports can determine whether NESTs' contracts are renewed as well as their promotions and salary increases. However, Rona mentioned that '(.) Kevin deserves achieving a prize but it is annoying paper work for me'. Even though she was pleased with the good result, she regarded the evaluation process, including completing officially formatted documents, as additional workload. Jessica did not involve herself in assessing Matthew's teaching performance and, by not participating in evaluative work, she felt she was relieved from the burden of a potential challenge in their relationship. Mary and Rona had to manage two different and conflicting role relationships, which influenced their interpersonal relationships with their native team partners in positive or negative ways. The evaluative role of the LETs makes them politically more powerful than their NESTs. Such an asymmetric power relationship in the educational system and the scheme damages the opportunity for mutual trust and an honest relationship to develop between the two teachers.

Power issues are often negatively associated with domination, control, authoritarianism or unequal vertical relations. Yet with both team teachers having the upper hand in different aspects of their partnership, this might enable them to redress the balance of power and to have 'flexible equality' (Sturman 1992: 160) in their roles and responsibilities. As Mann (2005) states, symmetrical (peer) relationships in team teaching do not always guarantee success. Each team teacher pairing can experience a diversity of challenges, problem-solving processes and power differences in their contexts. Therefore, team teachers need to be sensitive to possible challenging issues of relationship management with their team partners and find ways to negotiate and mitigate tension and conflicts in an unequal working relationship.

Suggestions for team teachers

On the basis of the discussion above, this chapter proposes some practical implications for NEST schemes, schools and team teachers in EFL contexts. First of all, along with enhancing LETs' pre-service and continuing professional development, it is necessary to recruit well-qualified NESTs. For example, NIIED has recently enhanced the recruitment system to ensure that EPIK applicants are selected thoroughly and with appropriate standards. In a significant policy change in force as of the autumn of 2015 (EPIK, 2015), TEFL/TESOL/CELTA certificates are now mandatory for any applicant who does not have one of the following: a Bachelor's degree in Education; Master's degree in Education; a Major in an Education field; a Teacher's Licence; or one year of TaLK experience. It is potentially helpful for LETs to implement team teaching with well-qualified NESTs. Secondly, it would be necessary to systematically develop in-service training for both LETs and NESTs with a focus on team teaching. As team teaching needs two teachers who share responsibilities, it would be desirable to train the two teachers together at the start of a new term or during a vacation. Regular in-service training should be designed for and provided to team teachers to promote their learning and professional development through interacting with team parttners and creating a network of other LETs and NESTs with whom to exchange ideas and find solutions to the challenges of team teaching. In pre- and in-service training programmes, LETs and NESTs should be trained both separately and jointly (Park, 2008) and well prepared for team teaching with a better understanding of their partner (or potential partners), learners, curriculum, materials and teaching contexts. Thirdly, it is necessary for team teachers to maintain a good relationship with each other in order to foster teacher collaboration. As mentioned earlier, interpersonal factors play a critical role in relationship-building or rapport management between team teachers in intercultural team teaching. In particular, when team teachers have a diversity of conflicts and tensions with their partner, the way they communicate with each other and work out possible solutions together could develop or hinder their relationship. Team teachers need to know their partners, understand individual and cultural differences and have an open mind in order to communicate with each other. Thus, individual team teachers should be aware of the need to develop interpersonal skills and sensitivities, such as 'willingness to compromise', 'empathy for the views of the partner' (Carless and Walker, 2006: 473) and 'professional respect' (Tsai, op cit: 188).

Conclusion

As emphasised by Eisen (2000: 9), 'no two teams are exactly alike because they operate along a continuum representing countless variations in goals, team membership and members' relationships'. Consequently, team teachers need to explore, create and develop their own team strategy appropriate for their teaching conditions and contexts. A team strategy based on mutual understanding and agreement enables both teachers to operate not only their team teaching but also their relationship management effectively and harmoniously. To do this, team teachers need to be aware of problematic issues or constraints which they confront in their situations, discuss them with their team partners with an open mind and diagnose issues connected with their teaching practice by themselves. Along with support from outside the school, teachers ultimately need to be proactive in changing, learning and developing their team teaching skills and professionalism as English teachers. Furthermore, there should be communication between the participants involved in NEST schemes (scheme administrators, recruiters, policy makers, trainers, educators, team teachers, etc.) in order to improve the current scheme and teaching practice.

References

Brown, P and Levinson, C (1987) *Politeness: Some universals in language usage.* Cambridge: Cambridge University Press.

Butler, DL, Novak Lauscher, H, Jarvis-Selinger, S and Beckingham, B (2004) Collaboration and self-regulation in teachers' professional development. *Teaching and Teacher Education* 20: 435–455.

Carless, D (2004) *JET and EPIK: Comparative perspective.* Paper presented at the KOTESOL Conference, October 2004, Busan, Korea.

Carless, D and Walker, E (2006) Effective team teaching between Local and Native-Speaking English Teachers. *Language and Education* 20/6: 463–477.

Eisen, J (2000) The many faces of team teaching and learning: An overview. *New Directions for Adult and Continuing Education* 87: 5–14.

EPIK (English Programme in Korea) (2011, 15 November) Retrieved from http://www.epik.go.kr/contents.do?contentsNo=84&menuNo=334

EPIK Policy Changes Fall 2015 (2015, 30 January) Retrieved from http://www.epik.go.kr/board.do?menuNo=271&boardConfigNo=77&action=view&boardNo=1673

Fujimoto-Adamson, N (2005) A comparison of the roles of two teachers in a team teaching classroom in a Japanese junior high school. *The Journal of Asia TEFL* 2/1: 75–101.

Kang, D (2008) The classroom language use of a Korean elementary school EFL teacher: Another look at TETE. *System* 36: 214–226.

Mann, S (2005) The language teacher's development. *Language Teaching* 38/3: 103–118.

Mann, S and Tang, H (2012) The role of mentoring in supporting novice English language teachers in Hong Kong. *TESOL Quarterly* 46/3: 472–495.

Ministry of Education, Science and Technology. (2009) *Policies on reforms to English education in Korea.* School Policy Sector. Seoul: MEST.

Miyazato, K (2009) Power-sharing between NS and NNS teachers: Linguistically powerful AETs vs. culturally powerful JTEs. *JALT Journal* 31/1: 35–62.

National Institute for International Education (NIIED) (2012) Available online at: www.niied.go.kr (accessed 23 February 2016).

Park, J (2008) EPIK and NEST-NNEST Collaboration in Korea Revisited. *English language & Literature Teaching,* 14(4): 141–160.

Richards, JC and Farrell, T (2005) *Professional development for language teachers: Strategies for teacher learning.* New York, NY: Cambridge University Press.

Shin, SK (2012) 'It Cannot Be Done Alone?': The Socialization of Novice English Teachers in South Korea. *TESOL Quarterly* 46/3: 542–567.

Spencer-Oatey, H (2013) Critical incidents. A compilation of quotations for the intercultural field. *GlobalPAD Core Concepts.* Available at GlobalPAD Open House on http://go.warwick.ac.uk/globalpadintercultural

Sturman, P (1992) 'Team teaching: A case study from Japan' in Nunan, D (ed) *Collaborative language learning and teaching.* New York, NY: Cambridge University Press, 141–161.

Tripp, D (2011) *Critical incidents in teaching (Classic Edition): Developing professional judgement.* Hoboken, NJ: Taylor & Francis.

Tsai, JM (2007) *Team teaching and teachers' professional learning: case studies of collaboration between foreign and Taiwanese English teachers in Taiwanese elementary schools.* Unpublished PhD thesis, The Ohio State University, USA.

Wang, LY (2012) Preparing NESTs and NNESTs for team teaching at the pre-service level. *Studies in Literature and Language* 4/1: 32–37.

10

Managing relations in cross-national team teaching pairs: insights from rapport-sensitive incidents

Trần Thị Minh Khánh, Nha Trang University, Vietnam
Helen Spencer-Oatey, Centre for Applied Linguistics, University of Warwick, UK

Introduction

Research has shown that team teaching between Native English-Speaking Teachers (NESTs) and Local English Teachers (LETs) has numerous benefits, including helping create a more authentic English language environment, improving students' English competence and promoting teachers' personal and professional development (Sturman, 1992; Tajino and Walker, 1998; Lai, 1999; Carless, 2002; Gorsuch, 2002; Carless and Walker, 2006). Yet previous studies have also revealed that many difficulties can occur between teachers in team teaching, such as cultural conflicts (Carless, 2002); communication breakdowns (Moote, 2003 in Carless, 2006); and lack of shared understanding and philosophies (Storey et al., 2001 in Carless and Walker, op cit). According to Carless (2006: 345), intercultural team teaching is particularly challenging because 'it requires a lot of enabling features', including pedagogic, logistical and interpersonal elements. This chapter focuses on this intercultural component and explores it by analysing 'rapport-sensitive incidents' obtained through case study research.

The chapter starts with a review of earlier work on NEST and LET team teaching, paying particular attention to the interpersonal challenges that team teachers have experienced. It then describes how data was collected over the course of a semester from three Vietnamese and NEST team teaching pairs working at two Vietnamese tertiary institutions. The aim was to explore how their working relationship developed over time. In this chapter, we focus on a number of 'rapport-sensitive incidents' that they reported, notably those that seemed to stem primarily from cultural differences. We use the term 'rapport-sensitive incidents' to refer to problematic situations and events in which one or both of the teachers felt annoyed, confused or face-threatened because of unexpected behaviour or events in their interactions with their team teaching partner (Spencer-Oatey, 2002). We describe and analyse the incidents from the perspectives of each of the participants, commenting on the impact each of the incidents had on the pairs' classroom team teaching and/or on their relationship. The chapter ends by considering the implications of the findings for the training of team teachers, especially for those who engage in cross-national team teaching.

Previous work on NEST and LET team teaching
Some background information

In the field of foreign language education, team teaching is typically arranged by pairing local and foreign teachers as an intercultural team to teach EFL students (Chen and Cheng, 2010). This kind of collaboration first became a popular teaching approach within the Japanese Exchange Teaching (JET) programme and then in EFL classes in Korea with the EPIK (English Program in Korea) and Hong Kong (Native-speaking English Teachers Scheme). The schemes have various aims, including improving the English proficiency of local students and teachers, changing English teaching methodology, developing cultural exchanges and facilitating integration. Accordingly, a variety of studies have been undertaken, primarily in these countries, in order to investigate how team teaching has been executed and its impact on the teachers and students as well as factors influencing team teaching success (e.g. Crooks, 2001; Gorsuch, op cit; Hasegawa, 2008). In particular, much has been written about the issues of how it is beneficial in terms of creating an authentic English language environment, improving students' English competence and promoting teachers' personal and professional development (Sturman, op cit; Tajino and Walker, op cit; Lai, op cit; Carless, 2002). On the other hand, there have been widespread reports on the numerous challenges that EFL team teachers have faced, including insufficient time for lesson preparation and the English proficiency level of local teachers (Kachi and Lee, 2001); role ambiguity (Tajino and Walker, op cit; Mahoney, 2004); lack of professionalism (Choi, 2001; Hasegawa, op cit); and lack of shared understanding or common teaching philosophy (Storey et al., op cit in Carless and Walker, op cit).

More recently, another aspect that has attracted the attention of team teaching researchers is the relationship between teachers as 'key to the efficacy of its practice' (Mastropieri et al. in Thielemann, 2011: 5). If teachers are to develop good relations, they need to devote adequate time and attention to working collaboratively with each other as well as to building their interpersonal relationship. Several studies have shown that, when they do this, positive experiences result (e.g. Carless, 2006; Carless and Walker, op cit; Dormer, 2006; Lee, 2009). However, studies have also revealed that if they do not, negative issues can develop in terms of cultural conflicts (Carless, 2002), communication breakdowns (Moote, op cit in Carless, 2006) and lack of shared understanding and philosophies (Storey et al., op cit in Carless and Walker, op cit).

Clearly, these interpersonal difficulties can prevent teachers from achieving their professional goals as well as from maintaining harmonious relationships. It is extremely important, therefore, for us to gain a good understanding of the nature of these difficulties and so the following section reports some empirical studies that identify interpersonal challenges (i.e. challenges from a relationship point of view) that teachers have encountered in their team teaching practices.

Interpersonal challenges of team teaching

In spite of the many beneficial elements that team teaching schemes bring for both teachers and students, empirical studies in Japan, Korea and Hong Kong have also revealed a number of problems and challenges, many of which are associated with the team teachers' process of collaboration. For instance, in Japan, JETs (Japanese English Teachers) and NETs (Native English Teachers) were found to face numerous difficulties in their collaborative interactions, such as lack of joint preparation time (Sturman, op cit; Kachi and Lee, op cit; Moote, op cit); confusion over each other's roles and responsibilities (Tajino and Walker, op cit; Mahoney, op cit); and communication problems. These problematic issues are presented in more detail below.

The challenge of time constraints has been reported in Kachi and Lee's (op cit) interview research of two Local English Teachers (LETs) and three American Language Teachers (ALTs) on the JET programme. In particular, the LETs were found to have very busy schedules, with insufficient time for joint lesson preparation with the ALTs. As a result, ALTs felt that they were treated more as visitors than as insiders in the Japanese educational system. This suggests that when two teachers do not spend sufficient time working closely with each other or engaging in ongoing communication, their team teaching relationship tends to be problematic. This might lead to another issue – team teachers' uncertainty regarding their mutual roles and responsibilities or how to carry them out as their teaching partner expects. This is what Mahoney (op cit) reported after conducting a large-scale study with the use of open-ended questions to collect data from 1,400 teachers from all over Japan. In particular, the LETs and ALTs had totally different perceptions of what duties they were expected to undertake and felt uncertain about whether or not they were fulfilling their roles adequately. In addition, Mahoney pointed out that teacher-related conflicts arising from confusion over roles were quite common. In fact, the role conflict typically happened when what the teachers thought they were supposed to be doing was not congruent with what they found themselves doing in reality (Mahoney, op cit: 225). As a result, many ALTs felt unhappy when they perceived that they were being treated by LETs as a 'human tape recorder' rather than as a real teacher (Tanabe, 1990 in Tajino and Tajino, 2000; Mahoney, op cit).

In line with Mahoney (ibid.), Ogawa (2011) has more recently maintained that ALTs often do not have a clear understanding of their duties, and that, as a result, some of these duties are not implemented. She further comments on the role ambiguity of both LETs and ALTs: saying that LETs 'sometimes do not know how to effectively make use of the ALTs and conversely, ALTs do not know what to do to meet the LETs' expectations' (ibid.: 474).

Another major challenge for intercultural team teaching pairs, experienced by a few LETs and NESTs and identified in Moote's (op cit) interview study, was communication problems. The reasons for these related to differences in communication styles and lack of ability in each other's native languages.

Other studies have found minimal levels of collaborative working. For example, in an investigation based on Storey et al.'s (op cit) study of teacher collaboration in Hong Kong secondary classes, Carless and Walker (op cit: 465) report that they did not work closely with each other and that there was 'a lack of genuine collaboration' between NESTs and LETs. As a result, there was little mutual understanding and sharing between the team teachers. In particular, there were some tensions in their educational philosophies and practices, such that they could not find a common voice in the practice of their team teaching. For example, the NESTs reported that the LETs' teaching approach was more textbook-based and focused on correcting the students' errors. In addition, they thought that it would be more useful to spend time on helping the LETs with their professional development rather than spending a great deal of time on extensive testing and marking, as the LETs usually wanted them to do (ibid.).

Carless (2002) also found such issues in Korea. He describes many different problems between the EPIK teachers and Local Teachers in their cooperation, including:

- cultural conflicts between NESTs and Korean LETs

- difficulties in cooperation for team teaching e.g. struggling to find time to plan together; reluctance on the part of some LETs to team teach with a NEST

- lack of understanding of the rationale and practice of team teaching.

As can be seen, a number of issues emerge repeatedly, but the cultural conflicts are particularly worth noticing here, as they could be a significant source of challenge in several respects. When team teachers come from different countries, they can potentially hold different values, beliefs and teaching philosophies as well as having preferences for different teaching methods and working styles. However, the impact of such cultural differences on the relationship between team teaching pairs has rarely been explored in detail. This chapter reports a study that has included this focus and takes a preliminary step in addressing this need. First, though, we explain briefly our stance on the concept of culture.

Conceptualising culture

There are numerous definitions of culture, but in this study we use that of Spencer-Oatey (2008: 3):

> Culture is a fuzzy set of basic assumptions and values, orientations to life, beliefs, policies, procedures and behavioural conventions that are shared by a group of people, and that influence (but do not determine) each member's behaviour and his/her interpretations of the 'meaning' of other people's behaviour.

In line with this definition, the American Council on the Teaching of Foreign Languages (ACTFL, n.d) conceptualises culture in its World-Readiness Standards for Learning Languages in terms of Products, Practices and Perspectives, a line that Moran (2001) takes up. *Products* are the 'concrete' or 'codified' aspects of culture, which, in this case study, could include the teaching timetable and the facilities in the classroom. *Practices* are the patterns of behaviour that we display, or desire, and include our patterns of speaking and our preferences for particular styles of interaction or classroom management. They typically reflect the rules, conventions and norms of the social group in which we are interacting, and they influence how we handle our cultural products, such as how we arrange the furniture in the classroom. *Perspectives* are the deep-seated and often unconscious attitudes, values and beliefs that we hold about life and our profession, such as respect for authority, the need for modesty and assumptions about time management.

There are many different perspectives and almost infinite numbers of practices. Each influences the other, but often without our awareness. As a result, if people's preferred/habitual practices and perspectives are different, misunderstandings, misperceptions and misattributions can result and relationship problems can develop. Thus, familiarity with cultural products, practices and perspectives, and their interrelationships, are important and, for this reason, they are named as such in the World-Readiness Standards for Learning Languages developed by the American Council on the Teaching of Foreign Languages. We take that approach to culture in this chapter.

The study design
The site and teacher participants
Our study was carried out at two Vietnamese tertiary institutions with the participation of three teaching pairs. The LETs were local Vietnamese English teachers who had been trained in TESOL/TEFL and who had worked long term in this context, while the NESTs were foreign volunteers coming to the university and college on a short-term visit from the US and Australia. As part of a broader study, we collected a wide range of data on a longitudinal case study basis and analysed it from different perspectives. For the purposes of this chapter, we focus on the rapport-sensitive incidents that occurred for the three team teaching pairs. More details about the pairs are presented below.

Ron and Dao
Ron was an American volunteer who came to Vietnam in 2010 to work as a teacher of English and as a writer. He was in his late 50s and it was his first year of teaching at the university. He had a PhD in Psychology from the US and two UK teaching certificates.

Dao was a Vietnamese English teacher who had been working long term at the university. She was 32 years old, had an MA degree in TESOL and had been teaching English to EFL students for six years. She had had numerous team teaching experiences with NESTs before working with Ron.

Sarah and Na
Sarah was an Australian volunteer in her late 40s with a Bachelor's degree in Drama. She had extensive work experience in a professional field and was assigned to work in a department of the Vietnamese university that was associated with this field. She had never done any team teaching before, so this was a completely new experience for her.

Na was in her late 40s and an experienced LET with an MA degree in TESOL. She had been working at the university as a teacher of English for almost 20 years and, at the time of the study, held a senior position in the faculty. During her teaching years, she had had numerous opportunities to teach with NESTs, from whom she had received valuable support for her professional development.

Jack and Tram

Jack, 23, was a young American volunteer teacher who was born in Vietnam but left at the age of two because his Vietnamese parents emigrated to the US. He was a new graduate but had taken a rigorous teacher training programme as part of his degree.

Tram, 29, was a LET with an MA degree in TESOL who had been working at the college since 2007. Before that, she had had extensive experience of team teaching English with NESTs at an international school for children.

Methods

A longitudinal case study was carried out during one school semester (from September 2011 to December 2011), with the first author using the following data collection methods: observations, semi-structured interviews, informal talks, note-taking, a researcher's diary, audio/video-recording, and document and email collection. The observations took place in two different settings: in the team teachers' lesson-planning meetings and in their team-taught classes, where data was collected by note-taking as well as audio/video-recording. The interviews were conducted with each teacher participant at three different stages of their team teaching: at the beginning, the middle and the end of the semester. In addition, informal chats were carried out whenever it was convenient in order to obtain additional insights. Documents were gathered, such as email exchanges between the teaching pairs and, where available, diary entries from the teachers. The first author (henceforth, the researcher) also kept a diary.

As explained earlier, we use the term 'rapport-sensitive incidents' to refer to problematic situations and events in which one or both of the teachers felt annoyed, confused or face-threatened because of unexpected behaviour or events in their interactions with their team teaching partner. This is similar to the concept of 'critical incident', but we prefer the term 'rapport-sensitive incident' in the context of this study because of our focus on interpersonal relations (Spencer-Oatey, op cit; Spencer-Oatey, 2013; Spencer-Oatey and Harsch, in press).

Whenever participants reported specific problems or challenges in their team teaching pairs, the researcher (drawing on the various sources of data) noted down the factual issues that had occurred in each incident and how the teachers felt and reacted in those situations. She also noted down the ways in which the individuals handled the annoyances or disagreements, and considered whether there were any potential cultural differences associated with the incidents.

Analyses of rapport-sensitive incidents

We report five rapport-sensitive incidents that occurred within the three team teaching pairs and that seem to be related to cultural issues. Two key themes recur: attitudes to advance planning and the personal/professional divide.

Incident #1: Last-minute information about the teaching schedule
What happened
Ron was due to start team teaching two classes per week with Dao at the beginning of October 2011. They met for their first pre-course planning meeting on

14 September, after which they exchanged a few emails about the syllabus, technical facilities, teaching resources, teaching methods and so on. On 23 September, Ron ended his email with the following question: 'Do you know when the first class is and what day or days of the week and when we will be teaching?' He did not receive a reply to this email, and so one week later, on 1 October, he sent another email, making some suggestions as to what elements he could teach and then asking for clarification about his involvement. He clearly wanted to start preparing his classes, which were due to start in a few days (the week beginning 3 October), as can be seen from this extract from his email: 'In periods 1 and 2, how much time are you planning on me teaching in each class? This will give me an idea of what to prepare.' However, in all his emails, he maintained a positive tone, ending this one, for example, with 'We will have fun, I think so'. Dao responded the same day as follows:

1   *Hi Ron*

    I think that's a great idea. If we can organize all classes like that, we

    save time a lot and we don't have to repeat this action 4 times.

    However, according to the schedule of 4 classes, 2 classes are on the

5   *mornings, 2 classes are on the afternoons. They also have to go to*

    class except Sundays. So we only do that on Sundays and I heard that

    maybe the total number of 4 classes is about 200 students. No room

    for all of them. So? In periods 1 and 2, maybe the first 5 minutes, we

    will introduce ourselves and I'll introduce the book, some class rules,

10 *and the examination.*

    15 mins. Later. You will tell them the problem

    5 – 7 mins: I will tell the importance of EPP

    20 mins: you will introduce the IPA

    The rest of time we can show them the videos.

    Let me know what you think. I am excited too.

    See you soon, Dao.

(Data Extract 1: Email from Dao to Ron, 1 October 2011)

Her description of in-class arrangements seems clear (lines 8–13), but the information about the times and number of the classes and when they were scheduled (lines 4–7) is very muddled. As a result, Ron still did not know when the four classes were scheduled to take place, so he replied to Dao's email immediately as follows:

1   *Hi Dao*

    I'm a little confused. Are there 4 classes and 4 periods for each class

    for each week? That can't be right, that would be 16 periods a week.

    Or is it one class with 200 students, 4 times a week. That doesn't

5   *sound right either. Also, you said 'we could do that on Sunday'. What is*

   that that we would do on Sundays?

   Your class organization sounds good. I'm sure we will have to adjust as we go
   along, but I think all will go smoothly and we will have fun.

   Ron

(Data Extract 2: Email from Ron to Dao, 1 October 2011)

The next day, which was a Sunday evening, Dao sent Ron a text message to say that their first class was at 7.40 the next morning. However, Ron did not see it until the next morning and so was late arriving for his first class.

Reactions and explanations

Ron reported this incident in an email to the researcher and was clearly confused as to why he had not been told clearly in advance when his classes were. However, superficially at any rate, he did not seem too upset:

1   *... So far teaching with Ms. Dao is great. She is a good teacher and I*

   think we will get along very well. We had a miscommunication about

   when classes started. I did not know until Sunday night that

   there was a class on Monday morning and Monday afternoon.

5   *I don't know why I wasn't told. I kept asking when the classes,*

   and all I got was that she sent me the schedule, but I never got it.

   I wish she just sent an email saying we will be teaching Monday

   morning at 7:30 and afternoon.

(Data Extract 3: Email from Ron to researcher, 4 October 2011)

He commented again on this in his interview in December, so it had clearly made a deep impression on him.

For Dao, this did not seem to be an issue. In an email to the researcher, she explained that she had asked the university for a teaching room which was suitably equipped for teaching pronunciation, and so this may well have been the main cause of the delay, as she had to wait for longer than usual to hear whether she could be allocated a suitable classroom.

   Since there are some things related to the teaching schedule which was
   informed a bit late by the university and he didn't read my email carefully about
   that, he was likely to be unhappy. However, after I had explained that to him, he
   felt OK. (Data Extract 4: Email from Dao to researcher [translated], 6 October
   2011)

As can be seen from Data Extract 4, Dao also maintained that Ron did not read her emails carefully. In fact, she was aware that she sometimes had difficulty explaining herself clearly in English and acknowledged that several times in her interviews. She also acknowledged that she found Ron's frequent emails a bit uncomfortable, as can be seen from the following interview comment:

I sometimes felt a bit uncomfortable at the beginning of the term as Ron sent me many emails, so I don't feel very comfortable. However, at that time it was because we did not understand each other very much. (Data Extract 5: Interview comment from Dao [translated], 14 November 2011)

Evaluation and Impact

From Ron's point of view, it would no doubt have been helpful for Dao to have told him that she was still waiting to hear back from the university, and it is not clear why she did not do this. It seems that she simply expected Ron to get ready for their first team teaching that week, despite not knowing the exact teaching schedule. In our experience, it is relatively common in Vietnam for teachers to be informed of the teaching schedule at very short notice, so she was probably unaware that advance notice was so important to Ron. She might also have felt it would have shown the university in a bad light if she had acknowledged that she did not yet know the schedule.

However, Ron did not seem to dwell too much on the issue and the incident passed without any further noticeable consequences.

Incident #2: Last-minute change of lecture content
What happened

Na went to Sarah's house for a lesson-planning meeting, as per usual. The purpose of their meeting that day was to discuss in detail their in-class teaching responsibilities based on the lecture content that had been mutually agreed beforehand. During their meeting, it emerged that Na had revised the lecture slides they had previously agreed on, but Sarah was unaware of these changes until they met to plan the lesson.

Sarah was dissatisfied with the changes for several reasons: the new material was not part of the syllabus, she felt it was too difficult for the students to understand and she was unhappy about the short notice. She pointed out to Na that these changes would require her to spend several additional hours of preparation, and since the class was the next day, there was no time for this. She reiterated her point three times and her tone of voice indicated her level of annoyance at the change. The pair negotiated over it for a while and at times their discussion became heated. Na repeatedly tried to argue that the changes were not very substantial and that it would thus not be too difficult for Sarah to familiarise herself with the added materials. However, Sarah took a firm stance and did not want to compromise. She maintained that it was impossible for her to rework the new lecture in time, saying 'I [would] need to spend another three hours tomorrow to prepare for the three-hour lecture ... I don't think I can work on it.' In other words, Sarah clearly stated that it would be costly for her in terms of time and effort to use the revised version, since their team-taught class was scheduled for the next day. Eventually, they agreed to use the original version, but Sarah apologised to Na and took a conciliatory attitude, asking twice, 'Is that OK with you?'.

Reactions and explanations

Sarah was clearly very annoyed about the last-minute change, as can be seen from the following informal comment to the researcher:

Ms Na changed the wording and actually changed the content of the lecture of what it was about and it didn't fit in the whole programme, which would be fine, but one of the difficulties was, it was Tuesday afternoon until evening and the class was the next day. (Data Extract #6: Informal chat with Sarah, 26 September 2011)

Sarah also noted her frustration in her diary. In addition, she expressed uncertainty as to what her team teaching partner really wanted and claimed that changes in course content took place regularly:

Lesson plan with Ms Na is very frustrating. I am very conscious of trying to maintain respect and also provide my opinions and suggestions for change, I do not really know if Ms Na wants change or is just saying she does.

Changing course content happens regularly

½ day notice for course changes

(Data Extract #7: Extract from Sarah's diary, 7 October 2011)

The unexpected disagreement is likely to have been face-threatening for Na, since, as module leader and a senior member of staff in the faculty, she might have expected Sarah to comply with her wishes. However, if those were her feelings, she downplayed them in her email to the researcher:

We encountered a difficulty in preparing for the lecture because of having different ideas, so we could not really find a common voice. Therefore, the two teachers had to review the issue and consider whose idea is more reasonable and appropriate. (Data Extract #8: Email from Na to the researcher, 2 October 2011)

Evaluation and Impact
Both Sarah and Na were clearly annoyed and frustrated with each other, but their conciliatory attitude (Na's willingness to revert to the original version and Sarah's concern as to whether Na minded doing this) helped, at least superficially, repair the relationship between them. Their in-class teaching went smoothly that week and they had a pleasant time talking cheerfully with each other in the staffroom about Sarah's housewarming dinner party.

Incident #3: Last-minute 'summons' to a singing practice
What happened
It was around 7.45 a.m. on Sunday morning. Sarah had just started her breakfast and her husband was still in bed. She received a phone call from Na, who said that they were having a singing practice at 8 a.m. to prepare for Vietnamese Teachers' Day, and that Sarah and her husband should join them at the departmental office. Sarah agreed to go, but she had to cancel a meeting with friends at 9 a.m. and had to take a taxi to the university instead of a bus, since time was so short.

Reactions and explanation
Although Sarah was happy to learn more about the school culture and spend time with other staff, she did not feel comfortable about the way Na had 'forced' her to take part in the activity at the last minute, especially since it was the weekend.

This can be seen from Sarah's comments in an interview and during an informal chat.

> *I am happy to be part of the faculty and the community. I felt grateful for being allowed to participate. I am learning that in Vietnam you don't necessarily get told things, you have 15 minutes, I have a phone call 7.45 on Sunday morning when I started breakfast to have song practicing at 8 a.m. in Australia, it's certainly no one asks you with that without that notice and we don't have that sort of activity, it's harder to have extra curriculum activities which are not totally voluntary (.) a couple of times, in the end, it didn't matter but there are times in the process I found a bit frustrating.* (Data Extract #9: Interview comment from Sarah, 2 December 2011)

> *This made me feel uncomfortable because my husband was still in bed and we had to take a taxi which costs a lot of money compared with going by bus. In addition, we had to cancel a meeting with friends at 9 a.m. – this may disappoint them.* (Data Extract #10: Informal chat with Sarah, 6 December 2011)

Evaluation and impact
Na's invitation was beneficial for Sarah in one respect (integration into the community), but it was costly on a personal level, especially because of its last-minute nature and because it occurred on a Sunday. Of course, Sarah had the right to turn down the invitation/request, but she decided to go in order to maintain a good relationship with Na, as well as to get more involved with the other teachers. However, her patience in this respect was tested a second time in the same week, as the next incident shows.

Incident #4: Last-minute invitation to a departmental party
What happened
Sarah had arranged to travel to another city for a week. She had asked Na's permission to do this several months in advance and had received Na's approval. She then booked and paid for the trip. However, much nearer the time, it turned out that the department was having a party on the last day of Sarah's trip, so Na asked Sarah if she could change her itinerary and come back earlier for the party. She made comments like 'we organised this party for you, [Sarah]. Please try a little bit to change.' However, Sarah refused.

Reactions and explanations
Na's invitation to join the departmental party made Sarah feel uncomfortable. She had obtained permission for the trip, had already booked and paid for it, and so felt it was unreasonable to be asked to change her arrangements at the last minute. She regarded Na's style of invitation as 'emotional blackmail', commenting as follows:

> *She's a very clever lady, Ms Na. She's very good at getting what she wants. I don't mean it in a bad way and she can be manipulative, she applies emotional blackmail, like we organise this party for you, oh please try a little bit to change* ...(Data Extract #11: Interview comment from Sarah, 2 December 2011)

Evaluation and impact

On this occasion, Sarah risked annoying Na, but did this deliberately so that she wasn't taken advantage of. In an informal chat, she commented as follows:

> It is not the end of the world, just things that happen differently from what would happen in Australia ... I said no to that because we booked and paid for the trip and we have told Ms Na a couple of months ago. It was not new. I checked if it was OK for her. I think you need to give in a little bit but you need to maintain saying no sometimes. It will continue 'can you do this, that?'. (Data Extract #12: Informal chat with Sarah, 6 December 2011)

These out-of-class issues frustrated Sarah. In her interviews and informal chats with the researcher, she began to reveal some resentment over Na's demands, which related not only to these last-minute requests but also to the increasing teaching pressures that Na was putting on her. However, the observational data showed that Sarah tried her best to be accommodating and, superficially at any rate, their interaction continued to proceed smoothly.

Incident #5: An unexpected visit at home
What happened

One day, when Jack was at his godmother's restaurant, Tram went there to find him because she wanted to ask him some questions about the lesson they were going to teach. It was 5 p.m. and when she arrived, Jack was trying on his tuxedo and was playing with his godsisters.

Reaction and explanation

Jack was not happy that Tram visited him in a non-work context and without any advance notice. He reported it in an interview as follows:

> She [Tram] came to my godmother's restaurant. She walked up and asked my godmother where I was and told me, 'Sorry I need to talk to you. How about the lesson plan?' I was in the middle of the restaurant. She didn't call me or give me notice. I was at the back with my godsisters, trying on my tuxedo, and she asked about what kind of pumpkin we should buy for the lesson. (Data Extract #13: Interview comment from Jack, 6 January 2012)

He also added,

> It is very unprofessional. I didn't like her from this side.

Evaluation and impact

From Tram's point of view, it was probably natural to drop in. It was the end of the day and she had just finished her teaching. She was on her way home and simply dropped by to see Jack at his godmother's house, which was near the campus. She presumably thought it was fine to check with Jack quickly about buying a pumpkin for their class.

However, Jack was unhappy about it. From an interpersonal point of view, the incident (and another similar one) had a major impact on his relationship with Tram and he reported: 'Outside the classroom, I don't talk to her [Tram].' However, he did not say anything directly to Tram about any of this and, within the class, he kept relations cordial. It seems that their team teaching performance was not affected by the incident(s).

Discussion
Cultural practices and perspectives
Two themes run through these five rapport-sensitive incidents: advance planning and the personal/professional divide.

As we noted earlier, previous studies have identified time management as an issue for NESTs and LETs. However, in those cases, it has been the LETs' busy schedules and their lack of time to meet with the NESTs for planning purposes that was identified. Such difficulties also occurred in our data, but the critical incidents reported above point to another issue relating to time that seems to have a cultural basis: people's preferences/level of comfort with last-minute invitations, requests or planning of events, compared with longer-term scheduling. Exploring this from a practice and perspective viewpoint may throw some light on the issue.

We all hold fundamental beliefs about time and its management, and several researchers (e.g. Hall, 1976; House et al., 2004; Trompenaars, 2012) have argued that there can be noticeable differences across cultures in these beliefs. People's time orientations can be long term or short term, and can be more past-focused, present-focused or future-focused. In other words, people may hold different perspectives on time, and these can manifest themselves in different practices, such as in preferences and norms for punctuality, multitasking and planning. In all of the rapport-sensitive incidents reported above, the NESTs demonstrated a preference for advance planning and a dislike for last-minute information, changes or requests, while the LETs were all much more comfortable with the latter.

Another perspective difference that emerged in several of the rapport-sensitive incidents was the boundary between personal and professional aspects of life. Trompenaars (2012: 101) labels this 'diffuse versus specific orientation' and explains it as 'the degree to which we engage others in *specific* areas of life ... or *diffusely* in multiple areas of our life' [emphasis in the original]. In other words, for people with a specific orientation, work life and private life are sharply separated, while for people with a diffuse orientation, the two are much more blurred. These differences in perspective are reflected in different practices, such as in the normative amount of disclosure of personal information in professional contexts, normative amount of contact between staff outside of work and management's right to expect staff to participate in social or extracurricular events. In Incidents #3–5, there were differences between the NESTs and the LETs in these respects. Both Sarah and Jack perceived less separation of the personal from the professional on the part of their LET partners, and Jack found that particularly difficult to accept.

Strategies for handling rapport-sensitive incidents
A key challenge for all of the NESTS that emerged from the rapport-sensitive incidents was whether or not to express their dissatisfaction to their LET partner. Sarah made clear her own preferences with regard to the issue at hand in two of the incidents. In Incident #2 she argued against changing the lecture content and in Incident #4 she refused to change her plans. However, she, Ron and Jack all

covered up any personal dissatisfaction with their partner's behaviour and any impact it had had on their interpersonal relationship. They all made a clear distinction between their professional relationship and any personal likes or dislikes, and this undoubtedly helped them carry out their team teaching responsibilities more effectively. All of them were able to keep their feelings mostly in check and were able to maintain a good, professional relationship with each other, at least superficially.

Implications for NEST/LET team teaching

Nevertheless, rapport-sensitive incidents, such as those reported in this chapter, were found to put significant strain on the team teaching pairs from time to time. We would argue, therefore, that the more both NESTs and LETs can understand and appreciate about each other's practices and perspectives, the better they will be able to work together harmoniously, effectively and rewardingly.

The World-Readiness Standards for Learning Languages (ACTFL, op cit: 1) identify the following as one key goal for language learners: 'Interact with cultural competence and understanding'. They then unpack this as follows:

> *Relating cultural practices to perspectives: Learners use the language to investigate, explain, and reflect on the relationship between the practices and perspectives of the cultures studied.*

> *Relating cultural products to perspectives: Learners use the language to investigate, explain, and reflect on the relationship between the products and perspectives of the cultures studied* (ibid.)

If this is important for language learners, then clearly it is also very important for language teachers. This does not mean that NESTs and LETs should learn essentialist (and potentially unreliable) information about their partner's cultural background. Rather they need to build awareness of the following:

- common continua of differences in cultural perspectives, such as beliefs about hierarchy (high–low power distance) and orientations to time

- ways in which cultural perspectives can influence practices, such as how beliefs about hierarchy can influence communication style preferences such as degree of formality and levels of directness–indirectness

- ways in which the products, practices and perspectives of a particular cultural context (organisational, professional and/or national) interrelate, such as how beliefs about hierarchy may influence (a) conventions within the school/ university on levels of formality between teachers and students and between teachers and their line managers, and (b) the choice of furniture for the classrooms and arrangements of office space for staff.

We suggest that collecting, analysing and discussing rapport-sensitive incidents such as those reported in this chapter is a helpful way of building such cultural awareness and sensitivity. For example, in order to help LETs and NESTs become more aware of cultural and interpersonal issues as well as develop problem-solving skills in their team teaching with each other, trainers could include some rapport-sensitive incidents in their training seminars in which both parties could have an opportunity to share their feelings and opinions about them and discuss how they would deal with them. Underlying reasons for their varying feelings and reactions could be explored, with discussions as to whether they reflect personal idiosyncrasies, cultural differences in preferred products, practices and preferences, or in fact a combination of these. If a large enough bank of rapport-sensitive incidents can be built up, this may also help us explore the extent to which common themes emerge for team teachers working in different national and organisational cultural contexts.

References

American Council on the Teaching of Foreign Languages (ACTFL) (n.d.) *World-readiness standards for learning languages*. Available online at: www.actfl.org/sites/default/files/pdfs/World-ReadinessStandardsforLearningLanguages.pdf (accessed 25 February 2016).

Carless, DR (2002) *Conflict or collaboration: Native and nonnative speakers team teaching in schools in South Korea, Japan, and Hong Kong*. Paper presented at the English in South East Asia Conference (ESEA), Hong Kong.

Carless, DR (2006) Good practices in team teaching in Japan, South Korea and Hong Kong. *System* 34: 341–351.

Carless, DR and Walker, E (2006) Effective team teaching between local and native-speaking English teachers. *Language and education* 20/6: 463–477.

Chen and Cheng (2010) A case study on foreign English teachers' challenges in Taiwanese elementary schools. *System* 38: 41–49.

Choi, Y (2001) Suggestions for the re-organisation of English teaching program by native speakers in Korea. *English Teaching* 56: 101–122.

Crooks, A (2001) Professional development and the JET program: Insights and solutions based on the Sendai City Program. *JALT Journal* 23: 31–46.

Dormer, JE (2006) *A perfect blend?: A study of co-worker relationship between NES and NNEST in two school sites in Brazil and Indonesia*. Unpublished PhD thesis, University of Toronto, Canada.

Gorsuch, G (2002) Assistant foreign language teachers in Japanese high schools: Focus on the hosting of Japanese teachers. *JALT Journal* 24: 5–32.

Hall, ET (1976) *Beyond culture*. New York, NY: Doubleday.

Hasegawa, H (2008) Non-native and native speaker teacher's perceptions of a team-teaching approach: case of the JET programme. *The International Journal of Language Society and Culture* 26: 42–54.

House, RJ, Hanges, PJ, Javidan, M, Dorfman, PW and Gupta, V (eds) (2004) *Culture, leadership, and organizations. The GLOBE Study of 62 Societies*. London: Sage.

Kachi, R and Lee, C (2001) *A tandem of native and nonnative teachers: Voices from*

Japanese and American teachers in the EFL classroom in Japan. Paper presented at the Annual International Conference on Language Teacher Education, Minneapolis, MN.

Lai, M (1999) JET and NET: A comparison of native-speaking English teachers schemes in Japan and Hong Kong. *Language, Culture and Curriculum* 12: 215–228.

Lee, KWY (2009) *Pathways to collaboration: A case study of local and foreign teacher relationships in a South-eastern Chinese university.* Unpublished Master's thesis, University of Toronto, Canada.

Mahoney, S (2004) Role controversy among team teachers in the JET Programme. *JALT Journal* 26/3: 223–244.

Moote, S (2003) Insight into team teaching. *The English Teacher: An International Journal* 6/3: 328–334.

Moran, PR (2001) *Teaching culture. Perspectives in practice.* Boston, MA: Heinle.

Ogawa, C (2011) 'Perceptions about team teaching: From Assistant Language Teachers and Japanese Teachers of English' in Stewart, A (ed) *JALT 2010 conference proceedings.* Tokyo: JALT.

Spencer-Oatey, H (2002) Managing rapport in talk: using rapport-sensitive incidents to explore the motivational concerns underlying politeness. *Journal of Pragmatics* 34: 529–545.

Spencer-Oatey, H (2008) *Culturally speaking. Culture, communication and politeness,* 2nd edition. London: Continuum.

Spencer-Oatey, H (2013) Critical incidents. A compilation of quotations for the intercultural field. GlobalPAD Core Concepts. Available online at: http://go.warwick. ac.uk/globalpadintercultural (accessed 25 February 2016).

Spencer-Oatey, H and Harsch, C (in press) 'The critical incident technique' in Zhu, H (ed) *Research methods in intercultural communication.* London: Blackwell.

Sturman, P (1992) 'Team teaching: A case study from Japan' in Nunan, D (ed) *Collaborative language learning and teaching.* New York, NY: Cambridge University Press, 141–161.

Tajino, A and Tajino, Y (2000) Native and nonnative: What can they offer? Lessons from team-teaching in Japan. *ELT Journal* 54: 3–11.

Tajino, A and Walker, L (1998) Perspectives on team teaching by students and teachers: Exploring foundations for team learning. *Language, Culture and Curriculum* 11: 113–131.

Thielemann, ES (2011) *Teachers' perceptions of their co-teaching relationships.* ETD Collection for Fordham University.

Trompenaars, F and Hampden-Turner, C (2012) Riding the waves of culture. *Understanding cultural diversity in business,* 3rd edition. London: Nicholas Brealey.

11

From an assistant to a team member: a perspective from a Japanese ALT in primary schools in Japan

Chiyuki Yanase, J.F. Oberlin University, Tokyo, Japan

Introduction

Due to rapid globalisation, in 2011 the Ministry of Education, Culture, Sports, Science and Technology (MEXT) in Japan proposed new educational reforms aimed at English education in elementary, lower and upper secondary schools. In the plan, MEXT addressed the need to obtain human resources, including expanding the number of Assistant Language Teachers (ALTs) in order to help develop the communicative competence of students throughout schools in Japan, including in primary-level education. As an intervention to meet the demands of MEXT, the local Board of Education (BOE) of a city district in Tokyo extended the eligibility criteria for ALT positions in primary schools in the area to include Japanese candidates with expertise in language teaching. Thus, having acquired a high communicative competence in English and over 20 years of experience teaching in small classrooms in private language schools, and while studying for a Master's in Teaching English for Young Learners (TEYL) as a distance-learning student at Aston University, UK, I was hired by the BOE as one of the first wave of Japanese ALTs. In the primary schools, I was required to work collaboratively with Home Room Teachers (HRTs), who do not have expertise in language teaching. In spite of my familiarity with TEYL, I have struggled with the lack of support available to help me to develop my practice as a Japanese ALT, as there are few guidelines and almost no academic literature on the subject.

In the hope of establishing guidelines which can be of use for teachers who will be – or are – in similar contexts, this chapter focuses on my unique case of team teaching and shares my personal journey as a Japanese ALT.

First of all, I will illustrate the challenges I found when team teaching with HRTs in various primary school classrooms and how I felt about and coped with the challenges. I will also describe some successful cases of team teaching and provide my analysis of the factors for success. Then I will address what can be done to improve the current team teaching system based on my auto-ethnographical observations in the form of a teaching diary written over a one-month period. In the conclusion, I will suggest how a Japanese ALT as a team member can foster an alternative model of team teaching and contribute to the development of teachers at the primary level of English education in Japan.

Current level of primary English education in Japan

Since April 2011, one weekly 45-minute English language class (35 in a year) has been incorporated into the schedule of fifth and sixth graders (ages 10–12) in all primary schools throughout Japan (MEXT, 2008). The guidelines of the new policy emphasise the importance of oral communication and were designed to promote interest in and motivation towards intercultural communication among children via activity-based communicative language teaching (ibid.). In order to realise the objectives MEXT has set, team teaching by HRTs and ALTs has been utilised. In general, young native speakers are hired as ALTs from Inner Circle countries (Kachru, 1992), such as the USA or the UK, unless such native speakers are unavailable (Machida and Walsh, 2014).

Current roles of ALTs in team teaching and issues

Team teaching can be defined as an instructional approach in which two or more teachers are involved in the planning, instruction and evaluation of learning experiences (Sandholtz, 2000). Jang (2006: 180) suggests that the team's primary concern should be 'the sharing of teaching experiences in the classroom, and co-generative dialoging with each other'. In many countries, team teaching is the prerogative of English language classrooms and the team comprises a Local English Teacher (LET) and a Native English-Speaking Teacher (NEST). The method of joint instruction between the NEST and the LET is considered as a 'potentially ideal' (Tajino and Tajino, 2000: 3) means of language teaching in Japan, where the NEST is often designated as the ALT. The latest ALT Handbook, published by MEXT in conjunction with the British Council in 2013, highlights the presence of a native English speaker as an opportunity for students to make immediate and authentic use of the target language as a communication tool (MEXT and British Council, 2013). It also establishes the role of the ALT as the LET's assistant and describes some of the ALT's fundamental responsibilities, such as joint lesson planning with the LET, assessing lessons, assisting classroom activities and motivating students to learn the target language. However, the guidelines mainly address ALTs working in junior high and high schools, where LETs are the norm. In primary schools, however, the job of teaching English falls to the HRT, who may or may not have English language skills.

In spite of the view expressed in the handbook that NESTs perform a unique and useful role, numerous studies argue that LETs are actually more effective, having the advantage in terms of being good learner models; providing effective language learning strategies; being able to offer scaffolding in the learner's first language (Medgyes, 1994); having a more accurate knowledge of the local educational system (Cook, 2005); and understanding learners' linguistic and cultural needs (Phillipson, 1996). Jeon (2009), on the other hand, argues that NESTs are often considered superior teachers due to the lack of linguistic skills of LETs. However, neither of these positions is wholly sustainable, as neither represents the reality of many LETs and NESTs; not all LETs have inferior linguistic skills and not all NESTs lack pedagogical experience. In fact, I am one of the exceptions as I have over 20 years of teaching experience, many of these with young learners, and sufficient linguistic skills.

Project design

This study is an auto-ethnography, which is a form of self-reflection and writing that explores and analyses the researcher's personal experience systematically with the aim of understanding wider cultural, political and social meanings (Holman Jones, 2005). In other words, auto-ethnography can utilise personal narrative, including journaling, looking at institutional or personal records, interviewing oneself and using writing to generate a self-cultural understanding (Ellis, 2004). The entries from my own teaching journal are the primary data for this project, which were recorded after each lesson over a period of one month, from approximately 27 October to 5 December 2014. The aim of this project is to explore the potential contributions of and challenges faced by the ALT (me) and the HRTs in the current team teaching context in state elementary schools in Tokyo, and to develop guidelines for these partners when they come to work together.

The teaching diary was recorded chronologically over a period of a month after each class, so that by nature it reflects my personal insights and interests, including my emotions, which might bias my conclusions. The approach of auto-ethnography, however, acknowledges subjectivity, emotionality and the influence of the researcher rather than hiding or denying their presence in the research (Ellis et al., 2011). Therefore, I sensitised my insider perception and recorded 'epiphanies', that is, the most memorable moments perceived as significant for my team teaching life in the journal writing (Bochner and Ellis, 1992). In order to avoid excessive subjectivity in my analysis of the data, an interval of a few weeks was left between the data collection and analysis. After allowing this distance in time, I identified negative comments and positive comments from the diary data and colour-coded them. I then examined the colour-coded comments and classified them into three main themes which emerged from the data as follows:

1. Classroom dynamics and management
2. The author's evaluation of the HRTs' behaviour and roles in class
3. The teacher-training role of the bilingual ALT.

Then I selected the most challenging obstacles in team teaching to include, as well as the most positive comments depicting successful factors in team teaching.

Setting and participants

Generally, in Japanese primary schools, HRTs are required to team teach English with NESTs or Non-native English-Speaking Teachers (with native-like English proficiency) who are from overseas and hired through the Japan Exchange (JET) Program (Amaki, 2008). HRTs play a major role in developing students' academic and career skills as they teach all the subjects except music, art, physical education (PE) and other lab-related activities (Ito, 2011). They are also responsible for developing students' interpersonal skills by leading activities such as class meetings or school events like sports days or school festivals (in which students collaborate on art or drama projects). Furthermore, they organise student responsibilities such as cleaning the classroom, serving lunch to other students or creating a classroom newspaper for students, as well as many other activities that require effective interaction among students (ibid.). As English is not currently part of the assessed curriculum in Japan, teaching certification at primary level does not cover language teaching skills. Therefore, the majority of HRTs have limited English language skills and little idea about how to teach English. In some cases, anxiety about teaching English leads to HRTs taking early retirement or suffering severe stress (Machida and Walsh, op cit). Therefore, ALTs have been dispatched to cover the needs of HRTs and avoid issues related to the implementation of English education in primary schools.

I was hired by the BOE in Tokyo and assigned to assist HRTs in conducting weekly 45-minute English classes for fifth and six graders at four state elementary schools, using the textbook *Hi Friends* and through activity-based communicative language activities.

According to the BOE, this radical change in the hiring policy of the city to include Japanese bilingual ALTs was made due to prior serious miscommunications between the former ALTs (non-native English speakers from the Philippines) and Japanese HRTs which had been caused by language barriers and cultural differences. According to an HRT who taught with one of the former ALTs, it was challenging for the ALT to adapt to the needs of Japanese young learners. From this information, I assumed that I was expected to be proactive in discussions regarding English classes with HRTs, taking advantage of my bilingual and bicultural identity.

Another unique characteristic of my position is my dual responsibility as an ALT and a teacher trainer. According to the BOE, these dual roles were assigned based on my qualifications and skills in language teaching, which I have developed over twenty years. My teacher training duties included delivering input sessions on language teaching methodology to primary teachers, some of whom I worked with.

In general, the number of classes that ALTs are assigned to conduct and the styles of team teaching they have to adopt vary according to each local school. In my context, the number of classes I conduct in each school varies depending on the number of students in the school. For instance, at one of the schools, they assign one of the HRTs as the person in charge of all four English classes for fifth and sixth graders. As well as my working there, this school also hires a NEST once a week to provide a variety of learning opportunities for students, according to the teacher in charge of English classes at the school. Therefore, I usually have only two classes a day.

The English proficiency level of the HRTs also varies from absolute beginners to 'returnee' level. In fact, one of the HRTs spent his high school days in the UK with the aim of becoming a professional football player. It might be worth noting that he hid his bilingual identity due to the radical decline of his English ability since it has been nearly 20 years since he left the UK. Another HRT earned her Bachelor's degree in English literature and went on a homestay for three months when she was younger. Those with comparatively higher English proficiency were not necessarily the most involved team teachers, as they tended to neglect having a brief discussion prior to the class regarding the learning activities I had planned due to their confidence in their English comprehension. In contrast, one of the most enthusiastic and supportive team teachers, who always wished to create the easiest and the most welcoming classroom atmosphere for his students and for me, was among the lowest in English ability of the HRTs. Perhaps due to his lack of proficiency in English, he never failed to have a brief discussion before the class in order to understand the objective of the lesson and each activity as well as the procedure. In sum, I taught 18 classes a week at four local elementary schools with 16 HRTs, who had various levels of English proficiency and interest in English education in primary schools, and I conducted two to six classes a day at each school.

The style of team teaching varies slightly depending on the HRTs I work with in my classes. In my first year as an ALT, three HRTs took the role of main teacher: they planned the lessons, including activities, and requested that I assisted them in various ways (modelling key dialogues with the HRT or the pronunciation of key vocabulary) when needed. Currently, however, only two HRTs try to lead the English class due to their interest in, experience of and knowledge about English teaching, which they acquired in former teaching jobs. In many cases, I conduct the English classes as a main teacher with the HRT's assistance. In terms of lesson planning, all of the HRTs requested that I took on this responsibility, due to their insufficient experience in and knowledge about teaching English to young learners and lack of time to prepare English classes. My classroom responsibilities, therefore, range from lesson planning to classroom management (such as preventing disruptive student behaviour) and, in some cases, the assessment of students' progress. In spite of the lack of systematic guidelines to follow, I have welcomed the freedom to negotiate teaching methodology with the HRTs and have introduced a humanistic approach that values learner autonomy and active interaction among students and teachers as participants in the learning environment.

Research findings

In this section, the outcomes from the teacher's diary data will be explained under three categories. In each category, I first outline the key issue and then identify and describe both challenging and effective cases with reference to my personal narrative and relevant literature when needed.

Teaching diary of the ALT

Classroom dynamics and management

Each class has a different set of dynamics and culture, which reflect the HRT's teaching style and philosophy. In general, according to the principles established by MEXT, Japanese primary schools respect 'normative consciousness' (MEXT, op cit), which values order and obedience as well as the traditions and culture that have fostered this consciousness. Therefore, a top-down lecture style of teaching is common in classrooms rather than collaborative and interactive learning.

In contrast, English classes based on my teaching philosophy are more collaborative and interactive, with students and teachers actively involved in learning activities – doing pair- and group-work, for example. A physically and cognitively active class requires effective and appropriate classroom management skills in order to facilitate an interactive yet safe environment. Ensuring the physical safety of excessively energetic students in a large class was challenging, particularly in schools where the HRT did not take an active role in supporting these student-centred activities. These classroom management issues became the focus of many of my diary entries.

Challenging cases

This extract is from the first entry in the diary (27 October):

> The Japanese teacher (HRT) was not supportive in the class today, doing her own work and left the classroom while I was teaching the class. Boys went so noisy and out of control that some girls complained … Classroom management from the HRT can be a great help since I have no authority to control the class.

At a different school, a similarly challenging case was mentioned in the diary (11 November):

> The classroom management is so challenging. Students got so much potential but they tend to act up badly during activities. How can I enjoy activities with certain control with misbehaving students? Students can't concentrate much with very short spans for focus. I need to think of more suitable activities for this class. The HRT forgot to set up the PC for the class. It's a small thing but it represents her attitude towards the English class. No classroom management she has done at all.

My classroom management issues were compounded by three factors. The first was the activities I set for the class. These had worked well in the small classes I was used to teaching in a private institution, but this was not the case here. I realised I needed to rethink the activities to ensure that they did not encourage out-of-control behaviour.

The second factor was lack of cooperation from the HRT. From my perspective, the HRTs were not well prepared for the class and did not value the class enough to take part. As an ALT, I had limited experience in disciplining students in a large class and struggled to do so effectively. From my point of view, the HRTs were not playing their part in the team teaching partnership, leaving me to do all the work.

The third factor leading to classroom management issues was that the majority of classes had an English-only policy. This was set by the HRTs in order to provide maximum exposure to English, but because of this policy, I was not allowed to utilise the L1 I shared with the students. Usually, I could manage to convey my ideas via body language, facial expressions and using other visual aids. However, in the case of giving instructions and discipline to misbehaving students, the language policy interfered with my authority and with my ability to manage the class effectively. L1 usage in L2 classrooms is still a controversial issue, especially in English as a foreign language classrooms. Researchers, however, argue that using L1 can be an important resource and claim the need for further research and discussions from bilingual teachers like myself (Copland and Neokleous, 2011).

The presence of misbehaving students, coupled with inappropriate activities, the ban on my using Japanese to control these students and the uncooperative attitudes of HRTs were listed as the causes of unsuccessful classroom management. Among these causes, the lack of cooperation by the HRTs in classroom management was perceived as the major factor in these challenging cases, as their intervention would ensure that activities ran smoothly and also that children behaved.

Effective cases

In contrast, a completely opposite and positive sentiment was mentioned in the diary after a dynamic and enjoyable class (11 November):

> We had a fun class and got passive and apathetic students involved in the pair activity because of the HRT. He created funny classroom atmosphere. He speaks English which makes everything so easy as he can give L1 support when students need. He also gets involved and enjoys activities with students.

In this case, the cooperation of the HRT in classroom management by facilitating a 'funny classroom atmosphere' was the determining factor in the success of the class. The HRT constantly created an informal and relaxed atmosphere in his classroom by interacting with outgoing students in a humorous manner and encouraging shy students to get involved. He articulated a simple rule to avoid excessive misbehaviour: listen when needed. He often used 'shush!' as a cue for students to understand that it was time to listen.

In another case, the mutual respect built between the HRT and me, and her constant cooperation in classroom management, were stated, as shown below (11 November):

> This class is noisy but the relationship with HRT is good since this is the second year to work with her. We built mutual respect and she's been supportive and appreciative with my work.

As the examples above show, when HRTs do not take responsibility for classroom management, the class become challenging, which is an excessive drain on my energy and causes me extra stress. On the other hand, rapport between the HRT and me, cooperative effort aimed at achieving more effective language classes and guidance from the HRTs based on their expertise in primary school education in Japan reduce my workload and help to ensure order in the classroom. These elements are, therefore, essential in an effective team teaching partnership.

HRTs' behaviours and roles

In the previous year, I had not requested any formal meetings with teachers except once at the beginning of the academic year. Because of the unfamiliarity of my new working environment, I focused on trying to understand the different systems and regulations of the four different schools in addition to recognising the large number of students and co-workers. My L1 ability enabled me to ask for help from school office workers and other part-time teachers. Due to their generous support and guidance, I was able to adapt to the new environment faster than I expected. There were four HRTs who were also assigned responsibility for English classes and were supposed to provide me with the guidance and support I needed. However, only one of the HRTs made time for regular discussion, took care of lesson planning and led classes as the main teacher. Luckily, by working with her and observing her English classes, I learned some effective classroom management skills and the appropriate level at which to pitch learning activities for primary school students.

Based on my experiences in the previous year, at the beginning of the current 2014 academic year I requested a meeting with the teachers in charge of English classes in all the primary schools I worked in. We discussed and agreed the following roles:

The ALT should:

- be the leading instructor in English classes
- plan and conduct activities
- assist the HRT in assessing the students' progress.

The HRT should:

- be the facilitator of his or her class
- participate in activities
- act as a role model for the students' language learning.

In spite of this discussion, the roles adopted by HRTs varied depending on their perceptions about and capabilities in language teaching. The following sections will explain the challenging and successful cases.

Challenging cases

This extract is from a class where I work with a teacher who has no previous teaching experience. On that particular day (20 November), he appeared to be absent-minded and paid no attention to what was happening in the class. Due to the HRT's behaviour, a sentiment of distress was evident in the diary:

> With the teacher's support, those kids can do much more … I wonder if he understands my instructions to the students in English. Working with him is like giving him training.

In the comment above, my scepticism and cynicism towards the teaching skills of the HRT was due to the inappropriate behaviour I felt he showed in the class. A similar sentiment was expressed about a different HRT when he did not show up to the class and gave no explanation in advance (20 November):

> In this class, the HRT can speak English quite well and understand my instructions. But the first half of the class, he didn't come to the class for no reason. Some explanations for his absence would be nice and supportive.

In any class, no matter how motivated students might be, the psychological or physical absence of HRTs from the classroom often provokes negative sentiments in me due to my belief that team teaching can be a powerful approach when both teachers contribute their skills equally in order to achieve the shared goal. Otherwise, for me, team teaching can be a source of stress; it can cause constant issues in the classroom and tension between the teachers due to the lack of cooperation and communication.

Another challenging case was when the team teacher became an onlooker, leaving everything except serious class management issues to the ALT. The sense of frustration and resentment were noted in the following extract (5 December):

> The HRT depends on the ALT 100%. Her help or encouragement to students can be helpful. Yet at the end of a year, teachers tend to be busy and absent-minded. This is the time when the class becomes challenging because students could be distracted as well.

The HRT's apathy and lack of support caused issues in class such as misbehaviour from the students. In fact, this HRT repeatedly said I did not need her support as I could manage the class on my own. What she failed to recognise was that her physical and psychological presence could assist in classroom management in a large interactive class due to her rapport with and knowledge of each student. It was challenging for me to establish a safe environment in which to conduct dynamic activities with plenty of physical and linguistic interaction among students. Neglecting one's role in team teaching may develop into a serious issue, since successful team teaching requires 'mutual satisfaction of self-interest, willingness to compromise and complementarity' (Carless and Walker, 2006: 473). This situation was even more distressing given that we had agreed roles and responsibilities at our meeting. I felt I had fulfilled my commitments but that these HRTs had not fulfilled theirs.

Effective cases
On the other hand, empathetic behaviours from HRTs can encourage me to improve my practice and appreciate the presence of the HRTs as partners. The extract demonstrates the author's perceptions when support was offered by an HRT (1 December):

> She (the HRT) was a great assistant today ... She started to take more active roles in the class ... The HRT knows how to discipline students and her presence, talk and classroom management skills were very supportive. I can learn from her how to elicit more responses from students.

As mentioned in the comment above, I learned appropriate types of questions and scaffolding for students depending on their abilities. For instance, the HRT provides either closed or open-ended questions depending on the personality and ability of the students. She also knows exactly when students need her support and what kind of support (linguistic, pedagogical or social) is required. Without daily interaction with students, developing such a deep understanding of students' needs, preferences and potential in a large class is challenging.

The following extract reflected a similarly positive shift in another HRT's behaviour (3 December):

> At the beginning, I thought he (the HRT) was too passive and dependent, leaving everything to me. But as he got used to working with me, he started participating in the class through controlling too wild boys or helping slow leaners to understand what to do.

These classes were evaluated as 'successful' due to the active participation and sufficient support of the HRTs. An HRT's active participation gives rise to mutual respect and better collaboration with me. The following extract (3 December) also shows how essential the HRTs' active involvement is in the class:

> This teacher had previous experience in team teaching with ALTs. She respects the meetings and is active in a supportive way in facilitating a dynamic yet manageable classroom atmosphere. She has also been a wonderful participant and supporter in activities as she willingly gets involved in any activities, using English.

Another extract (2 December) demonstrates the value of voluntary involvement of the HRTs:

> This HRT is so supportive in participation in activities and classroom management. It's been a pleasure to see students' development in language in a comfortable, safe and good setting with some orders ... He's a young teacher with very low level of English ability but pedagogically speaking, one of the best. This class is also one of the best with enthusiasm and discipline.

When team teaching with me, the HRTs' high linguistic competency in English is not perceived as essential because of my English language ability. The supportive behaviour that HRTs show in the classroom, such as active participation and constant encouragement of the students, are much more appreciated and valued since the HRTs are the most influential people in the classroom. Equally, spontaneous and approving comments from HRTs such as *ore mo yaro* ('I'm going to do it too') (December 1) and *omoshiroi* ('it was fun') (3 December) added 'a positive influence' in the class for the students. Moreover, the enthusiasm of HRTs and students towards learning English motivated me to develop more relevant, meaningful and enjoyable learning experiences. These HRTs demonstrated that taking on the roles they had agreed to in our meeting resulted in effective team-taught English classes.

My bilingual and bicultural identity: the affordances

My fluency in Japanese and understanding of Japanese cultural norms was useful. It meant I could easily interact with teachers in the teachers' room. I asked them questions in order to understand the school culture and began to better understand the personalities of the HRTs I worked with in classes. During lunchtime, stories I heard from other workers such as librarians, school nurses and other part-timers were the best source of essential information about issues such as which students needed extra support, events that were happening and the reputations and tendencies of the HRTs. The information I got was especially useful for event-planning with HRTs, which was part of my role as 'adviser' for teacher training. This role was assigned to me by the BOE due to my practical and theoretical knowledge in TEYL. Usually, the role required me to conduct special lessons (which were usually story-reading sessions with relevant learning activities for lower grades) and teacher training sessions. Knowing Japanese meant I could successfully communicate with the teachers despite the short planning time allotted for these activities. The following extract depicts the positive outcomes of one of the special lessons, a story-reading event for first graders (27 October):

> At the end of the session, the children waved their hands and kept saying 'good-bye' until I turned the corner and disappeared … The HRT was so happy that she told other teachers about this story-reading session. I got more requests from other grades.

My responsibility as an ALT is to teach English to fifth and sixth graders. However, as a teacher-trainer, I found that organising special events with other groups of teachers for their students was the most rewarding and productive way of acknowledging the needs of teachers and learners of English in primary schools.

Another noteworthy event as a teacher-trainer was a visit from a young American potter from New York. He was staying at the home of one of the HRTs for three months in order to study Japanese pottery. When I heard this, I immediately thought of using him to provide students with an opportunity for more authentic communication. Therefore, I suggested that we invite him to take part in two classes with sixth graders. Prior to the class, I provided him with a brief tour of the school, introduced him to teachers and discussed what we would do in the class. During the lessons, I encouraged students to ask questions about the potter's hometown, job, hobbies and life in the US. After a series of questions from students, I asked students to recommend places for him to visit or food to eat in Japan. There were unique suggestions including 'dinner at my home', followed by laughter. The interactions between the students and the guest were recorded in my diary as follows:

> His presence might change students' lives. We had so much fun. He was very interesting and peaceful person. He loves and enjoys Japanese culture and its people.

The positive attitude towards Japan and its people expressed by this guest inspired a sense of pride in the Japanese students in the class. For me, it was also an opportunity to realise the potential role afforded to me by my bicultural identity, enabling me to bridge the linguistic and cultural gap between the participants in such an event.

My bilingual ability and bicultural knowledge were also beneficial in the teacher-training sessions. For the first time since the implementation of English education in the city, three teacher-training sessions were held at three elementary schools in September and December 2014 and January 2015. The sessions were conducted mostly in Japanese, due to the lack of English proficiency of the teachers and the language anxiety expressed by the majority of them. As a language learner, I could empathise with the sentiment and utilise the shared L1 as the most effective tool for interaction. The two sessions were well received by the HRTs and helped to build further respect and trust with them. It is worth noting that the rapport the HRTs built through these training sessions enabled me to suggest pedagogically and linguistically effective approaches and engaging events for students. More interactions among us also lessened the tension that the HRTs felt in English classes. As a result, at the end of the 2014 academic year, I received several requests from HRTs to conduct activity-based interactive English classes with other groups of students.

In contrast, the experience of another Japanese ALT, whom I discussed in a different study, suggested that insufficient communication with HRTs causes issues in creating a collaborative and productive team teaching partnership for language learning. According to the ALT, a novice language teacher, the HRTs have substantial authority and control over the overall English programme and her proposals for lessons are often rejected. She says:

> I would like the HRTs to offer more chances for students to do more challenging activities as I suggested. I would like to establish more clear roles for me in the class. I also would like to have more time to discuss about classes with HRTs.

The challenges she experienced in team teaching differ from mine since I have few issues regarding my pedagogical skills, such as in planning lessons or in my role as a lead teacher. However, building mutual understanding though interactions with HRTs is extremely important. If the success of team teaching depends on building mutual understanding as suggested, the shared language and culture can be considered advantages of local ALTs as it can stimulate more interaction in order to achieve a solid working relationship with HRTs.

Discussion and guidelines for team teaching

The auto-ethnographical data from my teaching journal depicts both the challenges and positive aspects of team teaching, and offers guidelines as to what can be done to improve co-teaching between HRTs and local ALTs at primary school level.

The challenges are as follows:

a   perceived uncooperative behaviour of HRTs

b   HRTs' apathy or anxiety regarding English classes

c   HRTs' excessive reliance on ALTs in English classes

d   lack of time for discussion

e   discrepancies in pedagogical beliefs.

The unwillingness of the HRTs to cooperate in the class (a and b) is in opposition to one of the essential factors for effective team teaching, which is 'a willingness to compromise for a benefit of team harmony' (Carless and Walker, op cit: 464). Bennett et al. (1992) list five factors required for effective co-teaching:

1 a genuinely equal relationship among all members

2 equal contributions of diverse theoretical and practical knowledge

3 equal commitment in ongoing dialogue and mutual inquiry

4 opportunities to experience other's reality in a mutually supportive environment

5 opportunities to discuss issues that arise.

One-sided reliance (c) breaks the first and second conditions, which are an equal relationship and equal contributions in co-teaching. Inadequate time for discussion (d) means that conditions 3, 4 and 5 cannot be fulfilled, as they require the team members to dedicate sufficient time. Differences in pedagogical beliefs (e), such as teaching styles (including L1 usage), are commonly found in intercultural team teaching and can be addressed through more open discussions and negotiations (5) among the teachers involved (Storey et al., 2001). Nunan (1992) also claims that effective collaboration between the teachers can be realised when teachers develop relevant skills and are provided with both time to implement innovative team teaching and administrative support. Thus, the provision of sufficient training, supportive organisation and the allocation of time for discussions among team members (Sturman, 1989) may help to overcome the current issues stated above and help to build an effective team teaching team.

This study also depicts the advantages of team teaching as follows:

a extra support in classroom management

b positive influence on and motivation for the students

c opportunities to discuss classroom issues together

d the contributions of the diverse skills of each team member.

These advantages were apparent when both the ALT and the HRT made efforts to offer an inspiring model for communication for students in the class (b), worked collaboratively on matters regarding English classes (a and c), and contribute their diverse abilities, such as language learning strategies (ALT) and classroom management strategies (HRTs) (d). In other words, the success of team teaching depends on the equal commitment of the team members to improving their students' language learning (ibid.).

Once the strength of each member had been recognised, a potentially effective team teaching style emerged in my context. With this model, the ALT has the primary responsibility for planning and teaching, while the HRT moves around the classroom helping individual students and observing their behaviour. HRTs take responsibility for classroom management and for the assessment of student learning due to their expertise in the class culture, knowledge of individual student characteristics and understanding of the current assessment criteria in Japanese primary education. By giving team teachers more specific roles in classroom, this model can establish an equal contribution from both ALTs and HRTs, utilising the strengths of each member and compensating for weaknesses, as Carless and Walker (op cit) advocate.

The study has also suggested that local bilingual ALTs may have a number of advantages over their NEST counterparts, at least in the first months of team teaching. For example, they have cultural awareness of both local school systems and social norms. Furthermore, they can speak the local language. My cultural knowledge and linguistic ability enabled me to deliver pedagogically rewarding teacher-training events and helped to lower barriers between my co-workers and myself. Thus, instances of isolation or of miscommunication with HRTs, which Ohtani (2010) argues is the main issue in intercultural team teaching, were less of an issue for me.

To sum up, if HRTs and ALTs recognise each other's skills, appreciate each other's presence as valuable team members in the classroom and learn from one another by making sufficient time for meetings and discussions and by organising events utilising the shared language, an empowering team can be the result. Furthermore, a successful team can interdependently develop effective approaches to language learning for their students and enhance collaborative learning among students as they model effective collaboration (Tajino and Tajino, op cit).

Conclusion

According to Machida and Walsh (op cit), in order to participate in team teaching in primary schools in Japan, ALTs should be required to hold appropriate teaching qualifications and have sufficient linguistic ability to communicate with the HRTs. This claim matches the outcome of this study. My bilingualism and pedagogical knowledge in TEYL made distinct contributions to collaborative teaching. Thus, basic communicative competence in Japanese and external certification in language teaching would be strongly recommended when hiring ALTs to teach in primary schools in Japan.

Further research investigating various styles of team teaching between HRTs and bilingual ALTs in other teaching contexts is needed to discuss potential contributions and issues at the primary level of English education in Japan. Moreover, there also needs to be a radical reconsideration of the hiring criteria and working conditions for ALTs in order to establish more appropriate and effective guidelines for team teaching within the current contexts in state primary schools.

In conclusion, this auto-ethnography of a Japanese ALT suggests that positive collaboration between HRTs and ALTs, in which each party contributes their own individual strengths to the team, has the potential to create an inspiring, interactive and collaborative language learning environment for all the participants: the HRTs, the ALTs and the students.

References

Amaki, Y (2008) Perspectives on English education in the Japanese public school system: The views of foreign assistant language teachers (ALTs). *Educational Studies in Japan: International Yearbook* 3: 53–63.

Bennett, RV, Ishler, MF and O'Loughlin, M (1992) Effective collaboration in teacher education. *Action in Teacher Education* 14/1: 52–56.

Bochner, AP and Ellis, C (1992) Personal narrative as a social approach to interpersonal communication. *Communication Theory* 2/2: 165–172.

Carless, D and Walker, E (2006) Effective team teaching between local and native-speaking English teachers. *Language and Education* 20/6: 463–477.

Copland, F and Neokleous, G (2011) L1 to teach L2: complexities and contradictions. *ELT Journal* 65/3: 270–280.

Cook, V (2005) 'Basing teaching on the L2 user' in Llurda, E (ed) *Non-native language teachers: Perceptions, challenges and contributions to the profession.* New York, NY: Springer, 47–61.

Ellis, SC (2004) *The ethnographic I: A methodological novel about autoethnography.* Walnut Creek, CA: AltaMira Press.

Ellis C, Adams, ET and Bochner, PA (2011) Autoethnography: An Overview. *Forum: Qualitative Social Research* 12/1: 1–18.

Holman Jones, S (2005) 'Autoethnography: Making the personal political' in Denzin, NK and Lincoln, YS (eds) *Handbook of qualitative research.* Thousand Oaks, CA: Sage, 763–791.

Ito, A (2011) Enhancing school connectedness in Japan: The role of homeroom teachers in establishing a positive classroom climate. *Asian Journal of Counselling* 18/1&2: 41–62.

Jang, S (2006) Research on the effect of team teaching upon two secondary school teachers. *Educational Research* 48/2: 177–194.

Jeon, M (2009) Globalization and native English speakers in English Programme in Korea (EPIK). *Language and Culture and Curriculum* 22/3: 231–243.

Kachru, BB (1992) *The other tongue: English across cultures.* Urbana and Chicago: University of Illinois Press.

Machida, T and Walsh, JD (2014) Implementing EFL policy reform in elementary schools in Japan: A case study. *Current Issues in Language Planning.* DOI: 10.1080/14664208.2015.970728

Medgyes, P (1994) *The non-native teacher.* London: Macmillan.

Ministry of Education, Culture, Sports, Science, and Technology, Japan (MEXT) (2008) *Shougakou gakushu shidou yoryo* [Course of study for elementary school education]. Available online at: www.mext.go.jp/component/a_menu/micro_detail/_icsFiles/afieldfile/2009/04/21/1261037_12.pdf (accessed 26 February 2016).

Ministry of Education, Culture, Sports, Science, and Technology (MEXT) and British Council (2013) *ALT handbook*. Available online at: www.britishcouncil.jp/sites/britishcouncil.jp/files/alt-handbook-en_0.pdf (accessed 26 February 2016).

Nunan, D (1992) *Collaborative Language Learning and Teaching*. Cambridge: Cambridge University Press.

Ohtani, C (2010) Problems in the Assistant Language Teacher system and English activity at Japanese public elementary schools. *Education Perspectives* 4/1&2: 38–45.

Phillipson, R (1996) English only worldwide or language ecology? *TESOL Quarterly* 30/3: 429–452.

Sandholtz, JH (2000) Interdisciplinary team teaching as a form of professional development. *Teacher Education Quarterly* 27/3: 39–50.

Storey, P, Luk, J, Gray, J, Wang-Kho, E, Lin, A and Berry, RSY (2001) *Monitoring and evaluation of the native-speaking English teacher scheme*. Unpublished research report: Hong Kong Institute of Education.

Sturman, P (1989) Team-Teaching in Japan: The Koto-ku Project. *JALT Journal,* 11/1: 68–76.

Tajino, A and Tajino, Y (2000) Native and non-native: what can they offer? *ELT Journal* 54/1: 3–11.

12

Problematising the paradigm of 'nativeness' in the collaboration of local (NNEST) and foreign (NEST) teachers: voices from Hong Kong

Mary Shepard Wong, Azusa Pacific University,
Southern California, US
Icy Lee, The Chinese University of Hong Kong, Hong Kong
Xuesong (Andy) Gao, University of Hong Kong, Hong Kong

Introduction

The dominance of Native English-Speaking Teachers (NESTs) in the profession of TESOL is gradually eroding due to the increase of Non-native English-Speaking Teachers (NNESTs), who outnumber NESTs, and the development of the non-native speaker movement, which has raised awareness of prejudicial attitudes towards non-native-speaking teachers (Mahboob and Golden, 2013). Advocates for the cause of non-native speaking teachers (e.g. Braine, 2010; Medgyes, 1992; Moussu and Llurda, 2008) have argued convincingly that non-native teachers should be treated on an equal footing with NESTs due to their unique and valuable contributions in English language teaching. However, the problematic native-speaker paradigm still remains and inhibits productive collaborative practice between the two groups of teachers, also referred to in this chapter as foreign and local teachers respectively.

Studies have investigated the seemingly complementary assets and liabilities of both native and non-native teachers to show that collaboration can make the most of their unique contributions (see Dormer, 2010, 2012; Liu, 2008). However, categorising teachers simply as native and non-native, and focusing on this one distinction among many others for the purposes of fostering collaboration among teachers, may have contributed to reinforcing a false dichotomy between these two groups of teachers, framed solely within the paradigm of 'nativeness'. Therefore, more research is needed to determine the value of basing collaboration on the constructed and contested notion of 'nativeness'.

To examine the potential and problems of collaboration based on the native-speaker paradigm, the authors examined the factors that foster and inhibit collaboration between local and foreign teachers in Hong Kong, where an established history of collaborative practice between the two groups has taken place and where collaboration is supported by governmental policies and funding (see Griffin et al., 2006; Griffin and Woods, 2009). With the support of a Fulbright grant, the lead author completed 20 observations and conducted 25 interviews with over 40 local and foreign teachers and school heads in eight schools (four primary and four secondary) in Hong Kong over a period of five months. For the purposes of this chapter, one primary school and one secondary school were selected from the larger study to provide insights that problematise the paradigm of 'nativeness' as a basis of collaboration.

The context of the NET Scheme in Hong Kong

Due to the importance of English in Hong Kong and other sociopolitical factors that led to the questioning of the standard of English possessed by students and teachers, the Hong Kong government announced the Native-speaking English Teacher (NET) Scheme in 1997, implementing it first in secondary schools in 1998 and then in primary schools in 2002.

Apart from enriching the English language learning environment and enhancing students' language learning, the scheme aims 'to strengthen teaching capacity through school-based professional development and *collaboration between NETs and English Panel* (department) *Members'* [our italics] (Hong Kong Education and Manpower Bureau[1]). The NETs in primary schools are also expected to '*help local teachers develop* innovative learning and teaching methods, materials, curricula and activities' and 'disseminate good practices in language learning and teaching through region-based teacher development programmes such as experience-sharing seminars/workshops and networking activities' [our italics] (Hong Kong Education and Manpower Bureau[2]). The NET Scheme has attracted research attention ever since its inception (e.g. Carless and Walker, 2006; Tong, 2010; Trent, 2012). One reason for this is that some teachers have contested the inherent unequal power relationship in which local teachers are positioned as the ones in need of 'development' by the NETs, who do not always have as much teaching experience or as high a level of qualifications as the local teachers (Boyle, 1997; Lee, 2005).

Research on collaboration between NETs and local teachers in Hong Kong has revealed some promising results in primary schools, while less so in secondary schools. For example, Carless and Walker (op cit) report only modest gains in student learning and motivation related to collaboration in their study on secondary school teachers, while Carless (2006a, 2006b) reports more significant gains in teacher development in primary schools. This may be due in part to the Primary Literacy Programme – Reading and Writing (PLPRW) used in some primary schools, which supports collaboration, and the tendency for secondary teachers to work more on their own. It should also be noted that these studies sought out 'best practices' and focused on schools where collaboration was working well.

Formal evaluations of the NET Schemes commissioned by the Education Bureau of Hong Kong (Griffin et al., op cit; Griffin and Woods, op cit) indicated that the

1   http://www.edb.gov.hk/en/curriculum-development/resource-support/net/enet-objectives.html
2   http://www.edb.gov.hk/en/curriculum-development/resource-support/net/pnet-objectives.html

positive gains in student learning and teacher development that the NET Scheme had first envisaged were somewhat elusive, apart from those found in lower primary school pupils. Many factors may account for difficulties in collaboration, both external and internal to the NET Scheme. One such external factor is the examination requirement, which, according to Tong (op cit: 232), produces a culture of 'reluctant compliance'. Tong states that while teachers engaged in some critical reflective practice with colleagues, collaboration was often 'poorly conceived and imposed on teachers by school leaders', resulting in what Hargreaves (1992) calls 'contrived collegiality' and which served to undermine instead of support the curriculum reforms (Tong, op cit: 235).

Trent's (2012) study found that the relationship between NETs and local teachers in Hong Kong was constructed by policy discourses and that this discursive positioning hampered collaboration. In an attempt to understand the discursive positioning of NETs and positioning by other actors as part of the dynamic process of identity formation, Trent (2012) noted that some local teachers found the NET Scheme threatening to their professionalism, as it implies deficiencies in their language competence and pedagogy (see also Boyle, op cit; Walker, 2001). In contrast, the NETs displayed strong ideological beliefs in engaging with what they consider 'real' teacher activities (drama, games, etc.) as opposed to 'traditional' teacher activities (exam drills, worksheets, textbook work, dictations, etc.). Trent (op cit) identified an ideological divide between NET and local teachers:

> The identity categories of real and traditional teacher appeared to exist in antagonistic relation. This ideological divide is apparently irreconcilable as NETs were found to have considered it impossible to be a 'real' teacher and a 'traditional' teacher simultaneously.' (Trent, op cit: 120)

Ma's (2009, 2012) findings on students' perceptions of NETs and local teachers in Hong Kong revealed that students valued local teachers and in some cases preferred them to NETs. Although students in Ma's (2012) study noted both negative and positive aspects of local teachers, several advantages stood out (see also Cheung and Braine, 2007; Lasagabaster and Sierra, 2005). A noteworthy finding from Ma's (2012) study was that students viewed the local teachers' use of L1 as an advantage. Local teachers' ability to codeswitch and provide L1 equivalents or grammar explanations was valued, and contributed to students' feeling that local teachers were easier to understand and communicate with than their NET counterparts. While the findings of Ma's (2012) study confirm that NETs and local teachers have some complementary attributes, knowledge and skills, Trent's (op cit) study points to the difficulty in collaboration based on the 'antagonistic relation' that the 'nativeness' distinction creates, as expressed in the previous quote. Further investigation is needed to determine what hinders collaboration between these groups and what can foster more effective collaboration so that student learning can be improved. To better understand collaboration between native and non-native teachers, Moussu and Llurda (op cit) call for research that involves pairing them in the same classroom and observing how they distribute their roles. This was one of the data collection methods of this study, as described below.

Procedures and participants

We adopted case study as the methodological approach in this inquiry into what fosters and inhibits collaboration between NETs and local teachers in Hong Kong. The study examined views of NETs, local teachers and panel (department) chairs involved in collaboration in one primary school and one secondary school in Hong Kong. We used convenience sampling as the schools were identified through personal contacts, which provided us access to the schools. The schools were similar in size (both about 1,000 students), location (both within the New Territories) and type (both government subsidised schools). A total of six participants – two NETs, two local teachers and two panel chairs were interviewed and at least one class in which the NET and a local teacher team-taught was observed at each school.

Interviews

Six hour-long interviews were conducted with the NETs, the local teachers and the English panel chairs. An interview guide was used for these semi-structured interviews and it consisted of 24 questions within five categories. Six questions covered preliminaries and background information, six questions asked about impressions of collaboration, two questions were on the type and extent of collaboration and support services, and ten questions were on the successes and challenges of collaboration together with suggestions. The interviews were conducted in English and audio-recorded.

Observations

Four observations were conducted, two at each school. At the primary school, two double class sessions (90 minutes each) were observed in which team teaching took place with a different local teacher but the same NET in each session. At the secondary school, one team-taught class was observed and another observation took place in the teachers' shared office space, where collaboration was reported to occur. Field notes were taken during all the observations.

Data analysis

The six interviews were transcribed verbatim and double-checked by the lead author to ensure their accuracy. Data analysis of the qualitative data involved listening to each of the recorded interviews numerous times, reading the transcripts and field notes of observations, and coding the data repeatedly over several months. The lead author conducted the data collection and all three authors took part in data analysis. The three researchers met on several occasions during the study to discuss the findings and compare their analyses of the data, enhancing the reliability of the data analysis process.

The two schools and six participants

To provide a context for the findings, a brief description of the two schools and each of six participants will be given before the findings are discussed. These descriptions include a supporting quote from each of the participants to provide a sense of who they are and their views on collaboration.

The primary school

The primary school in this study enrolled close to 1,000 students, with test scores that 'were never below the standard', which, according to the panel chair, made this school somewhat competitive. The collaboration in this primary school could be considered 'successful' based on the fact that the NET had a positive relationship with the local teachers, panel chair, principal, students and parents, and because he could articulate specific ways that collaboration supported student learning. At primary levels 1–3 (P1–3), team teaching took place on a weekly basis and co-planning meetings took place about once a month. Support for collaboration was provided by governmental funding that paid for the NET and by the NET Scheme's PLPRW curriculum, which was designed with specific guidelines to foster collaboration in P1–3. Although there was some tension about how much time should be spent on the PLPRW curriculum (which the NET was charged to oversee) and how much time on the General English (GE) curriculum (which the local teachers taught and was the basis of the exams given in Primary 3 and 6) overall, the school seemed to have developed a collaborative practice that was, as a local teacher described it, 'comfortable'.

The NET at the primary school

The NET who was interviewed and observed at the primary school had had his two-year contract renewed three times. He described the school as 'wonderful' and his relationship with the school as 'a perfect marriage' in its eighth year. Yet the interview and observations provided insights into the problematic nature of 'nativeness' as the basis for collaborative practice. For example, interestingly, this NET was not a native speaker at all, which demonstrated that a non-native teacher could successfully fulfil the role of a NET in Hong Kong's NET Scheme. English was not his first language, which was evident from his Eastern European accent. However his command of English won over the NET Scheme interviewers and he was hired, and in the end it was this shared identity with his local teachers and students that he thought was one of the main reasons for his success, as he implies here:

> And it is even – the kids – one of the reasons they do not want to speak is the fear of maybe making mistakes. The same goes to the local teachers. When I arrived here the first time, it was kind of like … silence in the room. And I told them, I told them, listen guys. English is my second language. I also make mistakes. And then you know you could really feel like ahhh [a sigh of relief]. So they felt really relaxed.

The local teacher at the primary school

The local teacher who was observed and interviewed at the primary school had been there for seven years and had the dual role of the disciplinarian and local teacher. She brought the role of 'discipline mistress' into her co-teaching with the NET, which took place at least once a week. In the co-taught observed lesson, her comments to the students were entirely discipline-related, such as 'sit properly' and 'pay attention', with no comments related to English teaching. This segregation of roles was 'comfortable', as she called it, but it did not take full advantage of what might have been gained through a more mutual collaborative arrangement. She felt that she did not have time for a more equal sharing of teaching roles during the team teaching, as planning was limited to one meeting per month and she had many other tasks. From the interview it was learned that she felt the NET and local teachers had somewhat conflicting goals; while the NET was more concerned with the PLPRW programme that focused on reading and writing and what she called 'fun', the priority was to prepare students for the exams through the GE programme, as stated here:

> For example, if the local teacher is concerned about the progress of the GE lesson – because it is, we are very busy, actually. But if the NET is concerned about the PLPRW program, then maybe conflict occurs.

Even though the NET's collaboration with local teachers in this primary school was apparently smooth, their different roles, as institutionalised by different programmes, positioned them in opposition. The local teacher's less sanguine reflection on her collaboration with the NET tempered the more optimistic depiction of collaboration that the NET expressed.

The panel chair at the primary school
The panel chair at the primary school provided interesting insights during his interview regarding the negative attitude of many Hong Kong people towards the local teachers' level of English and regarding the 'normal' practice of hiring NETs. In spite of his ease in speaking in English, he acquiesced that NETs were needed due to this negative attitude in Hong Kong that gives preference to NESTs, as he states here:

> My English standard is only the normal one. Lots of [local] teachers here have good English. It is not a matter of English ability, it is a matter of … the attitude.

He noted that the ultimate aim of the NET Scheme was that 'one day there will be no need to have a NET', but he did not see that as happening soon, as the deployment of NETs had become 'normal practice'.

The secondary school
The secondary school selected for this study was a subsidised Christian school with about 1,000 students who were mostly from local housing estates and included students from 'the lower end of the economic scale', as one interviewee put it. Secondary schools in Hong Kong are placed in three bands, with Band One representing the highest level. The panel chair said her school was 'at the lower end of Band One' and noted that it considered itself an 'EMI' (English-Medium Instruction) school, although several classes, teacher meetings, memos and morning and weekly assemblies were all conducted in Cantonese. The school had a history of mistrusting NETs; they preferred to use the governmental NET funds to hire a team of five 'temporary' NETs for just one month to help students prepare for their oral exams instead of one NET for an entire year, as they had heard 'horror stories' about NETs from other schools. As the panel chair explained:

> I think our school has been very careful about the choice of NETs because we have heard all kinds of stories, like unpleasant experiences. Especially school principals. They heard from other schools about the kinds of NETs they got. And so our school has been careful.

However, the school had hired two full-time NETs in its history, and the NET interviewed for this study was in her second year of her contract at that school.

The NET at the secondary school
The NET at the secondary school was raised in a Chinese home in North America and was able to understand and speak Mandarin and some Cantonese. She had taught in Hong Kong for seven years, including three years at this school, but at that time she was not hired as their NET, since she was not eligible to be hired in the NET Scheme at that point. Several years later, after she completed her Master's in TESOL, she was invited back as their NET because they thought they could trust her. In this new role, the courses she taught were limited to just oral classes. Like most NETs, and in contrast to local teachers, she had minimal marking to do. She also had the extra benefit of a travel allowance to fly to and from the West and a housing allowance. In this school, the NET's main task was to teach a few oral English classes and oversee the 'English Day' each Thursday and other English events each semester. She felt somewhat isolated and lonely, unsure of her identity as a NET due to having to hide her ability to speak Chinese, as she notes here:

> I think it would help if I use Cantonese, speak Cantonese, like use more Cantonese. I have had teachers who say to me, oh, don't you feel bored or don't you feel lonely because people don't really want to talk to you in English. So, yeah. I was told that you cannot use Chinese, no matter what, I just don't and I can only use English.

As can be inferred from the quote, she found that her identity as a NET undermined her socialisation and her efforts to integrate into the school community.

The local teacher at the secondary school
The local teacher who was interviewed and observed at the secondary school was a former student at the school and, at the time of the interview, she had taught at the school for seven years. She had a Master's degree from a local university and was completely fluent in English. For her, collaboration took place when she asked the NET questions about culture or grammar, or when they discussed issues in meetings. Actual team teaching was rare and was not the focus of their collaboration. In the one-hour class that the first author observed her team teaching with the NET, the local teacher made only one opening announcement and whispered twice to the NET about her observations of students. When asked about this limited role, she said they had not planned how to team teach and she noted that this was her first year working with a NET. When asked what she gained from the relationship, she said:

> I learn from [the NET's] character to be outspoken in a way [if] you really want to make things better ... you voice out something. So I kind of feel that maybe I learned from her that style [of saying what you mean].

The panel chair at the secondary school

The panel chair who was interviewed at the secondary school had been at that school for 20 years and had well-defined views about the role of the NET, as seen in this quote:

> Since our first NET here we have been very, very, clear about the role of the NET in our school. That is to improve students' speaking abilities. We never ask the NET to teach a regular English class. We want the NET to focus on improving students' speaking abilities and improving the school English environment because [local] teachers would be focusing on reading skills, writing skills, listening skills – tests, exam papers or marking. So, in that sense there is not much collaboration. Once we have agreed on what we want her to help us with, then she is pretty much on her own to develop materials.

The quote clearly defines the roles of NETs and local teachers as separate, and assumes that 'not much collaboration', as she said, will (or should) take place. The NET was expected to help with the improvement of students' speaking abilities, limited to just that narrow role and left 'pretty much on her own'. The chair felt the NET had a specialised, restricted role, but from the NET's perspective, this left her ostracised and isolated, as she states here:

> I found out that other local teachers, they went shopping and they didn't even ask me to go! And it was my idea, too! And I was like, why didn't you ask me?!

Limitations of the native-speaker paradigm as a basis for collaboration

In this section, we examine the nature of collaboration in the study and discuss the limitations of the native-speaker paradigm as the basis of collaboration. As Ryan (2014) confirms in this quote, the native-speaker paradigm is contested by many scholars and found to be problematic in that it does not embrace the dynamic and complex nature of language, learners and the language learning process:

> A growing number of scholars argue that the native speaking paradigm presents a problem in foreign language education if the emphasis is on a standard linguistic norm and a standard uniform sociocultural world. Intercultural theorists and educators who recognize language and culture learning as a complex cognitive, social, and emotional process have expressed strong opposition to what they consider an outdated native-speaker paradigm in FL teaching (Alvarez, 2007; Byram, 1997; Holliday, 2005; McKay, 2002; Sharifian, 2009). (Ryan, op cit: 423–424)

In our two case studies, we found some collaboration between the local teachers and the NETs, more so in the primary school due perhaps to support for the team-teaching-based curriculum and co-planning meetings, and less so at the secondary school due in part to the restricted role of the NET. But more importantly, in both cases, the type and extent of collaboration was limited by the native-speaker paradigm, which affords more status and power to native speakers. Specifically, three types of limitations to collaborative practice related to the native-speaker paradigm emerged in this study: linguistic, pedagogical and professional. These limitations will be elaborated on below.

Linguistic limitations

The goal of language education in Hong Kong is to produce students who are trilingual (in Cantonese, Mandarin and English) and biliterate (in Chinese and English). With this in mind, one would think that a trilingual NET (a teacher who could speak English, Mandarin and Cantonese) would be an ideal teacher and role model. However, in the secondary school in this study, the trilingual NET was told to conceal her multilingual ability from students and colleagues, and to speak only in English, even while in the teachers' room. This linguistic 'muzzling' impacted her ability to form deep relationships with colleagues and students, and undermined her efforts to deepen collaboration with local teachers through effective socialisation. The school's attempt to keep her trilingualism from students backfired when one student overheard her ordering food in a restaurant in fluent Cantonese. Soon more students heard about this and expressed their feelings of betrayal through social media like Facebook, saying she had lied to them.

We use the metaphor of the 'paper doll' to convey this two-dimensional or limited linguistic role that the native-speaker paradigm can place on NETs who are hired only for their English abilities. In the secondary school, the local teacher said that she was asked to deceive the students about the NET's multilingual abilities, as she states here, perhaps coming to the realisation for the first time that this was a lie.

> Yes, that's a fact [that the NET has to pretend not to understand any Chinese phrases] because the students, maybe if they know that she knows Cantonese [students would not speak to her in English], but we have to tell them – I don't know if we have to tell them that – wait, yes, [we do and] actually that is a lie. We were told not to talk to [the NET] in Cantonese in the public area.

Due to the 'NET phobia' that existed at the secondary school, as described earlier, they gave only a narrow role to their carefully selected NET, that is, oral English only, as the panel chair in the secondary states:

> Our NET is doing very well here, playing her role to stick to English and not speak any Chinese. If students ever discovered that she is fluent in Mandarin and she can understand Cantonese very well, students would not bother to go to her and speak English. I can be quite sure about that!

This response is puzzling and resulted in the following questions. If Hong Kong's goal is to have trilingual citizens, then shouldn't teachers model trilingualism and not conceal it? If the point of education is to encourage and inspire students to learn, why should the school turn a blind eye to the NET's trilingual abilities and encourage her to lie to students instead of asking students to engage in trilingualism with her? Shouldn't learning how to be a trilingual in Hong Kong, with discussions about when to use English, Mandarin or Cantonese, and if and when to code-mix, be something that should take place in language classrooms with their language teachers?

While the NET was linguistically 'muzzled' by the limited pedagogical role afforded her at the secondary school, local teachers are equally constrained by the discourses that value 'nativeness', as we found at the primary school. Two different local teachers were observed co-teaching with the same NET at the primary school, revealing two different collaborative styles using the same PLPRW curriculum. The first teacher, the disciplinarian, stayed within her disciplinarian role, speaking only during about five per cent of the class time and peppering the class with phrases like 'sit properly' and 'pay attention'. The second local teacher used English and Cantonese not only to help with discipline but also to provide instructions in the L1, which made the transition to seatwork go more smoothly than it had in the first observation with the disciplinarian local teacher. Nevertheless, in both cases, the NET was the lead teacher, while local teachers acted like 'police officers', although the second local teacher engaged a lot more in the actual teaching process, participating in close to 50 per cent of the teaching.

To summarise, we have used two metaphors to represent the linguistic limitations that were found arising from the native-speaker paradigm. The metaphor of the 'paper doll' calls to mind the two-dimensional limitation imposed on the NET in the secondary school, who was 'flattened' by the instruction never to speak Chinese or even admit she could speak Chinese. Meanwhile, the 'police officer' metaphor refers to the local teacher's self-imposed limitation of tending to manage students rather than teach them when team teaching with the NET.

Pedagogical reductions/limitations
The NET at the secondary school was not only linguistically muzzled but was also marginalised because she was not given 'real' classes (those with grades) to teach and was asked instead just to focus on helping improve students' speaking abilities as they prepared for competitions, to form English clubs and to host special events. We likened this to Pinocchio, the wooden puppet who longed to be a real boy. In the NET's words:

> Because I feel, partially why I felt I so frustrated was because I couldn't teach. I couldn't do what I wanted to do. I couldn't teach. I really love teaching and I couldn't use my gift for teaching. ... Because I don't think they really know what to do with me [but] I find stuff to do.

The local teacher confirmed that students did not take the NET seriously or consider her a real teacher, as she states here:

> Maybe students would think that she is not, like, what can I say – a real teacher. They would just talk to her when they need to and when she is carrying out activities in the lessons that would think just for fun. Maybe they don't really take it very seriously.

Yet this same local secondary teacher did not take on a significant teaching role herself when they team-taught (there are further descriptions below).

In the observation of team teaching at the secondary school, the local teacher's role was clearly that of an assistant. She made a brief opening announcement in

English, took attendance, whispered to the NET about student behaviour on two occasions and cleaned the board at the end of class. When asked about this in the interview afterwards, she said: 'We haven't really talked about the way we teach them.' It seems the lack of planning for co-teaching resulted in the local teacher assuming a role akin to that of a 'magician's assistant'.

In the observation at the primary school, even the second, more active, local teacher at times slipped into the role of an assistant, but when the PowerPoint failed to work, she snapped out of it and was able to take on the role of lead teacher, almost seamlessly reviewing a previous point while the NET took care of the technical difficulties and then resumed his lead role.

The NETs in the study said that they wanted local teachers to take on more active roles when team teaching, but that it was hard to achieve due to the heavy demands on local teachers. It was sometimes easier for the NETs just to take over when team teaching. In these two case studies, the team teaching worked better at the primary school, especially for one team. This may have been due to the fact that the primary school curriculum (PLPRW) was designed for team teaching and to the required monthly co-planning meetings. But even with these meetings in place, one local primary teacher chose not to take an active role. Moreover, having different curricula for the different types of teachers was somewhat problematic, as placing teachers in opposing roles in charge of different programmes (NETs in charge of PLPRW and local teachers in charge of GE), each with different goals, positioned them in a competitive struggle, each vying for more time to be spent on their respective programmes.

The panel chair at the primary school agreed that the PLPRW curriculum helped teachers share roles when team teaching, but noted that they had to make it more 'natural', as he states here:

> Our NET is a very good teacher. And as you know [local] teachers are very busy here in Hong Kong. And he prepared all the lesson plans beforehand. When we have to co-plan, he prints out all the lesson plans beforehand. So we just go and enjoy. ... In the past, for example the one-hour lesson, we put – it is very clear. The first 10 minutes, X – you have to speak. Like this. And then the next 10 minutes, Y, I have to – like this. But we find this does not work. In reality we cannot have X talking and then stop. My turn. It's quite hard. So we have to throw the ball to each other naturally. Naturally. Yeah.

In summary, pedagogical limitations of the native-speaker paradigm took two forms and were expressed through two metaphors. Just as Pinocchio wanted to be a real boy, our secondary school NET longed to be a real teacher but was denied that status due to the limited oral-English-only teaching role imposed on her by the school. As she states here: 'Because I feel, partially why I feel so frustrated last year was because I couldn't teach. I couldn't do what I wanted to do', or as noted in the previous quote, 'I really love teaching and I couldn't use my gift for teaching'. The metaphor of a 'magician's assistant' was used to illustrate the second limitation, the unequal partnership that sometimes occurred in team teaching. One of the local teachers in the primary school and the one in the secondary school had a self-imposed reduced pedagogical role in the observed team-teaching classes and did not take full advantage of the opportunity to engage in actual teaching when the NET was in the classroom. We contend that a contributing factor to these limitations is the emphasis 'on a standard linguistic norm and a standard uniform sociocultural world' that the native-speaker paradigm maintains and that, as Ryan (op cit) notes, many scholars find to be outdated and problematic.

Professional reductions/limitations

The panel chair at the primary school noted the importance of the NET in the promotion of the school in the following quote:

> Um, also for the parents, [we] also remind him that after school, after school, say good-bye to the students. It is a kind of promotion. It is not just teaching English. If you have a NET outside of your school, especially in front of the school gates, saying good-bye to the students, then the parents will pick up their students like this – 'Hi Mr X' – it is kind of an advertisement. And he does it very well.

While this promotional role at this school – what we call that of a 'poster child' – was not the NET's only function, it has the potential to commandeer the more essential role of language educator and reduce the NET to a selling point for the school.

Related to the poster child role, but more menacing, is the positioning of local teachers in contrast to a reified White native expert speaker. This positioning focuses on the contrasts between the local teachers and the NET in terms of being or not being a native speaker, having or not having 'gold hair' and having or not having 'blue eyes' (see interview extract below). This limited construction positions the local teacher not only as non-native but also as non-White and non-expert.

Although the NET at the primary school was actually a non-native speaker himself and had a distinct Eastern European accent, his appearance as a White Westerner mitigated his 'non-nativeness' and afforded him some of the prestige and power of a native speaker. During the interview with the primary panel chair, it was mentioned that the NET was a 'non-native', and the panel chair said the following:

> Sometimes I just – it is not a complaint. No matter how hard I work in the field of English, my face, my hair, it is not gold hair, I do not have blue eyes. So when I talk to others in English, they may not trust me in this way. But for our NET or other NETs, whatever they say in English, the Chinese will believe because they think it is their mother tongue.

As the quotes above and below reveal, the native-speaker paradigm sets up the native speaker as superior, with 'advantages' and 'exciting moments'. The panel chair at the primary school said the following:

> Sometimes, we also have the feeling with the NET ... to let him talk more because you can see the **advantage**. For the students they meet the local teachers every day. So during that **exciting** moment then they would like to hear the NET more and this would be great for them to learn the accent from him [our emphasis].

This was also expressed by the local teacher interviewed at the primary school, who felt that NETs are better teachers in some cases, as if interesting teaching was intrinsic or unique to NETs.

> Yeah. For the reading and speaking part maybe the NET is better because they, I think, NETs can teach English in a funny way. And for me I can't – I am very straight. And sometime they have an interesting way to arise people's interest.

To summarise, two more limitations to collaboration that the native-speaker paradigm puts on teachers were found, and these we classified as professional limitations, as they related to the teachers' image and persona. We described the first limitation in terms of the 'poster child', that is, when the NET is hired to be the face on the website, the image in the brochure and the person to meet and greet when prospective and current parents come to the school. A 'monkey on the stage' is how the primary NET put it, hired more for the image and status he provided the school rather than for his actual contribution to learning. But the more sinister professional limitation placed on local teachers occurs when the native-speaker paradigm positions local teachers as the inferior other, the non-White, non-native, non-expert, focusing on who they are not, instead of who they are and what they can do.

Towards a new paradigm: native and non-native teachers as English language educators with multiple and changing identities to draw from and develop

In these two case studies, although there was some evidence of collaborative practice, it was hampered by a native-speaker paradigm that limited the participating teachers' roles linguistically, pedagogically and professionally. The native-speaker paradigm, which is based on a deficit and difference model of 'nativeness' essentialises teachers for their 'native and non-nativeness' and fails to recognise and embrace the fluidity of teachers' identities and the complexity of language, learners and the language learning process.

Linguistically, the multilingual identities of all teachers need to be fully acknowledged and utilised to benefit student learning. In the study, the desire to hide the secondary NET's abilities to speak Cantonese and Mandarin resulted in a no-win situation in the school, where the NET was seen as a liar, the local teachers – and the entire school – were incriminated and the students suffered from a sense of betrayal. In Hong Kong society, where trilingualism and biliteracy are celebrated, a monolingual approach to language education is not productive. The local teachers' use of L1 to help students' with English learning, for instance, should not be seen as an intrusion into the English classroom. In fact, there is a plenitude of literature that points to L1 as a powerful resource for L2 learning (Forman, 2010; Mahboob, 2010).

Pedagogically, teachers, whether native or non-native speakers, are unique individuals that bring with them varied beliefs, experiences and practices that influence language teaching in different ways. When a native speaker works alongside a non-native speaker or they team teach in the classroom, it is important that the collaboration brings out the best in each of them, instead of putting one (most often the native speaker) on a pedestal at the expense of the other. In collaboration, an equal relationship that taps the potential of each teacher is crucial. When basing collaborative practice solely on the native-speaker paradigm, it is difficult to overcome the inherent bias in favour of the native speaker.

For more productive and equitable collaboration to occur, native and non-native teachers should be valued equally. Discourse and policies that position the non-native as inferior, deficient in language and in need of outside expertise for professional development needs to be challenged. Local teachers should be seen as a valuable resource for Hong Kong's English language advancement. It must also be noted that such discourses do not give NETs clear advantages. Instead, they grant limited roles to them, including the role of personifying the target English language. Though the native-speaker paradigm places NETs in a highly privileged position, it also discourages them from actively participating in professional dialogues concerning these critical language issues with colleagues and students, which may profoundly shape pedagogical practices in classrooms.

Therefore, there is a need to build a workplace and profession of equity, where native and non-native teachers collaborate as professionals. Professional collegiality among local and international colleagues can be found at the university level, where differences in professors' various linguistic and cultural backgrounds are viewed as just some of the many strengths they bring to collaborative work. Although universities are, of course, different from primary and secondary schools in many ways, this more robust view of identity and professional respect and collaboration might serve as a model for primary and secondary schools to consider.

Possible future directions for research, practice and policy
Possible future directions for research are to explore how practice and policy might support the good work that local teachers are already doing as the foundation of English language teaching in Hong Kong. If NETs continue to be hired and placed in schools, how might a more equitable collaborative practice be encouraged? How can the myth be challenged that 'gold hair and blue eyes', as one local teacher put it, makes for better English teachers? And finally, what can be done to replace the native-speaker paradigm as the basis for collaboration with one that takes into account a more robust, fluid and complex understanding of teacher identity and that supports Hong Kong's goals – of providing trilingual and biliterate citizens as well as those of parallel native speaker programmes in other countries? These questions provide good food for thought and interesting avenues for further research.

References

Alvarez, I (2007) Foreign language education at the crossroads: Whose model of competence? *Language, Culture and Curriculum* 20/2: 126–139.

Boyle, J (1997) Native speaker teachers of English in Hong Kong. *Language and Education* 11/3: 163–181.

Braine, G (2010) *Nonnative speaker English teachers: Research, pedagogy, and professional growth*. New York, NY: Routledge.

Byram, M (1997) *Teaching and assessing intercultural competence*. Clevedon: Multilingual Matters.

Carless, DR (2006a) Collaborative EFL teaching in primary schools. *ELT Journal* 60/4: 328–335.

Carless, DR (2006b) Good practices in team teaching in Japan, South Korea and Hong Kong. *System* 34/3: 341–351.

Carless, DR and Walker, E (2006) Effective team teaching between local and native-speaking English teachers. *Language and Education* 20/6: 463–477.

Cheung, YL and Braine, G (2007) The attitudes of university students in Hong Kong towards native and non-native teachers of English. *RELC Journal* 38/3: 257–277.

Dormer, JE (2010) 'Strength through difference: Optimizing NEST/NNEST relationships on a school staff' in Mahboob, A (ed) *The NNEST lens: Nonnative English speakers in TESOL*. Newcastle Upon Tyne: Cambridge Scholars Publishing, 285–304.

Dormer, JE (2012) 'Shared competence: Native and nonnative English speaking teachers' collaboration that benefits all' in Honigsfeld, A and Dove, M (eds) *Co-teaching and other collaborative practices in the EFL/ESL classroom: Rational, research, reflections, and recommendations*. Charlotte, NC: Information Age Press, 229–238.

Forman, R (2010) 'Ten principles of bilingual pedagogy in EFL' in Mahboob, A (ed) *The NNEST lens: Nonnative English speakers in TESOL*. Newcastle Upon Tyne: Cambridge Scholars Publishing, 54–86.

Griffin, P and Woods, K (2009) *Evaluation of the Enhanced Native-speaking English Teacher Scheme in Hong Kong Secondary Schools*. Assessment Research Centre, The University of Melbourne.

Griffin P, Woods, K Storey, P, Wong, EKP and Fung WYW (2006) *Evaluation of the Native-speaking English Teacher Scheme for Primary Schools in Hong Kong 2004–2006*. Assessment Research Centre, The University of Melbourne.

Hargreaves, A (1992) 'Cultures of teaching: A focus for change' in Hargreaves, A and Fullan, MG (eds) *Understanding teacher development*. London: Cassell, 218–240.

Holliday, A (2005) *The struggle to teach English as an international language*. Oxford: Oxford University Press.

Lasagabaster, D and Sierra, JM (2005) 'What do students think about the pros and cons of having a native speaker teacher?' in Llurda, E (ed) *Non-native language teachers: Perceptions, challenges and contributions to the profession*. New York, NY: Springer, 217–241.

Lee, I (2005) 'English language teaching in Hong Kong Special Administrative Region (HK SAR): A continuous challenge' in Braine, G (ed) *Teaching English to the world: History, curriculum, and practice.* Mahwah, NJ: Lawrence Erlbaum Associates, 35–45.

Liu, J (2008) 'Empowering nonnative-English-speaking teachers through collaboration with their native-English-speaking colleagues in EFL settings' in Liu, J (ed) *English language teaching in China: New approaches, perspectives, and standards.* New York, NY: Continuum, 133–152.

Ma, LPF (2009) 'Student perceptions of native English teachers and Local English Teachers' in Mahboob, A and Lipovsky, C (eds) *Studies in applied linguistics and language learning.* Newcastle Upon Tyne: Cambridge Scholars Publishing, 325–348.

Ma, LPF (2012) Advantages and disadvantages of native- and nonnative-English speaking teachers: Student perceptions in Hong Kong. *TESOL Quarterly* 46/2: 280–304.

Mahboob, A (2010) *The NNEST lens: Nonnative English speakers in TESOL.* Newcastle upon Tyne: Cambridge Scholars Publishing.

Mahboob, A and Golden, R (2013) Looking for native speakers of English: discrimination in English language teaching job advertisements. *Voices in Asia Journal* 1/1: 71–81.

McKay, SL (2002) *Teaching English as an international language.* Oxford: Oxford University Press.

Medgyes, P (1992) Native or non-native: Who's worth more? *English Language Teaching Journal* 46: 340–349.

Moussu, L and Llurda, E (2008) Non-native English-speaking English language teachers: History and research. *Language Teaching* 41/3: 315–348.

Ryan, P (2014) 'The English as a foreign or international classroom' in Jackson, J (ed) *The Routledge handbook of language and intercultural communication.* NewYork, NY: Routledge, 422–433.

Sharifian, F (ed) (2009) *English as an international language: Perspectives and pedagogical issues.* Bristol: Multilingual Matters.

Tong, SYA (2010) Lessons learned? School leadership and curriculum reform in Hong Kong. *Asia Pacific Journal of Education* 30/2: 231–242.

Trent, J (2012) The discursive positioning of teachers: Native-speaking English teachers and educational discourse in Hong Kong. *TESOL Quarterly* 46/1: 104–126.

Walker, E (2001) Roles of native-speaker English teachers in Hong Kong secondary schools. *Asia Pacific Journal of Language in Education* 4/2: 51–77.

13

'Almost' native speakers: the experiences of Visible Ethnic-Minority Native English-Speaking Teachers

Eljee Javier, University of Manchester, UK

Introduction

In TESOL, professionals are often categorised in terms of being either 'native speaker' (NS) or 'non-native speaker' (NNS). These terms are problematic because their meanings are imprecise, yet they remain widely used in English language teaching to place value on individuals. There is a need to problematise the NS/NNS binary distinction to address the inequality embedded within these labels. In order to do so, this chapter draws attention to the existence of Visible Ethnic-Minority Native-English-Speaking Teachers (VEM-NESTs), whose identities are not easily categorised within such a binary distinction. This topic developed out of my personal experiences (as a Canadian-Filipino) of working as an English language teacher (see Javier, 2010). Generally speaking, I am often considered 'almost' a native speaker of English. On the one hand, I speak English with an American accent, so for some I sound like a 'real' NS. However, I began to learn that I do not look like a native speaker because of my racial identity as a Filipino.

In this chapter, I begin with a brief discussion of the way racial and ethnic identities are embedded within the NS/NNS binary distinction by drawing upon the concept of 'Whiteness' from Critical Race Theory. I then discuss how the association between 'White' racial identities and 'native speaker of English' can affect the way VEM-NESTs are perceived in specific contexts. To illustrate this relationship, I present data from two VEM-NEST participants. The data used in this chapter was part of my doctoral study (see Javier, 2015) that examined how individual VEM-NESTs used the binary distinction as a reference point to negotiate identities that are recognised within TESOL yet challenge the blunt categorisation of NS/NNS labels.

'Native speaker' as linguistic and professional benchmarks for quality

The NS/NNS binary distinction has its roots in the continued appeal of using a specific definition of NS as a benchmark to measure the linguistic ability and, by extension, professional ability of TESOL practitioners. On the surface, having a benchmark is regarded as a 'common sense' view (Davies, 2003: 2) but this rationale is not adequate because the common markers for an NS are not fit for purpose. On the one hand, there is Halliday's (1978) notion that the term 'native speaker' is defined as someone who has learned a language in childhood, but this definition is questionable because highly proficient users of a language who have learned a language at a later stage in their lives would not be considered an NS on this basis, regardless of their language ability (Cook, 1999). On the other hand, the NNS term emphasises the 'non' aspect, implying a deficiency as a language user (Medgyes, 1999) and this helps to highlight the superior status accorded to native speakers of a language.

These labels are closely attributed to competency; the native speaker is defined in relation to mastery of the language and is assumed to have a subconscious and intuitive understanding of the language (Stern, 1983). This positions the NS as a linguistic model: as Hackert (2012: 1) argues:

> the native speaker intuitions are not only tapped as a data source but also as the final arbiter of the grammaticality and acceptability of particular syntactic structure.

One of the inherent problems of this way of looking at language learning is that language learners are regarded as imitators of native speakers rather than language users in their own right (Cook, op cit). From this view, NNSs are regarded as linguistically handicapped (Nemtchinova, 2005) and, as Widdowson (1994: 387) argues, this perceived deficiency is extended to their professionalism:

> Native-speaker expertise is assumed to extend to the teaching of the language. They not only have a patent on proper English, but on proper ways of teaching it as well.

Thus, competency in the English language, and its associations with teaching ability, remains a key feature in defining the NS/NNS categories.

The NS/NNS binary distinction continues to influence how the ELT industry has developed around the world. This categorisation has left a legacy on the historical development of language policies in former colonies (see Rapatahana and Bunce, 2012) and influenced the racialised identity expectations of NESTs (Native English-Speaking Teachers) in TESOL. Pennycook (1994) contends that the use of English in educational and political systems has mainly served the interests of the elites, as a language of inclusion for the few and of exclusion for the many, setting up a system in which for linguistic imperialism to take hold and flourish. However, the domination of the English language cannot be easily described as merely a simplistic, top-down imposition process by quasi/neo-colonial organisations because the complexities are related to the various Englishes that can be found in the world today (Rapatahana and Bunce, op cit).

Racial identities as embedded in the NS/NNS binary distinction

NS/NNS have largely been defined on a linguistic basis. However, there have been more recent discussions on how race is an additional feature of this binary definition (e.g. Kubota and Lin, 2006; Harris and Rampton, 2003; Clark, 2013). One approach to understanding the theoretical relationship between race and NS/NNS binary distinction is through the concept of 'Whiteness' used in Critical Race Theory (Delgado and Stefancic, 2001). Whiteness is viewed as a structural social norm that considers the racial category 'White' as an invisible standard against which all other racial identities are measured.

The NS/NNS binary distinction is affected by the concept of Whiteness through the way the racial category of White is associated with 'Western' English-speaking countries. Using essentialised definitions of NS/NNS and White/non-White, I argue that White NSs remain the standard to which, according to Ruecker and Ives (2014), positive associations, such as competency in the English language and professionalism in English language teaching, are automatically attributed. Conversely, it can be argued that 'non-White' NNSs work on a deficit model in which their linguistic competency and characteristics associated with their racial identities are measured against criteria associated with White NSs (see Amin, 1997). This binary distinction continues to be problematic because it bluntly categorises individuals based on reductionist views of 'NS', 'NNS', 'White' and 'non-White'. My argument here is not that individuals should be restricted from identifying with these labels but rather that these labels need further questioning so that we can acknowledge the existence of identities that go beyond these categories.

'Visible Ethnic-Minority' Native English-Speaking Teachers (VEM-NESTs)

Visible Ethnic-Minority Native English-Speaking Teachers, or 'VEM-NESTs', constitute a category of teacher that does not easily fit in the NS/NNS binary distinction because their linguistic identities as NESTs are perceived to be at odds with 'non-White' racial and ethnic identities. For example, a VEM-NEST may be considered 'almost a native speaker' in the sense that the individual sounds like a native speaker of English but does not look like one. VEM-NESTs are compelled to use the binary distinction as a reference point because these labels are recognised in TESOL, yet, in doing so, they often go through a great amount of effort to explain who they are. In considering these views, I would like to offer the perspectives of VEM-NESTs whose experiences serve as examples of how this particular group of teachers negotiate their identities in light of the linguistic and racial expectations of the NS/NNS binary distinction.

Narrative-based approach: restoried narratives of experience

The examples presented in this chapter were part of a larger study using narrative data generated for my doctoral thesis (see Javier, 2015). A narrative-based approach considers the stories people tell of themselves as a way for the audience to access how individuals come to understand their own experiences as well as their own identities (see Lieblich et al., 1998; Riessman, 1993). The telling of stories is a meaning-making process in which narrators come to understand their experiences and, in doing so, can open up the possibility of a better understanding of themselves.

The data used in my thesis was individual restoried narratives. Restorying is used in narrative research as a way of organising data into a particular format. The final format is dependent on the processes undertaken and the extent to which the original data is manipulated. On the one hand, some narrative approaches are considered re-presentations because the final format is very different from the original data (Glesne, 1997). For example, poetic renderings of narrative data (e.g. Gallardo et al., 2009) aim to focus more on presenting the aesthetic qualities of the narratives and consequently establish a different orientation in the relationship between the reader and the narrator.

Other restorying approaches focus on organising data into a narrative format. Observation field notes and interview transcripts are some examples of data that is put into a narrative format for the purpose of the analysis. Often this involves a complex set of analytic procedures based on the central feature of restorying a story from the original raw data (Ollerenshaw and Creswell, 2002). Different approaches to restorying focus on different features, such as 'problem–solution' (e.g. Yussen and Ozcan, 1996), particular elements of experience (e.g. Clandinin and Connelly, 2000) or structural forms (e.g. Riessman, 2008).

The data used for this study were restoried narratives, which are defined as single narratives developed through combining written narrative content and semi-structured interview data. I did not have an a priori relationship with any of the participants that took part in the study and was therefore unsure if I would be able to access sufficient data from a single encounter (e.g. one interview). Taking these concerns into account, I designed a methodological approach that had two potential storytelling opportunities, the data from which I could combine into a single story. Below is a summary of the data generation process undertaken with the participants in my study.

Stage 1
First, I wrote my own story of my VEM-NEST experiences, which included a brief description of my background, an account of a specific situation that made me aware of my VEM-NEST identity and my reflections upon this situation. In a very real sense, the participants were as unknown to me as I was to them, and I felt that I needed to go one step further to create some kind of relationship if they were to share their stories with me. I needed to 'explain' myself (Clandinin and Connelly, op cit) in a way that presented who I am and how this study is related to who I am. My story was autobiographical in nature and included a description of my linguistic and ethnic background, which are aspects of my identity closely tied to my awareness of being a VEM-NEST.

My story was broadly organised under three headings: 'Background', 'Critical incident' and 'Reflection'. In the first story-writing experience, the participants were asked to read my story and then write their own story of their VEM-NEST experiences. The participants were not restricted to using my story as a model; however, the majority of the participants seemed to organise their story in a loosely similar way.

Stage 2

I developed a set of interview questions based on the content of their written stories and arranged to meet individual participants over Skype to conduct a one-to-one interview (Robson, 2002; Mishler, 1986). This interview lasted approximately an hour and was recorded with the participants' consent.

The second storytelling opportunity focused on clarifying the content of the participants' written stories. The interview questions were generated to sequentially follow the content of the written narratives and were designed to elicit further details and/or clarify information.

Stage 3

This final stage was the process of creating the restoried narratives. First, the interviews were transcribed in their entirety on a word processor. Next, I proceeded to delete my portion of the interview (e.g. questions asked) and any pauses or fillers from the transcription so that only the participants' responses remained. Then I began the process of restorying, which involved combining the participants' interview responses with the content of their written stories. I focused on matching descriptions of particular situations with the participants' reflections and/or evaluations of the situation. After the content was 'matched', I proceeded to organise the content chronologically, from the earliest situation to the most recent.

This restorying approach situates the storytellers' reflections on their experiences at particular points in the narrative. Placing the written and interview data chronologically presented the participants' experiences in a more coherent format and allowed the analysis to focus on one data set rather than two.

For the purposes of this chapter, specific extracts from the restoried narratives of two VEM-NESTs are presented. The data was chosen on the basis of how clearly it illustrated the process the participants undertook to negotiate their VEM-NEST identities in their specific contexts.

Li's Story 1: VEM-NEST as considered 'foreign enough'

Li identifies herself as Chinese-Canadian. She was born in Hong Kong and had spent a considerable amount of her childhood moving between Hong Kong and Canada. Li is fluent in both English and Cantonese, and is a highly proficient user of Mandarin Chinese. However, she considers herself a native speaker of English partly because of her identity as a Canadian but more so because she learned English from a young age.

After graduating from an undergraduate programme at a Canadian university, Li first taught English as an unqualified teacher in Hong Kong. This experience meant that she became interested in pursuing a career in teaching. To this end, she completed a CELTA (Certificate in English Language Teaching to Adults) course and has now had experience teaching in EFL contexts, first in South Korea and then in China. At the time of the study, she was working in Hong Kong as a qualified EFL teacher on a casual, non-contractual basis.

Li's story is an example of how she negotiated an identity that was associated with being a foreigner in order to be accepted as a NEST in her specific context. The following is an excerpt from Li's restoried narrative, and this specific situation took place while she was working in a private language school in South Korea.

I always knew that being an Asian meant it would be immensely difficult for me to teach English as a second language because of the general impression and bias Asians carry around. Most parents do not believe that you are a native English speaker with an Asian face. This simply cannot be true in their world (my own parents have the same impression).

My very first day at my first English teaching job in South Korea, I realised how true this notion was. I stepped into the office, and my Korean manager spoke to me in Korean and asked me if I was a parent of one of the children. Our Korean support team had to explain to her that I was an English teacher and that I was Canadian, not Korean.

I had the exact same reaction from the children the first time I stepped into the classroom:

Children (in Korean):	*Heh? I thought this was English class time? Why is the Korean teacher here?*
Me (in English):	*No Korean in class!*
Children (in English):	*Teacher not Korean? English teacher?*
Me (in English):	*Yes, I'm the English teacher. I'm Canadian.*
Children (in English):	*Do you speak Korean? Are you Korean?*
Me (in English):	*No, I'm Canadian. I speak English.*
Children (in English):	*But teacher look Korean. Are you Korean?*
Me:	*No ... I'm ... I'm Chinese.*

It's a little bit hard for them to accept that you're not White but you're from Canada. So it just doesn't register. With them it takes like five or six times before they start saying 'Oh, she's Canadian' and then next time they come to class they forget again, but if you tell them you're Chinese then immediately they're like, 'Oh she's Chinese' and then they all get it. Well, they'd ask questions like 'Do you know how to write this in Chinese?' or 'Do you know any Korean?' or 'Why is your English so good?' Many times in South Korea I found that admitting I was Chinese was much easier than convincing children that I was Canadian. Questions stopped and an expression of understanding would dawn on their faces. It was something very useful to me.

The concept of NEST as a foreigner was a topic that Li explored. In this situation, Li was aware that foreigners were generally considered non-Korean people from abroad and, in particular, that NESTs were viewed as White foreigners. As a non-Korean, 'non-White' foreigner, Li encountered difficulty explaining her identity. She was aware that NESTs were generally associated with 'White foreigners' and subsequently tried using different approaches, such as introducing herself as

Chinese to distinguish herself as a 'non-Korean type of foreigner'. This distinction was key because, in this specific context, Korean teachers (e.g. non-foreigners) were not afforded the same status as White and, to a lesser extent, 'non-White' foreign teachers.

First, Li introduced herself as Canadian because she observed that in her teaching context, NESTs were associated with countries such as Canada. However, she quickly realised her students expected Canadian NESTs to be White, which made it difficult for Li's Canadian identity to be accepted by her students. Instead, she chose to emphasise her Chinese identity as a way of explaining that she wasn't Korean but was still a foreigner and therefore 'foreign enough' to be considered a NEST. As a VEM-NEST, Li's goal was not to look foreign per se, but rather to be considered 'not Korean'.

Li's Story 2: The advantage of being a 'non-White foreigner'

In a seemingly contradictory view, Li felt that being considered a 'non-White foreigner' was something of an advantage. The example presented here is from her reflections on her teaching experiences in mainland China.

> So whenever I would go into a new class with the higher level students they'd go 'Oh I thought this was a foreign teacher class' and I'd be like 'No, I am a foreign teacher' and because these students were all adults it took more explaining but it hits them that I'm Chinese-Canadian and I do speak all three languages and they do know that but they're completely fine with it because they're there to learn English and they're actually people paying to learn English so they don't speak Chinese to you. They find it actually to be a little bit of an advantage as well because sometimes they have questions that they just don't know how to ask in English so they give you the word in Chinese and I can translate that for you and I can explain that in English for you as well.

This excerpt recounted a situation that took place in China and described the actions Li took when she met students for the first time, usually during the start of a new class. There was certainly some explaining on her part, but Li felt that the students eventually accepted her because she was someone they could relate to in different ways. The following is Li's reflection on the perceptions of her Chinese students:

> Having an Asian face and teaching in China was not a barrier for me. In fact, it was the greatest advantage I could ever have asked for. Other than the initial, expected, shock and awe reactions from the students, I realised that they really appreciated having an Asian native-English speaker as their teacher.

> Often, I would have students (especially younger ones) come up to me and say how relieved they were to see an Asian face and that they were really intimidated by the other foreign teachers because they were 'truly foreign'. Some would even come and ask how it is that I could speak English so well, without any Chinese accent at all. For all those compliments, I am truly grateful for my background and the advantages it has brought me. It was a lot easier for them to ask questions and actually some of them were really confident speaking

to me as opposed to speaking with an actual person with coloured eyes or different coloured hair because they're like what if they say something wrong and offend the other person and because I have the same face they feel I have the same culture and they can say anything and it's OK to make mistakes because I would understand better than anybody else.

Li's journey of becoming 'foreign enough' saw her turn potentially negative perceptions of her as a 'non-White foreigner' into an identity that she used to her advantage. Li has learned to expect her VEM-NEST identity to be rejected in EFL teaching contexts through her own upbringing (e.g. her parents believe Asians cannot be English NS). This expectation has informed the way she has gone about negotiating an identity that has been acceptable in her specific contexts. In the situation in South Korea, Li learned that she was more readily accepted as a Chinese foreigner and chose to negotiate her NEST identity in this way. In the situation in China, she experienced a similar line of questioning but, by this point, she felt that being a Chinese foreigner made her more accessible to her students. Proving her NEST credentials did not seem to be as important in the light of being considered Chinese because her students felt that, as someone like them, she could relate to their struggles and their experiences.

Andrés's story: the 'almost Asian'

Andrés identifies himself as a Mexican-American and studied Mandarin Chinese to a high level of proficiency at university. At the time of this study, Andrés was working in China as an EFL teacher. His facial features mark him out as 'Asian' despite his being of Mexican descent and consequently, when working in China, he was often mistaken for an 'ABC' (American-Born Chinese). Andrés's experiences working in China made him aware that in certain situations he could potentially pass as ethnically Chinese.

Living in China further confirmed that many people thought I was some mix of Chinese or had an East Asian background. I would always explain to cab drivers or locals I randomly had conversations with that I was Mexican-American and that neither of my parents are Asian. It never bothered me and it still doesn't. Sometimes people I meet know right away that I am Latino, other times they think I am a mix or have an Asian background.

This was an example of how Andrés was mistaken for a person of Chinese descent both inside and outside an EFL context. Attempting to engage with local people in Mandarin Chinese usually marked him out as a foreigner because of the way he spoke, but other times it did not. Regardless, his intention was not to blend in but rather to communicate with the local community. Unlike other participants, Andrés was able to use the local language to establish himself as a foreigner and, when necessary, explain his VEM-NEST identity. The following excerpt is an example of how Andrés negotiated his VEM-NEST identity in an EFL context.

It wasn't until I taught in China that I was aware of my visible ethnic minority status. All of the Chinese staff members were very curious to know my background and when they would randomly find out I knew how to speak

Mandarin, it was assumed I was an 'ABC' – American Born Chinese. I was asked and talked about and I knew exactly what they were saying – none of it was offensive and I've never taken offence, I was just interested in the fact that they were so curious.

And then the questions began:

'So is your mum or dad Chinese?'

'What about your grandparents – where are they from?'

'Did you leave China and grow up in America?'

With the students, being so young, they speak Mandarin to any teacher. They are too young to distinguish what I am and then decide whether to talk to me in what little English they know or nothing at all. They will ask where I'm from and I tell them America – so from that point, they just assume I know English and there isn't any further questioning from my students.

Andrés felt that questions about his ethnic identity were asked out of curiosity and consequently, he did not take any offence because he did not view this line of questioning as a challenge. In the example above, the people he was interacting with were not sure where Andrés fitted into a NS/NNS binary distinction. However, explaining that he was American allowed him to meet their linguistic NEST expectations, which then allowed him to gain acceptance as a VEM-NEST. Andrés reflects on the change in perception in the following excerpt:

I think that when students or parents see this programme they want to see a White American, you know, with blond hair, blue eyes. That's what they want. When they see someone from a different background or someone who's not some perfect teacher like in the pictures we display with a big smile, I think it doesn't sit well. I'm not sure what they think but when they come and want to see a White person to be their teacher ... you just want to prove them wrong, 'Relax, I can teach.' I think that's what they want. They just assume 'America' so you're native. English is what you know, so you say American and put that out there and they're like 'Cool he's American' and then it goes from that to something superficial – 'OK cool, he's American but why isn't he blond and White' or something.

Andrés's story is one in which he does not view justifying his VEM-NEST identity as negative, but rather views these encounters as opportunities to engage with local people. However, he is aware of the underlying identity assumptions that affect the way NESTs are expected to be foreigners – individuals who are not from China and who do not look Chinese.

The questioning of VEM-NEST identities

One aspect of the direct and indirect questioning of their NS identities is the VEM-NESTs' approach to answering these queries. VEM-NESTs in this study learned through experience to expect this line of questioning, and while the intention behind the questions was interpreted differently, the participants were nonetheless prepared to answer inquiries related to their NEST identity.

The stories presented are examples of how VEM-NESTs negotiated their identities in countries where learners, teachers and parents had few experiences of living multiculturally. This undoubtedly exacerbated differences and brought the issue of race to the foreground. Thus, when attempting to use their Canadian and American identities, both Li and Andrés were met with some resistance because these identities are generally associated with White foreigners. This resistance often materialises in the form of VEM-NESTs being questioned about their identity (e.g. 'Where are you really from?').

The questioning of VEM-NEST identity was a common event experienced by the participants and indicates how normal it is to question NESTs if they are not White. This shows that, to an extent, the nationalities of 'Inner Circle' countries (Kachru, 1992) remain associated with the providers of English native speakers and their racial identity continues to be assumed as White. In TESOL, the combination of Whiteness, native-speakerism and the colonial history of ELT form a well-established frame in which this line of questioning is normal.

From 'almost' to 'a different type'

Questions focused on the participants' backgrounds were attempts made by other people to understand where VEM-NESTs could fit within an NS/NNS binary worldview. In the examples given, the participants were usually questioned when first meeting a new audience. During these initial encounters, the potential for change was realised in the form of acceptance of the VEM-NEST as a different type of NEST. Sometimes this acceptance was achieved through the VEM-NEST presenting alternative definitions of what constituted a 'real' NEST. For Li and Andrés, their respective VEM identities challenged the stereotype of NESTs as White foreigners. What is not clear is the extent to which the VEM-NESTs were considered as equals to their White counterparts. In Li's situation, she found that the people in her context did not accept her as a Canadian because she was not White. Through highlighting her Chinese identity, she was able to negotiate a VEM-NEST identity that was more acceptable in that context.

The NS/NNS binary distinction remains a major way of categorising individuals and it is difficult to imagine TESOL without it. Acknowledging the variety of categories that already exist is a way of challenging the inequalities that result in the way the binary distinction is usually foregrounded. The examples presented in this chapter draw attention to the existence of VEM-NESTs, individuals that do not easily fit into the binary distinction because of their racial and ethnic identities. Andrés and myself are examples of how VEM-NESTs emphasise their nationalities as a way of being placed into the NS/NNS binary distinction. In Andrés's specific context, his American identity had the highest value. In many of my own experiences, foregrounding my Canadian identity was met with acceptance. In contrast, Li's example illustrates that sometimes one's nationality is not enough to explain one's NEST identity. In her context, the possibility that a NEST could be 'non-White' was difficult to accept. In response to this rejection, Li chose not to align herself with the notion of 'NEST as Canadian' but portrayed herself as a 'Chinese foreigner' in order to be considered an EFL teacher.

The stories shared by Andrés and Li (as well as my own story) are examples which demonstrate how we have been accepted as a different 'type' of NEST – one that conforms to the linguistic expectations yet challenges the racial and ethnic identity stereotypes. What is not clear is whether we were attributed equal status to White NESTs or regarded as exceptions. Our experiences reveal a range of different categories of professional identities that exist within the NS/NNS binary distinction that ought to be acknowledged if TESOL is to be as inclusive as it appears to be (Holliday, 2005).

Further considerations

Problematising the NS/NNS binary distinction is a process that needs to be addressed theoretically and practically. The theorisation of race and professional identities in TESOL would benefit from further exploration using *theoretical standpoints* (e.g. Critical Race Theory). Doing so would aid in examining the hierarchical structures that affect the way race and racism are understood.

This chapter focused on examining the experiences of English language teachers. Further research could examine the perspectives of different stakeholders (e.g. students, English language centre managers or recruitment agents) and would enable researchers to examine how different groups perceive the racial identities of TESOL professionals. Moreover, perspectives of White NESTs, White NNESTs and VEM-NNESTs would be a welcome addition to understanding how race is perceived in the NS/NNS binary distinction. Further research might well be conducted in a way that focuses on the influence of contextual factors, such as limiting the geographical location of the participants to one country.

Secondly, but just as importantly, research might explore how to practically raise awareness of the issues regarding race on an individual and institutional level, both within the classroom and out in the broader field of TESOL. Research into areas such as teacher development curriculum design, the hiring practices of English language providers and reflexive awareness of one's own racial and ethnic identities would be beneficial.

Racial and ethnic identities need to be foregrounded as a way of further problematising the NS/NNS binary distinction in discussions regarding the teacher identities of professionals in TESOL. Discussing race-related topics typically arouses discomfort and a sense of threat in both everyday and academic discourses because it is an emotive and potentially divisive area of research. This study engages with topics that are viewed by some as uncomfortable. However, increased awareness and discussion in this area is an important step towards developing a more inclusive and equitable field for all.

References

Amin, N (1997) Race and the identity of the nonnative ESL teacher. TESOL *Quarterly* 31/3: 580–583.

Clandinin, D and Connelly, F (2000) *Narrative inquiry: Experience and story in qualitative research.* San Francisco: Jossey-Bass Publishers.

Clark, U (2013) *Language and identity in Englishes.* Milton Park

Cook, V (1999) Going beyond the native speaker in language teaching. *TESOL Quarterly* 33/2: 185–209.

Davies, A (2003) *The native speaker: Myth and reality.* Clevedon: Multilingual Matters.

Delgado, R and Stefancic, J (2001) *Critical race theory: An introduction.* New York, NY: New York University Press.

Gallardo, H, Furman, R and Kulkarni, S (2009) Explorations of Depression: Poetry and Narrative in Autoethnographic Qualitative Research. *Qualitative Social Work* 8/3: 287–304.

Glesne, C (1997) That rare feeling: Re-presenting research through poetic transcription. *Qualitative Inquiry* 3/2: 202–221.

Hackert, S (2012) *The emergence of the English native speaker: A chapter in nineteenth century linguistic thought.* Berlin: De Gruyter Mouton.

Halliday, M (1978) *Language as social semiotic.* London: Arnold,.

Harris, R and Rampton, B (2003) *The Language, Ethnicity and Race Reader.* London: Routledge.

Holliday, A (2005) *The struggle to teach English as an international language.* Oxford: Oxford University Press.

Javier, E (2010) 'Foreign-ness, race and the native speaker' in Nunan, D and Choi, J (eds) *Language and Culture: Reflective narratives and the emergence of identity.* New York, NY: Routledge, 97–102.

Javier, E (2015) *Narratively performed role identities of visible ethnic minority, native English speaking teachers in TESOL.* Unpublished PhD thesis. University of Manchester, UK.

Kachru, B (1992) World Englishes: Approaches, issues and resources. *Language Teaching* 25/01: 1–14.

Kubota, R and Lin, A (2006) Race and TESOL: Introduction to concepts and theories. *TESOL Quarterly* 40/3: 471–493.

Lieblich, A, Tuval-Mashiach, R and Zilber, T (1998) *Narrative research: Reading, analysis and interpretation.* Thousand Oaks, CA: Sage.

Medgyes, P (1999) 'When the teacher is a non-native speaker' in Braine, G (ed) *Non-native educators in English language teaching*. Mahwah, NJ: Lawrence Erlbaum Associates, 177–196.

Mishler, E (1986) *Research interviewing*. Cambridge, MA: Harvard University Press.

Nemtchinova, E (2005) Host teachers' evaluations of non-native English speaking teacher trainees: A perspective from the classroom. *TESOL Quarterly* 39/2: 235–261.

Ollerenshaw, JA and Creswell, JW (2002) Narrative research: A comparison of two restorying data analysis approaches. *Qualitative Inquiry* 8/3: 329–347.

Pennycook, A (1994) *The cultural politics of English as an international language*. New York, NY: Longman.

Rapatahana, V and Bunce, P (eds) (2012) *English language as Hydra: Its impacts on non-English language cultures*. Bristol: Multilingual Matters.

Robson, C (2002) *Real world research: A resource for users of social research methods in applied settings*. Chichester: Wiley.

Riessman, C (1993) *Narrative analysis*. Newbury Park, CA: Sage.

Riessman, C (2008) 'Looking back on narrative research: an exchange' in Salmon, P, Riessman, C, Andrews, M, Tombukou, M and Squires, C (eds) *Doing Narrative Research*. London: Sage, 78–85.

Ruecker, T and Ives, L (2014) White native English speakers needed: the rhetorical construction of privilege in online teacher recruitment spaces. *TESOL Quarterly*, 49(4), 733–756.

Stern, H (1983) *Fundamental concepts in language teaching*. Oxford: Oxford University Press.

Widdowson, H (1994) The ownership of English. *TESOL Quarterly* 28/2: 377–389.

Yussen, S and Ozcan, N (1996) The development of knowledge about narratives. *Issues in Education* 2/1: 1–68.

14

Opinions and positions on native-speakerism

Sue Garton, Aston University, Birmingham, UK
Fiona Copland, University of Stirling, UK
Steve Mann, Centre for Applied Linguistics, University of Warwick, UK

Introduction

The preceding chapters of this book have addressed a wide range of themes, bringing a plurality of voices and views to bear on this challenging and under-examined area of English language teaching. Some, for example, have explored particular NEST schemes, providing a lens through which to view the classroom realities of team teaching (e.g. Khánh and Spencer-Oatey; Lin and Wang) while others (Yanase; Javier) have addressed native-speakerism and, in doing so, have challenged our understandings of the term, or provided alternative readings of it. In this final chapter, we build a dialogue around the issues raised by introducing the views of leading figures who have been, over the years, major influences on research and theory in this area. Each contributor was approached by email with the following message:

> We have recently been asked by the British Council to put together a collection around the broad topic of 'native-speakerism' in language teaching. We will have a number of full-length chapters, which will be written by people currently involved in the field. However, we would also like to include a number of short 'opinion' pieces from well-known figures who have had a major influence on research and theory in this area. We would therefore like to invite you to provide such a piece of between 250–500 words on any aspect of the above topic. The topic of your piece might include, for example, identifying key issues, critical reflections on concepts and ideas, summaries of current developments, important recent research, and areas for future research.

We are delighted that so many of those we approached responded positively, with insightful and thoughtful pieces which picked up on many of the themes identified in the chapters (although not always sticking to the 500-word limit!). In what follows, we provide the contributors' full texts with a brief linking commentary.

In the first opinion piece below, Andy Kirkpatrick indirectly raises a key theme that has been apparent in a number of the chapters in this book: the disconnect between academia and the 'real world'. The main criticisms of native-speakerism, such as the belief that NS norms should be the model for language learners, discriminatory hiring practices and, indeed, the relevance of the term itself, are well rehearsed in academic circles. However, these issues often remain unquestioned 'at the chalk face'. Indeed, at a recent TESOL Convention, Lia Khami-Stein noted that much progress has been made in promoting the role of the LET in terms of research, publications, conference presence and so on, but that LETs still face considerable challenges in the job market, especially in the private sector. In his piece, Kirkpatrick succinctly summarises the main issues concerning native-speakerism today.

Just because I'm a native speaker
Andy Kirkpatrick, Griffith University, Brisbane, Australia

While it is now accepted that the great majority of English speakers in today's world are people who have learned English as an additional language and are first language speakers of languages other than English, the belief that the native speaker should remain both target and model for the language learner remains remarkably resilient. At the same time, the most preferred teacher of English in today's world remains the native speaker. Native speakers of English command higher salaries and superior working conditions than their non-native counterparts in many countries, language teaching institutions and schools. It indeed remains possible for native speakers of English to be employed as English teachers solely on the grounds that they are native speakers. In many cases, they may not even need any teaching qualifications or relevant experience. Thus, native speakers with no qualifications or relevant experience can be employed ahead of fully qualified and highly experienced non-native-speaker teachers. This hiring of people solely upon the accident of birthright remains a major source of prejudice and discrimination, yet it is one that is not only allowed but openly encouraged in many settings. While no one could conceivably now hire (or refuse to hire) an employee solely on the basis of race, religion or gender, it remains apparently acceptable to hire (or refuse to hire) someone solely on the basis of their native language.

This practice of hiring language teachers solely on the basis of their linguistic birthright is not only prejudiced; it is also ill informed. Native speakers of English now constitute a minority of English speakers. There are fewer than 400 million native speakers today, compared with well over a billion speakers for whom English is an additional language. Many of these multilingual speakers of English routinely use English, not with native speakers, but with their fellow multilinguals. Many use English to talk about topics and values that are of central concern to them. Naturally, these topics and values may be based in, for example, African and/or Asian contexts and cultures. Thus, the majority of today's speakers of English are multilinguals who use English to communicate with each other and who discuss topics that are based in cultures which have little or nothing to do with the 'Anglo' cultures of native speakers. Yet, the notion that the most appropriate teacher for these people is the native speaker remains firmly embedded. It goes without saying (or should) that, in today's multilingual world, multilinguals with multicultural experience are more likely to prove effective language teachers than monolinguals with little cross-cultural experience.

> Surely it is time, on the grounds both of natural justice and of practicality and effectiveness, to cast aside the prejudice which privileges the native-speaker teacher and to move to hiring teachers based solely on their skills, qualifications and experience.

Kirkpatrick's main point is that the persistent 'myth of the native speaker' (Medgyes, 1992) leads to a continued preference for native-speaker models of language and consequently discriminatory hiring practices. Given our increasingly multilingual and multicultural world, the monolingual native speaker should not be regarded as a norm to be emulated. Yanase (this volume) offers evidence that, in providing a model for children learning language, a bilingual teacher can be as effective as a monolingual teacher, if not more so. However, the fact that she has to hide her bilingual identity shows that the myth continues to be pervasive.

In his personal and historical account, Robert Phillipson argues forcefully that teachers need to know more than just English in order to be successful. Like Kirkpatrick and also Kim (this volume), he believes qualified and experienced teachers are central to successful language learning. In addition, Phillipson points to the economic and ideological interests that surround ELT and reinforce native-speakerism.

Native-speakerism has tragic consequences
Robert Phillipson, Professor Emeritus, Copenhagen Business School

Native-speakerism means a blind faith in the superiority of one language, culture and pedagogy. One should only be in ELT if one loves languages (in the plural) and has personal experience of successful foreign or second language learning and language use.

I am a native speaker of English and have taught English since 1964. I use five languages professionally and in private life. I am not against English per se but I am against many of the uses to which English has been put over the past 500 years – and still is – in education systems in many countries and in many other contexts. Native-speakerism is part of the problem of teaching English, not the solution, with major negative ideological and structural consequences.

I worked for the British Council from 1964 to 1973. All recruits were sent to learn Spanish before teacher training in Madrid. I was posted to Algeria because my French was fluent. In Yugoslavia, as 'English Language Officer', learning Serbocroat was necessary. At this time, applied linguistics and theories of language learning were relatively underexplored. The dominant ELT paradigm was dogmatic, behaviourist, monolingual and misguided.

Since 1973, I have worked in Scandinavia, where foreign language learning is relatively successful. Obtaining employment in schools and higher education is dependent on qualifications rather than your origin. Native speakers of English as teachers are not needed for the successful learning of English, here as elsewhere.

After becoming involved in Scandinavian 'aid' for Namibian refugees from apartheid, I studied how education had evolved in former British colonies. I was appalled at how British 'expertise', in alliance with comprador elites, strengthens English and no other languages. It remains disconnected from multilingual cultural realities. This led to the analysis elaborated in *Linguistic Imperialism* (Phillipson, 1992). One detailed chapter denounces five fallacies in British ELT: monolingualism, native-speakerism, the early start, maximum exposure and subtractive fallacies. These falsehoods are still central to the US-UK ELT business and most World Bank education policies. They are not postcolonial, they are neoimperial (Phillipson, 2009).

Dispatching underqualified native speakers to teach English in schools and language schools (for instance, in Asia) is unprofessional. Employing monolinguals as consultants or teacher trainers on language-related projects worldwide is illegitimate, as research has shown. The British Council is increasingly run as a business to make money worldwide out of the teaching and examining of English and native-speakerism. That the British, a notoriously monolingual bunch, can sort out the language learning problems in education in India, Africa, Latin America, etc. is commercially driven pseudo-academic opportunism. The 'expertise' often operates within a narrow paradigm – neoliberal, consumerist and detached from local educational realities. Native-speakerism fraudulently legitimates a hierarchy of political dominance. It continues linguistic imperialism in new forms, does not contribute to social justice and interlocks with racist hierarchies, with tragic consequences (Rapatahana and Bunce, 2012).

Phillipson's views are similar to those set out in Edge (2006) and Block et al. (2012) among others. While it is beyond the scope of this volume (or indeed this chapter) to fully debate the issues, the chapters by Rivers and Lawrence remind us that they are multifaceted and complex, and that native-speaker teachers can also be the victims of the ELT charge.

One common assumption is that the 'native speaker' is a monolithic entity, incapable of learning another language or developing intercultural skills. Constant Leung, in our third opinion piece, maintains that it is no longer so (if indeed it ever was the case). He draws a contrast between the 'native speaker' used as a model for language teachers and learners and the reality that there is considerable diversity amongst native speakers themselves, who are rarely monolingual or monocultural.

The native speaker
Constant Leung, King's College, University of London, UK

The notion of the 'native speaker' has remarkable longevity in second/modern language education, despite sustained critical scrutiny in the past 25 years. One of the reasons for this is that the term captures many of the speaker qualities and capacities that language teachers are keen to promote. Another reason is that, in the real world, there are people who identify themselves as 'native or mother-tongue speakers of Language Y'. For many language professionals, the 'native speaker' is a reference model that sets the benchmarks for the language knowledge and communicative repertoires to be taught and learned. Put like this, the term has some practical value. However, the use of this term is often associated with a set of problematic assumptions such as 'all native speakers of a language are the same', 'the features and uses of language attributed to the native speaker are unchanging' and 'native speakers are monolingual speakers of the focal language'. These assumptions are unhelpful. Firstly, native speakers of a language are extremely diverse in terms of age, ethnicity, gender, social position and cultural affiliation, and this diversity is reflected in their language repertoires. Secondly, the lexico-grammatical resources and pragmatic conventions of any language are not fixed; they develop alongside changes in sociocultural practices. Thirdly, native speakers are not necessarily bound by monolingual resources and practices. Increasingly in ethnolinguistic diverse communities, native speakers are multi-glossic and plurilingual. Perhaps it would make sense to always pluralise the term and try to convey the idea of 'native speakers of a community/ies'.

Leung's call for the diversity of native speakers to be recognised and for there to be a shift towards the idea of 'native speakers of a community/ies' is an important one. However, as Javier (this volume) shows, the expectation that the native-speaker teacher should be both monolingual and White is pervasive. Recently, issues such as race and sexuality in English language teaching have begun to attract academic attention. See, for example, Kubota and Lin (2009) on race and the recent series of 'Queering TESOL' seminars run by John Gray (Gray et al., 2014).

In her piece, Claire Kramsch brings together many of the themes discussed so far and extends them. Like the authors of the previous pieces, she notes the persistence of the native-speaker model, especially in hiring practices. However, like Leung, she questions the existence of the monolingual native speaker in reality. Interestingly, she also takes the discussion beyond native speakers of English to native speakers of other languages and offers a perspective that sees national and economic interests not only supporting the native-speaker-driven ELT industry but also defending the native-speakerism of other languages.

Native-speakerism in language teaching
Claire Kramsch, UC Berkeley, USA

The native speaker was declared dead 30 years ago (Paikeday, 1985) but has been very much alive and kicking since then. In fact, it has become a desirable commodity in a job market that now sells linguistic purity and cultural authenticity as sources of symbolic capital, and intercultural communication as the condition of economic survival. What has happened to the privilege of the non-native speaker (Kramsch, 1997)?

With the rise of English as a Lingua Franca and economic globalisation, the native speaker has once again come under fire. Not only are there many more non-native speakers of English than there are native speakers, but the idea of a monolingual native speaker has become ludicrous. NSs of English nowadays speak many different languages, with various accents, grammars and vocabularies. In ELT, the unravelling of the monolingual, mononational, monocultural native speaker has led to such bold proposals as 'disinventing languages' (Makoni and Pennycook, 2007: 1) and using 'truncated repertoires' (Blommaert, 2010: 103) in a cosmopolitan practice where English as a Lingua Franca meshes culturally and socially with all other languages (Canagarajah, 2013). In other words, we are all non-native speakers. So is the issue of the native speaker finally moot?

Quite the contrary. What we witness nowadays is an increasing backlash both from the individual states who for reasons of national pride do not want to relinquish native-speakerism, and from the global corporations who for reasons of economic profit hold on to native-speakerism as an economic strategy. More than ever, tourism sells. While recognising the benefits of being non-native speakers of English, speakers of other languages realise the political and economic advantages of being perceived as native speakers of historically identifiable national cultures like French, Chinese, Russian or Persian. In fact, the global spread of English has, if anything, reinforced the symbolic profit of distinction of the local native speakers of languages other than English on the world stage.

In this era of global mobility and hybrid identities, what we need are not icons of local authenticity nor cosmopolitan global brands but a much more complex understanding of multilingual individuals. As Mary Louise Pratt wrote in *The Traffic in Meaning: Translation, Contagion, Infiltration:*

> *In talking about cross-cultural meaning making, it's essential to attend to fractures and entanglements, their makeup, asymmetries, ethics, histories, interdependencies, distributions of power and accountability.* (Pratt, 2002: 33)

We need linguistic and cultural mediators who have experienced displacements and their asymmetries, fractured identities and the interdependence of histories; multilingual speakers who are able to reflect on their paradoxical experiences, conceptualise them and pass them on to younger generations. The subjective turn in SLA should be an opportunity for English and foreign language teachers around the world to rethink what they are teaching these languages for.

The point that the native-speakerism debate affects languages other than English is well made. However, in the applied linguistics literature, discussions seem to focus almost exclusively on the English language (the terms 'NEST', 'NNEST' and 'LET' all include the word 'English'). Given the rise of languages such as Spanish, Chinese and Arabic (Graddol, 2006) it will be interesting to see if current debates will, in future, extend to other languages. Together with Leung's idea of 'native speakers of a community/communities', Kramsch's calls for recognition of the importance of multilingual individuals and the role that linguistic and cultural mediators can play in language learning indicate a way forward.

The gap between academia and the rest of the world can be clearly seen in Jennifer Jenkins's piece. In a piece which suggests that parallel universes exist in academic institutions, she describes a situation in which she is appointed Chair of Global Englishes at the same time as native-speaker teachers on an English language pre-sessional course are unable to contemplate that students might prefer a non-native speaker teacher to teach them.

Jennifer Jenkins,
University of Southampton, UK

My starting point is something that a Syrian PhD student of mine, Abdul Tahhan, said to me during a supervision meeting. His PhD focuses on orientations to the English of non-native English-speaking students in university presentations, both pre- and in-sessional, and last summer, as a means of supporting himself financially as well as gaining first-hand experience of his research field, he worked on a pre-sessional English language course for several weeks.

Abdul told me that his team had consisted of himself and two other teachers, one Scottish and the other Northern Irish. At one point, the Scottish teacher had asked their (mostly Chinese) students which of the three teachers they found easiest to understand. Like her Irish colleague, she was 'shocked' when the students unanimously said 'Abdul'. After all, Abdul's English, while fluent, was clearly not 'native-like', and he had an unmistakable Arabic accent. The other two teachers asked Abdul why he thought the students found him more intelligible than them. But when he explained that he, for example, avoided the use of British English idioms, slang, phrasal verbs and the like, they criticised him for such practices.

While this account is anecdotal, I believe it demonstrates that a number of extremely outdated beliefs about non-native English and its users are still in circulation in these days of global superdiversity. I will restrict myself here to just three of them. Firstly, these two native English-speaking pre-sessional teachers, like many other EAP teachers of my acquaintance, apparently have a seriously limited understanding of intercultural communication. This leads them to assume that native English is, by definition, the most intelligible kind of English for diverse first language contexts in which English serves as a lingua franca – as is undoubtedly the case on an English language pre-sessional course, wherever in the world it takes place, including the UK.

Secondly, they seem to have no conception of the part played by cultural baggage such as local idiomatic language in diminishing intelligibility for those who are outside the culture. And finally, these two teachers are by no means alone in believing that native English and its speakers with various (if highly selective) accents, including their own Scottish and Northern Irish accents, are superior to non-native. Meanwhile, their non-native English-speaking students are by no means the first to find another non-native English speaker easier to understand than his native English counterparts, and are unlikely to be the last.

Jenkins's piece also shifts the emphasis of the argument from the negative aspects of native speakers to the positive attributes of LETs. The arguments in favour of LETs have been well rehearsed in the literature and a number of chapters in this volume reiterate versions of this argument (see, for example, Heo and Tang's chapters). Jenkins's discussion provides a concrete example of the gap between the 'abstract' world of academic argument and the 'real' world in which NESTs and LETs live and work.

Like Leung and Kramsch, Enric Llurda (see also González and Llurda, this volume) challenges the very notion of the native speaker and questions whether such a person has ever existed. However, he also points to the damage that such a concept can cause, not only in the practical sphere of hiring practices but also to the perception that LETs can have of themselves (see, for example, Tatar and Yildiz, 2010).

Native-speakerism, native speakers, non-native speakers
Enric Llurda, Universitat de Lleida, Spain

Native-speakerism presupposes the existence of an illusionary category of speakers that hardly has any correspondence with real life. Very few so-called 'native speakers' could claim they possessed all the properties often associated with the 'ideal native speaker', which include being an educated and articulate speaker of standard language, one hundred per cent intelligible to all other speakers of the language and capable of producing highly elaborate and proficient speech in a fluent and effortless manner.

Both (real) native and non-native speakers are victims of the extraordinarily powerful native-speakerist ideology within applied linguistics and also among people with no linguistic background, and they need to jointly combat the rigid categorisation and separation imposed on individuals who would otherwise consider themselves users of the language without any further labelling in terms of the native- or non-native-speaker condition. Paikeday and Chomsky (1985) proclaimed the 'death' of the native speaker 30 years ago, but now it would probably be much more accurate to claim that native speakers, as they are commonly marketed and advertised in the ELT industry, were never born and have never existed in real life. So-called 'native speakers' are rather complex individuals, subject to a set of circumstances which define their idiosyncratic reality beyond idealised formulations of 'the native speaker'.

Obviously, the negative effects of native-speakerism are more keenly felt by people who have learned Language X after previously having learned other languages, as people who learned Language X as their first language can normally benefit from the societal bias in favour of the ideal category of the 'native speaker' and so may be offered more jobs and higher salaries. This is why, in the field of language teaching, there has been a specific sensitivity to this issue and a desire to raise awareness among so-called 'non-native teachers' of the discrimination suffered in some instances and the need to overcome feelings of limitation and lack of self-confidence that some teachers suffer from. Acknowledging the lack of relevance of order of acquisition of a language in the development of professional capacities in relation to that language is a necessary step to overcoming native-speakerism and applying fairer practices in language-related professional activities.

Llurda argues that LETs need to be coached to develop confidence in their own abilities and not to feel cowed by native-speaker colleagues, who, as Lawrence (this volume) shows, rarely lack confidence in their own abilities.

The need to value the role and contribution of LETs, largely ignored for many years, led to the NNEST movement. The history and the role of this movement in TESOL is outlined in detail in Selvi's chapter in this volume, but Ahmar Mahboob, in his opinion piece, not only succinctly summarises the history of the movement but also picks up a theme addressed by Kirkpatrick, Leung and Kramsch: the need to reconceptualise TESOL in terms of multilingualism, multiculturalism and multinationalism. This is a promising area for further contributions as traditionally, the worlds of TESOL and those of bi- and multilingualism have rarely met; TESOL has tended to be concerned with teaching internationally for social and academic purposes, whereas bilingualism has tended to focus on teaching migrant communities or those who operate in different languages in their home and school lives. In addition, as Mahboob points out, the TESOL world, at least in its public-facing institutions, has tended to be dominated by native English speakers; multilingualism is more diverse in both its institutions and leading scholars. In our increasingly superdiverse world, this dichotomy has become less sustainable and, as Mahboob argues, a reorientation towards viewing the dichotomy through the 'NNEST lens' is needed in order to ensure that LETs are more equally represented in TESOL.

The NNEST movement: aims and goals
Ahmar Mahboob, The University of Sydney, Australia

The recent surge of interest and scholarship in NNEST issues should not come as a surprise to TESOL and applied linguistics experts. NNESTs comprise (and have historically comprised) the large majority of English language teachers. Howatt (2004) points out that, as early as the 1500s, refugees in the UK were teaching English to their people. In the British colonies, the local teachers were also the ones teaching English to other locals. Thus, even in the early days of ELT, NNESTs were a visible and major contributor to ELT. However, over time, the centre of research and development in ELT shifted to native speakers in Inner Circle countries (Mahboob and Lin, in press).

This shift resulted in practices and theories that were monolingually oriented and did not consider the contributions or the needs of NNESTs. As a consequence of this limitation, native-speaker norms and models became dominant in the ELT discourse and resulted in beliefs that native speakers were ideal teachers. It is this body of literature and the resulting beliefs and practices that the NNEST movement has been working to counter. The NNEST movement wants ELT theory and practices to be inclusive and to support the needs of all ELT professionals, regardless of their first language. In order to achieve this goal, NNESTs have questioned the monolingual bias in TESOL (Kachru, 1994) and promoted the notion of the 'NNEST Lens' (Mahboob, 2010) in carrying out research in applied linguistics and TESOL.

The term 'NNEST Lens' comes from the title of an edited volume, *The NNEST Lens: Nonnative English Speakers in TESOL* (ibid.) and is defined as:

> *a lens of multilingualism, multinationalism, and multiculturalism through which NNESTs – as classroom practitioners, researchers, and teacher educators – take diversity as a starting point, rather than as a result.* (ibid.: 1)

By questioning the monolingual assumptions and power relationships between native and non-native English speakers, the NNEST Lens, in a broader context, can be understood as one aspect of a much larger critical movement that has focused on questions of power, equity and access in social sciences. And, in the context of our field, the NNEST Lens is a way of understanding and supporting the development of theory and practice in linguistics, applied linguistics and TESOL which questions and responds to a monolingual bias in the discipline and associated professions. This critical and multilingual orientation promotes research and practice which aims to break monolingual and native-speaker biases in the field. The implications of the NNEST Lens are far-reaching and its goal is not only to impact hiring discrimination in the field (which has been a focus of research on NNESTs) but also to question some of the key assumptions made in the applied linguistics and TESOL literature. This aim of the NNEST movement is reflected in the concluding remarks of a recent review of literature on NNESTs, where Llurda (2014: 113) states that the NNEST Lens 'entails a new way of approaching recurrent problems in language, language teaching, and language-based research.'

When looking to the future and to the ways in which native-speakerism can be overcome, our contributors have identified two key imperatives. The first is to combat the notion that a monolingual native speaker is the ideal teaching model. Instead, in order to offer the best support to learners, language teachers should aspire to be multilingual and multicultural. If this were the case, the distinction between NESTs and LETs would no longer be as relevant. The second is to ensure that language teachers are valued and hired on the basis of their experience and qualifications, not purely on the basis of their so-called first language. In this volume, Rivers offers an analysis of advertisements in Japan in which being a native speaker or having native-speaker expertise figure prominently. In our next opinion piece, Aya Matsuda takes up the point raised by Kirkpatrick concerning the practice of hiring unqualified teachers by virtue of the fact they are native speakers. She proposes an alternative approach where teachers are hired because of their qualifications, focusing on what teachers need to know and what they need to do.

Reconceptualising teacher qualification
Aya Matsuda, Arizona State University, USA

Native-speakerism, and the concept of 'native speaker' in general, has been criticised extensively in the field of applied linguistics. Traditional definitions of native speakers (NSs) are found to be insufficient in capturing the linguistic resources of multilingual users and their complex relationship with languages. Uncritical application of such inadequate definitions has resulted in native-speakerism, especially in (although not limited to) the way we think about teacher qualification. In light of this, some scholars (Brutt-Griffer and Samimy, 2001; Davies, 2003; Liu, 1999) have attempted to redefine the concept so that it is more useful and meaningful in understanding language use and learning. While I share their concerns and appreciate their effort, the notion of NS, in my view, does not have a legitimate place in the field of ELT any more.

This is not to deny the fact that native-speakerism continues to have a strong presence in the field of ELT. But when we envisage the ELT of the future – what it could be, rather than what it is – the concept of NS has nothing to offer. Take the practice of teacher hiring, for example. 'Native English-Speaking Teachers' are often preferred over their 'non-native' counterparts because they are believed to have a stronger knowledge of the language and culture, but as I and other scholars have pointed out (e.g. Matsuda, 2014), this is not always the case. In other words, using 'being a native speaker' as the criterion is a risky way of recruiting because there is no guarantee that 'native English-speaking' candidates actually possess the qualities they are expected to have.

An alternative approach would be to define the teacher criteria in terms of what we want our teachers to know and to be able to do. Once we start conceptualising teacher qualifications using their actual – and not expected – knowledge and ability, it becomes clear that the idea of 'native speakers' can be left out all together. I should also clarify that not requiring 'nativeness' in teacher qualification does not mean we would tolerate someone less. In fact, being more precise about what we need may end up raising the bar for some – i.e. some of those considered native speakers of English may no longer qualify for the position. This 'what they know and what they can do' criterion helps us reach out more directly to those whose qualifications match our needs than an approach that is based on the fuzzy concept of 'native speakers'.

Matsuda's call is particularly salient as qualifications in English language teaching are non-aligned. In the British system, for example, there is no unified set of qualifications which clearly indicates proficiency in English language teaching. What is more, the qualifications that are available in the UK are very different from qualifications that teachers might achieve in education systems in other countries. For example, courses such as the Cambridge University CELTA (Certificate in English Language Teaching to Adults) and DELTA (Diploma in English Language

Teaching to Adults) are designed to provide strategies for teachers working with small groups of adult learners, generally in multilingual groups. In contrast, many state-issued qualifications in European countries focus on developing abstract knowledge about linguistics and improving students' command of English. This is considered appropriate and ample training for teachers who are going to work in secondary and primary schools. Given this range, identifying the skills to be included in the 'what they know and what they can do' toolbox will take some very heated discussion.

Julian Edge also recognises the importance of establishing minimum qualifications for ELT teachers as a way of combating native-speakerism. However, Edge also goes beyond formal qualifications and calls for a future where both teachers and learners are supported in doing what they do well, rather than encouraged to attain targets that are unattainable.

On native-speakerism
Julian Edge, University of Manchester, UK

I remember listening once to Peter Medgyes, who did so much to shape the (N)NS debate in ELT. Just listening to Peter's voice in English was always pleasure enough, evocative, as I found it, of a picture-book-serene England of thatched cottages, Beefeaters and cricket on the wireless. On this occasion, however, he was also making an important point. He was explaining that he sent his school-age son to English classes in England each summer. This was to improve the boy's English generally and, more particularly, to help him acquire British pronunciation. A Hungarian colleague of Peter's also went to Britain each summer, where he taught English to foreign students. 'I would not be amused,' Peter commented drily, 'were I to discover that my colleague were teaching my son!'

It is so tempting to revisit the old arguments, to pick among the linguistic, educational, political, commercial, exploitative and self-serving stances that have shouted past each other over the years …

However, space presses. As someone who bangs on about continuing development, I nevertheless have to admit that my basic thinking has not really changed since I wrote this in 1988:

> When I stood in front of a class of Turkish schoolchildren, there was clearly only a very restricted sense in which I could act as a model for them in social, cultural, emotional or experiential terms, with regard either to their past or their future. The person who could act as such a model would be a Turkish teacher; and, if we believe that reference to the social, cultural and emotional experiences, awareness and aspirations of our pupils is important in learning, then this is the ideal model. (Edge, 1988: 155)

At this point, therefore, I prefer to turn to the future with three questions that seem to me to be of particular interest:

- Is a brain that has been shaped monolingually susceptible to subsequent language learning in ways identifiably different to a brain that has been shaped bi/multilingually to the extent that this might influence language teaching methodology as this involves both learners and teachers? Is such a question (albeit better formulated) on a neuroscientific research agenda?

- Are we still committed to an NS-derived approach to language teaching, to which all teachers and students need to be adapted? Or, to the extent that we are talking only about a teacher's level of language ability, are we prepared to say that below a certain level, we might usefully explore the question of what it is that this teacher can teach well and how that might best be achieved? Or the question of what it is that these students can do well, such as rote learning, and how that might best be turned to good account?

- If we would like to combat native-speakerism by establishing minimum teaching qualification standards in ELT that would apply also in the private sector, how can we best pursue that goal in a British context in which the government has removed the requirement for teaching qualifications in the general education of our children?

Edge references Peter Medgyes, who was one of the first to bring issues around native-speakerism to the attention of the TESOL world with his *ELT Journal* article (Medgyes, op cit). In this piece, Edge suggests that even people like Medgyes, who recognise the inherent injustice of NESTs being preferred over LETs, can still be attracted by a pitch-perfect RP accent. Edge shows that English language teachers live with seeming contradictions with regard to the native-speakerism; likewise Lawrence (this volume) reflects on sympathising with the views of both NESTs and LETs in his discussion of team teaching in Japan. These two cases demonstrate that although we have come a long way in the last 25 years or so – evidenced by a flourishing NNEST movement, a substantial amount of research into native-speakerism and an ever-growing number of publications – in changing attitudes and behaviours in daily practice there is much more to do.

All the opinion pieces so far have focused almost exclusively on native-speakerism in English, with the exception of Kramsch. Our penultimate piece, by Hywel Coleman, extends the debate into new territory by asking what happens in contexts where there is no native language. Coleman also shows that debates around native-speakerism and, in particular, language as the medium of instruction, are not just limited to English. His account of the situation in Morocco raises a number of new issues that are beyond the scope of this volume, but which cannot be ignored. In particular, language-in-education policies in multilingual contexts where the medium of instruction is different from the shared language of teachers and children are beginning to attract the attention of researchers (e.g. Tembe and Norton, 2010).

The native-speakerness of learners and the non-existence of native speakers: the case of Morocco
Hywel Coleman, University of Leeds, UK

Discussions of 'native-speakerism' focus on how native-speakerness can be defined, whether the teacher being a native speaker helps or hinders learners' learning and whether being a native speaker increases the teacher's face validity in the eyes of learners. But there are two adjunct issues which also demand attention: the native-speakerness of learners and the phenomenon of languages which have no native speakers at all. Morocco provides a context in which both issues can be explored.

Morocco has 12 languages. Darija (Moroccan Arabic) has more native speakers than the other languages. Darija also has large numbers of L2 speakers and it is the country's de facto lingua franca. Three Berber languages, unrelated to Arabic, also have substantial numbers of native speakers: Tachelhit, Tamazight and Tarifit. None of these four languages has an official role in education.

In contrast, Morocco's education system prioritises three different languages, none of which has native speakers (not, at least, in Morocco). Standard Arabic is the medium of instruction from Year 1, French is taught from Years 2 to 12 (and is the medium of instruction in higher education), while Standard Amazighe is taught from Years 1 to 6. Amazighe is the product of an attempt to produce a standard Berber which will be acceptable to speakers of the various Berber languages. In practice, however, Amazighe is not understood by speakers of the Berber languages. Thus, teachers and learners alike are not native speakers of the three languages prioritised in education.

This language-in-education policy prevents children and their teachers from talking to each other in the languages that they share. Although Standard Arabic plays a crucial role as the language of Islam, many pupils and teachers do not master the language sufficiently to be able to learn and teach other subjects through it. French has almost no native speakers in Morocco and many young people resent the language. Meanwhile, the artificially created Amazighe has never had native speakers. No appealing native-speaker models are available and there is no immediately apparent need to learn the language (as with Latin in some UK schools until fairly recently and Sanskrit in some Indian states until today).

It is probably not a coincidence, therefore, that Moroccan children achieve some of the lowest scores in the world in international comparative tests of reading, science and mathematics. These results reinforce arguments in favour of using children's mother tongue as the medium of instruction, at least in primary school. A corollary is that so-called 'content and language integrated learning' is risky if it is the default educational approach and if it is used at too early an age.

The implementation of Morocco's language policy is in crisis. Status decisions regarding Standard Arabic, Amazighe and French have not been supported by appropriate acquisition planning. Consideration needs to be given to alternative ways of developing language competence. Making use of learners' and teachers' native languages offers such an alternative.

Coleman suggests that other concerns related to native-speakerism need to be considered in discussions about language of instruction. Content and language integrated learning (CLIL), which has become so popular in recent years and which again favours native speakers of the target language, is considered less than ideal as a methodology. Like many experts in child education, Coleman suggests that teaching in the children's first language is the ideal pedagogical choice, although it is not always possible to identify a child's first language and it might be impossible in many urban classes which are populated by children from many different language groups.

Our final piece is by Alastair Pennycook. It closes the chapter by bringing together many of the themes that have been discussed so far but also by opening out the discussion to the question of how to address the complex issues in an academic setting. Pennycook details the aspects of native-speakerism that he addresses, including discrimination against LETs, the economics of native-speakerism and the racism it involves, before concluding with an interesting proposal for a new distinction.

On thinking before we speak
Alastair Pennycook, University of Technology Sydney, Australia

In a recent graduate class I teach on global Englishes, we came back to the difficult and contentious subject of native speakers. It is a challenging issue not only because it is theoretically messy but more importantly because this is about the unequal world these students live in. The majority of the students in that class speak English as a second language, covering anything from highly fluent speakers of English who have grown up in Australia but speak another language at home to newly arrived students from overseas who are struggling to relate their prior success at home as English learners to the new and difficult environment of being a graduate student in Australia. But all these students know they face a massive difficulty in competing in the international job market against so-called native speakers. It has been a number of years since Canagarajah (1999: 77) spoke of the 'absurdity of an educational system that prepares one for a profession for which it disqualifies the person at the same time', yet this is still very much the way things operate.

We do a lot of work in the class to unpack the notion of the native speaker, showing its historical emergence in the middle of the nineteenth century, its relation to the notion of 'standard' English, with its particular class orientations (educated speakers), and the context of Anglo-Saxonism, 'one of the most powerful historical-political ideologies' of the late nineteenth and early twentieth centuries (Hackert, 2012: 88). We consider the mistaken assumptions about what being a native speaker entails, especially the misconception that relates being a native speaker to speaking a standard variety. Indeed, as Piller (2001: 112) points out:

> a native speaker of Standard English is logically impossible! A native speaker is supposedly born into the language while the standard is supposedly attained through superior education.

We take Rajagopalan's (2007: 203) contention seriously that the native speaker is

> [only as real] as Mickey Mouse and Batman are real. In the multi-billion dollar EFL industry, the figure of the native speaker is a product of intense and very successful marketing indeed.

We discuss the development of ELT dogmas, in combination with the economic interests of the vast ELT industry, that proscribed translation, emphasised the use of only English in the classroom and maintained the idea that the goal of learning English was somehow to emulate the mythologised native speaker. We draw attention to the work that has sought to redress inequitable hiring practices, taking up Kirkpatrick's (2007: 57) argument that 'multilingual speakers themselves should provide the linguistic models for language learners, rather than native speakers' or Modiano's (2005: 26) point that:

> the NNS practitioner has certain advantages over the NS instructor – not only because they have knowledge of the linguistic complexities of the mother tongue and the target language in contact – but more importantly because the NNS practitioner is well suited to provide students with a pluralistic cultural perspective'.

And we discuss some of the other ways of thinking about what is at stake here in terms of expertise (Rampton, 1990) or resourceful speakers (Pennycook, 2012, 2014).

We do all this work, but like a consciousness-raising exercise to understand the conditions of one's own oppression, it leaves everyone feeling rather bereft of options. Everyone in the class gets a bit uncomfortable here. The small group of people who speak English as first language have been challenged in relation to their bilingual qualifications: should a basic qualification to teach English as a second language not at the very least be bilingualism? Students are also very aware that the NS construct easily slides into other forms of prejudice, that 'the tendency to equate the native speaker with White and the nonnative speaker with non-White' is as important as any linguistic prejudice in explaining the 'discrimination against nonnative professionals, many of whom are people of colour' (Kubota and Lin, op cit: 8). They know that the colour of their skin may already make finding a job as an English teacher harder. Like Alim and Smitherman's (2012: 55) observation that the 'somber reality for many African Americans is that, still, no matter how "articulate" yo ass is, upon visiting in person, can't nuthin fool the landlord now, baby – you Black, Jack!', so the well-trained and articulate NNS teacher turning up for a job interview can no longer fool the employer.

And all are aware too that the unequal terrain of language use is played out in the classroom, as some people get to speak much more than others. As we discuss this, someone points to the well-known problem that as a second language speaker you so often have to pause to think before you speak (by which time the chance may have gone) while more fluent speakers are happy to speak up.

This problem will surely resonate for anyone who has taught classes such as this, or indeed for anyone who has had to function at a reasonably high level in a second language. So perhaps, we suggest, the real division is between those who speak before they think (SBT) and those who think before they speak (TBS). Perhaps the SBT/TBS division is just as useful as this NS/NNS divide.

It at least makes a few helpful points. First, it turns the tables on the NS/NNS divide by reversing the focus of the supposed deficit: the TBS speakers, sorting their thoughts carefully before they utter them, become the preferred model over those whose linguistic fluency gets in the way of forming a more judicious response. Second, the division is as useful as the NS/NNS divide in that both are ultimately rather messy and unhelpful: there are those who think before they speak and still may not have that much to say, and those whose quick words are on the mark. The point is that the TBS/SBT division is more or less as good as the NS/NNS division, and I wouldn't want either to carry too much weight in deciding who should teach. And finally, there are a couple of other lessons here about thinking before we speak, pausing, allowing space for others, considering the uneven playing field created by the global spread of English and also perhaps not letting the terms native or non-native speaker pass our lips ever again.

Pennycook's final call still seems a distant reality. Not only is there much work to do among TESOL professionals to alert them to the issues and myths surrounding native-speakerism – such as teachers' bilingualism, race and discrimination (see the chapters in this volume by Yanase, Javier and Rivers respectively) – but it is also unlikely that the general public will ever understand how imprecise and divisive the term is. Nevertheless, there is no reason why our field cannot develop a stronger sensitivity and begin to answer Pennycook's call. Native-speakerism should be a topic on the curriculum of every teacher preparation course. Advertisements for teachers should list the teaching skills or qualifications required (rather than the level of proficiency) and publishers should be mindful of ensuring that course materials represent a broad range of Englishes, accents, peoples and cultures. Steps such as these, though small, may help to accelerate the arrival of a level playing field for those who want to teach English. And it won't be before time.

References

Alim, HS and Smitherman, G (2012) *Articulate while Black: Barack Obama, language and race in the US.* Oxford: Oxford University Press.

Block, D, Grey, J and Holborrow, M (2012) *Neoliberalism and applied linguistics.* London: Routledge.

Blommaert, J (2010) *The sociolinguistics of globalization.* Cambridge: Cambridge University Press.

Brutt-Griffer, J and Samimy, KK (2001) Transcending the nativeness paradigm. *World Englishes* 20/1: 99–106.

Canagarajah, S (1999) 'Interrogating the "native speaker fallacy": Non-linguistic roots, non-pedagogical results' in Braine, G (ed) *Non-native educators in English language teaching.* Mahwah, NJ: Lawrence Erlbaum Associates, 145–158.

Canagarajah, S (2013) 'From intercultural rhetoric to cosmopolitan practice: Addressing new challenges in Lingua Franca English' in Belcher, D and Nelson, G (eds) *Critical and corpus-based approaches to intercultural rhetoric.* Ann Arbor, MI: University of Michigan Press, 203–226.

Davies, A (2003) *The native speaker: Myth and reality.* Clevedon: Multilingual Matters.

Edge, J (1988) Natives, speakers and models. *JALT Journal* 9/2: 153–157.

Edge, J (2006) *(Re-)locating TESOL in an age of empire.* Basingstoke: Palgrave.

Graddol, D (2006) *English Next.* London: British Council.

Gray, J, Baynham, M and Cooke, M (2014) *Queering ESOL: Towards a cultural politics LGBT issues in the ESOL classroom.* ESRC funded seminar series.

Hackert, Stephanie (2012) *The emergence of the English native speaker: A chapter in nineteenth-century linguistic thought.* Berlin: De Gruyter.

Howatt, APR with Widdowson, HG (2004) *A history of English language teaching,* second edition. Oxford: Oxford University Press.

Kachru, Y (1994). Monolingual bias in SLA research. *TESOL Quarterly* 28/4: 795–800.

Kirkpatrick, A (2007). Language variation and the multilingual speaker of English: Implications for English language teaching. *The New English Teacher* 1/1: 44–60.

Kramsch, C (1997) *The privilege of the non-native speaker.* PMLA May 2007. New York, NY: Modern Language Association.

Kubota, R and Lin, A (2009) 'Race, culture, and identities in second language education' in Kubota, R and Lin, A (eds) *Race, culture and identities in second language education: Exploring critically engaged practice*. New York, NY: Routledge, 1–23.

Liu, J (1999) 'From their own perspectives: The impact of non-native ESL professionals on their students' in Braine, G (ed) *Non-native educators in English language teaching*. Mahwah, NJ: Lawrence Erlbaum Associates, 159–176.

Llurda, E (2014) 'Non-native teachers and advocacy' in Bigelow, M and Ennser-Kananen, J (eds) *The Routledge handbook of educational linguistics*. New York, NY: Routledge, 105–116.

Mahboob, A (2010) *The NNEST lens: Nonnative English speakers in TESOL*. Newcastle upon Tyne: Cambridge Scholars Publishing.

Mahboob, A and Lin, A (in press). *Using Local Languages in English Language Classrooms*.

Makoni, S and Pennycook, A (2007) *Disinventing and reconstituting languages*. Clevedon: Multilingual Matters.

Matsuda, A (2014) Beyond the native speaker: My life as an NJS, NNES, and bilingual user of Japanese and English. *NNEST Newsletter: The Newsletter of the TESOL NNEST Interest Section*. Available online at: http://newsmanager. commpartners.com/tesolnnest/issues/2014-09-09/2.html (accessed 27 February 2016).

Medgyes, P (1992) Native or non-native: who's worth more? *ELT Journal* 46/4: 340–349.

Modiano, M (2005) 'Cultural studies, foreign language teaching and learning practices, and the NNS practitioner' in Llurda, E (ed) *Non-native language teachers: Perceptions, challenges and contributions to the profession*. New York, NY: Springer, 25–43.

Paikeday, TM and Chomsky, N (1985) *The native speaker is dead! An informal discussion of a linguistic myth with Noam Chomsky and other linguists, philosophers, psychologists, and lexicographers*. Toronto and New York: Paikeday Publishing.

Pennycook, A (2012) *Language and mobility: Unexpected places*. Bristol: Multilingual Matters.

Pennycook, A (2014) Principled polycentrism and resourceful speakers. *The Journal of Asia TEFL* 11/4: 1–19.

Phillipson, R (1992) *Linguistic imperialism*. Oxford: Oxford University Press.

Phillipson, R (2009) *Linguistic imperialism continued*. London: Routledge.

Piller, I (2001) Who, if anyone, is a native speaker? *Anglistik* 12/2: 109–121.

Pratt, ML (2002) *The traffic in meaning: Translation, contagion, infiltration. Profession 2002.* New York, NY: Modern Language Association.

Rajagopalan, K (2007) Revisiting the nativity scene. Review of A Davies, (2003) The native speaker: myth and reality. *Studies in Language* 31/1: 93–205.

Rampton, B (1990) Displacing the 'native speaker': expertise, affiliation, and inheritance. *ELT Journal* 44/2: 97–101.

Rapatahana, V and Bunce, P (eds) (2012) *English language as hydra: Its impacts on non-English language cultures.* (Vol. 9) Multilingual Matters.

Tatar, S and Yildiz, S (2010) 'Empowering nonnative-English speaking in the classroom' in Mahboob, A (ed) *The NNEST Lens: Nonnative English speakers in TESOL.* Newcastle upon Tyne: Cambridge Scholars Publishing, 114–128.

Tembe, J and Norton, B (2010) 'English education, local languages and community perspectives in Uganda', Chapter 6, in Coleman, H (ed) *Dreams and realities: Developing countries and the English language.* London: British Council.

Contributors

Fiona Copland

Fiona Copland is Professor of TESOL at the University of Stirling, Scotland. She has worked as a NEST in Nigeria and Hong Kong and as a teacher trainer in Japan and the UK. She has also been Course Director of Master's programmes in TESOL at UK universities and supervises PhD students in a range of areas. Fiona has researched and published in the areas of teacher education, teaching English to young learners and linguistic ethnography.
fiona.copland@stir.ac.uk

Xuesong (Andy) Gao

Xuesong (Andy) Gao is an Associate Professor in the Faculty of Education at the University of Hong Kong. His current research and teaching interests are in the areas of learner autonomy, sociolinguistics, language learning narratives and language teacher education. His publications appear in journals including Applied Linguistics, Journal of Education for Teaching, Journal of Multilingual and Multicultural Development, Language Teaching, Language Teaching Research, Studies in Higher Education, System, Teaching and Teacher Education and TESOL Quarterly. He is co-editor of System: An International Journal of Educational Technology and Applied Linguistics and serves on the editorial boards of The Asia Pacific Education Researcher, the Journal of Language, Identity and Education and Teacher Development. He was a recipient of the 2013 TESOL Award for an Outstanding Paper on NNEST Issues (with Wong and Lee) and was President of the Hong Kong Association for Applied Linguistics in 2013–2014.
xsgao@hku.hk

Sue Garton

Sue Garton is Director of Postgraduate Programmes in English at Aston University, Birmingham, UK, where she teaches TESOL modules to both undergraduates and postgraduates as well as supervising PhDs. Her research interests include teaching English to young learners, language policy and planning, language teacher education and classroom discourse. She has published books and articles in the area of English language teaching, including *From Experience to Knowledge in ELT* with Julian Edge in the Oxford Handbooks for Teachers series and Professional *Encounters in TESOL* with Keith Richards. She is currently series editor, with Keith Richards, of a major new 15-volume series called *International Perspectives on ELT* published by Palgrave Macmillan.
s.garton@aston.ac.uk

Adriana González

Adriana González is a Professor at the School of Languages of the Universidad de Antioquia in Medellín, Colombia. She teaches an introductory course on second language acquisition and qualitative data analysis in the Master's programme in

Foreign Language Teaching and Learning. In the undergraduate programme in foreign language teaching, she has supervised students in the Practicum and taught Methods of TESOL. Her areas of research and publication in national and international journals and books include the professional development of foreign language teachers, language policies, SLA and task-based language teaching and learning. She holds a doctoral degree in Linguistics (TESOL) from State University of New York at Stony Brook and an MA in Language Sciences from the Université de Nancy II, France. She served as Vice-president and Secretary of the Colombian Association of English Teachers from 2006 to 2012. She belongs to the editorial committees of the journals PROFILE, Colombian Applied Linguistics, Lenguaje and IKALA.

adrianamariagonzalez@gmail.com

Jaeyeon Heo

Jaeyeon Heo is an English instructor who currently works at Chungbuk National University in South Korea and is also involved in teacher training programmes for secondary English teachers and university lecturers at Mongolia International University. She holds an MSc in TESOL from the University of Bristol and a PhD in English Language Teaching and Applied Linguistics from the University of Warwick, UK. Her research interests include NEST schemes, teacher training and development, teaching writing and writing feedback.

jenny_jyheo@yahoo.co.uk

Eljee Javier

Eljee Javier is an experienced English language teacher who has worked in China, Australia and the UK. Throughout her teaching career, her identity as a Canadian-Filipino has been perceived both positively and negatively, which has raised some interesting issues that she discusses in her chapter. She moved to the UK to complete an MA in TESOL and then a PhD at the University of Manchester. Her previous teaching experiences have helped to shape her current research interests in racial and ethnic identities, native-speakerism and performativity in narrative-based research. She currently works as the Researcher Development Officer for the Faculty of Humanities at the University of Manchester.

eljee.javier@manchester.ac.uk

Greg Keaney

Greg Keaney is CfBT's Head of English Language Teaching Partnerships as well as the Programme Director for the CfBT NEST project in Brunei, the world's largest and longest-running PPP NEST scheme. The Brunei NEST project recruits approximately 300 Native English-Speaking Teachers to work in government schools across Brunei. The project is charged with improving student proficiency in English and student involvement in English-medium academic and extracurricular activities, as well as with capacity building of CfBT and Bruneian Local Teachers in every government school across the country. Greg has more than 30 years' experience in the management and administration of ELT and NEST projects in a variety of contexts, including Malaysia, Indonesia, Japan, Australia

and, for more than 14 years, Brunei. He has a PhD in International Education Management from Sydney University as well as a Master's in Applied Linguistics from Macquarie University.
gkeaney@cfbt.org

Trần Thị Minh Khánh

Trần Thị Minh Khánh is an EFL teacher and has been working as a lecturer at Nha Trang University, Vietnam, for over ten years. She has an MA in English Linguistics from Dalarna University, Sweden, and a PhD in Applied Linguistics from the University of Warwick, UK. Her PhD research was on team teaching between NESTs and LETs, with a particular focus on their relationship management and development.
m_khanh79@yahoo.com

Sung-Yeon Kim

Sung-Yeon Kim is Professor in the Department of English Education at Hanyang University in Seoul, Korea. She has a PhD in TEFL and a Master's degree in Linguistics and Instructional Technology. She has taught for more than 15 years in higher education settings. Her research interests include teacher education, teaching reading, teaching writing, language testing, language policy and computer-assisted language learning.
sungkim@hanyang.ac.kr

Luke Lawrence

Luke Lawrence has taught English in Japan for over 12 years. From 2010 to 2015, he worked for the British Council Japan, where he spent three years working as a team teacher in public secondary schools on the project described in this chapter. His research interests are primarily concerned with sociocultural issues in language teaching and the classroom as a microcosm of culture and society. These include debates surrounding native-speakerism and use of L1 as well as aspects of social psychology and group dynamics. He now teaches at Yokohama City University in Kanagawa, Japan.
lukejlawrence@gmail.com

Icy Lee

Icy Lee is a Professor in the Department of Curriculum and Instruction of the Faculty of Education at The Chinese University of Hong Kong. Her main research interests are in second language writing and second language teacher education. She was formerly President of the Hong Kong Association for Applied Linguistics and Chair of the Nonnative English Speakers in TESOL (NNEST) Interest Section of TESOL International Association. Her publications have appeared in numerous international journals, such as the Journal of Second Language Writing, TESOL Quarterly, Language Teaching, the ELT Journal, System and Language Teaching Research. She was a recipient of the 2013 TESOL Award for an Outstanding Paper on NNEST Issues (with Wong and Gao), the 2010 TESOL Award for Excellence in Teaching and the 1999 TESOL Award for Excellence in the Development of

Pedagogical Materials. She was also a recipient of the 2008 Journal of Second Language Writing Best Paper Award for her article 'Understanding teachers' written feedback practices in Hong Kong secondary classrooms'.
icylee@cuhk.edu.hk

Tzu-Bin Lin

Tzu-Bin Lin is an Associate Professor in the Department of Education at the National Taiwan Normal University. Prior to his current post, he was a researcher at Bournemouth University, UK and Assistant Professor at the National Institute of Education, Singapore. His research interests include education policy and leadership, media literacy education, English teaching and multicultural education. In the past five years, he has published more than 20 papers and chapters in international peer-reviewed journals and books in the above-mentioned areas. He is also the first editor of the book *New Media and Learning in the 21st Century: A Socio-Cultural Perspective* (2015, Springer).
tzubin_lin@ntnu.edu.tw

Enric Llurda

Enric Llurda is a Lecturer and current Head of the Department of English and Linguistics at the Universitat de Lleida, Catalonia, Spain. He teaches courses on applied linguistics, intercultural communication and research methods. His research interests are multilingualism, language attitudes, English as lingua franca, language awareness and non-native teachers' identity. He edited the book *Non-native Language Teachers: Perceptions, Challenges and Contributions to the Profession* (2005, Springer), which has received wide international attention and has been translated into Arabic (King Saud University, 2012). He has also co-authored two books in Spanish: *La conciencia lingüística en la enseñanza de lenguas* (2007) on the promotion of language awareness in language education; and *Plurilingüismo e interculturalidad en la escuela: Reflexiones y propuestas didácticas* (2010) on the development of multilingual and intercultural competence in secondary education. He has also published around 60 articles in edited volumes or specialised journals, including the International Journal of Applied Linguistics, International Journal of Bilingual Education and Bilingualism, Journal of Multilingual and Multicultural Development, Journal of Psycholinguistic Research, Language Awareness, Language Teaching and System.
ellurda@dal.udl.cat

Steve Mann

Steve Mann is Associate Professor at the Centre for Applied Linguistics at the University of Warwick, UK. He previously lectured at both Aston University and the University of Birmingham. He has experience in Hong Kong, Japan and Europe in both English language teaching and teacher development. Steve supervises a research group of PhD students who are investigating teachers' education and development. The group's work considers aspects of teacher development, teacher beliefs and the development of knowledge, the first year of teaching,

mentoring, blended learning and the use of technology in teacher development. He has published various books including *Innovations in Pre-service Teacher Education* (British Council).
steve.mann@warwick.ac.uk

Damian J. Rivers

Damian J. Rivers is an Associate Professor at Future University Hakodate, Hokkaidō, Japan. He holds an MA and PhD in Applied Linguistics and an MSc in Social Psychology. His research interests include critical applied linguistics, discourses of authority in educational contexts, rhetoric and knowledge representation, the native-speaker criterion and the management of multiple identities. In addition to being the author of numerous international journal publications, he is co-editor of *Native-Speakerism in Japan: Intergroup Dynamics in Foreign Language Education* (2013, Multilingual Matters) and *Social Identities and Multiple Selves in Foreign Language Education* (2013, Bloomsbury) with Stephanie Ann Houghton. He is also editor of *Resistance to the Known: Counter-Conduct in Language Education* (2015, Palgrave Macmillan).
www.djrivers.com

Ali Fuad Selvi

Ali Fuad Selvi is Assistant Professor of TESOL and Applied Linguistics in the Teaching English as a Foreign Language programme at the Middle East Technical University, Northern Cyprus Campus, and the Immediate Past Chair of the NNEST Interest Section in TESOL International Association. His research interests include the sociolinguistics of English language teaching with special emphasis on the global spread of English as an international language and its implications for language learning, teaching, teacher education and policy/planning; issues related to non-native English-speaking professionals in TESOL; and second language teacher education (particularly teacher cognition, the notion of praxis and the interplay between second language acquisition and second language pedagogy). He is the co-author of *Teaching English as an International Language* (2013, TESOL Press).
selvi@metu.edu.tr

Helen Spencer-Oatey

Helen Spencer-Oatey is Professor and Director of the Centre for Applied Linguistics at the University of Warwick, UK. Her primary research interests are in intercultural interaction and intercultural pragmatics. She has published extensively in these fields, for example *Culturally Speaking* (2000/2008, Continuum) and *Intercultural Interaction* (Palgrave, 2009) with Peter Franklin. She has also developed extensive resources for practitioners, many of which are freely available via the University of Warwick's Global PAD website.
helen.spencer-oatey@warwick.ac.uk

Elaine Hau Hing Tang

Elaine Hau Hing Tang completed her MA and PhD in English Language Teaching at the University of Warwick, England. She has been an English teacher and instructor in Hong Kong and China for more than eight years, teaching students from secondary to tertiary levels. She is now a part-time Instructor with the English Language Teaching Unit of the Chinese University of Hong Kong, teaching mainly business and social science students business and academic writing.
elainetang@cuhk.edu.hk

Li-Yi Wang

Li-Yi Wang is a Research Scientist in the Office of Education Research, National Institute of Education (NIE) Singapore. His PhD looks into the transmission of professional identity of non-native English teachers in the context of teaching English as a foreign language (EFL). Since joining NIE Singapore, he has extended his research interests to include school-based curriculum innovation and education policy. He is also involved in research projects in relation to teacher efficacy and the pedagogical and affective needs of academically low-achieving students.
liyi.wang@nie.edu.sg

Mary Shepard Wong

Mary Shepard Wong is Professor at Azusa Pacific University in Southern California, where she directs the field-based graduate TESOL programme. She has taught for over three decades in the US, Thailand, China and Myanmar. Her publications appear in several international journals, including Frontiers of Education in China, Language Education in Asia, Forum on Public Policy, Education and Society and the CATESOL Journal. She has edited two Routledge books on teachers' spiritual identity and ELT, one co-edited with Suresh Canagarajah and the other with Zoltán Dörnyei and Carolyn Kristjansson. She also has a forthcoming book co-edited with Ahmar Mahboob on spirituality and ELT under contract with Multilingual Matters. In 2012 she was a Fulbright scholar in Hong Kong, where she conducted research with Icy Lee and Andy Gao on the collaboration of foreign and local teachers, resulting in a presentation which won the 2013 TESOL Award for Outstanding Paper on NNEST Issues.
mwong@apu.edu

Chiyuki Yanase

Chiyuki Yanase is a language school owner and an ALT in public elementary schools in Tokyo, Japan. She has been teaching English to young learners in Japan for over 20 years and is a graduate of the MSc TEYL program at Aston University, UK. She also started teaching at universities in Tokyo in 2015. Her research focuses on collaborative learning and literacy development in young learners. She has been an active member of the Japan Association for Language Teaching since 2011, has presented at numerous conferences and is the co-author of the textbooks *Guinness World Records 1* and *2* (2013, Macmillan).
chicosunny_e@yahoo.co.jp

Acknowledgements

We would like to thank all the authors for their patience and their commitment throughout the project. Our thanks also go to colleagues who responded to our rather odd request to send 500 words on their current thinking on NEST issues for inclusion in the final chapter. Finally, thank you to the team at the British Council for seeing this work through to publication.